ENLIGHTENMENT AGAINST EMPIRE

ENLIGHTENMENT AGAINST EMPIRE

Sankar Muthu

PRINCETON UNIVERSITY PRESS

PRINCETON AND OXFORD

Copyright © 2003 by Princeton University Press
Published by Princeton University Press, 41 William Street,
Princeton, New Jersey 08540
In the United Kingdom: Princeton University Press, 3 Market Place,
Woodstock, Oxfordshire OX20 1SY
All Rights Reserved

Library of Congress Cataloging-in-Publication Data

Muthu, Sankar, 1970–
Enlightenment against empire / Sankar Muthu.
p. cm.
Includes bibliographical references and index.
ISBN 0-691-11516-8 (alk. paper) —ISBN 0-691-11517-6 (pbk. : alk. paper)
1. Imperialism.   2. Political science—Europe—History—18th century.
3. Enlightenment.   I. Title.

JC359.M87   2003
325'.32'01—dc21   2002042717

British Library Cataloging-in-Publication Data is available

This book has been composed in Galliard

Printed on acid-free paper. ∞

www.pupress.princeton.edu

Printed in the United States of America

10 9 8 7 6 5 4 3 2

ISBN-13: 978-0-691-11517-7

ISBN-10: 0-691-11517-6

For my parents

After the city or town comes the world, which the philosophers identify as the third level of human society. They begin with the household, progress to the city, and come finally to the world. And the world, like a gathering of waters, is all the more full of perils by reason of its greater size. First of all, the diversity of tongues now divides man from man. . . . It is true that the Imperial City has imposed on subject nations not only her yoke but also her language, as a bond of peace and society, so that there should be no lack of interpreters but a great abundance of them. But how many great wars, what slaughter of men, what outpourings of human blood have been necessary to bring this about! Those wars are now over; but the misery of these evils has not yet come to an end.

(*Augustine*)

Contents

ACKNOWLEDGEMENTS ─────────────

THE INITIAL research for this book was made possible as a result of generous funding by the Social Sciences and Humanities Research Council of Canada. I also thank the Mellon Foundation for a dissertation completion grant. The Center for European Studies at Harvard University provided me with an intellectually stimulating and elegant environment for my last two years of dissertation research and writing and also for the spring semester of 2000, while I was on a research leave from the New School. While at the Center, I enjoyed spirited discussions with dozens of faculty associates, visiting scholars, and graduate student affiliates; I thank in particular Tom Ertman, Josep Fradera, Stanley Hoffmann, Susan Pedersen, Dana Villa, and Patrick Weil. I would also like to acknowledge the wonderful staff there, especially Abby Collins, Lisa Eschenbach, Anna Popiel, George Cumming, and Sandy Selesky.

Once as fellow students and now as colleagues, I am very fortunate to have the intellectual advice and friendship of Arash Abizadeh, Gary Bass, Ben Berger, Chris Brooke, Peter Cannavò, Mark Duckenfield, Sam Ewing, Michaele Ferguson, Jim Fuerst, Mala Htun, Nancy Kokaz, Karuna Mantena, Jason Niedleman, and Tim Shah. I especially want to thank Patchen Markell and Andy Sabl both for their friendship and for countless conversations about the variety of issues that I discuss in this book. I would also like to single out the original '6 Marie gang': Libra Hilde, Jamie Jones, Paul Talcott, and Kim Reimann, as well as Geoff Herrera, for their support and laughter. I am indebted to all my friends from Canada and from college for their camaraderie.

Presentations at a variety of conferences and colloquia helped me to sharpen my arguments and provided welcome opportunities to reflect upon thoughtful criticisms; many thanks to all those who offered comments on my research. I thank Morris Kaplan for many conversations and for his invitation to give a lecture at SUNY-Purchase. Ian Shapiro kindly invited me to present at the Yale Political Theory Colloquium. I also thank David Johnston for his support and an invitation to present my work at the Faculty Seminar in Social and Political Thought at Columbia University. I benefited from many discussions after having presented a paper at a conference on 'Europe and Empire' at the Center for European Studies at Harvard University. Thanks also to the participants of 'The Enlightenment and Its Legacies' conference, sponsored by the Conference for the Study of Political Thought, at Yale University, and especially to Richard Falk for his perceptive comments there. I am indebted as well to questions and suggestions that I received on a panel about liberalism and rights at the International Society for the Study of European Ideas conference in Bergen, Norway. I thank Anthony Pagden, J.G.A. Pocock, Alan Ryan, and Bernie Yack for participating in a panel that I organized about 'Pluralizing "the" Enlightenment', as part of the 1999 American Political Science Association conference in Washington, D.C.; I learned much from their papers and comments. Alan Patten offered illuminating questions about my chapter on Herder at a panel on Enlightenment political thought and nationalism, organized by Patricia Nordeen, at the 2002 APSA conference in Boston.

At two conferences, I presented papers based on the research for my next book on Enlightenment debates about transnational commerce and globalization, but the thoughtful commentary I received there helped me in my final revisions for this book. I thank Kirstie McClure for inviting me to the conference on 'Inside/Outside Constitutionalisms: Rights, Revolutions, Empires, c. 1640–1848' at the Clark Center of the University of California at Los Angeles, and for her cogent questions and comments. While at the Clark Center, I had many valuable conversations with J.G.A. Pocock, who offered encouragement and much erudite advice. I thank Erik Bleich, Stéphane Dufoix, and Patrick Weil for inviting me to present a paper at a conference on "The Legacy of Colonization and Decolonization in Europe and the Americas", sponsored by the Centre d'Étude des Politiques Immigration, d'Intégration et de Citoyenneté (CEPIC) of the Sorbonne (Université de Paris, I).

An early version of some of the arguments that I make in chapter 7 was published as "Enlightenment Anti-Imperialism" in *Social Research*, vol. 66 (1999). "Justice and Foreigners: Kant's Cosmopolitan Right", in *Constellations*, vol. 7 (2000), contains a previous version of some parts of chapter 5.

The Graduate Faculty of the New School for Social Research was an exciting intellectual home. Its unusual commitment to interdisciplinary thinking, scholarship, and conversation has been an inspiration for my work. I am indebted to Nancy Shealy's tireless efforts at forging order out of chaos. I thank my undergraduate students for their enthusiastic interest and lively participation in my seminars on the history of debates over slavery, empire, and international justice, and the excellent graduate students at the New School for innumerable discussions about the issues under study in this book, many of which helped me to refine my arguments. I owe much to all of my New School colleagues, but I especially would like to acknowledge my comrades in the Department of Political Science: Nancy Fraser, Vicky Hattam, Mala Htun, Courtney Jung, Jacob Landynski, Jim Miller, David Plokte, Addie Pollis, Adolph Reed, Jr., and Ari Zolberg. I am also very grateful for the encouragement given to me by my colleagues in the Department of Philosophy, in particular Richard Bernstein, Jay Bernstein, Agnes Heller, Dimitri Nikulin, Charles Taylor, and Yirmiyahu Yovel. I offer a special thanks to my extraordinary junior faculty colleagues across all of the departments at the Graduate Faculty.

Judith Shklar's exemplary scholarship on Enlightenment political thought, which first drew me to Harvard's Department of Government, has served as a model for my feeble efforts. As I developed my dissertation prospectus, I received helpful comments from Peter Berkowitz, Daniel Gordon, Bonnie Honig, and Tzvetan Todorov. Linda Zerilli offered constructive comments on an early version of my writings about Diderot's understanding of Tahiti. I have also gained much from incisive conversations about Enlightenment political thought with Istvan Hont, George Kateb, Gordon Lawson, Steven Lukes, John McCormick, Michael Mosher, Bhikhu Parekh, Corey Robin, and Alan Ryan. Michael Suarez, S.J., has been both a kind friend and has served as an example of scholarly integrity. I am grateful to Melvin Richter and Bernard Yack for having read my book manuscript and for offering insightful advice. In addition, I thank the anonymous readers of my book for their conscientious, detailed, and invaluable commentary. Many thanks to Terence Moore at Cambridge University Press for his generous support of this project. I am indebted to Linda Truilo for her thorough and expert copyediting and to Maria denBoer for her careful preparation of the index. Ian Malcolm, my editor at Princeton University Press, has been a joy to work with; his excitement about this book and his attention to its every detail have aided me in innumerable ways.

Anthony Pagden, to whom all scholars working on questions about empire in modern political thought are deeply indebted, kindly read the whole manuscript and, over the years, has offered consistently sage advice. Richard Tuck read drafts of many chapters and gave me excellent suggestions over many conversations. At the University of Wisconsin at Madison, Marcus Singer offered encouragement and expert knowledge in moral philosophy and the philosophy of law. At Harvard, Pratap Bhanu Mehta provided a wealth of always intelligent advice on a wide range of issues in addition to friendly support. Seyla Benhabib, my principal adviser, was enthusiastic about this project from the outset and has shown tremendous care for even the smallest details of my arguments; I have benefited greatly from her insightful and learned advice. It is because of Patrick Riley that I first cultivated a passion for the study of political thought. He has gone above and beyond the call of duty in providing me with an astonishing amount of philosophical advice, scholarly criticism, and good cheer.

My sister and brother-in-law, Uma Muthu and John Vlahoplus, have been a constant source of encouragement and affection. My niece, Phoebe

Tharaka Vlahoplus, has also encouraged me by asking repeatedly, "Are you finished your book?" It also gives me great pleasure to thank Lawrence and Mary Pitts for their kind and caring support.

Jennifer Pitts has read virtually every draft of every chapter of this book. She has consistently offered me profound advice as a fellow scholar and political theorist; as my best friend and lifetime partner, she has enriched my life with her compassionate disposition, good humour, and steadfast love.

I owe my parents, Jeya (Rajavel) Muthuchidambaram and Subba Pillai Muthuchidambaram, much more than words can express. I dedicate this book to them.

ENLIGHTENMENT AGAINST EMPIRE

One

Introduction: Enlightenment Political Thought and the Age of Empire

IN THE late eighteenth century, a number of prominent European political thinkers attacked imperialism, not only defending non-European peoples against the injustices of European imperial rule, as some earlier modern thinkers had done, but also challenging the idea that Europeans had any right to subjugate, colonize, and 'civilize' the rest of the world. This book is a study of this historically anomalous and understudied episode of political thinking. It is an era unique in the history of modern political thought: strikingly, virtually every prominent and influential European thinker in the three hundred years before the eighteenth century and nearly the full century after it were either agnostic toward or enthusiastically in favour of imperialism. In the context of the many philosophical and political questions raised by the emerging relationships between the European and non-European worlds, Enlightenment anti-imperialist thinkers crafted nuanced and intriguingly counter-intuitive arguments about human nature, cultural diversity, cross-cultural moral judgements, and political obligations. This study aims both to pluralize our understanding of the philosophical era known as 'the Enlightenment' and to explore a set of arguments and intellectual dispositions that reorient contemporary assumptions about the relationship between human unity and human diversity.

Throughout this book, I use the term 'Enlightenment' as a temporal adjective; in this sense of the term, Enlightenment political theory simply refers to the political thought of the long eighteenth century (that is, the late seventeenth to the early nineteenth centuries). As I argue in the concluding chapter, more substantive and conventional understandings of 'the Enlightenment' usually occlude more than they illuminate the writings about non-European peoples and empire by eighteenth-century political thinkers. This study, then, is neither a defence of 'the' Enlightenment nor an attack upon it, for an investigation of the anti-imperialist strand of eighteenth-century writings is meant to broaden our understanding of Enlightenment-era perspectives, rather than to redescribe 'the' Enlightenment or an overriding 'Enlightenment project' that ostensibly typified this age of philosophical thought. As with other historiographic terms of convenience, 'the Enlightenment' groups together an

extraordinarily diverse set of authors, texts, arguments, opinions, dispositions, assumptions, institutions, and practices. Thus, I begin this book
with the presumption that we should diversify our understanding of Enlightenment thought.[1] On this understanding, rather than categorizing
'the' Enlightenment *as such* or constructing ideas of a single 'Enlightenment project' that one must defend or reject, I take Enlightenment anti-
imperialist arguments, which are themselves multifaceted, to represent
only some of many, often conflicting, discourses in eighteenth-century
moral and political thought.

In the following chapters, I interpret the relationship among theories
about the constitutive features of humanity, explanations of human diversity and historical change, and political arguments about European imperialism.[2] In exploring the rise of anti-imperialist arguments in Enlightenment political thought, I concentrate upon the philosophically robust
and distinctive strand of such arguments made by Denis Diderot (1713–
84), Immanuel Kant (1724–1804), and Johann Gottfried Herder (1744–
1803). These thinkers are not usually grouped together; indeed, they
could be viewed as fundamentally antithetical, as representing some of
the contrasting ideal-types of eighteenth-century political thought: athe-
istic materialism, enlightened rationalism, and romantic nationalism. To
begin with, such labels grossly distort their actual philosophies. Moreover, as I will argue, viewing these thinkers through the lens of debates
about international relations that concerned them deeply, in particular
those about the relationship between the European and non-European
worlds, brings out the remarkable extent to which their political theories,
though obviously unique to be sure, are nonetheless cut from the same
cloth.[3] Diderot's immense philosophical influence in this period with regard to questions of imperialism explains in part the shared intellectual
disposition about the immorality of empire and the related philosophical
ideas upon which this disposition often rested: theories of human nature;
conceptualizations of human diversity; and the relationship between universal moral and political norms, on the one hand, and a commitment to
moral incommensurability, on the other. As we will see, Diderot's anti-
imperialist contributions to Abbé Raynal's *Histoire philosophique et politique des établissements et du commerce des Européens dans les deux Indes*
[*Philosophical and political history of European settlements and commerce
in the two Indies*], one of the most widely read, 'underground' nonfiction
works of the eighteenth century, appear to have left their mark on both
Kant and Herder. Behind them all, I will argue, lie Jean-Jacques Rousseau's writings, in particular the two *Discourses*, which exerted both a
negative and a positive influence upon the development of this aspect of
Enlightenment thought, for Diderot's, Kant's, and Herder's anti-imperialism rested crucially upon both an appropriation as well as a rejection of

particular elements of Rousseau's philosophical anthropology and political thought.

In this chapter, I elaborate the historical and philosophical distinctiveness of Enlightenment anti-imperialist political thought. I also note briefly some of the philosophical sources and legacies of Enlightenment anti-imperialism, which I examine in more detail in the concluding chapter. As I will contend, a number of the conventional distinctions that are deployed by many contemporary political theorists—for instance, between universalism and relativism, or essential and constructed identities—fail to do justice to the arguments made by Enlightenment anti-imperialists, who often treat such supposed opposites as interrelated features of the human condition. A study of Enlightenment anti-imperialism offers a richer and more accurate portrait of eighteenth-century political thought and illuminates the underappreciated philosophical interconnections between human unity and human diversity, and between moral universalism and moral incommensurability.

Enlightenment Anti-imperialism as a Historical Anomaly

Enlightenment anti-imperialist political theory has been the object of far less study than the anti-slavery writings of the same period.[4] Some of the best contemporary scholarship on slavery details the rising tide of philosophical opinion against it, and the emergence of a humanitarian ethic that provided the concepts and languages that newly formed anti-slavery societies and activists deployed in their controversial, lengthy, and ultimately successful campaigns. In their studies about slavery, David Brion Davis and Robin Blackburn attempt to discern why an institution that is universally decried today underwent no sustained opposition from a critical mass of thinkers and political actors until the eighteenth century.[5] The same question can plausibly be asked with regard to imperialism, for it is only in the latter half of the eighteenth century that a group of significant European political thinkers began to attack the imperial and colonial enterprise as such. To be sure, in surveying the philosophical and political debates that followed the European discovery of the New World, one encounters discussions about the hypocrisy of European imperialists,[6] humanitarian attacks upon the practice of Amerindian slavery and other cruelties perpetrated by the conquistadors in the New World,[7] and romanticized (though, as I argue in chapter 2, ultimately dehumanizing) accounts of noble savages in travel, literary, and philosophical texts. Before the late eighteenth century, however, those who sympathized with the plight of colonized peoples and those who launched explicit criticisms of Europeans' relations with the non-European world (including the most morally impassioned accounts, such as Bartolomé de Las Casas' arguments against the Castilian crown in the mid-sixteenth century) generally decried the abuses of imperial power, but not the imperial mission itself. Imperial rule, however it may have been perceived and justified (inter alia, in light of religious conversion, the civilizing mission of imperialism, economic and other commercial benefits, or the more rational use of otherwise supposedly wasted natural resources), was widely endorsed even by the most zealous *critics* of the violence perpetrated by Europeans in the New World.

Truly anti-imperialist political philosophy emerges in the late eighteenth century among a broad array of thinkers from different intellectual and national contexts. A significant group of European political thinkers rejected imperialism outright as unworkable, dangerous, or immoral—for economic reasons of free trade, as a result of principles of self-determination or cultural integrity, due to concerns about the effects of imperial politics upon domestic political institutions and practices, or out of contempt over the ironic spectacle of ostensibly civilized nations engaging in despotism, corruption, and lawlessness abroad. In confronting the steadily expanding commercial and political power of European states and imperial trading companies over the non-European world, the diverse group of thinkers who assailed the injustices and countered the dominant justifications of European imperialism include Jeremy Bentham, Condorcet, Diderot, Herder, Kant, and Adam Smith.[8] Moreover, such denunciations of what Herder liked to call "the grand European sponging enterprise" were complemented by more specific attacks upon European imperial or quasi-imperial activities in particular regions. Along these lines, the most notable efforts are Edmund Burke's legislative attempts to curtail and to regulate the activities of the East India Company and his lengthy, zealous prosecution of the impeachment of Warren Hastings, a senior East India Company official and the Governor-General of Bengal.[9] Burke argued that the British had failed to respect the sovereignty of local Indian powers, and had accordingly enriched themselves through illegal and unjust means, contributing not one iota, in his view, to the well-being of Indians themselves. In making such arguments, Burke was not a lone voice in the wilderness; rather, he raised concerns that were shared by a number of his contemporaries, a fact that has been neglected even by incisive scholars who have studied the connections between modern political theory and empire.[10] Of course, such anti-imperialist political thinkers fought an uphill battle, for defences of European imperial rule were still prevalent; the Enlightenment era is unique not because of the absence of imperialist arguments, but rather due to the presence of spirited attacks upon the foundations of empire.

Enlightenment anti-imperialism is understudied most likely because of its failure to take root both in the broader political cultures in which it was presented and in the intellectual writings of later thinkers, including those who in some sense saw themselves as heirs to the tradition of progressive thinking of the eighteenth century. Here the contrast with anti-slavery writings is especially stark. Anti-slavery writings of the eighteenth century, from Montesquieu onward, provided much of the political language and principles that were used by anti-slavery activists and by newly formed anti-slavery societies; accordingly, the immorality of slavery became a common (though, of course, by no means a universal) presumption of nineteenth-century European social and political thought. Eighteenth-century anti-imperialist arguments, on the other hand, almost always went unheeded, not only by political, religious, and commercial authorities (as one would expect), but also by later political thinkers, including some of the most progressive social and political reformers of the nineteenth century. Those who crusaded against the fraud and oppression of imperial rule and the activities of commercial trading companies were generally ridiculed and ultimately defeated in their efforts. Burke's efforts in the Hastings trial are particularly suggestive of the failed political results of anti-imperialist crusades; Hastings was found innocent, and Burke's refusal to compromise on the India issue damaged his standing not only with his parliamentary colleagues, but also with the press and the general populace.[11] And although the French Revolution gave an impetus to eradicating slavery, revolutionary and post-revolutionary France, as Benjamin Constant noted, was firmly committed to a form of imperialism, one of conquest within Europe, in order to spread the ideals and institutions of the revolution.[12] Strikingly, with regard to intellectual opinion, anti-imperialist sentiments largely fell by the wayside as the eighteenth century came to a close. The anti-imperialist writings of the latter half of the eighteenth century failed to rally later thinkers to the cause of exposing imperialist injustices, defending non-European peoples against imperial rule, and attacking the standard rationales for empire. None of the most significant anti-imperialist thinkers of the eighteenth century can be matched with any nineteenth-century anti-imperialist thinker of a comparable stature. By the mid-nineteenth century, anti-imperialist political thinking was virtually absent from Western European intellectual debates, surfacing only rarely by way of philosophically obscure and politically marginal figures.[13] Indeed, the major European political theorists of the immediate post-Enlightenment period either were ambivalent about European imperialism or were quite often explicitly in favour of it.

Thus, while imperialist arguments surface frequently in eighteenth-century European political debates, this period is anomalous in the history of modern political philosophy in that it includes a significant anti-

imperialist strand, one moreover that includes not simply marginal figures, but some of the most prominent and innovative thinkers of the age.
In this respect, the nineteenth-century European political and philosophical discourse on empire marked a return to the frequently held imperialist
sentiments of pre-Enlightenment political thought. While the dominance
of languages of race and nation in the nineteenth century was new, the
virtual consensus about the necessity and justice of imperialism among
European political thinkers recalls the pre-Enlightenment discourse on
empire. It is perhaps by reading popular nineteenth-century political
views of progress, nationality, and empire back into the eighteenth century that 'the Enlightenment' as a whole has been characterized as a
project that ultimately attempted to efface or marginalize difference, a
characterization that has hidden from view the anti-imperialist strand of
Enlightenment-era political thought.

Synopsis

The following chapters proceed chronologically, and they are also linked
biographically. Rousseau and Diderot were, for a time, friends who influenced one another's political writings, in particular the texts under study
in this book. As Kant himself famously attested, his philosophical commitments and intellectual disposition were deeply shaped by Rousseau's
writings. In addition, I will argue that Diderot's most radical political and
historical writings appear to have informed Kant's and Herder's anti-
imperialism. As is well known, Herder studied under Kant at Königsberg,
and held him in great admiration even after Kant had written critical
book reviews of the first two installments of Herder's masterpiece, *Ideen
zur Philosophie der Geschichte der Menschheit* [*Ideas Toward a Philosophy of
History of Humankind*]. Approaching some of the philosophically most
incisive and innovative currents of eighteenth-century political thought
on human diversity and European imperialism reveals the overlapping
and intersecting character of such writings and debates. The rapidly pro-
liferating literature about human unity and diversity in the Enlightenment era reflects a cross-fertilization of concepts, arguments, and perspectives from diverse intellectual contexts.[14] Whatever the conclusions
and assessments that one draws from their diverse writings, it is clear that
many social and political reformers of the eighteenth century saw their
efforts as part of a broad, though also a diffuse and contentious, multina-
tional effort. Such a 'Republic of Letters', to use a phrase that was employed often in the eighteenth century, aimed to identify and to check
oppression not only within Europe, but often also in light of what a
number of eighteenth-century thinkers viewed as Europe's tyranny over

other continents. Hence, the specific grouping of thinkers in this book illuminates both a cohesive set of arguments about international justice and cultural pluralism as well as a set of influences, both negative and positive, across national and ideological lines.

The rise of anti-imperialist political theory in the late eighteenth century depended upon far more than a universal ethic that ascribed value or dignity to every human being. In addition to the fact that the indigenous inhabitants of the New World had been considered by many Europeans, from the fifteenth century onward, to be subhuman, it is crucial to note that even when their humanity was accepted, they failed to win recognition as free and self-governing peoples. Within the modern natural right and social contractarian traditions, Amerindians in particular were almost always deployed as empirical examples of pure humans, that is, as beings who inhabit a state of nature and who thus exhibit purely natural qualities, such as natural sentiments or an unmediated knowledge of natural laws and rights. Ironically, however, for reasons that are philosophically revealing and that I will later discuss, the profoundly influential natural right theorists of the seventeenth and eighteenth centuries, such as Grotius and Vattel, as well as the social critics who celebrated Amerindians as noble savages, categorized Amerindians as the most purely human of humans, while also according them the weakest possible (and sometimes even a nonexistent) moral status in the face of European imperial power. The idea of what it meant fundamentally to be human went through a transformation before an anti-imperialist political theory could emerge. Human nature had sometimes been viewed as a stable category, one that is unchanging and that serves as a foundational essence upon which more ephemeral, particular features of human life (mores, institutions, social practices) are layered. This account came to be replaced—at times, no doubt, unwittingly, but largely in conscious opposition to naturalistic and unitary understandings of human nature—by the view that humanity is marked fundamentally by cultural difference. This is what I will call the view of *humanity as cultural agency*, which in varying ways animates the thinking of Diderot, Kant, and Herder.

By using the term 'cultural agency', I am not suggesting that Enlightenment anti-imperialists believed that there are different cultures, that non-Europeans are members of distinct cultures, and that such cultures are of worth equal to that of all other cultures. Enlightenment anti-imperialism is not 'multiculturalist' in this conventional (and contemporary) sense because eighteenth-century thinkers did not write of culture in the plural. This was a development that would occur in European writings of the nineteenth century, when 'cultures' would begin to signify (sometimes only certain) peoples. The Enlightenment anti-imperialists under study in this book, by contrast, believed that human beings are fundamentally cultural creatures, that is, they possess and exercise, simply by virtue of being human, a range of rational, emotive, aesthetic, and imaginative capacities that create, sustain, and transform diverse practices and institutions over time. The fact that humans are cultural agents, according to these writers, underlies the diverse mores, practices, beliefs, and institutions of different peoples. My use of the term 'cultural' is only somewhat anachronistic, since the philosophical use of the term 'culture' itself, in particular to denote some aspect of the differences among humans, emerges in a number of late eighteenth-century German writings. *Kultur*, like the English 'culture', derives from the Latin *cultura*, which referred to cultivation generally and often to agricultural practices, a fact that (as we will see) is by no means unimportant for appreciating some imperial understandings of cultural development. Even in its earliest uses, 'culture' was a highly ambiguous term, for it could refer to a particular social or collective lifestyle (usually sedentary and agricultural) or to an aesthetic sensibility that was posited either as an ideal or as a reality that had been achieved by only some peoples or individuals.[15] It could also, however, connote the constitutive features of humankind; in this book, I use the term 'cultural agency' in this most expansive sense, in order to indicate those qualities that humans have in common and that also account for many of their differences. The concept of 'cultural agency', then, signifies how Enlightenment anti-imperialists anthropologically employed the term 'culture' or its near equivalents and analogues. These include the French *mœurs*, which both Rousseau and Diderot employ in the context of theorizing human diversity, and the language of 'sociability', under which many eighteenth-century thinkers discussed the varied capacities, activities, and values that today would often be categorized by the word 'culture' and its variants.

Diderot, Kant, and Herder were all profoundly influenced by Rousseau's account of human history and social life, of his conception of humans as free, self-making creatures, whose very freedom creates and perpetuates diverse psychological needs, social inequalities, and political constraints, while also serving potentially as a source for a less unjust society. But they argued, contra Rousseau, that humans are constitutively social and diverse creatures, that they are cultural agents. Thus, they appropriated Rousseau's social criticism and much of his accompanying account of freedom, but jettisoned his attack on the idea of natural sociability. Diderot, Kant, and Herder all elaborated the view that, to use Edmund Burke's concise formulation, "art is Man's nature".[16] Having appreciated Rousseau's searing indictment of European mores, social institutions, political power, and economic inequality, they were loathe to recommend European societies as models for other peoples. But they were also unwilling to classify any people or set of peoples as virtually natural, as free from artifice. For them, the art (or culture) that constitutes human practices, beliefs, and institutions is necessarily diverse and also, importantly, in many respects, incommensurable. Consequently, non-Europeans, including nomadic peoples who were often viewed as exotically uncultivated and purely natural, were members of societies that were artful, or cultural; they were simply artful in a different manner, one that could not be judged as intrinsically superior or inferior. At certain moments of Enlightenment thought, as cultural differences came to be viewed as the results produced by interactions of human freedom and reason with diverse environments—rather than as pathological aberrations from a single true way of life as represented by some set of European mores, practices, and institutions—Europeans' brutal treatment of foreign peoples evoked an outpouring of moral indignation and protest. Intriguingly, as the particularity and partial incommensurability of human lives came to the fore in a number of late eighteenth-century political writings, the moral universalism that occupied a formal, but ultimately hollow, position in earlier political theories became more genuinely inclusive.

In the following chapters, I examine the core philosophical assumptions and arguments that underlie the anti-imperialist political theories of Diderot, Kant, and Herder. In chapter 2, I examine a series of French writings that constitute what in retrospect can be identified as a tradition of noble savage thinking, which exerted an enormous influence upon many eighteenth-century thinkers, including Diderot. Focusing principally upon understandings of 'natural men' in Montaigne, Lahontan, and Rousseau, I then turn toward Diderot's appropriation and subversion of noble savagery in his account of Tahitian society in the *Supplément au Voyage de Bougainville*. Diderot's philosophic dialogue upsets the standard assumptions of noble savagery—most notably, the presumption of the existence and philosophical usefulness of 'natural' humans, who were thought to be free, or nearly free, of artifice or culture. Diderot's subversion of noble savagery and his attendant account of humanity as fundamentally cultural would help to ground many aspects of his anti-imperialist political thought. In chapter 3, I analyze Diderot's myriad arguments against empire and conquest in his influential contributions to Raynal's *Histoire des deux Indes*, many of which reemerge in later Enlightenment attacks upon empire. In chapter 4, I examine Kant's understanding of 'humanity' in order to elucidate a key and often misunderstood concept of his political philosophy that has profound consequences for his writings on international and cosmopolitan justice. In Kant's view, humans were not at bottom metaphysical essences from whom one could abstract all social and cultural attachments, but rather they were fundamentally cultural agents. I offer an account of the understandings of reason and freedom that he associated with 'humanity' and I show how this influenced his views of history and society. In chapter 5, I interpret Kant's account of plural values in order to examine how he defends an anti-paternalistic conception of human development. I then turn to his understanding of human diversity and his attacks upon European imperialism in light of his account of humanity and ideal of cosmopolitan justice. In chapter 6, I provide an interpretation of Herder's political thought that emphasizes both its distinctiveness and its deep similarities to Diderot's and Kant's anti-imperialist political philosophies. Underlying Herder's account of pluralism and independent nationalities, I contend, is a nuanced and complex understanding of 'humanity' (*Humanität*) that is at once anthropological, moral, and political. Finally, in the concluding chapter, I present the key philosophical sources and legacies of the strand of Enlightenment anti-imperialism under study in this book. I argue that Diderot's, Kant's, and Herder's incisive and hitherto underappreciated arguments against empire provide us with an opportunity to rethink prevalent assumptions about our understandings of 'the' Enlightenment and about the relationship between human unity and diversity, and between universal moral concepts and pluralistic ethical commitments. Common understandings of 'Enlightenment universalism' fail to come to terms with the complicated and intriguing manner in which Diderot, Kant, and Herder interweave commitments to moral universalism and moral incommensurability, to humanity and cultural difference. Such universal and particular categories in their political philosophies not only coexist, but deeply inform one another. Thus, as I will show, their arguments against empire treat the affirmation of a wide plurality of individual and collective ways of life and the dignity of a universal, shared humanity as fundamentally intertwined ethical and political commitments.

Two

Toward a Subversion of Noble Savagery: From Natural Humans to Cultural Humans

THE DEVELOPMENT of anti-imperialist political thought in the late eighteenth century is attributable only partly to the development of the natural rights doctrine or, indeed, to any other version of the idea that humans as such deserve moral respect. It is a much noted feature of modern political theory that proponents of egalitarian doctrines of equal rights and liberty regularly flouted such norms when reflecting upon the social and political status of women, nonpropertied males, and those who were deemed foreign or exotic, among others. At times, this reflected a gross inconsistency between prima facie humanistic norms and self-serving or prejudicial arguments that sought to exclude certain categories of humans from having full social, legal, and political standing. This seeming paradox, however, could also follow from the specific characterization of universal principles themselves; as I will argue in this chapter, even on the assumption that non-Europeans or New World peoples were human, particular understandings of humanity were less likely (and, conversely, other understandings were more likely) to undergird political arguments in favour of the rights and liberties of non-European peoples. This tension between moral universalism and the politics of exclusion was overcome to a certain extent by anti-imperialist thinkers who framed the relationship between human nature and cultural pluralism differently from previous thinkers (and from some of their contemporaries); their view that imperial rule was manifestly unjust, and their inclination to defend a variety of non-European peoples against imperial policies and institutions, in part developed out of an understanding of humanity as cultural agency, a view that was distinct from that of a number of their most obvious forebears.

In this chapter, I investigate the philosophical and political assumptions and arguments that made this outlook possible in part by contrasting this view, as we find it in Diderot's understanding of Tahitian society, from the influential image of New World peoples as 'noble savages'.[1] This idealized conception of what were usually taken to be nomadic peoples sought to counter the most pejorative characterizations of foreign peoples as barbaric and fundamentally inferior. As David Brion Davis has plausibly speculated, the celebration of so-called primitives may well have "partially weaken[ed] Europe's arrogant ethnocentrism and create[d] at

least a momentary ambivalence about the human costs of modern civilization".[2] Yet, ultimately, as much as this may have helped to elicit the
intellectual groundwork for the humanitarianism of anti-slavery thinking,
a *rejection* of noble savagery was necessary before a more meaningful and
substantive moral commiseration with non-Europeans could develop, in
particular one that could help to engender an anti-imperialist political
philosophy. As I will argue, the peculiar understanding of the relationship
between human nature and culture in noble savage writings yielded
a virtually dehumanizing exoticism, despite the best intentions of the
thinkers who chose to celebrate what they saw as the 'purely natural'
specimens of humanity in the New World. In order to understand how
Diderot drew upon the mode of social criticism distinctive to the tradition of noble savagery, while also ultimately subverting its core presump-
tions about the character of New World peoples and indeed of humanity
itself, we must first examine the exponents of this tradition who most
shaped the relevant aspects of his intellectual milieu.

The interpretations of New World peoples inherited by eighteenth-
century thinkers vary widely and are not reducible to any one doctrine,
although theories that were based upon the purported genetic, behavioural, or cultural inferiority of Amerindians were by far the most influential and dominant at the outset of the century, by which time European
colonial and imperial activities were well entrenched and steadily expanding. Given its complicated influence upon the group of anti-imperialist
thinkers discussed in later chapters, I focus here largely upon the heterodox noble savage literature that, in contrast, celebrated New World peoples as intrinsically pacific and benevolent natural beings, free from the
corruption not only of modern life but indeed of culture itself. The sixteenth-century essayist Michel de Montaigne plays a central role in the
philosophical history of theorizing Amerindians, although he both deploys the idea of a noble savage and at times undermines it. While in this
respect his writings foreshadow Diderot's views, they also reveal the deep
philosophical tensions of noble savage theory, which Montaigne never
comprehensively or directly explored. These tensions are even more glar-
ing, and consequently the exoticism inherent in noble savagery is thrown
into even sharper relief, in the writings of Baron Lahontan. At the turn of
the eighteenth century, Lahontan, a French imperial officer who lived in
Quebec and studied the Huron, Algonquin, and Iroquois peoples, was
among the most influential noble savage theorists in the French tradition.
Like other noble savage accounts, Lahontan's writings offer an amalgam
of anthropological interpretations and radical social and political criticism. Rousseau's *Discourse on Inequality* is heavily indebted to Lahontan
and Montaigne and to this tradition of social criticism in general, which
highlighted and elaborated idealized representations of Amerindians from

New World ethnography. As with previous attacks on European social practices and political institutions that used the Amerindian as a pure and natural foil, European imperialism itself was never the sustained object of Rousseau's trenchant criticism. Paradoxically, as I argue later, identifying indigenous Americans as purely human resulted ultimately in their dehumanization, making the possibility of any meaningful commiseration with their oppression remote. Nonetheless, the subtlety and power of Rousseau's account of humans as self-making (and self-enslaving) agents shaped the political thought of Diderot, in addition to the writings of Kant and Herder. When the critical features of Rousseau's account of freedom and history were conjoined to a philosophical anthropology that, contra Rousseau, viewed social and cultural differentiation as central to the human condition, it became more likely that at least some thinkers would engage in sustained intellectual assaults upon European state power not only in a domestic or intra-European setting, but also as it was exercised in imperialist ventures abroad. Thus, Rousseau looms over the latter half of the eighteenth century as an ambiguous figure who both impedes and enables the development of anti-imperialist political thought. To understand this better, however, and to appreciate the innovation of thinkers such as Diderot, Kant, and Herder, it is crucial to begin with the accounts of noble savagery that most informed Rousseau's (and through Rousseau, Diderot's) understanding of New World peoples.

The accounts of many of the earliest encounters between Europeans and Amerindians contain reactions toward New World peoples that implied, or more directly offered, praise for what was perceived to be their 'natural' manner of living. Idealized portrayals of Amerindians in these writings reflect the varied, and at times conflicting, fables about faraway lands and peoples across the seas that shaped the expectations of the late-fifteenth- and early-sixteeth-century explorers, missionaries, and soldiers who travelled to the Americas. Imagined visions of distant lands occupied by magical creatures, instantiations of mythological 'wild men', or members of a golden age who were celebrated in song and in lyrical poetry no doubt helped to occasion moments of what can be described in hindsight as noble savagery.[3] To the extent that early accounts contained any positive assessments of Amerindians, they typically offered only fleeting moments of adulation of Amerindians' rusticity, which could then turn rapidly to outright disgust at what appeared to explorers and settlers as manifestly backward and barbaric appearances and behaviour. Still, these occasional nonpejorative expressions of wonder often became widely circulated and redescribed, eventually forming a vivid image of the Amerindian that served many rhetorical purposes for imperial administrators, church officials, theologians, social critics, and the humanist literati. One of the origins of noble savage sentiments, for instance, can be found in missionaries' writings that lauded Amerindians' simple nobility and reasonableness both in an effort to persuade European political authorities that they could be converted and to censure sinful behaviour within modern European societies.[4] More sustained noble savage accounts, however, broadly attacked Europe's moral standing—and that of all civilizations—rather than supporting the more conventional social and political aims that inspired many of the isolated fragments of wonder and praise in the earliest travel literature and theological commentaries. The distinction between nature and artifice, which plays such a central role in Montaigne's influential essay, "Des Cannibales" ["Of Cannibals"] (1578–80), was crucial to such modes of radical social criticism.

Noble Savagery in Montaigne's "Of Cannibals"

One especially significant instance of the proliferation of noble savagery can be traced to Amerigo Vespucci's *Mundus Novus* (1503), a letter that became one of the most popular essays on the New World in the sixteenth century.

> They have no cloth of wool, linen, or cotton, since they need none. Nor have they private property, but own everything in common: they live together without a king and without authorities, each man his own master. They take as many wives as they wish, and son may couple with mother, brother with sister, cousin with cousin, and in general men with women as they chance to meet. They dissolve marriage as often as they please, observing no order in any of these matters. Moreover, they have no temple and no religion, nor do they worship idols. What more can I say? They live according to nature, and might be called Epicureans rather than Stoics. There are no merchants among them, nor is there any commerce. The peoples make war among themselves without art or order.[5]

The lack of "art or order" among beings who live simply according to nature is a trope that emerges in nearly every idealized conception of Amerindian life, although the specific manner in which such "natural" lifestyles are presented and explained differ from thinker to thinker. A key philosophical assumption of such portrayals is that a human life *could* be simply natural (or very nearly so), free from the 'artificial', regular social practices and constructed institutions that shape human expectations and form the horizon of possibilities—free, that is, from what would now most often be described as 'culture'. Montaigne paraphrased Amerigo's celebrated description, but set it in the context of a more extensive discourse about the corruption of European societies and the superior excellence of nature's treasures, which included for him most of the indigenous inhabitants of the New World who had hardly strayed from their "original naturalness" (153).[6]

Montaigne's essay is often interpreted as an ingenious attempt at complicating the very idea of savagery, for he directly challenges the view that Amerindians are savage in any pejorative sense.[7] A proper understanding of the term *sauvage*, in his view, shows that Europeans who have altered themselves and their environments are in fact savagely artificial, rather than naturally pure. As Montaigne argues,

> Those people [Amerindians] are wild [*sauvage*], just as we call wild [*sauvage*] the fruits that Nature has produced by herself and in her normal course; whereas really it is those that we have changed artificially and led astray from the common order, that we should rather call wild [*sauvage*]. The former retain alive and vigorous their genuine, their most useful and natural, virtues and properties, which we have debased in the latter in adapting them to gratify our corrupted taste. (152)

Yet, while this challenges the moral superiority associated with cultivation or civilization (though he himself does not use the latter term in this context), his analysis of the term "savage" serves only to replicate antecedent understandings of Amerindians as noble savages. Amerindians are savage, Montaigne argues, not in the sense that they are inferior, but only in the sense that they are natural, closer to what human beings are like in a pure, undeveloped state, and thus without the largely corrupting layers of artificiality that constitute modern humans. This is, of course, what a number of previous and seemingly nonpejorative descriptions of Amerindians had asserted. Montaigne makes the simple naturalness of Amerindians explicit when he concludes that "[t]hese nations, then, seem to me barbarous only in this sense, that they have been fashioned very little by the human mind, and are still very close to their original naturalness." (153) It is precisely to underscore this point that Montaigne paraphrases Amerigo's celebrated description of Amerindian life. Montaigne declares,

> This is a nation, I should say to Plato, in which there is no sort of traffic, no knowledge of letters, no science of numbers, no name for a magistrate or for political superiority, no custom of servitude, no riches or poverty, no contracts, no successions, no partitions, no occupations but leisure ones, no care for any but common kinship, no clothes, no agriculture, no metal or use of wine or wheat. (153)

By way of John Florio's English translation of "Des Cannibales", this passage would emerge yet again, and the attendant understanding of Amerindians as pure, undeveloped natural humans would be further popularized through yet another literary form in Shakespeare's *The Tempest*.[8]

The initial amazement that New World peoples led seemingly pristine lives developed over time into a tradition that understood Amerindians according to recurring, naturalistic themes, albeit with minor (and sometimes instructive) variations. Montaigne's effort at unravelling the meanings and implications of a 'savage' existence, one that could in many respects be celebrated over and against European ways of life, rests principally upon an examination of what specifically constituted a 'natural' life. Montaigne does not systematically study this question, but his characteristically subtle and meandering thoughts on the topic outline the range of meanings of a 'natural' existence that many later thinkers would draw together into theories about human nature and the origins of human societies.

For Montaigne, a natural life consists of the most simple physical and psychological needs. "They [the Amerindians] are still in that happy state of desiring only as much as their natural needs demand; anything beyond this is superfluous to them." (156) On this view, Amerindians are not corrupted by an attachment to material goods (or, even worse, by a fondness for luxury), as Montaigne suggests in his discussion of wars among Amerindian nations. The wars that New World peoples fight among each other are motivated not by base material concerns but by an elevated sense of courage; while this might not excuse them for engaging in the horrors of war, it nevertheless offers a sharp contrast, he implies, to the self-interested motives that appear to lie behind the European conquest of the Americas.

> Their warfare is wholly noble and generous, and as excusable and beautiful as this human disease can be; its only basis among them is their rivalry in valour. They are not fighting for the conquest of new lands, for they still enjoy that natural abundance that provides them without toil and trouble with all necessary things in such profusion that they have no wish to enlarge their boundaries. (156)

Montaigne contrasts what is savage or natural and what is artificial and conventional not only at an individual but concomitantly at a social level, for the lack of superfluous personal desires helps to maintain a relatively egalitarian society. He contends that Amerindians appear to live in entirely (or largely) communal societies that tend to shun private property and that distribute all (or nearly all) goods in common.

> They generally call those of the same age, brothers; those who are younger, children; and the old men are fathers to all the others. These leave to their heirs in common the full possession of their property, without division or any other title at all than just the one that Nature gives to her creatures in bringing them into the world.[9] (156)

The near absence among New World peoples of what were taken to be artificial hierarchies and inequalities, in particular those of political authority, would be asserted by virtually all of the foremost social contract thinkers in the European tradition, from Grotius and Hobbes to Locke and Pufendorf (though not, as we shall see, by Kant), for this supposed anthropological fact about Amerindians buttressed the philosophical claim that all humans are naturally equal and that political power is thoroughly artificial and constructed. As with later thinkers who would deploy the image of noble savagery, Montaigne connects these two ideas of simple desires and egalitarianism with a third: the moral health of a nonhierarchical and simple life engenders physical health. Drawing his information, we are told, from a European friend who lived for a time in Brazil, Montaigne contends that "it is rare to see a sick man there" (153). Conversely, as we will see with Lahontan and later Rousseau, Europeans' diseases are said to result most often from either their luxury or their poverty, both of which rest upon artificial desires and social, legal, and political inequalities that are minimal in the New World.

What animates the behaviour of savage peoples, given that they purportedly lack culture? The concepts that best address this aspect of noble savagery in Montaigne can be derived from the schema that he borrows from Plato to defend the idea that what is "natural" is often superior, more perfect (or less imperfect), and more praiseworthy than what is artificially created: "All things, says Plato, are produced by nature, by fortune, or by art; the greatest and most beautiful by one or the other of the first two, the least and most imperfect by the last." (153) As we have seen, for Montaigne, New World peoples—with the exception of the Mexica and Inca nations that he discusses toward the end of a later essay, "Des Coches" ["Of Coaches"] (1585–88)—are altered by hardly any cultural artifice. This nearly acultural understanding of New World peoples leaves the work of the creation and maintenance of these societies largely to fortune and nature. The role of climate, a key category in the analysis of human diversity not only in Montaigne's time but through the Enlightenment period, was central to his understanding of the role of fortune in helping to bring about and to maintain savage societies. New World peoples were blessed by a favourable climate and an abundance of natural resources that afforded sustenance without the need of complex social organizations and intensive industry, "without toil and trouble" (156). "[T]hey live in a country", Montaigne explains, "with a very pleasant and temperate climate. . . . They have a great abundance of fish and flesh . . . and they eat them with no other artifice than cooking." (153) But the primary ordering principle, or source, of such savage lives is nature itself. "The laws of nature still rule them, very little corrupted by ours" (153). For most, perhaps even all, noble savage accounts, savagery is largely a function of naturalness, which is generally seen as the anti-thesis of artificiality and of culture, that is, of any of the modes of think-ing, acting, imagining, and creating that are at all conventional, that vary over time and place, and are performed differently by various peoples and even by different individuals.

If New World peoples are 'natural' and 'savage', there remains the difficult question of how such peoples exercise their rationality and whether their rationality generates and revises practices and institutions through the use of reason, memory, imagination, and other creative fac-ulties. No proponent of noble savagery as a method of understanding the peoples of the New World doubted their capacity to foster such cultural agency in the future—if they became cultivated, for instance, by Euro-peans who would introduce supposedly artificial ways of life to them. In their allegedly natural condition, however, before what proponents of noble savagery would consider largely corrupting foreign conventional practices and institutions were introduced to them, a savage or natural life is driven either by natural instincts that mechanically motivate indi-viduals and even whole societies, or by the innate knowledge and vir-tually automatic observance of natural laws. Many noble savage accounts moved back and forth, however inconsistently, between the two, with Amerindians and at times other New World peoples leading 'natural' lives sometimes by instinct and other times by rationally following the dictates of natural law. While the latter option would appear to partake of some sense of active rationality, noble savage accounts rarely attribute to New World peoples the act of choice or agency to follow or not to follow such laws. Indeed, it seems at times that such accounts do not even describe them as consciously following such laws or principles, or if so then only because a life oriented toward pleasure corresponds to them. It is telling that Amerigo notes that Amerindians are natural in the manner of Epi-cureans, rather than Stoics, for this implies that their natural lifestyle de-rives from following their most basic desires in order to meet their unar-tificial needs and thus to engage in healthy pleasures, rather than leading such lives from a more sober, self-disciplined, reasoned, or Stoic assess-ment of the superiority of a rustic way of life.[10] Montaigne writes that natural laws rule Amerindians, hence producing a "happy state of man" that "surpasses . . . all the pictures in which poets have idealized the golden age", rather than describing Amerindians themselves as cogniz-ing, understanding, and applying natural laws to their specific conditions (153). This is the manner in which nearly all noble savage accounts tend to reduce peoples to sets of hard-wired creatures who follow their most basic (and presumably naturally good) physiological drives or who in-stinctively put into practice the laws of nature, for such behaviour most closely conforms to the key claim of noble savage narratives: that a nonartificial, or acultural, life empirically exists. Montaigne himself notes that the greatest lawgivers, such as Lycurgus and Plato, would be incredulous that such societies in the New World could exist with virtually no consciously created and maintained order: "They could not imagine a naturalness so pure and simple as we see by experience; nor could they believe that our society [i.e., the one that we Europeans witness in the New World] could be maintained with so little artifice and human solder." (153)

This understanding of New World peoples at times creates tensions within noble savage accounts, for one of the central critical claims of these writings is that the prevalent idea that such peoples are inferior or barbaric is wrongheaded. Yet, in order to make this charge and hence to humanize these peoples, proponents of noble savage understandings would laud not only the naturalness but also on occasion the mental acuity and ingeniousness of such peoples. Thus Montaigne feels compelled to contest the view that

> all this [Amerindian behaviour] is done through a simple and servile bondage to usage and through the pressure of the authority of their ancient customs, without reasoning or judgement, and because their minds are so stupid that they cannot take any other course. . . .[11] (158)

To prove that Amerindians are not simply creatures of custom (note that he does not, of course, aim to challenge the view that they are largely creatures of *nature*), Montaigne cites two examples of "their capacity": a stirring song composed by an Amerindian prisoner of war in order to taunt his captors, and a love song, both of which demonstrate the lack of barbarity in Amerindians' character. Yet these stray examples of aesthetic creativity do not amount to a defence of the idea that New World societies are maintained first and foremost by creative powers, for this would undercut the naturalness that is integral to the idea of a praiseworthy savage. To be sure, Montaigne makes several claims about various kinds of creativity and excellence in "Of Coaches", but with regard to the Mexica and Inca—that is, with reference to sedentary, agriculturally based, city-dwelling peoples, those who more easily fit the prevalent understandings of what constituted 'civilized' society. From the late fifteenth century onward, in European ethnographic writings and other texts that drew upon them or from direct experience in the New World, the less complex societies of hunters, gatherers, fishermen, and pastoralists were almost always the referents for either the most depraved and barbaric or, in the hands of noble savage theorists, the most natural and praiseworthy peoples; these are the peoples Montaigne discusses in "Of Cannibals" and he presents them there almost without exception as unartificial, naturally driven humans. There is no doubt that on occasion Mon-

taigne acknowledged, in effect, that the simplest peoples could also manifest a kind of cultural agency, but, given the predominant assertion of the
cannibals essay, that "these peoples are fashioned very little by the human
mind" (153), this thicker view of Amerindian life emerges as a curious
and somewhat inconsistent footnote to the more central theme of the
"naturalness" of New World societies. The resulting paradox of an image
of purely natural humans who lack all artifice, yet who also appear im-
pressively at times to practise certain arts lies unresolved and undertheor-
ized in "Of Cannibals", as it is in later thinkers of the noble savage tradition. As we will see, this paradox takes shape in Rousseau's *Discourse on
Inequality*, since he presents New World peoples there both to flesh out
the image of a pure state of nature and to present empirical examples of
the middle (post-natural, but precivilized) stage of human development.
The manner in which Enlightenment thinkers responded, often tacitly, to
this paradox shaped their theories of the relationship between human
nature and culture, and led in some cases to the reconceptualization of
noble savage arguments and assumptions; in the case of Diderot, it
would even lead to what amounted to a rejection of the concept of noble
savagery.

Paradoxes of this kind were usually not explicitly taken up by noble
savage thinkers because the primary purpose of such accounts was not to
produce an accurate ethnography (although, to be sure, the rhetorical
power of these writings did much to shape Europeans' attitudes about
actual New World peoples), but to foster social criticism. First and foremost, the concept of the noble savage was a critical device that could
serve the interests of thinkers who sought to challenge a variety of orthodox doctrines. Two central normative claims run through most noble
savage writings: first, that one should be wary of judging others simply by
one's own, possibly parochial, standards and, second, that a sympathetic
analysis of the 'natural' peoples of the New World could place into particularly sharp relief the deep injustices of 'artificial' European societies.

These critical impulses find their expression most clearly in Montaigne's
response to the view that Amerindians are barbaric.

> [T]here is nothing barbarous and savage in that nation, from what I have been
> told, except that each man calls barbarism whatever is not his own practice; for
> indeed it seems we have no other test of truth and reason than the example and
> pattern of the opinions and customs of the country we live in. (152)

The plurality of perspectives from which one can make moral judgements
and the resultant appeals to tolerance and against narrow dogmatism are
among the best known features of Montaigne's thinking, but it is the
controversy regarding the barbarity of cannibalism in the New World that
afforded him with an especially propitious opportunity to develop the

most distinctive features of his moral thought. Despite the thoroughgoing scepticism of his most sustained attacks upon transcendent notions of truth and knowledge, in particular in the "The Apology for Raymond Seybond" (originally written 1575–76; revised 1578–80), Montaigne's ultimate object of scorn in most of his essays is self-serving, intellectual dogmatism and the prejudices that flow from it, and not the very idea of cross-cultural standards of judgement. Indeed, as he notes above, it only "seems" as if we have no other standard of truth than our own customs, and at the outset of the cannibals essay he intones that "we should beware of clinging to vulgar opinions, and judge things by reason's way, not by popular say." (150) In confronting the reported existence of cannibalism in the Americas (interpreted by Montaigne as a corollary of warfare among New World peoples, who at times kill and then eat certain prisoners of war), Montaigne seeks to balance the demands of judging by reason and engaging in a tolerant scepticism by arguing that the practice of cannibalism is indeed barbaric, but that Europeans, precisely by attacking cannibalism abroad, fail to notice and to criticize the barbaric cannibalism of religious and political persecution at home.

> I am not sorry that we notice the barbarous horror of such acts, but I am heartily sorry that, judging their faults rightly, we should be so blind to our own. I think there is more barbarity in eating a man alive than in eating him dead; and in tearing by tortures and the rack a body still full of feeling, in roasting a man bit by bit, in having him bitten and mangled by dogs and swine (as we have not only read but seen within fresh memory, not among ancient enemies, but among neighbors and fellow citizens, and what is worse, on the pretext of piety and religion), than in roasting and eating him after he is dead. (155)

If we are to judge others by defensible standards, then such standards should be used with reference to our own practices and institutions. In doing so, Montaigne suggests that New World peoples may well be described as engaging in barbaric practices, but that the standards by which such barbarity should be judged derive not from our own supposed excellence or goodness, but rather "in respect to the rules of reason". According to such standards, Montaigne asserts that Europeans surpass Amerindians "in every kind of barbarity", a claim whose general formulation would recur in many noble savage accounts: it is we who are the real (or the more fully realized) barbarians (156).

Montaigne's treatment of cannibalism, then, allows him both to attack what he sees as the predominant impulse to judge others simply according to one's own practices and customs and to draw upon New World ethnography in order to attack injustices within Europe. The mode of social criticism of European institutions and practices that was most dis-

tinctive to the noble savage literature, however, and one that was especially potent, was to speculate or to report upon what New World indigenous individuals themselves thought of Europeans and of Europe more
generally. Montaigne ends his essay with this classic device of criticism,
when he reports of a visit that he had personally witnessed (in 1562,
when he was a counselor to the Parlement of Bordeaux) of three Amerindians to the court of King Charles IX in Rouen. The puzzled reaction of
these visitors, Montaigne reports, concerned the curious sight of grown
men serving a child, and of the vast and persistent disparity of wealth in
France. The 'natural' lives of relatively egalitarian and communal individuals in the New World here directly confront the artificiality of hereditary
monarchical rule and the artificial inequalities of wealth of a supposedly
advanced society.

Philosophically, New World ethnography offered thinkers such as Montaigne, and those who would be influenced by him, with a rich trove of
empirical examples that could provide a reliable portrait of humans' fundamental properties. In this view, 'human nature' can be discerned ef-
fortlessly in the New World since it was thought to be populated by
'natural humans'. Thus, no longer would one have to rely solely upon
arcadian myths of pastoral simplicity and happiness, or past golden ages
as celebrated in poems, epics, songs, and pictorial representations, to reflect upon the innocent and simple nature of humanity. Such naturalness
actually exists today, noble savage proponents could argue; moreover,
their presence was said to be a living example of Europe's (and humanity's) own past. This temporal claim, that the New World was new not
only to European explorers, but new to the development of social and
political life itself, and that it represented the earliest stages of human
history that civilized societies themselves once inhabited, became a key
feature of many interpretive accounts of New World peoples. Those who
viewed them as fundamentally inferior could use such an assumption to
argue for their forced enslavement or civilization under imperial rule. In
contrast, noble savage writings presented the earliest stages of humanity, as
represented by Amerindians and others, as savage only in the sense, as Montaigne argues, that they are close to humanity's "original naturalness".

At the beginning of the discussion of the New World in "Of Coaches",
before focusing upon the Mexica and Inca nations, Montaigne describes
New World societies as part of an "infant world", apparently drawing
again upon Amerigo's vivid description in *Mundus Novus*.

> Our world has just discovered another world . . . no less great, full, and well-
> limbed than itself, yet so new and so infantile that it is still being taught its A B
> C; not fifty years ago it knew neither letters, nor weights and measures, nor

clothes, nor wheat nor vines. It was still quite naked at the breast, and lived only on what its nursing mother provided. (693)

The infantilization of New World peoples by noble savage writers was meant primarily as an attack upon the decrepitude of European civilization, which they generally viewed as well past its prime, and not as an attempt to lower the status of 'new' peoples. Again, such understandings gave further currency to narratives that were already well established, from the Biblical narrative of Eden to countless meditations upon the golden ages of the most ancient and (in such accounts) the happiest peoples. The states of nature described by modern social contract theories not surprisingly elaborated these themes, although the manner in which New World ethnography was interpreted differed according to the natural condition that was being justified. Regardless of the substantive anthropological claims in such arguments, it became a commonplace of such contractarian arguments of governmental power and natural rights to assert, as John Locke could with confidence in the 1680s, that "in the beginning all the World was *America*."[12]

The presentation of New World peoples that served as the anthropological basis of unorthodox, or even radical, moral and political claims ultimately came at the price of presenting them as largely hard-wired automatons, rather than as creative agents who were embedded within and who shaped and altered cultural systems of meaning and value; the latter belonged to the life of civilized artificiality, and not—most emphatically not in this view—of the natural, savage peoples of the New World. Still, it is important to note that the intent, and much of the power, of such accounts lay in their attempts to foster humanistic and tolerant moral judgements in addition to offering a sharper sense of the injustices of Europe's own social, religious, and political order. Although not by intent then, but nevertheless in effect, the irony of treating New World peoples as the earliest, least artificial, and most natural humans—the very attempt, that is, to humanize them or to turn their presumed savagery into a badge of honour—ultimately cast them as lacking the cultural agency that would have made them recognizably human. The closer to nature they were said to be, the more exotically and inhumanly foreign they appeared. As Montaigne himself notes of his portrayal of Amerindians, "there is an amazing distance between their character and ours." (158) Closing this distance, however, would involve not only reinterpreting the relevant ethnographic accounts, but also revising the accompanying philosophical arguments in noble savage writings—those that were either explicitly delineated or tacitly invoked—about human nature and its relationship to culture. Only then would some European thinkers more successfully humanize New World peoples.

Lahontan's Dialogue with a Huron

Notwithstanding Montaigne's stature among the *philosophes*, the most influential noble savage writer in the French tradition was Louis-Armand de Lom d'Arce, baron de Lahontan, who in 1703 published in a two-volume set a collection of letters that he had written while in Canada (*Nouveaux Voyages* [*New Voyages*]); a discourse on the lands, peoples, and colonial politics of the New World (*Mémoires de l'Amérique Septentrionale* [*Memoirs of North America*]); and an enormously popular dialogue ostensibly between Lahontan and a Huron (*Dialogues Curieux entre l'Auteur et un Sauvage de bons sens qui a voyagé* [*Curious dialogues between the author and a savage of good sense who has travelled*]). An army officer who commanded local garrisons in New France, Lahontan travelled widely within North America, created maps (though sometimes fanciful and highly flawed) of territories hitherto unknown to Europeans, lived occasionally with indigenous peoples, and eventually learned to speak Algonquin and Huron. In 1693, after a political controversy stemming from charges of insubordination, he fled to Amsterdam and, for a time, became a vagabond. His personal history and itinerant lifestyle were so obscure that some disputed his existence when his writings were published. In spite of such eccentricities, Lahontan reached a wide audience and popularized, probably more than any other single thinker in the French tradition, the image of the noble savage: Montesquieu, Diderot, Rousseau, and Voltaire (as well as Swift) were among those influenced by his writings.

Using a style that was imitated at times by such thinkers, Lahontan places almost all of his critical commentary about European societies in the mouths of Amerindians. Perhaps hoping to stave off any controversy that might have affected him personally (oddly, perhaps, given his practically fugitive status at the time of publication), Lahontan carefully presents criticisms of European mores and practices as descriptions of Amerindians' attitudes. Thus, his writings are full of editorial comments impugning such criticisms and asserting, however weakly, the obvious superiority of civilization to savagery. It is not insignificant that, in the *Dialogues*, the eponymous character Lahontan attempts to convince Adario, a Huron, of the benefits of European civilization and Christianity. Yet, despite this (somewhat transparent) caution and the partly confused tone that results, the upshot of Lahontan's dialogue is clear: recalling an identical point made by Montaigne, Lahontan writes that "the name of savages that we bestow among them would fit ourselves better".[13] Lahontan describes Amerindians' lives as happier and more fulfilling than those of Europeans; hence, despite the character Lahontan's arguments to the contrary, the *Dialogues* presents Adario's disgust with European society as entirely well founded.[14]

Lahontan's writings incorporate many of the staple elements of noble savage accounts. Hurons' simple lives are made possible, he writes, by their lack of attachment to material goods: the "Savages know neither thine nor mine, for what belongs to one is equally that of another." (95) Once again, as Montaigne had suggested, a vigorous and natural lifestyle ensures robust physical constitutions, free from most diseases and easily restored to health from common maladies (93–95; cf. 200–201). Behind the minimalism and good will of New World peoples lies a profound equality that Lahontan frequently contrasts with European societies. In a comment that encapsulates the purported egalitarianism of Huron life, Adario announces proudly that among his people "everyone is as rich and as noble as his neighbour; the women are entitled to the same liberty with the men, and the children enjoy the same privileges with their fathers." (228) Such sentiments fuel Lahontan's criticism of monarchies: in an absurd contrast to the freedom from rank and privilege in the New World, the French bend their knees to a single all-powerful ruler. Lahontan claims that Amerindians themselves "brand us for slaves" by noting that "we degrade ourselves in subjecting ourselves to one man who possesses the whole power, and is bound by no law but his own will" (96). In addition, Amerindians' supposed antipathy toward distinctions of rank and wealth forms the basis of a stringent assault on private interests and luxury that presage many of Rousseau's specific criticisms of civilized life. Separate, private interests that follow from the distinction between "mine and thine", Adario argues, are ultimately the roots of all evil; they are exacerbated by the existence of currency, the treacherous drive toward accumulating wealth, and the distinctions perpetuated by such means (199–201). Hurons are free because they are their own masters, enslaved neither by their appetites (in particular, the quest for social standing and wealth) nor by other people who claim superiority (the clergy, magistrates, nobles, and kings). As Rousseau would later argue at length, Lahontan's Adario asserts that this freedom from dependence is the source of true liberty, a quality unknown to modern Europeans, but at the heart of savage life (183–85).

The lesson that Lahontan could offer for Europe is potentially radical: dismantle civilization itself in order to live a humane and free existence. Indeed, Adario claims that Providence may lie behind Europeans' discovery of North America because they may now have an opportunity to correct their faults and follow the example of Amerindians. Moreover, Lahontan describes the values that Amerindians embody—innocence of life, tranquillity of mind, a communal existence free from selfish and parochial divisions—as *human* values and, thus, as universally applicable.

On this view, all humans should work toward them because they manifest
the fundamental goodness of human nature itself (181–83). Yet, as with
so many thinkers who used the image of the noble savage, Lahontan is
not a proponent of primitivism; he never claims that Europeans should,
as it were, return to the forests. His constructive advice is rather thin, and
consists largely of a call for the gradual levelling of social strata in Europe
in order to benefit the poor and to combat the petty, corrupting, and
selfish private interests that are based on distinctions of wealth (197–98).
The egalitarian impulse behind such ideas certainly has a utopian cast—
indeed, the tone of Lahontan's writings at times resonates with an almost
revolutionary fervour. But, in the final analysis, the power of his rhetoric
rests more in its social criticism than in its vague calls for reform.

Lahontan supplements Montaigne's classic account of Amerindians by
more comprehensively elaborating what had become the standard objections in the noble savage literature against European civilized society.
Moreover, he examines two subjects that would play a prominent role in
many later eighteenth-century noble savage writings: Christianity and the
status of women. Lahontan portrays Amerindians as believers in a "natural" religion, a claim that Montaigne briefly touched upon in "Of Cannibals" and that anti-clerical thinkers such as Voltaire and Diderot would
make as well. Lahontan presents a view of spirituality that rests solely
upon the rational cognition of a basic postulate: that a powerful being
created the Earth and instituted moral laws discernible through reason
alone (105–12). The existence of a hierarchy of clergy and of formal
religious institutions, he thus implies, are unnecessary and corrupting additions to the pure and simple faith that all humans should enjoy.[15] Under
the weight of a host of superfluous and sometimes contradictory rules
and obligations, Christians become hypocrites, especially in their role as
missionaries—preaching such doctrines to Amerindians, while acting
contrary to them (111–12).

The New World travel literature inspired a diverse range of arguments
about the role of women in society, and more generally about the themes
of love, marriage, and sexuality. A common theme in writings that appropriated New World ethnography in order to highlight the purported barbarism of New World peoples was that women in New World societies
were especially maltreated and subject to conditions of near slavery and
that Europe, in comparison, offered a civilized liberty to its women.
While this sentiment at times curiously emerged in writings that largely
celebrated the natural lifestyles of New World peoples and criticized European social and political attitudes, many noble savage writers challenged such conventional arguments by celebrating what they understood to be the relative equality of men and women in 'natural' societies.
More broadly, love and intimacy were at times interpreted through the
lenses of nature and artificiality in order to cast aspersions against Euro-

pean gender relations, though this could sometimes take the form of primarily criticizing European women for purportedly controlling men through their artificial and complex sexual charms. In a passage that recalls and may have inspired such a discussion about moral versus physical love in Rousseau's *Discourse on Inequality*, Lahontan contrasts the jealous, blind fury of European love to the simple good will of Amerindians' passions (115–16). The sexual relations between men and women among indigenous Canadians strikes Lahontan as more honest and sincere than the excessively formalized and Janus-faced discourse between the sexes in France. In addition, Lahontan chastises the sexism of French society by noting that only women bear the social costs of adultery, whereas men are often celebrated for their sexual prowess (226–27). In the New World, he argues, marriages are more secure and infidelity is rare. Moreover, in a critique of church doctrine on divorce, Lahontan notes appreciatively that, among the Huron, when marriages unravel, divorce can be initiated by either men or women for no other reason than a desire to become single again (120). In addition, the power of fathers to choose, or to veto, their daughters' potential mate in Europe is absent, Lahontan asserts, among Amerindians (222–23). Instead, he continues, young women are given complete autonomy to choose or to consent to potential husbands. The tendency for some reflections upon the New World to evoke relatively egalitarian ideas about gender relations arises again in some of Diderot's commentary about Tahitian society in the *Supplément au Voyage de Bougainville*. Other passages of the *Supplément*, however, and a number of Rousseau's assertions about women demonstrate that Amerindian peoples could inspire just as easily more traditional responses to the heated eighteenth-century debates about women's capacities and what roles they occupy, and ought to occupy, in society.

Since the idea of a radical difference between European and indigenous New World peoples—a difference in kind between natural and artificial societies—is a presumption of Lahontan's entire dialogue and of noble savage writings more generally, the simple fact of what was taken to be exotic difference did not in and of itself make a foreign society praiseworthy or useful for the purpose of social criticism. In contrast to political writings that incorporated the themes of noble savagery, the praise of the 'other' suggested by a variety of modern European thinkers' invocation of China consisted usually of lauding its ancient and sophisticated civilization. Whereas Lahontan and others praised the New World for embodying the values of naturalism, philosophers such as Voltaire, Leibniz, and the Leibnizian rationalist Christian Wolff placed China in the noble rank of a super-civilization, an extraordinary site of rationality incarnate with a political system overseen by enlightened mandarins, in contrast to the absolute despots who sat on most European thrones. Rather than attempt to civilize the New World, Leibniz suggested wryly in his *No-*

vissima Sinica (1697) that China ought to send missionaries to Europe.[16]
To undermine such enthusiasm, Adario, in response to Lahontan's boast
that the Chinese and Siamese who visit France appear to admire its civilization, castigates the Far East as even more interest-oriented, propertied,
and hence even more brutish than Europe (210–13). Rousseau closely
follows this line of thinking in the *Discourse on the Sciences and Arts*
(1750). From one angle, he criticizes civilization and its supposed wisdom by reference to the New World: "those happy Nations which do not
know even by name the vices we have so much difficulty in repressing,
those savages of America whose simple and natural polity Montaigne
unhesitatingly prefers . . . to everything that Philosophy could ever imagine as most perfect for the government of Peoples". From another angle,
he employs the resonant image of oriental despotism: "If the Sciences
purified morals, if they taught men to shed their blood for the Father-
land, if they animated courage, then the Peoples of China should be
wise, free, and invincible. But if there is not a single vice that does not
rule them. . . . [w]hat benefits has China derived from all the honours
bestowed upon them? To be peopled by slaves and evil-doers?"[17] The
twin themes of the praiseworthy naturalness of New World peoples and
the artificial despotism of Asia make clear, of course, the extent to which
the ethnography about the non-European world gave European thinkers
almost ready-made vehicles for their own political outlooks, predetermined, it would appear, by their antecedent beliefs about the practices
and institutions of European societies. To be sure, noble savage writings,
in particular, usually aimed not only to use New World ethnography to
engage in political debates about Europe, but also to humanize New
World peoples. Lahontan attacks the injustices of European life as well as
those Europeans who have denigrated and barbarized New World peoples. The former strategy gains rhetorical power and a seeming empirical
validity by pointing to supposedly natural beings in the actual world, but
ultimately at the expense of the latter strategy. For Lahontan's writings
(and, as we will see, Rousseau's *Discourse on Inequality*) make or presuppose philosophical arguments about human nature and its relationship to
culture that undermine the claim that New World peoples are fully human beings.

The paradoxical understanding of New World peoples' mental capacities in the noble savage literature discloses itself sharply in Lahontan's
writings. As Lahontan's discussion of natural religion implies, Amerindians are fundamentally rational creatures. It is precisely this standard of
rationality that Europeans fail to practise, given their prejudices, supersti-
tions, and their superfluous and often degrading institutions and practices. On this view, an understanding of "natural" New World societies
can enlighten Europe. Describing his approach toward understanding
Amerindians, Lahontan notes that he attempts to steer a middle course

between theologians who view them as incapable of reflection (and, thus, impossible to convert), and those, especially the Jesuits, who assert that they warmly embrace the Gospels (92). The former denies Amerindians the cognitive abilities that they quite clearly possess; the latter is mistaken since, in addition to appearing wholly satisfied with their lives, they seem, Lahontan contends, to abhor Christianity and the practices of European civilization. Lahontan's fictional Huron, Adario, is an especially perceptive interlocutor because he is portrayed to be, as the title of the *Dialogues* informs us, "well travelled". We learn that he has viewed English America and even France itself with his own eyes; his criticisms, then, are supposed to gain a credibility they may have lacked without such wide exposure. But Adario's powers of reason and speech are perfectly ordinary and typical of less cosmopolitan Amerindians, Lahontan insists, for when criticizing European life, they all prove themselves to be "great moralists" [*grands Moralistes*], drawing upon an extraordinary memory and employing impressive argumentative skills (104; also, 95–104). They speak acutely, with subtlety and imagination, in tribal council meetings during which matters of communal interest are at stake. It appears, at such moments, that they lead an artful and cultivated life, one that may be different from European peoples, but not fundamentally different, or different in kind. Yet, Lahontan's attempts to humanize Amerindians cannot stray too far from the notion that they are natural, largely free of the corrupting trappings of artifice. As we have seen, like other noble savage writings, the bulk of his social criticism rests upon the claim that such peoples live purely naturally, or very nearly so. Hence, he suggests that New World peoples reason and deliberate well *despite* "having no advantage of education"; these "truly rustic philosophers", in short, must be "directed only by the pure light of nature" (99).

The tensions raised by such comments result from Lahontan's practice of describing Amerindians' various customs, rituals, myths, and social practices at length without also being able to interpret them as non-natural, cultural forms of activity and self-understanding. Lahontan does not treat the inheritance and creative transformation of specific traditions and self-understandings over generations as a form of "education", even though he regularly witnessed such artful activities taking place among the Huron and other peoples in French Canada. As we have seen, such a move would not be easy to make for a thinker who has invested heavily in the principal anthropological claim of noble savagery: that New World peoples—however much they appear to be situated within and transform an array of practices, beliefs, and institutions—are ultimately free from artifice. Thus, Lahontan's Adario asserts that the Huron

live quietly under the laws of instinct and innocent conduct, which wise Nature has imprinted upon our minds from our cradles. We are all of one mind; our

wills, opinions and sentiments observe an exact conformity; and thus we spend
our lives with such perfect good understanding, that no disputes or suits can
take place amongst us. (188)

One important consequence of such a view is that throughout his writings Lahontan easily slips from discussing the Huron, or more generally
the indigenous peoples of Canada, to "savages" in general. Shorn of their
distinctive cultural systems of meaning and value and reduced entirely to
natural beings, Amerindians become an amorphous, undifferentiated
whole, even for someone like Lahontan, who learned a great deal about
Huron and Algonquin life. The danger of such a view is that, stripped of
all cultural attributes, New World peoples must inevitably be presented as
instinct-driven brutes whose basic humanity, though not formally denied,
becomes increasingly difficult to discern. As we shall see, Rousseau's conjectural anthropology engenders a theory of human nature and social
development that quite clearly fosters such paradoxes and unintended
results.

While noble savage accounts attempted in part to raise the status of
New World peoples and challenged the view that such peoples are fundamentally barbaric, the portrait of such peoples as artless and purely natural (and the corresponding belief that human nature itself consists of a
lack of artifice) yielded a fantastic and unreal understanding of them, one
that was unlikely to produce the moral understanding and commiseration
necessary for a thoroughgoing criticism of their subject status under European imperial power. David Hume's reaction to such accounts, focusing on the fact that supposedly natural beings in distant lands exhibit
only virtues and no vices, and also emphasizing that such narratives usually portrayed such people as lacking ambition (and, one might add, lacking all of the artfulness that ambition was thought to be linked with in
many eighteenth-century political writings), was precisely what noble savage writers inadvertently helped to foster:

> Should a traveller, returning from a far country, bring us an account of men,
> wholly different from any with whom we were ever acquainted; men, who were
> entirely divested of avarice, ambition, or revenge; who knew no pleasure but
> friendship, generosity, and public spirit; we should immediately, from these cir-
> cumstances, detect the falsehood, and prove him a liar, with the same certainty
> as if he had stuffed his narration with stories of centaurs and dragons, miracles
> and prodigies.[18]

Such a conception of foreign peoples was not only fanciful, Hume implied, but would also be clearly inhuman. Indeed, understandings of
New World peoples as *cultural* beings were more likely to yield a robust
affirmation of their status as *human* beings—this is borne out, I will

argue, both in the philosophical anthropologies of Diderot, Kant, and Herder, and concomitantly in their anti-imperialist political theories. Conversely, the *Realpolitik* of many of Lahontan's analyses of French imperial policies demonstrates that a noble savage celebration of Amerindian life not only sits alongside aggressive colonial schemes, but without as much contradiction as one might originally have thought. In the *New Voyages*, Lahontan argues against the complete "destruction" of the Iroquois not because of humanitarian concerns, but rather due to the probability that the enemies of the Iroquois would then turn against New France. Thus, Lahontan recommends playing off various Amerindian nations against one another. Ultimately, New France can sufficiently weaken the Iroquois and bring them into line, he argues, by virtually imprisoning them on a plot of land guarded by forts in order to "distress" them in times of war and "confine" them in times of peace. This should, Lahontan promises, "reduce them to one half of the power they now possess".[19] These elements of Lahontan's political thought place his glorification of Amerindians in a different light, and it indicates what were usually the ethical limits of such perspectives about humanity and New World peoples. In the eighteenth century, the full recognition of non-Europeans as humans who should rule themselves and who are in no need of European imperial rule takes root almost always among thinkers whose understandings of humanity explicitly or tacitly reject the tenets of noble savagery.

New World Peoples in Rousseau's Conjectural History

In the *Discours sur l'origine et les fondements de l'inégalité parmi les hommes* [*Discourse on the Origin and the Foundations of Inequality Among Men*] (1755), Rousseau contends that "[a]lthough the inhabitants of Europe have for the past three or four hundred years overrun the other parts of the world, and are constantly publishing new collections of travels and reports, I am convinced that the only men we know are the Europeans" (212).[20] Rousseau's complaint stems from his belief that the only way one can begin to understand humanity as such is to examine the broadest possible array of human diversity. As he notes in the *Essay on the Origin of Languages*, the

> great failing of Europeans is always to philosophize . . . in the light of what happens right around them. . . . When one proposes to study men, one has to look close by; but in order to study man one has to learn to cast one's glance afar; one has to begin by observing the differences in order to discover the properties.[21]

Given the increasingly vast range of cultural information housed in the travel literature of his day and the opportunities that it offered for a more accurate conception of humanity, Rousseau bemoaned the lack of a rigorous, philosophical study of such human diversity. Instead, he insists, one finds a mere chronicling of characters and mores in travel accounts without an attendant appreciation of the anthropological significance of such diversity, of how they might contribute to an understanding of the shared humanity of, and the genuine differences among, all peoples. Consequently, he argues that scholars' learned studies of human nature, even those that ostensibly draw upon the new knowledge of non-European peoples, are merely treatises about their own nations.

Rousseau argues that those who undertake the arduous journey to the New World produce anthropologically disappointing reports because of their prejudices, primarily those of their nation and of their particular occupation. "Sailors, Merchants, and Soldiers", he asserts, are hardly able to pronounce judgements of any philosophical import because of their narrow perspectives.[22] The fourth kind of traveller, the missionaries, perhaps have the educational training necessary for an incisive study of humanity, but, he cautiously notes, they are too "absorbed by the sublime vocation" of religious conversion to partake in a scholarly study of humanity. Indeed, according to Rousseau, the philosophical acumen required for such a study is rare even among those with the appropriate training and intellectual skills. All this leads him to call desperately for a profound meditation upon human diversity:

> Shall we never see reborn the happy times when Peoples did not pretend to Philosophize, but the Platos, the Thales, and the Pythagorases, seized with an ardent desire to know, undertook the greatest journeys merely in order to learn, and went far off to shake the yoke of National prejudices, to get to know men by their conformities and their differences, and to acquire that universal knowledge that is not exclusively of one Century or of one country but of all times and of all places, and thus is, so to speak, the common science of the wise? (213)

This yearning for the wisdom of ancient philosophers, in contrast to the tracts of "Europeans more interested in filling their purses than their heads", did not prevent Rousseau from appropriating a significant amount of material from modern travel writings. Indeed, it is not often noted that his celebrated call for a more genuinely philosophical appreciation of humanity and human diversity in note X of the *Discourse on Inequality* arises in the context of his attack upon travel writers' assertions that orangutans are not human—a claim not unrelated to his presentation of Amerindians (as we will see)—rather than from a concern about distorted judgements or understandings of New World peoples. Despite his misgivings, then, about the travel writings of his day, Rousseau drew upon them frequently. He also related many of the tropes of the then well-established philosophical and literary image of the noble savage to lend empirical support for what he knew would be controversial claims about natural humans.

The method that informs Rousseau's speculative history and the developmental sequence that he elaborates begin to explain the peculiar roles that New World peoples play in his narrative. Rousseau defends a theory of human nature that owes much to the tradition of noble savagery, but as part of an extended conjectural history that outlines stages of human development. Although he often simply contrasts "savage" and "civilized" life, Rousseau's conjectural history in fact outlines three stages of human development that mark distinct historical phases of social activity, scientific and technological complexity, and institutional development: a primordial condition (a pure state of nature); a primitive, middle stage; and the civilized condition of modern Europeans, a variety of ancient peoples, and some sedentary non-European peoples, such as the Chinese, who practise agriculture and metallurgy.[23]

On the assumption that the behavioural patterns, social institutions, and the political machinery of modern peoples are *artificial* constructs that have masked, or even altered, our underlying humanity, Rousseau asks in the preface to the *Discourse on Inequality*:

> how will man ever succeed in seeing himself as Nature formed him, through all the changes which the succession of times and of things must have wrought in his original constitution, and to disentangle what he owes to his own stock from what circumstances and his progress have added to or changed in his primitive state? (122)

Rousseau explicates his method by using the imagery of the statue of Glaucus, so encrusted and warped by the ravages of the seas, storms, and time that it resembles more a "ferocious beast" than a God (122). Rousseau's account of natural humans is the result, then, of peeling away the layers of society and culture that, in his view, obscure humans' underlying, universal nature. Such a thought-experiment reveals that the most fundamental characteristics of human behaviour are self-preservation and sympathy, or pity, for other sentient beings. After contending that previous political thinkers who used the category of the state of nature did not go back far enough in human history to describe a truly natural, precivil human condition, he describes at length an earlier state of nature that exemplifies these two essential springs of human action. Rousseau's natural humans preserve themselves without the fixed order of law and government because of their *amour de soi*, a peaceable self-love that involves no comparison or needless competition with others. For Rousseau, primordial humans' solitary existence is peaceful because of the bounty of their environment, their simple (that is, their natural, nonartificial) needs and desires, and their hard-wired (instinctive, natural) repugnance against human suffering. Given the method that informs his speculative history, it becomes clear why New World ethnography, as filtered through the lens of noble savagery, offered ideal resources for such an account of human origins. By removing from the distorted figure of 'civilized man' the purportedly corrupting layers of science, technology, art, sociability, and even language, in addition to the psychological states and passions that Rousseau contends they breed, the figure that remains is the natural human, a noble savage thoroughly free of artificiality.

Rousseau emphasizes in the exordium to the *Discourse* that the "[i]nquiries that may be pursued regarding this Subject ought not be taken for historical truths, but only for hypothetical and conditional reasonings; better suited to elucidate the Nature of things than to show their genuine origin" (133). Yet, in detailing the precivilized condition of humanity, Rousseau makes frequent use of the real-world examples of savages in order to bolster his assertions about 'savage man'. The confusion that results is indicative precisely of the tensions that run through the tradition of noble savagery, where thinkers would both trumpet the pure and largely animalistic naturalness of Amerindians while also at times detailing cognitive and institutional features of Amerindian life. In the context of Rousseau's developmental account, the related paradoxes arise because he categorizes New World peoples as part of the middle stage, while also using them to substantiate a number of his claims about the earlier, pure state of nature.

The movement from a pure state of nature to the middle stage, in Rousseau's conjectural history, involves the development of language, the transition from an entirely nomadic existence to an occasionally sedentary life, the origin of a limited amount of private property (largely in the form of objects that can be carried, rather than of land itself), the formation of family units, and the gradual emergence of nations that are "united in morals and character, not by Rules or Laws, but by the same kind of life and of foods, and the influence of a shared Climate." (169) Rousseau did not believe that a middle, post-primordial and precivilized, state was entirely free of corruption and conflict. Once humans become social creatures, in his view, a corruption of their natural, purely instinctive characteristics inevitably follows. The psychological transformation wrought by such behavioural and sociological changes is significant because they give birth to *amour propre*, or vanity, the vice at the heart of modern unhappiness and social injustice. Thus, Rousseau notes that violence is not uncommon among New World peoples, just as it is embedded, though far more pervasively, in European societies. Nevertheless,

New World peoples lead generally praiseworthy lives, for having reached only the middle stage of human development, they are still restrained partly by natural pity for other creatures. In *On the Social Contract*, he asserts that Amerindians practise a form of government that can best be classified as a "natural aristocracy", for their rulers are elders who are thus naturally unequal to others by virtue of the "authority of experience", rather than civilized aristocrats, who rule according to "instituted inequalities" such as "riches". He concludes that "[t]he savages of northern America still govern themselves this way in our day, and they are very well governed." (406) Most importantly, Rousseau argues that New World peoples are free of two pernicious technological developments— large-scale agriculture (and, in tandem with this, they lack a more extensive and fixed system of private property holdings) and metallurgy— which rely upon and breed a high level of interdependence that in turn signals the death knell of human independence and freedom (171–72). For Rousseau, most peoples of the New World live at precisely the "just mean between the indolence of the primitive state and the petulant activity of our vanity [*amour propre*]", a period during which humans are happiest and a condition that, simply stated, is the "best for man" (171).

Rousseau argues that the post-primordial, precivilized stage is not an ephemeral historical epoch that was achieved for a stunning but tragically brief moment. Instead, this relatively ideal form of human organization constituted the most stable, longest-lasting era of human history. He suggests that the very discovery of New World peoples at this level of social and technological development as late as the eighteenth century demonstrates its impressive durability. He writes that the

> example of the Savages, almost all of whom have been found at this point, seems to confirm that the Human Race [*le Genre-Humain*] was made always to remain in it, that this state is the genuine youth of the World, and that all subsequent progress has been so many steps in appearance toward the perfection of the individual, and in effect toward the decrepitude of the species. (171)

Given Rousseau's stark pessimism about the advanced stage of anthropological development and the fact that it might never have been reached but for a string of contingent factors, the fall from the relatively peaceful and content middle state constitutes the greatest tragedy of human history. As Rousseau explains in *On the Social Contract*, the establishment of a "civil state" would constitute genuine, unalloyed progress were it not for the degradation that civilized life engenders. The brute existence of the state of nature led to a civilized condition in which natural, animalistic beings who possessed a set of social virtues and faculties in potentiality (because of their 'perfectibility') happened to become, through a series of random occurrences that were by no means predestined, intelligent but also almost thoroughly corrupted and oppressed humans.

> Although in this [civil] state he deprives himself of several advantages he has from nature, he gains such great advantages in return, his faculties are exercised and developed, his ideas enlarged, his sentiments ennobled, his entire soul is elevated to such an extent, that if the abuses of this new condition did not often degrade him to beneath the condition he has left, he should ceaselessly bless the happy moment which wrested him from it forever, and out of a stupid and bounded animal made an intelligent being and a man. (364)

For this reason, Rousseau suggests that the arrival of the middle stage constitutes genuine progress, for it lacks the most egregious injustices of the civilized stage. A degree of humanization occurs in the movement toward the middle stage as the distinctively human faculty of perfectibility begins its operations, but without the corresponding dehumanizing conditions of extreme poverty, artificial inequalities, illness and disease, interdependence, and ultimately the despotic slavishness of the civilized stage.

Rousseau acknowledges that such a judgement is tantamount to the glorification of a golden age, one that exists far in Europe's past, but that continues to exist among the largely nomadic peoples of the Americas and Africa. In the "Last Reply" to the critics of his *Discourse on the Sciences and Arts*, he scorns the corrupt modern individuals who reject the notion of a golden age by asserting that in doing so they treat virtue itself as a mere fantasy: "I am told that men have long since been disabused of the chimera of the Golden Age. Why not also add that they have long since been disabused of the chimera of virtue?" (80) Indeed, the golden age and Rousseau's idealized presentation of the ancient city-state Sparta are the twin, and (as Judith Shklar has noted) in certain respects the mutually exclusive, exemplary ideals that animate much of his social and political thinking.[24] As with many earlier theorists of noble savagery, Rousseau asserts that the middle stage of human history cannot be resurrected in Europe, for the social and psychological changes that arise with the development of civilized societies are too great to be undone by an attempt to return to the rustic happiness of the golden age. Still, much of Rousseau's thought can be interpreted as a series of attempts to revive certain aspects of this age. One such attempt involves re-creating in the modern world, *mutatis mutandis*, elements of the life of a rustic city-state (see *On the Social Contract* and, to a lesser extent, *Considerations on the Government of Poland*). Another involves fashioning a less corrupt life in the midst of civilized society either by a highly regimented education from birth that attempts to inculcate and foster the natural sentiments that still animate (without any such education) the indigenous inhabitants of the New World (see, e.g., *Emile*, and *Emile et Sophie*), or by becoming an outsider on the margins of society whose immersion in the natural world provides a form of self-therapy (see, e.g., *Reveries of the Solitary Walker*).

To defend the empirical grounding that he had given in support of the middle stage, Rousseau challenges the common view that New World societies are sites of brutal passions and cruel social practices. Writings that extolled noble savages were always secondary in influence to pejorative understandings of the New World, the most detailed of which aimed not only to proclaim but also to explain the allegedly backward conditions and barbaric behaviour of Amerindians. Along with what can be termed *internal* explanations of their status and behaviour (of the kind that Francisco de Vitoria attacked, such as the view that Amerindians are examples of Aristotle's natural slaves), New World peoples were further encumbered, some argued, by *external* factors, the most important of which was climate.[25] Climate, a key concept in pre-nineteenth-century European social thought, was an umbrella category of the various characteristics of local environments (ranging from meteorological factors, such as the amount of sunshine and heat, to the landscape and other geographical features) that were said to shape social practices, psychological dispositions, and even political institutions.[26] Among French thinkers of the eighteenth century, Montesquieu was by far the most influential proponent of climatological social analysis. A lengthy section of *The Spirit of the Laws* (1748) is devoted exclusively to the behavioural and institutional effects of climate. With regard to moral behaviour, Montesquieu's analysis focused upon the purported effects of heat on the passions:

> You will find in the northern climates peoples who have few vices, enough virtues, and much sincerity and frankness. As you move toward the countries of the south, you will believe you have moved away from morality itself: the liveliest passions will increase crime; each will seek to take from others all the advantages that can favour these same passions.[27]

Such theories grounded a common view of most New World and also African peoples: physiologically, the torrid climates in which they lived boiled their "humours" (and consequently their passions) to degrees uncontrollable by their presumed meagre rationality. In this view, then, the combination of two structural constraints, one external (climate) and one internal to New World inhabitants' constitutions (their ostensibly limited cognitive powers), together were said to account for the barbarous social practices described in many New World travel writings.

In response to such charges of barbarism, Rousseau finds it "ridiculous to portray Savages as constantly murdering one another in order to satisfy their brutality" (158). Despite his scepticism toward those who assert that Amerindians are prone to violence because of their nature, their environment, or both, Rousseau does not deny the effects of climate on human behaviour. Indeed, the very need for a philosophical account of humanity, he maintains, stems from the "powerful effects of differences in Climates, air, foods, ways of life, habits in general and, above all, of the astonishing force of uniform causes acting continuously on long successions of generations." (208) It is for precisely this reason that, for Rousseau, theorizing a fully natural human existence requires stripping away the layers of social and cultural particularities to discern the pure elements of humanity, for modern individuals have been warped almost beyond recognition by a multiplicity of such contingent factors. Consequently, Rousseau attacks the view that primitive peoples are cruel and ferocious while, at the same time, accepting the climatology that had often supported the traditional representation of New World peoples. Thus, referring to the Caribs in particular, he asserts that they are "the most peaceful in their loves and the least given to jealousy, even though they live in a scorching Climate, which always seems to stir these passions to greater activity." (158)

Rousseau suggests that to the extent that episodes of cruelty and violence occur within noncivilized communities, they result not from the lack of civilization, but because the changes that might lead to a civilized condition have started to develop. Life in the middle stage has not yet reached the wretched interdependence of European civilization, and thus it constitutes the condition "best for man", but it is far from the natural isolation of a pure state of nature, which is the only sure guarantee of a complete freedom from cruelty in human life. The historical, and concomitant psychological, development from a purely natural condition, not the want of purportedly civilizing or refining elements of modern life, accounts for whatever strains of cruelty exist in primitive communities. Amerindians are sometimes cruel to one another because they have reached the stage of anthropological development at which one is exposed to the early stirrings of *amour propre*. Therefore, according to Rousseau, before too much civilization (and the interdependence it breeds) corrupts human life, the natural sentiment that makes doing evil repugnant to humans continues to counteract even the most powerful—and potentially degrading—climatic and social factors (156). As with its predecessors, noble savagery in its Rousseauian version, then, offered a counterpoint to the most pejorative understandings of New World peoples. In addition, Rousseau sought to balance his praise of the middle stage of human history, and concomitantly his celebration of New World peoples, with the understanding that such peoples had already been partly corrupted by the early development of sociability.

With a couple of exceptions (such as the Mexica, whom he categorizes as civilized in the *Essay on the Origin of Languages* [5:386]), Rousseau claims then that New World peoples exist at a middle stage of anthropological development. Accordingly, he acknowledges that even the Caribs, "which of all existing Peoples have so far departed least from the state of Nature" (158), are not entirely natural humans. Still, the tension that tends to surface in noble savage accounts—between theorizing an acultural (and, in Rousseau's case, also an asocial) natural human and celebrating the qualities of New World inhabitants as praiseworthy humans (who are not different in kind, but simply closer to the pure conditions of natural humanity than civilized humans)—arises also in Rousseau's conjectural history. For despite his explicit categorization of New World inhabitants as peoples who exist in the middle stage of human development, Rousseau most often discusses Amerindians and the Hottentots of southern Africa to support his account of purely natural humans in the original state of nature. Rousseau's speculative history may well conclude that the middle stage of development is the "best for man", but the earliest state of nature occupies a special place in his theory since it provides the starkest contrast between modern humans and human nature itself. Moreover, only an appreciation of natural humanity, in his view, can ultimately provide the basis for understanding the laws that motivate humanity or that should govern humanity: "so long as we do not know natural man, we shall in vain try to ascertain either the Law which he has received or that which best suits his constitution." (125) Thus, while he presents the pure state of nature as a period so far back in the history of humanity that no written records can attest to its features, the documents that detail the life of indigenous New World inhabitants offer a wealth of examples to support his conjectures about the original state of nature. One can only speculate as to the motivations behind this use of New World ethnography, given its inconsistency with Rousseau's own categorization of Amerindians. Nonetheless, given the influence of the writers from the noble savage tradition upon Rousseau, it should perhaps come as no surprise that natural humans and New World peoples would, in effect, be equated in his account of human nature. As the *Discourse on Inequality* demonstrates, Rousseau moves easily from discussing the 'savages' of the pure state of nature to the 'savages' of contemporary New World societies. Natural, or savage, existence—*la vie sauvage*—can, in part, be accurately described for Rousseau by studying savage, or primitive, humans, *les hommes Sauvage*. Thus, precisely in the manner of the noble savage tradition, Rousseau often cites New World peoples as examples of the impressive *physical* and meagre *mental* qualities of natural humanity. In addition, since Rousseau tends to conflate the boundary between New World humans and animals in this manner, his converse attempt to place orangutans at the level of natural humanity becomes especially noteworthy.

Physical qualities of natural humanity. The opening passages of the first part of the *Discourse on Inequality*, those meant to discern natural humans simply from their "physical" side before considering them from the "metaphysical and moral side", rely greatly upon New World ethnography to provide empirical evidence about the physical prowess of natural humans in the wild (141). To the extent that any animal becomes domesticated, argues Rousseau, it becomes timid and weak, lacking its original courage and vigour (139). After detailing the sharpness of sense and acuity of judgement of wild animals who live primarily according to self-preservation, Rousseau concludes, "Such is the animal state in general, and according to Travellers' reports, it also is the state of most Savage peoples." (140–41) Accordingly, Rousseau notes that "the Savages of America track the Spaniards by smell just as well as the best Dogs might have done" (141).

Rousseau's notes at the end of the *Discourse on Inequality* provide much of the ethnographic material that is meant to support his historical conjectures. Although most of the main text details the injustices of the civilized condition, sixteen of Rousseau's nineteen notes aim to elaborate and substantiate his claims about the pure state of nature and the middle stage of human development. In note VI, which marks one of the most intensive uses of travel literature in the *Discourse on Inequality*, Rousseau lists several examples of indigenous peoples' physical vigour and skill, from the Hottentots' fishing, hunting, and running and the accurate shooting of the "Savages of the Antilles" to the general strength and physical skills of the "Savages" and "Indians" of both North and South America. In note V, drawing upon François Corréal's *Voyage aux Indes Occidentales* (1722), Rousseau defends his thesis that humans are naturally vegetarian in part by relating the story of the primitive inhabitants of Lucayes, who, removed by the Spanish from their homes and taken to Cuba, Santo Domingo, and elsewhere, died because of eating meat; such "natural" physiologies, Rousseau implies, could not handle animal flesh (199). In note III, Rousseau uses both indigenous peoples and feral children to study the question of whether humans are naturally bipeds or quadrupeds. After noting that humans must *teach* their children to walk on two limbs, Rousseau asserts that since Caribs and the Hottentots both "neglect" their children by keeping them as quadrupeds for so long, for them, learning to become bipeds requires considerable effort. Even their adults, he writes, are sometimes found as quadrupeds. Rousseau considers the feral children of Europe, abandoned children who were discovered in rural areas and who often generated sensational publicity, as guides to the study of human nature.[28] Surviving in remote areas, and at times like the legendary Romulus and Remus allegedly raised by animals, feral children often elicited an enthusiastic response after their discovery in part because of their apparently 'natural' qualities. As if placed by fate in a laboratory experiment in which all the conventions of social life were eliminated, the feral child ostensibly exhibited the most primal, underlying characteristics of the human species. Accordingly, Rousseau cites five examples of feral children in order to elaborate the possibility that humans are naturally quadrupeds. In one passage, then, Rousseau manages to equate savages (understood as the earliest purely natural individuals of his conjectural history), the "Savage Nations" of the New World, and feral children (such as the "little Savage of Hanover") as natural creatures (196). Rousseau's frequent reliance upon supposedly empirical examples of "savages" in such cases indicates not only the centrality of New World ethnographic sources in his effort to discern humans' natural physical characteristics, but also the virtual animalization of New World peoples, however unintended, that this method risks.

Mental qualities of natural humanity. In conjunction with the physical animality of natural humans, Rousseau attempts to establish the *mental* simplicity of "savages" as well. It is important in his account, as it is so often in narratives of natural humanity and noble savagery, to defend the idea that the virtues of such lives result not from forms of education, institutions, or self-conscious and dynamic social practices, or indeed from any other form of what was understood to constitute artificiality, but rather from the uncorrupted instincts (or, for Lahontan and others, the laws) that Nature itself implanted in humans. Hence, Rousseau asserts that "one might say that Savages are not wicked precisely because they do not know what it is to be good; for it is neither the growth of enlightenment nor the curb of the Law, but the calm of the passions and the ignorance of vice that keep them from evil-doing" (154). Although the humans of the middle, precivilized stage lead partly settled lives with minimal amounts of private property, produce simple commodities, and thus undergo significant psychological changes and the development of a rudimentary sociability, he also argues that this middle stage is remarkably durable partly because such humans have not yet reached the cognitive state in which the imagination, curiosity, and foresight needed for deep reflection and for scientific and technological advances (in short, for the more extensive flourishing of human perfectibility) exists. In such a condition, humans have minimal (and still largely natural) needs that are

met by subsistence hunting and gathering and, at times, small-scale agriculture. Their minds work constantly at what is before them, never abstracting from their own life or looking ahead to future events.

After elaborating such speculative claims about proto-civilized humans,
Rousseau again illustrates them by noting the example of a New World
people:

> Such is still nowadays the extent of the Carib's foresight: he sells his Cotton
> bed in the morning and comes weeping to buy it back in the evening, having
> failed to foresee that he would need it for the coming night. (144)

Not merely primitive peoples' immediate social conditions and psychological dispositions, then, but also their cognitive abilities themselves, in
Rousseau's view, exist at an elementary level, a stage that ensures little
progress and therefore tremendous durability. Referring to "Savage man",
he asserts that "nothing must be so calm as his soul and nothing so
limited as his mind." (214) The physical prowess that Rousseau describes
with such relish—single-handedly subduing wild bulls, striking distant
and minute targets with stones, and swimming flawlessly in turbulent
waters—all come at a price. This praise sits alongside Rousseau's contentions that Amerindians' impressive physical characteristics flourish precisely because their mental capacity cannot go beyond the simple association of basic ideas at their stage of historical development. Any higher
form of reflection would lead to, and in part be a result of, interdepen-
dent social practices that over time would enervate humans' original, vigorous constitutions. Thus, the animality of natural humans is not only of
the body, but of the mind as well. As with other noble savage representations of non-European peoples, the analytic ability to make lasting connections between sets of ideas—in short, sustained cognitive reflection—
is nearly as absent in the human beings of the New World as it is in any
of the animals of the wild.

Orangutans as natural humans?   Since Rousseau's conjectural history conflates the boundary between the middle stage and what he himself describes as the animal condition of the earliest state of nature, it is
not entirely astonishing to read his speculation that certain primates may
very well be human beings.[29] Rousseau's representation of most New
World peoples mirrors, therefore, his anthropomorphic conception of recently discovered primates. In note X of the *Discourse on Inequality*, he
contends at length that orangutans, in particular, might be extant examples of the earliest and most primitive humans. After quoting a few passages about primates from one of his most frequent sources about non-
European societies, Abbé Prévost's twenty-volume compendium, *Histoire
Générale des Voyages*, Rousseau argues against travellers' accounts that

orangutans are definitively nonhuman.[30] These "Anthropomorphic animals", he argues, are so physically and even behaviourally similar to humans that "it is because of their stupidity" that voyagers have typically described them simply as animals (210). Rousseau muses sarcastically that if the travellers who make such claims had discovered a feral child with a human form but hardly any ability to reason or to speak, they "would have spoken about him learnedly in fine reports as a most curious Beast that rather resembled a man." (212)

Rousseau considers orangutans as likely humans in part because it was not adequately demonstrated, in his opinion, that they lack *perfectibilité*, the faculty of self-perfection that is a "specific characteristic of the human species." (211) In addition, Rousseau attempts to rebut the one argument that, in his view, is usually given to justify the assertion that orangutans are not humans: their lack of speech. In a claim about the history of human language, which he elaborates in detail in the unpublished *Essay on the Origin of Languages* (much of which was originally intended to be part of the second *Discourse*), Rousseau notes that orangutans' lack of any humanly comprehensible speech tells us nothing about the species to which they belong because the act of speech itself is not natural to humans. The earliest humans, in Rousseau's account, possess the "organ of speech" in an incipient form that then develops slowly in conjunction with a variety of social and psychological changes. Thus, orangutans— the word derives etymologically from two Malay words meaning "man of the woods"—could very well be examples of the earliest humans who managed to stay entirely uncultivated by dispersing themselves in remote forests eons ago (208). If this were true, then New World peoples presumably would no longer be the eighteenth-century humans best suited to model the original state of nature, since the primordial state itself would still be in existence in the forests of Asia. He notes cautiously, however, that with the dearth of information about, and lack of experimentation with, such creatures, his thoughts on this matter are purely speculative.[31] Notwithstanding such qualifications, Rousseau never retracts his orangutan hypothesis and consistently voices scepticism over travellers' judgements to the contrary. By the end of the *Discourse on Inequality*, Rousseau manages both to humanize certain animals and, though it was clearly not his purpose, to animalize certain humans. Both sets of creatures living in the wild or savage regions of the world come, therefore, to resemble one another.

THIS CURIOUS FEATURE of Rousseau's *Discourse on Inequality* becomes understandable when one considers the paradoxes underlying the tradition of noble savagery to which Rousseau's 'natural man' owes so much. Much of the admiration for New World peoples in this literature, as we have seen, concerns what is considered to be purely natural about them—

features that are often animalistic. Rousseau, of course, did not call for European societies to return either to the golden age he represented or, for that matter, to the condition of orangutans. The social and psychological changes that take place from one stage to the next, in his view, are too deep to allow for such movement. Although it is correct to note that Rousseau is therefore not a 'primitivist', it would be a mistake to conclude from this that Rousseau's treatment of New World peoples constitutes a fundamental departure from the noble savage doctrine.[32] Noble savage thinkers, such as Lahontan, tended to naturalize and animalize Amerindians in precisely the same manner as Rousseau—that is, without arguing that Europeans should, in some sense, return to the forests. It is the particular characterization of New World peoples, rather than the claim that humans should abandon civilization, that most accurately typifies what can be characterized as noble savagery, the tradition of theorizing New World peoples that most influenced Rousseau. On balance, there is no doubt that Rousseau considered New World peoples to be simple, but not wholly natural. He makes clear in the *Discourse on Inequality* that Amerindians and Hottentots, for example, occupy his middle stage of anthropological development. The paradox of his treatment of such peoples is that of the entire tradition of noble savagery: New World peoples are meant both to illustrate a pure humanity free of artifice and culture (and sometimes, as with Rousseau, free of all sociability), while they are also occasionally praised for their conventional practices and norms, such as martial virtue or the eloquence of their speech. Since New World peoples are meant to provide a foil to 'civilized' societies, the manner in which they are portrayed in noble savage accounts tends to veer back and forth between wholly naturalistic and cultural descriptions; they are said to be superior or happier usually because they lead natural lives, yet at times their nobility reveals itself in artificial conventions that are less corrupt or more egalitarian than those of Europe. Hence, they are usually categorized as different in kind and also at times as different in degree, that is, as beings who are also artificial or cultural, but more simply and decently so. As we have seen in Rousseau's account, this is evident in the manner in which he categorizes most New World peoples as occupying his middle stage, but nonetheless uses them most often to illustrate features of the earliest state of nature.

Notwithstanding the influence of the noble savage tradition upon Rousseau, he moves beyond previous accounts by conceptualizing New World peoples within a philosophically sophisticated speculative history that aims not merely to contrast savage and civilized life, but also to hypothesize at length about the complex development of injustice and inequality. In this respect, Rousseau exerts an enormous influence over Diderot, who would appropriate much of Rousseau's conjectural history and the incisive social criticism of European society that it made possible, while also rejecting the naturalistic (that is, the noble savage) elements of his philosophical anthropology. Moreover, like Montaigne, Rousseau was by no means indifferent to the imperial politics of his day. While expressions of sympathy toward the plight of New World peoples and criticism of the injustices of European imperial rule only infrequently emerge in Rousseau's writings, his contempt and anger toward the European subjugation of New World peoples is noteworthy. To be sure, Rousseau's early opera *La Découverte du Nouveau Monde* [*The Discovery of the New World*] offers not only praise for Amerindians' natural virtue and courage, but also a triumphal account of Columbus and the conquest of the New World, with the chorus declaring at the opening of the second act that the New World "is made for our chains".[33] This early writing (whose composition has been dated between 1739 and 1741) should not be taken, however, as a guide to his thinking about empire, given that it was not intended to offer a political analysis of imperial rule and especially since it precedes his turn toward more systematic and direct discussions of history, society, and politics. More significant is Rousseau's characterization of "the odious Cortés subjugating Mexico with powder, treachery and betrayal" in the "Last Reply" to the critics of the *Discourse on the Sciences and Arts* (91). Responding to his critics' view that "barbarians" engage in conquest because they are "most unjust", Rousseau writes,

> What, pray, were we during our so greatly admired conquest of America? But then, how could people with artillery, naval charts, and compasses, commit injustices! Am I to be told that the outcome proves the Conquerors' valour? All it proves is their cunning and their skill; it proves that an adroit and clever man can owe to his industry the success which a brave man expects from his valour alone. (91)

Accordingly, in *On the Social Contract*, Rousseau offers the conquest of the Americas as an example of the possession of land "by a vain ceremony". As he sarcastically asks,

> When Núñez Balboa, standing on the shore, took possession of the southern seas and of all of South America in the name of the crown of Castile, was that enough to dispossess all of its inhabitants and to exclude all the Princes of the world? (366)

Instead, he argues, "labour and cultivation" is the only "real sign of property which others ought to respect in the absence of legal titles." (366) While this might resemble agriculturalist arguments in favour of the appropriation of nomadic peoples' lands, in the early draft of *On the Social Contract*, now known as the *Geneva Manuscript*, Rousseau wrote a footnote ridiculing the idea that lands inhabited by nonagriculturalist "savages" should be viewed as open, unowned land. "I saw in, I think, a work entitled the *Dutch Observer*," he notes,

> a most amusing principle [offered by Jacob Moreau in favour of the French seizure of Amerindian lands during the Seven Years' War], which is that all land inhabited only by savages should be considered vacant, and that one may legitimately seize it and drive the inhabitants away without doing them any wrong according to natural right." (301)

Although Rousseau chose not to include this comment in the final text, there is no evidence to suggest that he changed his mind about the common imperial classification of Amerindian land as *res nullius*, as belonging to no one.

Rousseau never pursued such scattered observations at any length in order to craft what might have been a powerful anti-imperialist political philosophy, and he thus has much in common with the many modern European thinkers who promoted the idea of a 'natural man', stripped of all artificial, cultural attributes, but without offering in addition a sustained criticism of European empires and defence of the New World peoples who were used as examples of such noble savages. It is a striking fact that the thoroughgoing anti-imperialist political theories and most robust accounts of the injustice of European imperialism in the history of modern European political thought were virtually always grounded by the view that humans are cultural agents, and hence the rejection of the very category of a 'natural human', as this was understood by noble savage thinkers. As I will further argue in the final section of this chapter, this should come as no surprise, for while concern about the oppression of non-European peoples under European imperial rule is not precluded by descriptions of New World peoples as (or as very nearly) natural and acultural, the extensive commiseration with non-European peoples and sustained criticism and outright rejection of European empires that we find, among others, in Diderot, Kant, and Herder, follows more easily from the anthropological understanding that humans as such are cultural creatures.

Diderot and Bougainville's *Voyage*

Diderot's presentation of Tahitian society in the *Supplément au Voyage de Bougainville* [*Supplement to Bougainville's Voyage*] subverts the tradition of noble savagery, even as it draws upon some of its classic tropes. Diderot was influenced by the writings that I have discussed thus far in this chapter, which together constitute an identifiable modern European philosophical tradition toward thinking about New World and other nomadic, nonsedentary peoples. Like many of his fellow *philosophes*, Diderot viewed Montaigne as an exemplary hero whose scepticism, commitment to social criticism, and exposure of hypocrisies and injustices made him a model for enlightened thought.[34] Similarly, Diderot was also inspired by Baron Lahontan's *Dialogues curieux*, as well as other celebrated writings that idealized the pastoral themes of noble savagery but without any explicit reference to the New World, such as Fénelon's *Télémaque* (1699).[35] It was, however, Rousseau's *Discourse on Inequality*—in which the previous two centuries of noble savagery, and its attendant, distinctive form of social criticism, were distilled and transformed into a philosophically more complex conjectural history—that most captured Diderot's imagination. Unlike Voltaire, who wrote to Rousseau shortly after the publication of the *Discourse on Inequality* only to thank him sardonically for writing a treatise "against the human race", Diderot was moved by Rousseau's account of the origin of inequality.[36] Indeed, the two discussed the arguments of the *Discourse* as Rousseau composed it. Diderot recognized the depth of Rousseau's vision, one that drew upon, but also went beyond, previous attempts at social criticism that were based upon golden ages and primitive, natural men. In light of this tradition of social criticism, his friendship with Rousseau, and his admiration in particular of the *Discourse on Inequality*, Diderot's *Supplément* is often understood as a standard example of eighteenth-century noble savagery, a work that presupposes its essential philosophical and anthropological assumptions, varying only in ethnography and locale—in this case, Bougainville's travel narrative, *Voyage autour du monde*, and the South Pacific islands, the New World of the eighteenth century.[37] In fact, Diderot's *Supplément* sets forth a doctrine of human nature, sociability, moral judgement, and human diversity that stands in sharp contrast to the tradition of noble savagery.[38] The political consequences of Diderot's immanent subversion of noble savage assumptions are significant because the development of his anti-imperialist political thought was enabled by precisely this rejection of the traditionally primitivist understanding of 'natural man'.

As we have seen, when information about non-European peoples elicited genuine interest rather than contempt or puzzlement among European thinkers who were already critically disposed toward European religious and political institutions, the relevant ethnography became a weapon in the hands of such philosophers, poets, and other satirists. To the extent that such travel writings shaped the thinking of those who drew upon them, the variety of social forms and behaviour portrayed in these writings pointed to the relativity of European institutions, behaviour, and norms. In part, Rousseau's and Diderot's philosophical anthropologies sought to prove that the injustices and inequalities of European societies were not inevitable or permanent. For them, social, psychological, and technological transformations over time demonstrate humans' self-construction and malleability.[39] Notwithstanding Rousseau's pessimism about humans' opportunities for the future, one normative implication of his anthropology is that humans can, within bounds, alter their political conditions for the better. Similarly, the discovery of the New World, in Diderot's view, promoted crucial advances in moral thought because its diverse practices enabled thinkers to discern that the roots of political injustice, economic exploitation, and social ills were not divinely sanctioned or historically inevitable, but "only the product of time, ignorance, weakness and deceit."[40] (193)

Rousseau and Diderot were both critically disposed toward the political injustices of their own societies, and their one-time friendship led to a close working relationship about such issues at the time when Rousseau was composing the two *Discourses*. As Rousseau would later explain in a letter to Malsherbes, he was struck by an epiphany—that humans are naturally good and that they themselves are to blame for the institutions that corrupted them—during a journey to visit Diderot, who at the time was in prison for having written allegedly blasphemous material. As Rousseau recalls,

> I was going to see Diderot, at that time a prisoner at Vincennes; I had in my pocket a *Mercure de France* [the October 1749 issue of the popular periodical] which I began to leaf through along the way. I fell across the question of the Academy of Dijon ["Has the restoration of the Sciences and Arts tended to purify morals?"] which gave rise to my first writing. . . . Oh Sir, if I had ever been able to write a quarter of what I saw and felt under that tree, how clearly I would have made all the contradictions of the social system seen, with what strength I would have exposed all the abuses of our institutions, with what simplicity I would have demonstrated that man is naturally good and that it is from these institutions alone that men become wicked.[41]

As Rousseau describes it in his *Confessions*, Diderot noticed his agitation at Vincennes and, after discovering the cause, "exhorted" Rousseau to submit an essay to the Academy.[42] The *Discourse on the Sciences and Arts* was published in 1751 and launched Rousseau's career as a writer and social critic. As Rousseau himself notes, in his letter to Malsherbes, this led almost ineluctably to the following *Discourse*, which provided a deeper philosophical and anthropological grounding for his radical criticisms. As we have seen, Rousseau uses New World travel literature most thoroughly in the course of explaining and justifying the pure state of nature in the *Discourse on Inequality*. This was a work that, as Rousseau states, "was more to Diderot's taste than all my other Writings, and for which his advice was most useful to me".[43] As they grew apart, Rousseau ultimately changed his view of Diderot's help, accusing him eventually of inserting his own passages into Rousseau's text. He claimed, for instance, that Diderot had written into the *Discourse on Inequality* a passage that, Rousseau believed, made him appear harsh and overly critical.[44] Notwithstanding their eventual hostility toward one another, Rousseau had clearly influenced Diderot both by his use of ethnography about the non-European world and, philosophically, by his argument that the inequalities and injustices of human life were in fact humanly constructed (and, thus, amenable to human transformation), rather than rooted in the fundamental nature of human beings or human society.

Influenced by Rousseau, and most likely by Lahontan as well,[45] Diderot, too, engaged in a form of social criticism that drew upon New World travel literature, although, as I argue, his conceptualization of New World societies ultimately subverted the noble savage tradition, whereas Rousseau most often mirrored it. Diderot was especially captivated by the *Voyage autour du monde* [*Voyage around the world*], a travel narrative written by Louis Antoine de Bougainville, who had become the first French explorer to circumnavigate the globe, and the second European (shortly after James Cook) to visit Tahiti. At the time that he read Bougainville's book, Diderot was undertaking research for what eventually became his anti-imperialist contributions to Abbé Raynal's *Histoire des deux Indes*. He had also recently completed two short stories, *Ceci n'est pas un conte* [*This is not a story*] and *Madame de La Carlière*, both of which had explored the many tensions between conventional social and religious morality and sexual desires and practices.[46] At first, Diderot wrote a book review of Bougainville's *Voyage*, within which he expressed outrage that Bougainville's visit to Tahiti was most likely laying the groundwork for French colonization in the South Pacific. As Diderot exclaims,

> Bougainville, leave the shores of these innocent and fortunate Tahitians. They are happy and you can only harm their happiness. . . . This man whom you lay hold of as though he were a brute or a plant is a child of nature like you. What right have you over him? Let him have his morals [*moeurs*]; they are more decent and wiser than yours.[47]

Eventually, however, the combination of Diderot's recent literary endeavours, the ongoing development of his humanism, and the early stirrings of his anti-imperialist politics led to the composition of a more substantial work, the remarkable dialogue *Supplément au Voyage de Bougainville*.[48] Diderot's *Supplément* makes clear his view that further contacts with the New World provided an opportunity to reflect deeply and innovatively upon human unity and diversity, and in ways that could be turned against European mores and European political power. In part, the ingenuity of his response to the "discovery" of Tahiti was to construct a complex dialogue between two Europeans ("A" and "B") about the little-known supplement (written by Diderot himself) to Bougainville's published travel narrative—a supplement that contained further fictional dialogues among members of Bougainville's crew and Tahitians. The complicated structural and rhetorical features of the *Supplément* also allow Diderot to write in many voices and to offer a kind of running commentary throughout about relations between Europeans and non-Europeans, some of which ironizes the very myths that his fellow Europeans like Bougainville had constructed about Tahiti.[49]

In the second section of the *Supplément*, in which an elderly Tahitian scathingly bids farewell to Bougainville and his sailors, Diderot affirms the shared humanity of Tahitians and the French and deplores the domineering behaviour of French travellers. Paraphrasing earlier comments from Diderot's review of Bougainville's *Voyage*, the old Tahitian argues, "This inhabitant of Tahiti, whom you wish to ensnare like an animal, is your brother. Your are both children of Nature. What right do you have over him that he does not have over you?" (42) Fearing that future contact with the French will be violent and ultimately enslaving, the old man recalls angrily how justly his fellow Tahitians treated Bougainville's crew: "You came; did we attack you? Have we plundered your ship? Did we seize you and expose you to the arrows of our enemies? Did we harness you to work with our animals in the fields? We respected our image in you." (42–43) By presenting Tahitians and the French as kindred souls, or "children of Nature", Diderot emphasizes their shared humanity and, thus, grounds their comparison and moral equality; yet, it is ultimately their differences, in his view, that are most telling, for an encounter with a foreign society can serve to dislodge the prejudices of own one's country, the kinds of prejudice that must be checked both to learn from other peoples and to formulate a tenable conception of human diversity. Hence, he explains, through character "B" in the *Supplément*, how one's understandable partiality toward what is familiar can be shed by reading New World travel accounts, such as Bougainville's *Voyage*:

> The account of Bougainville's voyage is the only one which has ever drawn me to any country other than my own. Until I read it, I imagined that nowhere could one be as happy as at home, and I assumed that everyone on earth felt the same: a natural consequence of the attraction of the soil, itself bound up with the comforts it affords and which one doubts finding elsewhere. (40)

For Diderot, the underlying humanity of two societies serves to make their comparative study cognitively possible, while their differences help to curb the biases that are inevitably rooted in one's own national character. Throughout most of the *Supplément*, however, Diderot would go beyond such well-meaning platitudes to transform the philosophical relationship between humanity and cultural difference in the course of re-describing Bougainville's Tahitians.

In an early work, *Suite de l'Apologie de l'abbé de Prades* (1752), Diderot speculated briefly about humans' primordial existence. Such early humans, he conjectured, possessed an extremely limited cognitive capacity, were ruled by instinct, and lived in herds, rather than in consciously maintained societies.[50] As he wrote later in the *Observations sur le Nakaz* (a commentary on Catherine II's proposed social and political reforms for Russia), "Men gathered together in society by instinct, just as weak animals form herds. There was certainly no kind of primitive agreement." (124) Despite such speculations, Diderot generally viewed the idea of a "pure" state of nature, a condition entirely free of human arts, inventions, and institutions, as a fruitless category for political thought. Human life, for Diderot, is too closely bound up with a shared social existence and with ingenuity and skill to justify theorizing at length about asocial beginnings and animalistic primordial conditions. As he notes in the *Supplément*, "the bleak and savage state of man . . . is so difficult to imagine and perhaps exists nowhere" (69). As we shall see, Diderot's ambivalence about the category of a primordial condition and its consequent insignificance for his political thought are crucial both for his understanding of New World peoples and for the development of his anti-imperialism.

Diderot indicates several features of Tahitian life throughout the *Supplément* that throw doubt on an idealized conceptualization of the New World. Far from portraying Tahiti as an idyll free of all social or political problems, Diderot denotes features of Tahitian society that expose both the inevitable injustices of social life and the fundamental vices of human character. Although he chose to omit certain aspects of Tahitian society about which Bougainville speculated in his *Voyage* (such as human sacrifice), Diderot nevertheless follows Bougainville's account in describing Tahiti as armed for conflict with neighbouring "enemies", as prey to nearby "oppressors" to whom Tahiti must pay tributes of their own men, and as victims of environmental disasters and public health tragedies, including "calamitous epidemics" (45, 64). Diderot in effect discredits many of the classic assertions about the peaceful and healthful character of New World peoples that the noble savage doctrine propagated. Although he tends to praise Tahiti and Tahitians' character in the *Supplément*, in part to indicate that a set of non-European social institutions and practices are capable of being well-ordered and just, Diderot's writings on human nature evince his scepticism toward entirely laudatory or pejorative descriptions of the human condition. In the *Encyclopédie* article "Hobbism", for instance, after contending that both Rousseau's and Hobbes's conflicting theories of human nature are equally astute but one-sided, Diderot asserts that both "goodness and wickedness" are permanent elements of the human condition (28). It should come as no surprise, then, that Diderot does not characterize New World peoples as naturally good. As we shall see, Diderot argues that most of humans' potentially darker energies can be channelled into productive, nondestructive outlets if social institutions and mores are constructed and maintained such that human selfishness and the common good are not entirely at odds. Diderot's Tahiti, of course, is meant to be a concrete example—and thus a potent symbol—of such a society.

Diderot's Tahiti: Appropriating and Subverting Noble Savage Theory

I have argued that Rousseau's writings on New World peoples fall prey to the paradoxes of noble savage accounts. As we have seen, noble savage theorists, such as Lahontan, left unresolved a tension between describing Amerindians as, on the one hand, hard-wired, instinct-driven creatures and, on the other, as partly autonomous, cognitive creatures who both understand natural laws and consciously put them into practice. Rousseau's use of New World travel literature in the *Discourse on Inequality* reveals that he too moves back and forth between a purely natural, primordial, and indeed an animalistic account of New World individuals and an understanding of them as primitive, but recognizably human peoples in a praiseworthy middle stage of historical development. Diderot, on the other hand, disputes the view that Tahitians, or any other set of humans, could possibly live by the light of nature alone, whether understood as natural instincts or natural laws. Although noble savage theorists celebrate New World peoples, Diderot, by adopting the critical possibilities of the New World travel literature, yet subverting the basic idea of a noble savage, continues the tradition of cross-cultural social criticism while also preparing the way for an anti-imperialist political theory that would go well beyond the ultimately inconsistent and, at times, dehumanizing praise of New World peoples that the noble savage tradition offered.

Let us turn, then, to the details of Diderot's account of Tahiti in the *Supplément au Voyage de Bougainville*. I examine four key features of his interpretation of Tahitian society that demonstrate his subversion of noble savagery and that evoke broader themes in his political and moral thought: the constraints and opportunities afforded by climate; social welfare as the purpose of social organization; the knowledge and practical skills that are needed to sustain social life; and, finally, the relationship between self-interest and social (or 'general') goods.

Constraints and opportunities afforded by climate. Diderot incorporates the diverse influences of a variety of environmental factors on human behaviour and institutions in his presentation of Tahitian society. In a response to Catherine the Great's assertion that only the "savages" of the New World are dominated by their climate, Diderot argues forcefully in the *Observations sur le Nakaz* that all humans are affected profoundly by their particular environments:

> I find it very difficult to believe that climate does not have a great influence on national character; that the American overcome by heat can have the same character as the inhabitant of the North hardened by cold; that a people who live in the midst of frozen wastes can enjoy the same cheerfulness as a people who can stroll in a garden almost the whole year round. . . . This permanent cause will produce its effect on everything, not excluding the productions of the arts, laws, food, taste, amusements, etc. (100)

Nonetheless, in the same work, he argues that the form of government and its specific legislation can trump the influence of climate and other external forces that partly mould humanity into its diverse cultural forms. Accordingly, he declares,

> Manners [*moeurs*] are everywhere the result of legislation and government; they are not African or Asiatic or European. They are good or bad. You are a slave under the Pole where it is very cold, and a slave in Constantinople where it is very hot; but everywhere a people should be educated, free and virtuous. (85)

Political practices, then, traditionally conceived as comprising simply legislation and government, provide a partly nonenvironmentally determined, autonomous control over the affairs of our lives. Diderot often combines an emphasis on the human agency inherent in planning and maintaining social institutions with the determinative powers of a variety of structural or environmental factors. Accordingly, he employs climate in his analysis of Tahitian society, but interestingly reverses the prevalent assumption about its effects. Tahiti's warm climate gives rise to a lavish agricultural bounty, he notes, thus affording its inhabitants a healthy amount of leisure. The constant battle of feeding and providing for a polity, the daily struggle to afford basic sustenance, is reduced considerably because of Tahitians' immediate environment. According to Diderot, a tropical climate itself, then, far from being an impediment as Montesquieu had argued, may fortuitously help to generate and to sustain an ethically fulfilling and meaningful life for Tahitians (66). Concerning New World inhabitants' alleged cruelty, Diderot speculates that European travel writings may be mistaken in their accounts. Invoking the primacy of survival over all other considerations, Diderot argues that humans probably become cruel only when their preservation is threatened, and that such behaviour may be more common in the New World than in the Old because of geographical reasons: due to their proximity to entirely nondomesticated surroundings, he surmises, there must be a frequent need "to defend themselves against wild beasts". On the whole, however, he concludes that the New World inhabitant is "gentle whenever his peace and security are left undisturbed." (39)

Notwithstanding the structural factors in Diderot's thought, the voluntarist features of social life are most crucial for his understanding of society; thus, as we shall see, the most detailed component of his treatment of Tahitian society concerns the social planning required to achieve prosperity and happiness. For Diderot, in contrast to Rousseau, it is not the stage in human development that New World inhabitants occupy that explains whatever happiness they enjoy, but rather their ingenuity, the conscious use of their will to transform their fortuitous circumstances into a felicitous social condition. Unlike Rousseau, who attributes the peacefulness of New World peoples to their precivilized existence, Diderot argues that a combination of immediate geographical and climatic causes with long-term, thoughtful social planning enhances both individual and collective welfare in Tahiti.

Social welfare as the purpose of social organization.   Bougainville and his crew were so overcome by the lush beauty of Tahiti, the warm reception they were given, and the liberality of the Tahitians, in particular their sexual freedom, that they recalled the fabled Greek island Cythera.[51] Describing Tahiti with the aid of a familiar mythological referent helped Bougainville confront the radically distinct lifestyle that was led on these South Pacific islands. It also indicates the aspect of Tahiti that was most immediately striking, and that indeed is explored at such great length in Diderot's *Supplément*—the seemingly rampant libidinal pleasures of an exotic locale, evocative not of any real place, but only of the mythical birthplace of Aphrodite, the Greek goddess of love. Tahiti, then, was the New Cythera, *la Nouvelle-Cythère*. Diderot himself might appear to write the *Supplément* as if to convince his readers that Tahiti is such a mythic, island paradise, embodying the instinctual natural virtues of a primordial human life. He writes, for instance, that Tahitians faithfully adhere to the laws of Nature, instead of obeying false and arbitrary rules and institutions.

Diderot, however, slowly reveals the significant social planning that he hypothesizes might underlie the behaviour that Bougainville observed in 1768. The reader of the *Supplément* learns in greater detail throughout the dialogue how Diderot believes the Tahitians have *consciously* created and sustained a relatively efficient and just polity. The free and easy sexuality that is first described in a dialogue between the French chaplain of Bougainville's crew and a Tahitian native, Orou, in the third section of the *Supplément* is later exposed as a highly structured and socialized set of activities implemented in order to meet the goal of a steadily growing population. Diderot's interpretation of Tahitian life is generally congruent with Bougainville's two chapters on Tahiti in his *Voyage autour du monde*, but it adds much more detail about the mechanics of Tahitian social institutions in an attempt to unearth the sociology beneath Bougainville's surface impressions. On the whole, then, while Diderot's analysis is clearly inspired by Bougainville's first-hand account of Tahitian life, his conception of Tahiti is also an imaginative reconstruction of Tahitian society. Diderot himself understood perfectly well the partly constructed quality of the *Supplément* and of Bougainville's original account. In one of many ironic asides, character "A" notes dryly that the Old Tahitian's speech, written of course by Diderot though presented within the dialogue as part of a recently discovered supplement to Bougainville's *Voyage*, strikes him as oddly European in tone: "[t]he speech seems fierce to me, but in spite of what I find abrupt and primitive, I detect ideas and turns of phrase which appear European." (46) And earlier "A" asks his interlocutor suspiciously, "Are you falling prey to the myth of Tahiti?" (41) Concerning New World ethnography, "A" remarks that travellers are bound to present exaggerated descriptions of New World peoples:

> Since we're all born with a taste for the exotic, magnifying everything around us, how could a man settle for the correct dimension of things, when obliged, as it were, to justify the journey he's made and the trouble he's taken to travel so far to see them? (39)

Diderot makes clear, then, his own awareness of the partiality both of his account of Tahiti and of Bougainville's *Voyage*. Given the brief description of Tahiti in the *Voyage*, Diderot seeks to envision the broad range of moral values and institutional structures that might have engendered the social practices and beliefs of Bougainville's Tahiti.

In Diderot's account, Tahiti sustains legal, economic, and social institutions to effect the ultimate goal of enlarging the population. Uniform social practices and public sexual morality are maintained by domestic education. Parents clothe young boys in a tunic and girls with a white veil. After puberty, elaborate public ceremonies emancipate the young from rules strictly prohibiting sexual encounters and confer upon them their status as fully responsible members of Tahitian society (54–55). Both physical and intellectual maturity are needed, argues Orou, for men and women to participate orderly and responsibly in the Tahitian social system. That the entire system is oriented with a view to generating and raising children is clear from the prohibitions of sex between men and women who cannot conceive children. Genetically infertile and elderly women wear black veils and women "indisposed by their monthly pe-

riods" wear grey veils (60). Both veiled women and the men who consort
with them are punished by public censure. Legal sanctions, which include
exile to the north of the island, keep the young apart from one another
(62). In order to ensure that raising children would not create an undue
economic burden, Diderot describes a Tahitian scheme of distributive
justice in which one-sixth of every harvest is donated to the community
as a whole. This communal food supply is then distributed according to
the number of children in each family. Diderot argues that by enacting
and maintaining such a policy, Tahiti fosters an economic system that
provides tangible, material incentives for producing and nurturing children. Far from being based upon a set of institutions followed blindly
due to custom or upon a subservience to natural instincts, Diderot's Tahitians consciously mould the young in deliberate ways, maintain social
and legal sanctions, and run an economic program of distribution in order to encourage specific forms of social behaviour.[52] For Diderot, a carefully crafted social and political process—and at times a rather severe one
at that, far from a stereotypically licentious and carefree "natural" life free
from the pressures of "civilization"—is crucial for sustaining a social life
that is congruent with humans' most elemental behavioural traits and
desires, such as our sexual drives. It is this last aspect of Tahitian society
that leads Diderot to note on occasion that Tahitians lead a more natural
life than Europeans. The entirety of his account of Tahitian society makes
clear that, in his view, Tahitians live 'by nature' only in the sense that
they have created and maintained social institutions and norms that do
not conflict severely with basic human desires. For Diderot, the paradig-
matic example of a hegemonic and 'unnatural' set of norms, practices,
and institutions, and thus one of the central rhetorical targets of the *Supplément* is the Catholic church in France.

Diderot argues that by attending to "the value of every newborn child,
and the importance of population", Tahiti strives to ensure that its land
will contain as many people as it can sustain (63). As he notes, in assessing the welfare of France and Tahiti or indeed that of any country, one
should attend to its wealth in human resources; in comparing the social
practices of any two groups or specific polities, Diderot's Tahitian character Orou attempts to convince the French chaplain that if a land can feed
more people than it has, its mores are probably deficient and, by implication, it ought to be reordered toward the goal of a steadily rising population. (47–48) In characterizing population growth as one of the ultimate
ends of social organization, Diderot was not alone. Despite a few oppo-
nents to this view who presaged what is now a widespread response to
rapid population growth and its social effects (most notably Thomas Mal-
thus, who published his *Essay on the Principle of Population* in 1798), a
staple feature of a broad range of eighteenth-century political thought

was its insistence on population as the standard of a nation's economic, social, and political health.[53] Demographic estimates served as indicators of the prosperity, as well as the political stability, of a country. In this view, a nation free of wars, internal persecution, famine, and plagues while booming in trade and industry would lead to a steady growth in population.[54] Politically, this focus on population ultimately reveals the centrality of social welfare for many *philosophes*. The exploits of leaders and the wealth of the aristocracy or church establishment are incidental in determining a nation's political achievement; instead, freedom from persecution, healthful living conditions, access to shelter and basic sustenance, and other features of basic human welfare constitute the true measure of a nation's success. In the context of the eighteenth-century French discourse on social welfare and political health, therefore, Diderot's argument in the *Supplément* about Tahiti's demography, as peculiar as this might seem to a contemporary reader, constitutes among the strongest possible *political* praise that one could give to a society. By sketching the social practices and institutions that might have achieved the seeming lack of poverty that Bougainville noted, Diderot suggests that Tahitians have organized themselves toward enhancing their collective welfare. If Tahiti is a paradise, he implies, it is in large part a paradise constructed and maintained by Tahitians themselves.

Knowledge and skills for social life. Diderot's arguments in the *Supplément* about the role that "advanced" knowledge ought to play in improving society at first appear to conflict with his broader social and political thought. On the one hand, Diderot celebrates Tahitian society because of what he perceives to be Tahitians' successful social planning and cultural values. It is hardly astonishing that the primary editor of the *Encyclopédie* would favour an interpretation of Tahitian society that emphasizes its rationally ordered structures, practices, and goals. At the same time, however, Diderot notes explicitly in the *Supplément* that an analysis of Tahiti demonstrates that a nation can progress without many of the "higher" sciences, such as physics or anatomy, which the *philosophes* lauded and investigated in detail in the volumes of the *Encyclopédie* (56). That the leader of a project premissed on the view that cataloguing and disseminating the most advanced knowledge can benefit humanity at large is also able to champion, in the *Supplément*, a "primitive" society seems at first a contradiction.[55] Rousseau's thought, in contrast, offers a consistently critical view of the role that the arts, sciences, and technology have played in enslaving and tormenting Europeans and other 'civilized' peoples. His celebration of the New World in the *Discourse on Inequality* accords, therefore, with his earlier arguments in the *Discourse on the Sciences and the Arts*.

Coming to terms with this potential paradox in Diderot's thought reveals his balanced view of the role of advanced knowledge in social development. For Diderot, such knowledge is neither the panacea nor the curse of the modern age. Thus, he refrains from using Europe's level of technological and social complexity as a benchmark against which to assess the cognitive capacity or social organization of New World societies. He rejects the view, in short, that the spread of European sciences and technology, or, in general, of European 'enlightenment', will necessarily improve the condition of non-European peoples. Moreover, unlike Rousseau, Diderot did not view sophisticated technology or other advancements in human knowledge as necessarily degrading. Advanced knowledge neither necessarily corrupts nor necessarily liberates—instead, political and social institutions, behaviour, and practices are the crucial elements needed for a healthy polity. Advances in knowledge are useful only if their social costs and benefits are carefully weighed and ultimately integrated into an efficient and just political system. For Diderot, Tahiti is worthy of respect, therefore, *not* because it lacks sophisticated technology and science (thus, Rousseau would argue, avoiding the slavish interdependence that accompanies such human knowledge), but because it has indigenously developed a set of institutions and a national character that are durable, efficient, and just—*this* is the proper work of politics, in his view, regardless of a people's philosophical, scientific, or technological development. In the *Histoire des deux Indes*, Diderot contends that "[a]ll civilized people were once primitive; and all primitive people, left to their natural impulse, were destined to become civilized." (206) Human societies, he asserts, tend to become further differentiated and are characterized by increasingly complicated sets of institutions over time, yet such changes are not necessarily degrading. As we have seen, Diderot shares many of Rousseau's concerns about the social and political conditions of European nations, but Diderot ultimately does not praise Tahiti because it lies in a fixed stage of human history before civilization emerges. Rather, he views Tahitians as a people necessarily in flux; their measured growth, not their lack of development, becomes the key subject of his praise in the *Supplément*. The Tahitians, he argues, "remain unperturbed by too rapid an advance of knowledge." (66) Thus, Diderot argues that the progress of human knowledge should be kept at a level at which humans can reflect upon the social consequences of proposed scientific and technological advances. Diderot bemoans the fact that Tahiti will become Europeanized through the coercion of imperialism in part because of his fear that Tahiti will fail as badly as Europe in accommodating advanced knowledge within a robust social and political order. The failure is not inevitable but probable, given that Tahitians themselves will never have the opportunity to develop their institutions freely and methodically to incorporate such knowledge, as they have successfully done in the past—instead, they will be forced to plunge headlong into the labyrinth of the 'civilized' world under masters not of their own choosing.

Relationship between self-interest and social goods. Tahitian society, as presented in the *Supplément*, is in part grounded on the principle that personal, even selfish, interests need to be satisfied in order for political stability to take root and for justice to flourish. In Diderot's political thought, the assumption that human beings care primarily for themselves or their immediate friends and family, even in Tahiti, runs alongside his frequent claim that the general good must always be preferred to the particular. Thus, for Diderot, one of the primary goals of politics, properly understood, is to configure society such that the conflict between narrow interests and the general welfare is minimized, for "[y]ou can be sure that whenever a man is as attentive to his fellow-creatures as to his bed, health or peace of mind, his hut, harvests or fields, he will do his utmost to ensure their welfare."[56] (63)

In common with many other *philosophes*, Diderot held the view that individuals are fundamentally oriented toward their own existence and advantage and that this fact must be taken as a given in any descriptive or prescriptive account of society, politics, and ethics.[57] In Diderot's thought, both institutions and moral values play crucial roles in reconciling personal with social interests. Tahiti is a laudable society, in his opinion, not because Tahitians have transformed themselves into altruistic agents, but because their shared traditions and social institutions appear to channel self-absorbed individual energies into productive behaviour and attitudes that benefit the community at large. Diderot's emphasis on uniting the general and individual welfare is a crucial component of his political thought that finds a rhetorically powerful home in the *Supplément*. While Rousseau's Amerindians live in durable societies because of their good fortune in inhabiting a particular stage of anthropological development, Diderot's Tahitians maintain an impressive society over time by consciously ensuring that it is based on "self-interest", the sentiment that Diderot considers, throughout his political writings, to be altogether the most "energetic and durable" (61).

The New World as a Device of Social Criticism: The Overlapping and Rival Approaches of Diderot and Rousseau

Inspired in part by the noble savage themes in writings by Montaigne, Lahontan, and others (such as Fénelon), Diderot and Rousseau engage in a thoroughgoing criticism of European societies by pointing to the technologically and institutionally simpler and, in their view, less corrupted New World. In addition to works on noble savagery, many other popular writings used the trope of judging Europe from a non-European viewpoint. Perhaps most notably, Montesquieu's *Lettres Persanes* (published anonymously in 1721) offered what became a highly influential critical examination of French society from an ostensibly Muslim and Persian perspective. In general, the increasing stock of travel literature in the eighteenth century provided the grist for ever more radical analyses of European life, for more varied and insistent evaluations of European societies from an ethical perspective engendered in part by understandings of non-European peoples.[58] For Rousseau's and Diderot's philosophical anthropologies, this comparative dimension is most conspicuous in their treatments of human needs and property relations and the sentiment of love and the role of women in society. Although a number of Diderot's and Rousseau's criticisms of European societies are similar in spirit, upon closer examination, this aspect of their philosophical anthropologies also reveals the profound differences that exist between their theorizations of New World peoples. To be sure, both Diderot and Rousseau use the ethnographic literature about non-European peoples as a critical foil against which the injustices of European societies can be brought into view. Nonetheless, the manner in which they understand non-European peoples, even in those philosophical contexts in which they instrumentally serve a critical function that has more to do with Europe than with the non-European world, has an impact upon how robustly non-European peoples can be viewed as moral equals. The nature of Rousseau's criticism of European life often draws upon a highly exotic and naturalistic understanding of New World peoples, the pernicious (if inadvertent) consequences of which will be examined in the next section. Diderot, in contrast, offers a social commentary upon European societies that simultaneously humanizes non-European peoples and that therefore accords well with his deep concern about their subjected status, as we will see in the following chapter.

Human needs and property relations.   Rousseau argues that the true needs of humans are as simple as basic sustenance and rest: food, drink, and sleep are enough to satisfy the savage human (135; cf. 143). The most basic physical needs, then, are natural to humanity; all other desires are socially constructed and often harmful. In arguing against Hobbes's contention that the state of nature is prone to violence, Rousseau asserts that Hobbes's chief error was to attribute to humanity the need "to satisfy a multitude of passions that are the product of Society and have made Laws necessary" (153). Recalling earlier noble savage writings,

Rousseau links the development of socially engendered passions not only to a corrupt set of social practices, but also to poor physical health itself. In this view, a natural human is a "free being whose heart is at peace and body in health" (152). The creation and stirrings of human passions lead to unstable and unjust societies as well as enervated, sick bodies. Rousseau, therefore, identifies old age as practically the only real cause of death among New World peoples. He argues that civilized societies engender such strong passions and superfluous needs that the public health itself is in danger. Rousseau praises the strong constitutions and physical vigour of New World peoples and contrasts the maladies brought on by the luxurious idleness and dangerously rich foods of the civilized rich as well as the harsh labour and meagre sustenance that is afforded occasionally, if at all, to the poor in civilized nations (138, 203–4). According to Rousseau, in order to acquire basic necessities, natural humans learned "to overcome the obstacles of Nature" (165). In time, the establishment of a relatively sedentary lifestyle created the leisure with which the first "conveniences" were acquired; this, he writes, was the "first source of evils" in human history (168). Both the body and mind were enervated, and new, unfamiliar, and ultimately illusory needs soon became perceived as basic necessities. Perversely, with the softened characters of newly sedentary peoples, the pain of even contemplating the loss of these new commodities grew stronger than the joy of having them. As a result of the psychological changes wrought by a growing materialism—especially an increasing vanity (*amour propre*), a tendency to judge oneself according to the gaze of others—wealth eventually became the standard of comparison among individuals and groups (188–89). Luxury, the crowning height of materialistic depravity, results finally in depopulation. Farmers, squeezed by taxes and unable to manage a subsistence wage, flee to the cities, leaving barren fields, only to become destitute and to join the growing ranks of the wretched urban poor—"[t]hat is how the State, while it on one side grows rich, grows weak and is depopulated on the other" (206).

In a similar vein, Diderot castigates many civilized desires as "superfluous" and "factitious" (43). Thus, a deep suspicion of ever increasing commodities, other material trappings, and the attendant flourishing of selfish and degenerate passions in modern Europe runs throughout both Rousseau's and Diderot's writings. The most primitivist side of Rousseau's interpretation of the New World, however, posits a simpler, arguably *natural*, and presocial life as a benchmark against which the material excesses and passionate willfulness of civilized nations can be measured. In contrast, Diderot lauds Tahitians' *artful* (that is, cultural) efforts at maintaining a community that appropriates its surrounding environment prudently, for the benefit of enhancing human welfare rather than for the

sake of material production itself. Diderot, of course, often describes Tahitians as engaged in a "natural" life, but, as we have seen, he clearly
means by this that they have planned and sustained social relations in a
manner congruent with what he considers to be elemental (or natural)
needs and desires. He celebrates the importance that Tahitians have accorded to leisure in contrast to the torment of excessive toil or wanton
luxury in France. Tahitians themselves, in this view, have determined
what balance between work and leisure is most conducive to a healthy
lifestyle and polity. For Diderot, the narrative of development from a
primitive to a civilized society is thoroughly social from beginning to
end—it does not presume that human problems arise with social activity,
for he takes social life to be constitutive of the human condition. The
character of social practices and institutions, not the very existence of
sociability, is the crucial issue for Diderot's analysis of both European and
non-European peoples. The psychological changes and technological
momentum created by early efforts to make humans' environments habit-
able eventually foster social conditions that generate inflated needs and
conflicting, unstable passions. As Diderot contends, these forces of historical change drive "[man] well beyond his immediate objective; so that
when his need has elapsed he comes to be swept into the great ocean of
fantasy from which he cannot pull out." (66) Thus, humans' efforts to
survive in harsh surroundings foster a set of needs, desires, and passions
that compel them disastrously to attempt to master Nature itself. Diderot
argues that Europeans have impoverished their souls and societies by
adopting such a domineering attitude toward their environment. Accordingly, he argues in his *Observations sur le Nakaz* that

> it was the necessity of struggling against the ever-present, common enemy—
> nature—which brought men together. They became aware that they struggled
> to better effect together, than separately. The evil is that they went past their
> goal. They were not content to conquer, they wanted to triumph; they were
> not content to bring down the enemy, they wanted to trample him underfoot.
> (123–24)

For Diderot, the natural environment is an "enemy" only to the extent
that it raises impediments against human survival and flourishing. His
central concern is not that Europeans have cultivated and appropriated
their surroundings, since all humans out of necessity do this, but that
they have done so precipitously.

Rousseau's and Diderot's concerns about private property also highlight their different understandings of New World peoples. Diderot had
read in Bougainville's account that individual homes and the ownership
of basic goods exist in Tahiti, but, in Diderot's view, Tahitians' shared
values and communal institutions counteract whatever egoistic psycho-

logical changes and social inequalities arise as a result of a system of private property. For Rousseau, however, the opposite fact protects the New World from rampant corruption and injustice: it is the lack of interdependence, not the communal linkages among individuals, that ensures a "free, healthy, good, and happy" life, despite the existence of some private property (171). For Rousseau, then, Amerindians escape the ills of Europe's property relations for reasons largely outside of their control, while in contrast, for Diderot, a combination of environmental factors and humanly chosen and sustained social activities and institutions explain Tahitians' greater liberty and equality.

The sentiment of love and the role of women in society. Another criticism of European society through the comparative lens afforded by the New World concerns the status and the role of women. Diderot and Rousseau both contrast relationships between men and women and their social effects in the New World with those in European societies. Judging the latter in light of the purported superiority of the former is, however, one of the few similarities on this issue between them. Their writings reveal radically divergent positions on the status of women and about how encounters with particular New World peoples' moral values could inform European notions about sexual relations.

The *Supplément* is as much a work on sexual politics as on politics conventionally understood. Returning to the concept of property and its connection to the New World, Diderot berates Old World societies for treating women as either the de jure or de facto property of men. This "tyranny", Diderot argues, is one of several ways in which human sexuality is twisted into an almost criminal act in contemporary European societies. One of the central claims of the *Supplément* is that Tahiti is in part founded upon, and thus not inconsistent with, humans' elemental desires and needs. Thus, Diderot portrays Tahiti as a society at ease with the personal and social dynamics of human sexuality. In Tahiti, Diderot asserts, women are not confused with property and, thus, intimate relationships are more liberated and relaxed. The empirical evidence furnished by Bougainville about Tahiti, then, demonstrates for Diderot that a healthy, well-functioning community can exist with sexual mores significantly different from what the Catholic church, European states and their censors, and prevalent European social customs dictate are necessary to preserve a basic moral order. Diderot argues that in treating women as propertied objects, European societies have

> confused something which cannot feel or think or desire or will . . . with a very different thing that cannot be exchanged or acquired; which *does* have freedom, will, desire; which has the ability to give itself up or hold itself back forever;

which complains and suffers; and which can never be an article of exchange unless its character is forgotten and violence is done to its nature. (50)

The confused belief that reduces women to mere property, then, in addition to laying the groundwork for monogamy, rules of chastity, and other social practices that, in his view, violate humans' sexual passions, ultimately constricts liberty, thereby violating human dignity.

The subtitle of Diderot's *Supplément* foreshadows his position on the sources of European virtues and vices: "dialogue between A and B on the inappropriateness of attaching moral ideas to certain physical actions that do not accord with them". For Diderot, a whole host of purported vices and virtues are social constructs that are born of the mistaken impulse to restrict instinctive human desires that are often amoral. In the *Supplément*, a litany of such qualities of character are analyzed from the perspective of Tahitian social behaviour and mores. Diderot argues, for instance, that jealousy is exacerbated in civilized societies because of "false moral standards and the extension of property" to an entire class of human beings (68). He asserts that the most socially harmful consequences of jealousy and other personal vices are minimized in Tahiti because of the more liberal approach that it has chosen to adopt with regard to sexuality. In the old Tahitian's speech, Diderot contends that just as Christianity helped to breed shame and fear about sexual relations in Europe, it now unravels the healthy sexual attitudes of Tahiti through its missionary work (44).[59]

Diderot takes to task not only religious institutions, but also the secular legal code (in particular civil laws concerning marriage) and social customs that are bound up with the formalities and proprieties of aristocratic society (70–71). Thus, in the *Supplément*, Diderot relates a popular eighteenth-century story about a New England prostitute, Polly Baker, who is charged with becoming pregnant as a result of dissolute morals; the narrative takes the form of a speech purportedly given by Polly Baker at her trial in Connecticut.[60] Laws and social prejudices, she argues, change the nature of innocent, harmless actions into criminal offences. Instead, actions that truly "disturb public tranquillity" should be rightfully considered unjust criminal behaviour. And so, she adds, laws should be enacted that punish irresponsible *men*, the bachelors who impregnate, deceive, and neglect women and who even drive many of them to prostitution, not the responsible mothers who raise their children despite the social calumnies heaped upon them. Diderot notes the irony that although it is widely acknowledged that the nation as a whole benefits materially from the birth of children, single mothers like Polly Baker nevertheless become impoverished (57, 70–71). The social engineering that subverts the nature of actions and deems them to be sinful, criminal, or improper, Diderot implies, is a manifestation of the exploitative and unjust values that guide European societies. To be sure, Diderot's presentation of Tahitian life also exhibits its share of socialized communal values. But he insists that in Tahiti such habituated practices and social norms engender individual contentment and the broader social welfare much more effectively than in any European society because of an approach that seeks to make social institutions and their values compatible with the most basic human needs and desires. Just as Tahitian society arguably structures itself in accordance with, not against, self-interest, it also provides socially productive and nondestructive outlets for humans' sexuality and other fundamental drives and passions.

Rousseau elaborates a distinction between physical and moral love that manifests the profound differences between his and Diderot's conceptions of women and their position in society. "Savages", Rousseau argues, take part in physical love, a sentiment born of the most general sexual desires. Their limited ability to think abstractly and their inability to make comparisons, to focus vainly on appearances, beauty, or merit, preclude them from engaging in moral love, a passion unique to the civilized world that focuses humans' raw physical desires to a specific, preferred object. And so the Caribs, who have "departed least from the state of Nature", are the least susceptible to jealousy and "the most peaceful in their loves" (158). "Now it is easy to see", Rousseau adds in contrast, "that the moral aspect of love is a factitious sentiment; born of social practice, and extolled with much skill and care by women in order to establish their rule and to make dominant the sex that should obey." (158)

The critical ends to which Rousseau and Diderot deploy New World women also differ greatly. While Diderot's contentions about sexuality, love, and women sometimes reflect the conventional views of his time, Rousseau more typically exhibits the norms of his age. Diderot rejects the treatment of women as property in European societies, in which, he notes, it is clearly men who wield not only the most social, but also sexual power.[61] In contrast, Rousseau asserts that women deploy moral love to subjugate men. Diderot emphasizes the equal dignity of the sexes in order to counter the objectification of women; Rousseau endorses the view that women are naturally inferior and, thus, properly constituted to obey men.[62] Although Diderot and Rousseau, then, portray sexual relations in European societies as inferior to those found in the New World, they employ distinct moral vocabularies to explain such differences, and thus differ widely in their analyses and conclusions. Rousseau deploys Amerindians as instinctually loving creatures who are not yet ruled by the artificial sexual dominance of women, while Diderot chastises European patriarchal attitudes by celebrating Tahitians' consciously formed and

maintained sexual morality, one that, he believes, comes closer to affirm-
ing women's humanity. Overall, the contrast with Diderot's account of
sexuality in New World societies is striking, for Rousseau's naturalized
Amerindians can do *nothing but* engage in physical love. Diderot's Tahitians, on the other hand, form and maintain moral values and social institutions that accord with humans' sexual passions.

The intellectual cross-cultural encounters that New World travel literature brought about in Europe from the late fifteenth century onward
yield an ambiguous legacy. On the one hand, the rise of comparative
social theory and a growing interest in foreign peoples for their own sake
helped to create an awareness of the complexity of non-European societies.[63] On the other hand, the theme of the exotic noble savage remained strong throughout the eighteenth century, as the writings of
Lahontan and Rousseau make clear. Diderot, however, even when playing the New World against Europe for his own political purposes, acknowledges New World peoples as conscious, fully rational, and cultural
beings. Also, as we have seen, Diderot satirizes his imaginative reconstruction of Tahitian life. Such ironic moments indicate Diderot's self-
awareness about the idealized representation of Tahitian society that he
employs in the course of his social criticism of European practices and
institutions.[64] Most importantly, the substance of his characterization of
'primitive' life is almost always at odds with the mechanical and naturalistic conception of New World peoples that one finds most often in the
tradition of noble savagery. Ultimately, Diderot's vigorous anti-imperialism makes clear his ethical interest in non-European peoples for their
own sake, and distinguishes him from those who, however inadvertently,
present a nearly animalistic characterization of New World peoples. Diderot developed his multifaceted and subversive perspective of New World
peoples for the *Supplément* at about the same time as his anti-imperialist
contributions to Abbé Raynal's *Histoire des deux Indes*—indeed, some
passages in the latter are simply borrowed from the former.[65] Before turning to an examination of how Diderot's philosophical anthropology and
social theory shape his anti-imperialist political thought in the next chapter, I first conclude with some further observations about the ethical and
political consequences of theorizing 'natural humanity'.

The Dehumanization of Natural Humanity

Diderot deployed the noble savage strategy of thinkers such as Montaigne and Rousseau in criticizing Europe through the lens of the New
World, but his characterization of New World peoples challenged the
understanding of humanity and its relationship to culture offered by no-

ble savage thinkers. Moreover, he went far beyond most noble savage accounts in attending to the predicament of New World peoples themselves, especially in light of European imperialism. While only strains of this concern exist in Rousseau's thought, Diderot's writings resolutely attack the injustices committed against aboriginal peoples. Instead of focusing almost exclusively on the problems facing Europeans as the noble savage theorists did, Diderot details and decries the plight of New World peoples. Noble savage theorists occasionally criticized the corruption that Europeans could bring to 'natural' and 'innocent' peoples. The dehumanization brought about by these thinkers' exotic characterizations of Amerindians and others, however, undercut whatever possibilities existed in their thinking for cultivating a genuine cross-cultural sympathy with historically real, flesh-and-blood aboriginals who at worst were being systematically enslaved or massacred. The problems that motivated noble savage thinkers were almost always those of Europe—hence their need to place foreign peoples at the level of an idealized, 'natural' standard in order to decry European materialism, corruption, and injustice.

Rousseau and Diderot are among the eighteenth-century thinkers who developed a multidimensional social theory, one that approaches the study of societies by recognizing the complex interdependence of structural and voluntary features of human life.[66] The understanding of the human subject that such an account presupposes is that humans are *cultural agents*; that is, humans are partly shaped by and situated within cultural contexts, yet are also able to consciously and freely transform themselves and their surroundings. While Rousseau acknowledges this to be true for humans at particular stages of development, Diderot theorizes humans to be *constitutively* cultural agents. In their own ways, then, Rousseau and, under his influence, Diderot theorize the manifold and intricate relationships between our inherited institutions, practices, and beliefs and our ability to scrutinize and reconfigure them. Rousseau introduces the term "perfectibility" to philosophical discourse, arguing that this is one of the defining characteristics of humanity, while also formulating a subtle and profound analysis of the ways in which humans are psychologically moulded and constrained by technological and sociological factors not of their own choosing. Diderot, too, recognizes liberty to be a constitutively human trait, while also appreciating the costs and benefits of physiological, historical, and even geographic determinants. For Diderot and Rousseau, humans' partial autonomy is a universal feature of humanity in addition to being the ultimate source of particularity, of the multiplicity of human life. Their social analyses point to the interlocking web of voluntary and structural elements that comprise all societies. As we have seen, however, Rousseau tends to praise Amerindians and Hottentots for factors beyond their control—such as the inborn stirrings of natural pity—while Diderot theorizes Tahitians as individuals who have consciously formed and maintained social institutions that are in accord with their collective goals and natural instincts. Overall, Diderot conceptualizes humans as such (and thus New World individuals) as cultural agents, in contrast to Rousseau. While Rousseau usually uses Amerindians to illustrate the concept of a universal human subject, the pure natural humans of his earliest state of nature, it is Diderot's thicker and more particularized understanding of Tahitians that paradoxically prepares the way for a universal, inclusive anti-imperialist political theory, one that embraces both Europeans and non-Europeans.

Diderot's application of a multidimensional social analysis toward societies such as Tahiti is linked to his moral respect for, and his impassioned anti-imperialist defence of, New World peoples. As we have seen, despite Rousseau's potential for an anthropologically acute understanding of Amerindians, it is Diderot who attempts to understand New World inhabitants as cultural beings. We saw earlier that the influential and archetypal noble savage theorist Lahontan had been able to favour colonial policies that were explicitly destructive of Amerindian societies while also lauding these societies' practices and beliefs because his appreciation of Amerindians was ultimately very thin. Lahontan's account of the Huron, for example, rested fundamentally upon a *decultured* description of their life; in spite of his stated belief in their humanity and his arguments that they possessed impressive cognitive powers, Lahontan effectively dehumanized Amerindians in light of his often naturalistic representations of them, which denied their status as cultural agents. I have argued that Rousseau's political thought also manifests this connection between deculturation and dehumanization. As the *Discourse on Inequality* demonstrates, Rousseau moves easily from discussing the "savages" of the original state of nature to the "savages" of contemporary New World societies. Given that the 'savage condition' amounts to what Rousseau himself considered to be a nearly animal existence, his use of the New World travel literature to theorize the earliest state of nature results in precisely the same curious result created by earlier noble savage accounts: those celebrated as the most purely human appear as inhuman, instinct-driven, and mechanical animals.

In addition to the disturbing ethical consequences of portraying New World peoples in this manner, many eighteenth-century political thinkers believed that the very concept of a 'natural human' was indefensible. Today, significant contemporary gains in our knowledge of humans' biological inheritance and its complex relationship to environmental factors—knowledge derived in part through developments in genetics and evolutionary biology—indicate the incoherence of even the hypothetical idea of a human being shorn of all cultural attributes. We now know that humans, far more than other animals, are dependent upon extragenetic mechanisms—not merely environmental stimuli, but cultural signals that partly order and structure behaviour and expectations—because the genetic information humans inherit is far more diffuse than the narrower and more precisely ordered and effective genetic cues given to cognitively simpler animals. Cultural norms and expectations, in other words, provide humans with information without which they could not function. Evolutionary history in part explains our unique dependence upon cultural knowledge and may well demonstrate the centrality of culture to the human condition.[67] A variety of philosophers in the eighteenth century argued in a more speculative fashion that humans are unlike other animals in that they rely upon far more than their basic instincts and partly fashion the world themselves, thus living their lives according to the conventional worlds of their own making (and remaking). Those who defended the idea of human sociability as a constitutive element of humanity believed that humans not only *can* but *must* live according to more than their instincts, and the environmental stimuli that trigger them, in order to function coherently.

Natural humans, humans stripped of their cultural attributes, would thus be, as Clifford Geertz writes, "unworkable monstrosities with very few useful instincts, fewer recognizable sentiments, and no intellect: mental basket cases", far from the placid and well-ordered natural humans described at length in the *Discourse on Inequality*.[68] Like many contemporary scholars, Geertz mistakenly identifies the reductive concept of a natural man with what he calls "the Enlightenment view of man".[69] As I have argued (and will continue to argue with reference to the anti-imperialist political philosophies of Diderot, Kant, and Herder), there are important strands of eighteenth-century social and political thought that take humans to be intrinsically cultural agents who partly transform, and yet are always situated within, various contexts. Strikingly, anti-imperialist political theories in the Enlightenment era were almost always informed by such understandings of humanity.

Rousseau, then, followed the tradition of noble savagery in denying a crucial and indispensable feature of human nature: cultural agency, an element moreover that, at certain moments in the *Discourse on Inequality*, he appears to deny to a whole set of peoples—the indigenous inhabitants of the New World. To be sure, given Rousseau's theorization of perfectibility, he too believes that humans, in many respects, make themselves. But in his conjectural history, Rousseau does not theorize human beings *from the outset*—that is, by their very nature—as social and cultural beings. As we have seen, this has profound consequences for his interpretation of New World peoples. Rousseau's need to provide empirical examples for a supposedly hypothetical category transforms what might have been merely a heuristic (if implausible) concept of natural humanity into an ethically troubling and inadvertently dehumanizing rhetoric, one that replicates the paradoxes of the noble savage tradition. Pace conventional understandings of Enlightenment philosophy, since the relationship of art, ingenuity, and freedom to human life was a lively topic of debate in the eighteenth century, a number of Rousseau's contemporaries attacked his concept of a natural human in precisely this manner. As Adam Ferguson argued, with reference to the New World and Rousseau's *Discourse on Inequality*, and as part of his own conjectural history of humanity,

> We speak of art as distinguished from nature; but art itself is natural to man. He is in some measure the artificer of his own frame, as well as his fortune, and is destined, from the first age of his being, to invent and contrive. . . . If we are asked therefore, Where the state of nature is to be found? we may answer, It is here; and it matters not whether we are understood to speak in the island of Great Britain, at the Cape of Good Hope, or the Straits of Magellan. While this active being is in the train of employing his talents, and of operating on the subjects around him, all situations are equally natural. . . . But if nature is only opposed to art, in what situation of the human race are the footsteps of art unknown? In the condition of the savage, as well as in that of the citizen, are many proofs of human invention. . . .[70]

As we have seen, Diderot theorizes along these lines that humans are intrinsically social and cultural beings and, accordingly, conceptualizes New World peoples as such. For the eighteenth-century thinkers who explicitly or tacitly challenged the tradition of noble savagery, a multidimensional social theory—one that attends to the complex interplay between our structural and voluntary characteristics (which Rousseau undertakes in his radical analysis of European societies)—was crucial for an understanding not only of 'civilized peoples', but a fortiori of *any* group of human beings. Since Diderot understood non-European peoples as *cultural* beings, he therefore afforded them more genuine respect as *human* beings, a regard borne out most comprehensively in his anti-imperialist contributions to the *Histoire des deux Indes*.

An understanding of New World (and other non-European) peoples as social and cultural beings served as a key catalyst of the rise of anti-imperialist thought in the late eighteenth century. The exotic beings that classic noble savage accounts presented were too unreal (in part because they were presented as fully 'natural') to be considered as flesh-and-blood humans with whom one could sympathize and on behalf of whom one would challenge European imperialism. Diderot was powerfully influenced by the social and political criticism that Rousseau's device of natural humanity made possible, and he incorporated much of Rousseau's account of perfectibility and freedom into his increasingly humanistic political thought. But Diderot also challenged the view that humans were at bottom asocial, and rejected the view that humanity could be best understood by attempting to reveal a core, natural human that underlies the various cultural layers of human life. For Diderot, human beings are fundamentally social and cultural beings, and he thus interpreted Tahitian society in the *Supplément* as a set of constructed social norms and institutions that are amenable to conscious human transformation, rather than portraying Tahitians as natural humans who live by the light of nature alone. The moral and political significance of this is crucial, as an examination of Diderot's anti-imperialist writings in the following chapter will show.

Three

Diderot and the Evils of Empire:
The *Histoire des deux Indes*

ABBÉ Guillaume-Thomas Raynal, the man celebrated throughout Europe as the author of *Histoire philosophique et politique des établissements et du commerce des Européens dans les deux Indes* [*Philosophical and political history of European settlements and commerce in the two Indies*], was an iconoclastic Jesuit who edited and wrote parts of this extraordinary ten-volume work, a broad survey of global political and economic ties from the earliest Spanish conquests in the Americas to the colonial and commercial activities of, among others, the Danes, Portuguese, Dutch, French, and English.[1] In addition to providing a synthetic history, the *Histoire* also offered commentaries on European and non-European societies and launched numerous attacks on both the slave trade and imperialism. The intellectual genesis of the *Histoire* was in many respects analogous to the *Encyclopédie* that Denis Diderot coedited with Jean d'Alembert, for it included contributions from many writers. Unlike the latter, however, all of the contributions to the *Histoire* were anonymous, with Raynal alone listed as author of the entire text. With Raynal taking the cover, his contributors were able to make heterodox arguments that would likely have landed them in jail if their authorship had been known. Diderot, in particular, seemed to relish the opportunity to craft controversial moral and political arguments without the threat of expulsion or a return to Vincennes, where he had been imprisoned for having written allegedly blasphemous material. Many of the radical contributions, and indeed most of the anti-imperialist arguments, were written (as we now know) by Diderot in the 1770s.[2] Predictably, the *Histoire* was banned by the *parlement* of Paris and all known copies were ordered to be burned. That Edmund Burke knew of the *Histoire* and held it in high esteem (he called Raynal "one of the finest authors of the age"),[3] and that, significantly, both Immanuel Kant and Johann Gottfried Herder seemed to have read the *Histoire* as well and appropriated its attacks on the practices and traditional justifications of European empires, should come as no surprise. Despite its renegade status, Raynal's *Histoire* was one of the most popular eighteenth-century 'forbidden' publications, having gone through an astonishing thirty editions in seventeen years.[4]

The 1780 edition of the *Histoire* was published as ten volumes of text and one volume of maps and tables. The "two Indies" in its title refer to the East and West Indies, but this signifies almost everything east of Persia and south of Russia for the 'East Indies', and the entire Americas (not only the Caribbean islands) for the 'West Indies', all in addition to what was then known of Africa. Thus, the *Histoire* was no less than the history of Europe's interactions with virtually the entire non-European globe that had been traversed, and largely subjugated, by European explorers, missionaries, traders, armies, and imperial administrators from 1492 onward.[5] Diderot's contributions to this ambitious work were significant, amounting to roughly 700 pages in the 1780 edition. His contributions ranged in size from a single paragraph to essays of over thirty pages, and comprised a broad array of subjects such as (to take a sample from hundreds of topics) the history of taxation in Europe and its relationship to modern commerce and society; the songs, dances, and other artistic practices and crafts of the indigenous peoples of Canada; the religious philosophy of the Brahmins in India; and the social structure of the Inca civilization. In contemporary terms, Diderot's contributions fall under a range of subjects from cultural anthropology and social history to political theory and economics. Linking them all is a provocative and subtle ethical sensibility that contributes greatly to our understanding of modern political thought.

I begin here with an overview of some of Diderot's key claims about the nature of imperialism and his criticisms of the European imperial enterprise, the presuppositions and further details of which will be elaborated more comprehensively in the following sections. In Book IX of the *Histoire des deux Indes*, Diderot writes,

> National character is the result of a large number of causes, some constant and some variable. This part of the history of a people is perhaps the most interesting and least difficult to follow. The constant causes are determined by the part of the earth which they inhabit. The variable causes are recorded in their annals, and are evident from their effects. While these causes act in contradiction to one another, the nation is unconscious [of itself as a nation]. It only begins to have a character suitable to it at the moment when its speculative principles accord with its physical situation. It is then that it makes great strides towards the splendour, wealth and happiness which it can expect from the free use of its local resources. (IX, 1)

National character, a much discussed and highly contested term in eighteenth-century political thought, is for Diderot a kind of political culture that is best represented symbolically by a *mask*, for it is simply a set of societal tools that structures behaviour through incentives and norms toward (ideally) ethical, peaceful, and productive ends. Diderot stresses that national character "almost never determines the actions of individuals."

Rather, the "mask" of national character serves as a political culture that more subtly shapes and influences moral and political perceptions, practices, and institutions (IX, 1). The plurality of masks that we find among all peoples and social institutions also indicates a shared, underlying feature of human life, the "general will of humanity" for norms of respect and reciprocity, which manifests itself diversely according to time and place. The problem with colonial empires, according to Diderot, is that "[t]he greater the distance from the capital [of the empire] the looser the mask becomes. At the frontier it falls off. Going from one hemisphere to another, what does it become? Nothing." (IX, 1)

In the noble savage literature, as we saw in chapter 2, a decultured (and sometimes a desocialized) individual is a 'natural man', a being who ought to be celebrated for his independence, physical prowess, and pure uncorrupted instincts. Under the influence of such writings, in particular those of Baron Lahontan, Rousseau often elaborates his contentions about humans in the earliest state of nature (despite his own claim that most 'primitive' peoples exist in a middle stage between the state of nature and civilized society) by describing the supposed attributes of Amerindians and other New World peoples. For Diderot, however, the figure that most embodies an unmasked human is the European imperialist. Bereft of the social and cultural bonds that normally would have humanized him and that might have moderated his outlook and behaviour, the imperialist runs wild in the New World, clamouring for profit, brutalizing fellow human beings, and destroying foreign nations. Just as Lahontan's Amerindians are, from an anthropological standpoint, amorphous and undifferentiated wholes, Diderot's colonizers are, from an ethical standpoint, virtually indistinguishable. Still, the colonizers are human enough to act voluntarily and so are morally culpable. Diderot thus reserves much of his most rhetorically powerful and harshest criticism in the *Histoire* for their actions:

> Beyond the Equator a man is neither English, Dutch, French, Spanish, nor Portuguese. He retains only those principles and prejudices of his native country which justify or excuse his conduct. He crawls when he is weak; he is violent when strong; he is in a hurry to enjoy, and capable of every crime which will lead him most quickly to his goals. He is a domestic tiger returning to the forest; the thirst of blood takes hold of him once more. This is how all the Europeans, every one of them, indistinctly, have appeared in the countries of the New World. There they have assumed a common frenzy. . . . (IX, 1)

Diderot discusses three ethical principles of colonization at the opening of Book VIII of the *Histoire des deux Indes*. When a discovered territory is actually uninhabited (and not simply presumed to be so), it can then be colonized legitimately. If the territory is only partly occupied, then unless the entire land is necessary for the indigenous group's survival, the uninhabited portion can be justly settled. But in this situation, he warns, it is imperative that the newly settled community live alongside its neighbours in a peaceable and nonthreatening fashion. Employing again the symbol of a once domestic tiger now in the wild, a beast wholly freed from its domesticating and humanizing social and cultural environments, Diderot argues that

> [w]ith . . . reason, and with no offence against the laws of humanity and justice, that [indigenous] people could expel and kill me if I seized women, children and property; if I infringed its civil liberty; if I restricted its religious opinions; if I claimed to give it laws; if I wished to make it my slave. Then I would be only one more wild animal in its vicinity, and no more pity would be due to me than to a tiger. (XIII, 1)

Diderot astutely deploys the language of counteracting perceived future threats—a rationale that played a crucial role in justifications of imperial war and conquest—against the Europeans themselves by arguing that it is aboriginals who can justly attack colonists who settle a partially inhabited land in such a manner that the indigenous community's future safety and prosperity are in doubt. He stresses that not only actual injuries, but the likelihood of future incursions into an indigenous group's lands or potential disruptions of their ways of life legitimate aggressive responses. "Every people", writes Diderot,

> is justified in providing for its present and future safety. If I set up a stockade, amass weapons, and put up fortifications, a people's deputies would be wise if they came and said to me: 'Are you our friend? Are you our enemy? If a friend, what is the purpose of all these preparations for war? If an enemy, you will understand why we destroy them.' And the nation will be sensible if it immediately gets rid of a well-founded fear. (XIII, 1)

Finally, in the case of a fully inhabited land, explorers should at most trade peacefully and nonexploitatively with the indigenous population, who in addition are under no ethical obligation to engage in commerce, especially in light of Europeans' proven tendency to be untrustworthy in their commercial dealings with non-European societies.[6] Along these lines, presaging a similar argument by Kant (who was likely influenced by this section of the *Histoire*), Diderot explains that "[t]he Chinese may be bad politicians when they shut us out of their empire, but they are not unjust. Their country has sufficient population, and we are too dangerous as guests." (XIII, 1) It is obvious, Diderot then implies, that Europeans have failed to meet any of these principles. Accordingly, he ridicules the absurdity of the New World conquests in which Europeans claim lands to be their rightful property not because they are uninhabited, but because they are unoccupied by anyone from the Old World.

Diderot's understanding of European imperial activities as well as of New World peoples led him to doubt whether peaceful and just relations between the Old World and the New could ever be established. Diderot's attempt to imagine how a more noble and beneficial relationship might have developed stresses the value of shared learning and cross-cultural interaction. Diderot envisions a situation that might have been, a meeting of the Old and New Worlds in which small numbers of Europeans would settle among New World peoples and exchange both commodities and ideas. In addition to such commercial and intellectual exchange, through intermarriages, an entirely new people might have been created who would represent the fruits of this peaceful interaction: the European "men would have married the women of the country, and the women the native men. Ties of blood, the strongest and most immediate of bonds, would soon have formed a single family out of the natives and the foreigners." (IX, 1) Diderot realized, of course, that the chance for such learning to take place and for such communities to form had long passed and would not likely be taken up in the future given that Europeans in the New World and other non-European realms continued to arrive with "the imperious commanding tone of masters and conquerors" (IX, 1).

To appreciate further the nuances of Diderot's anti-imperialist political thought, the central themes of his contributions to the *Histoire* that bear upon his critical judgements of empire must be investigated. Accordingly, I first examine Diderot's flexible moral universalism that allows him both to trumpet the freedom and dignity of all humans and to consider a wide array of cultural practices and institutions (of *moeurs*) in the non-European world as rational, defensible responses to local needs and concerns. This will involve an analysis of his idea of a general will of humanity in relation to his related arguments about human sociability, the partial incommensurability of diverse ways of life, and the ethical and psychological dimensions of travel across borders and forms of hospitality abroad. Then, Diderot's anti-imperialist arguments will be analyzed by focusing upon arguments that European imperialism has been catastrophic for non-European peoples; the special role that commerce and trading companies occupy in imperial exploits; the destabilizing effects of empire upon European countries; and the idea that Europe itself is so degraded ethically and politically, and that its few genuine achievements are so fragile, that it is hardly a model of society that should be exported by force to the non-European world.

The General Will of Humanity, the Partial Incommensurability of *Moeurs*, and the Ethics of Crossing Borders

For Diderot, the "general will of humanity", the most fundamental ethical attitude that humans generally hold in their relationships, derives its need and efficacy in part from what he takes to be a universal and highly potent source: the emotions of "indignation and resentment" that humans share not only among themselves but also with other animals and that lie behind the vast array of practices, norms, and institutions that invoke "social laws" and carry out "public retribution". Hence, the "principles of the prescribed law" of civilized nations, the "social practices of savage and barbarous peoples", and even "the tacit agreements obtaining amongst the enemies of mankind" (the codes of honour and respect that keep relations among pirates and brigands, for instance, relatively stable and predictable, however arbitrarily violent their actions may be toward the rest of humanity) are all social phenomena that attend to our fundamental sense of injustice and our need as social beings to construct norms of *respect* and *reciprocity* that in content can vary widely over various times and different places.[7] The universality of the general will of humanity, the humanistic core of Diderot's moral thought, rests upon the similar desires that all peoples have to create workable rules of conduct that allow particular ways of life to flourish without themselves creating harsh injustices and cruelties. The struggle that all societies face to survive, adapt, and develop is the common feature among humans that forms the basis of a cross-cultural moral understanding, one that Diderot contends European imperialists routinely violate. This "similarity between the physical constitution of one man and another, a similarity which entails that of the same needs, pleasures, pains, strength and weakness", "the source of the necessity of society, or of a common struggle" (XIX, 14) underscores the physical vulnerabilities that draw humans together and that provide a common framework for the most basic ethical precepts (which themselves may well differ over time and place). Yet, morality as such does not flow from our physical natures unreflectively and deterministically; to be sure, Diderot writes of an innate principle of compassion (e.g., X, 5), but the general will of humanity, while it relates to humans' physical similarities and vulnerabilities, is a feature of life that humans recognize, discuss, and shape as they construct and alter their social and political institutions.[8] For animals, as Diderot notes in the *Encyclopédie* article "Droit Naturel" ["Natural Right"], the general will takes the form of a brute sense of injustice; for humans, it manifests itself

in the conscious development and transformation of social laws and practices over time. Diderot's account of morality in his later writings of the
1770s onward show the great extent to which he moved away from a
rigidly materialist ethics and embraced a humanistic morality that placed
human freedom at its core.[9]

The general will of humanity is the core ethical disposition, then, that
animates social and political institutions, rather than a determinative set
of laws that is meant to produce the same or similar social practices and
institutions. As Diderot argues, "all morality consists in the maintenance
of order. Its principles are steady and uniform, but the application of
them varies at times according to the climate and to the local or political
situation of the people" (XIX, 14). As he contends in "Droit Naturel",
humans' desire to be happy, their ability to reason, to communicate, to
transmit their "feelings and thoughts" to each other, and their equal vulnerability in the face of natural calamities and the unjust "hazards" that
humans can inflict upon one another all point to a shared basis: "a general and common interest", by which humans can legitimately seek to
prevent injustices and to protect basic freedoms. It is within the context
of these broader claims that Diderot asserts "the general will never errs",
a sentiment that Rousseau would later appropriate and transform in order
to theorize the general will of a self-governing community based upon
collective sovereignty, rather than a more universal general will of humanity.[10]

Clearly, for such an account of universal morality (which all humans
are said to share simply in light of being human) to be plausible, sociability must be taken as an elemental feature of the human condition. We
have seen already, in Diderot's presentation of Tahitian society in the
Supplément, which was composed at roughly the same time as his contributions for the third edition of the *Histoire*, that the 'naturalness' of
Tahitian life turns out to be, in his view, the result of a relatively complex
set of social norms and institutions that were constructed with specific
ethical and social purposes in mind. In the *Histoire*, Diderot criticizes
what is surely meant to be a description of Rousseau's state of nature:

> From considering the few wants that men have in proportion to the resources
> nature affords them; the little assistance and happiness they find in a civilized
> state, in comparison to the pains and evils they are exposed to in it; their desire of
> independence and liberty in common with all other living beings; together with
> various other reasons deduced from the constitution of human nature; from
> considering all of these circumstances, it has been doubted whether the social
> state was as natural to humanity as it has been generally thought. (XIX, 2)

Along these lines, Diderot continues, some have supposed that humans
were naturally isolated and that the eventual creation of government by

the founders of political authority was partly a response to an artificially created state of war. "Thus it is", he writes, again tacitly implicating Rousseau, "that the first founders of nations are satirized, under the supposition of an ideal and chimerical savage state." (XIX, 2) Diderot challenges what he views as a fantastical understanding of human nature; as he bluntly contends, "[m]en were never isolated in the manner here described. They carried within them a seed of sociability which tended continually to be developed." (XIX, 2) The deep bonds and reciprocal attachments between mothers and children that result from nurturing and mutual care, the many signs of communication and rudimentary forms of language, a variety of "natural events" that can "bring together and unite free and wandering individuals", and the accidental causes that get humans to meet and eventually to seek sustenance together all demonstrate that humans have a "natural tendency to sociability." (XIX, 2) Both settled and nomadic tribes are examples, in his view, of the mutual association that humans form for, at the very least, the purposes of survival. While for rhetorical effect, Diderot occasionally describes "men without society" as a foil to the socially complex, oppressive condition of civilized societies (e.g., XVII, 4), his extensive discussions of New World peoples and other nonsedentary peoples treat them explicitly as social beings with consciously created and maintained norms, customs, and collective practices. In the language that I have been using to summarize such claims, then, Diderot assumes that humans as such are cultural agents.

The social projects that exemplify the general will of humanity vary widely, according to Diderot, and represent a range of responses to the challenge of institutionalizing political rules and practices that foster the norms of respect and reciprocity. Diderot states repeatedly that different political institutions should be expected and may well be legitimate given differences in population, the extent of territory, the impact of a variety of local opinions, and external influences. For these reasons, it is simply not the case, he argues, that only the character of rulers can legitimately account for a plurality of political laws and practices. Perhaps only in the most absolutist and despotic governments, surmises Diderot, does the character of the ruler truly wholly shape the polity. Thus, "[t]he science of government does not contain abstract truths, or rather it does not rest upon one single principle that extends to all branches of public administration." (XIX, 2) The lack of a predetermined, universal theory of political authority and the law makes a detailed knowledge of local circumstances a prerequisite for sound and just governance. "The state is a complicated machine," he asserts, "which cannot be wound up or set into motion without a thorough knowledge of all of its components." (XIX, 2) As we will see, it follows for Diderot that imperial rule over far-flung territories is unlikely to yield just political institutions; foreigners will be unlikely to know the local circumstances better than indigenous peoples themselves. Moreover, no universally valid, privileged political ideology exists that could guide a would-be conqueror. Sound moral knowledge is not the province of one ruler, one nation, or one continent; moreover, it manifests itself differently over time and place in such a way that even the same actions are treated legitimately in distinct ways. "It is everywhere known what is just and unjust," he asserts, "but the same ideas are not universally attached to the same actions." (XIX, 2) In elaborating this claim, Diderot examines the differing rules concerning sexual behaviour and modesty in hot countries versus cold climates, the killing of animals in India, and when the killing of humans is permitted by the Iroquois and Huron. Rather than treating such remarkable instances of ethical diversity as fundamentally inconsistent or irrational, he concludes that "[t]he means that are the most opposite in appearance all tend equally to the same end, the maintenance and prosperity of the body politic." (XIX, 2) None of this implies moral relativism, for the general will of humanity itself is a universal ethical touchstone that embodies cross-cultural norms of mutual respect and individual freedom; rather, Diderot appears to balance a commitment to a plurality of cultural values and institutions with a humanistic concern for the equal dignity of all individuals. At times, his commitments to equality and freedom lead him to engage in cross-cultural judgements that point to the evils of non-European institutions, such as the fixed inequalities and oppression that he detests in the caste system of India, which he discusses at length in Book I (I, 8). Such judgements (which he makes against an array of European practices and institutions as well), for reasons that will be further explored in this chapter, offer no grounding, however, to the view that foreign peoples should be placed under European imperial rule. Diderot's moral philosophy is obviously nonsystematic, and his scattered observations and arguments about ethical thought owe much more in spirit to one of his heroes, Montaigne, than to the systematic and deductive ethical systems of some of his fellow *philosophes*, in particular those of radical materialists such as La Mettrie and Helvétius (whose *De l'homme* [1773] Diderot criticized at length).[11] It is in part due to Diderot's intellectual disposition that he provides no formula or easy recipe to determine how to balance the inevitable tensions between his commitments to moral universalism and pluralism, but the more substantive reason is that such moral and political judgements, in his view, require a complex and highly contextual knowledge of local histories, geographies, social norms, and other factors, and are thus not amenable to straightforwardly applicable, abstract rules.

For Diderot, aspects of the wide range of practices and institutions that constitute human diversity are amenable to strict moral censure by all humans, as they so clearly and egregiously violate the most basic norms of respect and reciprocity. Among them, as we will examine further in this chapter, are those associated with imperialism and slavery, the latter of which Diderot condemns at length in an influential section of the *Histoire*. Yet, in addition to such cross-cultural moral judgements, Diderot believes that a wide array of practices, institutions, and ways of life (pastoralism, hunting and gathering), as well as peoples themselves, are not condemnable in this manner, and in fact are, from a moral viewpoint, *incommensurable*. That is, there are no cross-culturally valid, defensible ways to rank order them definitively or to judge them either as simply superior or inferior. The pluralism that guides Diderot's survey of the relationship between the European and non-European worlds in the *Histoire* arises early, in a passage from Book I for instance, when he praises the multiplicity of religious worship that Hinduism appears to accept.

> Brahma delights in the distinct form of worship observed in different countries. . . . He is the intimate of the Muslim, and the friend of the Indian; the companion of the Christian, and the confidant of the Jew. Those men whom he has endowed with an elevated soul see nothing in the opposition of sects and the diversity of religious worships, but one of the effects of the richness he has displayed in the work of creation. (I, 8)

Accordingly, Diderot often attacks the lack of anything even resembling such pluralism among European imperialists. In a contribution that details the earliest Spanish conquests of the Americas, after having discussed the achievements of the "Tlascalans", an indigenous people of Mexico who had formed a republic before being laid waste by the conquistadors, Diderot concludes that the Spanish viewed even such complex and highly structured societies contemptuously because of the "national prejudices" that coloured their sentiments, judgements, and characters.

> Such were the people whom the Spaniards disdained to acknowledge to be of the same species with themselves. . . . They fancied that these people had no form of government because it was not vested in a single person; no civilization [*policé*] because it differed from that of Madrid; no virtues because they were not of the same religious persuasion; and no understanding because they did not adopt the same opinions. . . . This national pride, carried to an excess of infatuation beyond example, would have inclined them to consider Athens in the same contemptuous light as they did Tlascala. They would have treated the Chinese as brutes, and have everywhere left marks of outrage, oppression, and devastation. (VI, 9)

As Diderot's many contributions to the *Histoire* make abundantly clear, this is a judgement he makes not only with regard to the imperial officers of the Castilian crown, but against the dogmatism that informed every European nation engaged in conquest.

Part of the problem with such self-centred prejudices, in Diderot's view, is that they are so often based upon a willful ignorance of non-European societies. As he notes above, even other technologically complex and highly stratified societies like China—that, on the surface at least, resemble European countries—have been judged by Europeans to be patently inferior and backward. In a long section on China in the early editions of the *Histoire*, the unattributed contributor defends Chinese mores, social practices, and political institutions as part of a broader celebration of Chinese civilization. For the 1780 edition, Raynal inserted a following section, written by Diderot, that aimed to summarize the critical arguments made against Chinese civilization by European travellers and philosophers. Part of the point of this section was to present a broader range of views that readers could peruse in order to make a better informed set of judgements about the nature of Chinese society. But even these two sections put together would not be sufficient for the purposes of truly coming to terms with China. As Diderot writes,

> The several arguments of the partisans and of the calumniators of China are now submitted to the judgement of our readers, to whom it is left to decide: for why should we be so presumptuous as to attempt to direct their judgement? If we might be allowed to hazard an opinion, we should say that although these two systems are supported by respectable testimonies, nevertheless these authorities do not bear the marks of a great character that would inspire faith. Perhaps, in order to decide this matter, we must wait until some impartial and judicious men, who are well versed in Chinese writing and language, are permitted to make a long residence at the Peking court, to go through all the provinces, to live in the country villages, and to converse freely with the Chinese of all ranks. (I, 21)

Given Europeans' limited sources of knowledge about China, and that such sources were often based upon information from bureaucrats and administrators in Peking, Diderot concludes that at most one could make only very tentative and provisional judgements about the nature of Chinese society. Such a critical and modest intellectual temperament, of course, was precisely the antithesis of the hubristic mind-set that Diderot believed was at work among the most powerful Europeans who dictated the terms of contact with the non-European world—from members of royal councils and directors of the Indies companies to the authorities of the church and its religious orders.

Diderot's attempts at crafting relatively balanced accounts of non-European peoples, however, fostered other problems. He was especially concerned to counter the view—which he thought might be implied by his many sympathetic comments on hunting and gathering, and on pastoral and other nomadic, less structurally complex societies—that the 'savage' way of life was superior to the 'civilized' condition. In response to this anticipated reaction to his writings, he contends not that we are unable to judge aspects of foreign societies, but rather that there are such a wide array of features in any one society that it cannot be judged as a whole to be definitively better or worse than any other.

> It is not, however, that I prefer a savage to a civilized state. This is a protest I have made more than once. But the more I reflect upon this point, the more it seems to me that, from the rudest to the most civilized state of nature, everything is nearly compensated, virtues and vices, natural good and evil. In the forest, as well as in [civilized, sedentary] society, the happiness of one individual may be less or greater than that of another: but I imagine that nature has set certain bounds to the felicity of every considerable portion of the human species, beyond which we have nearly as much to lose as to gain. (VI, 23)

To assert that peoples themselves could be rank-ordered or that collective ways of life that structure whole societies, such as pastoralism or hunting and gathering, are fundamentally inferior or superior overlooks the fact that peoples are inherently too diverse and complex to judge in such a manner. Specific individuals could be happy or unhappy in a particular society, and, as Diderot's analyses of many European and non-European societies evince, particular institutions and practices in any society could be ineffective in promoting social goals or might reasonably be judged as manifestly unjust. However, whole peoples and the fundamental social choice of how to seek subsistence, in his view, cannot be treated as morally commensurable. As Diderot implies earlier, it makes no sense to assert baldly that pastoral societies are fundamentally inferior to agriculturalist societies or vice versa. Indeed, it would be absurd, he implies, to make such judgements about nomadic versus agriculturally based sedentary societies given that their development derives not from a supposedly objective rationality or reflection upon the abstract choice of how to organize a society, but rather upon the contingencies of the local environment. One "becomes either a shepherd or an agriculturalist, according to the fertility or barrenness of the soil he inhabits" and, for either collective way of life, a great deal of art and creativity will be involved in fashioning and maintaining such an existence, given that "humans are endowed with a power of accommodating" themselves "to the various modes of life that prevail in every climate" (I, 8).

Since Diderot militates so often against European political and religious institutions and other pernicious sites of social power and while he also comments at times upon the harshness of a nomadic lifestyle, he considers (most likely in order to respond to Rousseau's argument about the life "best for man") whether a middle ground between what was so often described as the 'primitive' and 'civilized' worlds would be the best possible condition for humans. As we have seen, Diderot himself occasionally engages in a wistful reverie about the life between the excesses of a corrupt and unjust civilized existence and the rustic travails of the most rudimentary societies that might have been created in the New World had Europeans not arrived with the intention of destroying indigenous societies and replicating their own, highly imperfect, institutions abroad. Diderot often characterizes history as an ultimately cyclical set of events and revolutions, and thus he notes frequently in the *Histoire* and elsewhere that the seemingly most stable and highly refined societies at some point collapse and disintegrate (the fall of the Roman empire was one of his favourite examples), just as simpler societies are by no means destined to stay the same, but rather are sure to develop more complex and hierarchically structured social and political practices over time.[12] In the final analysis, while he appears to be attracted to it, he ultimately expresses scepticism about the idea that a medium between these ways of life should be a goal toward which all humans should work.

> In all future ages, savages will advance by slow degrees toward the civilized state, and civilized nations will return toward their primitive state; from which the philosopher will conclude that there exists, in the interval between these two states, a certain medium in which the happiness of the human species is placed. But who can discover this medium, and even if it were found, what authority would be capable of directing the steps of man toward it, and to fix them there? (IX, 5)

This happy medium between the two—perhaps fleetingly captured on occasion as part of the cyclical process of history that Diderot theorizes— cannot be identified with any precision; nor could it be used as a model for a stable society. It remains in his political thought ultimately as a pessimistic reminder that almost all existing societies are highly imperfect and that any gains made by them are fragile, an assumption that, as we will see later in this chapter, undercuts much of the imperial ideology that aims to 'civilize' non-Europeans.

The discussions of ancient trading routes and imperial ties throughout the *Histoire* underscore the extent to which Diderot understood the crossing of borders and the interactions of peoples with distinct histories, *moeurs*, and political institutions to be continuing phenomena, rather than developments that were distinctive to the modern age; even so, the fact that such connections became global from the sixteenth century onward, and the sheer scale of travel in the modern imperial age, appeared to Diderot to create unique conditions abroad for voyagers.[13] Along these lines, he defines "hospitality" as "the offspring of natural commiseration" and argues that it was practised universally in the ancient world; the arduous and less frequent travels in ancient times depended crucially upon the hospitality of those in foreign lands. "It was," he writes, "almost the only thing that attached nations to each other. It was the source of the longest lasting and the most respected friendship, contracted between families who were separated by immense regions." (IX, 5) With increased contact among peoples, such "instances of humanity" have decreased. For Diderot, it is not simply technological developments, such as the compass and improved navigation, but the development of "social institutions", modern "commerce", and "the invention of signs to represent wealth" that led travellers to create their habitation abroad on their own terms, rather than relying upon the hospitality of indigenous hosts. He argues that the interactions among diverse peoples in the modern world are brought about by explorers, traders, missionaries, and other travellers, who are often "industrious, rapacious" men and who form

> settlements in all parts, where the traveller takes his place and commands and where he disposes of all the conveniences of life as if he were at home. The master, or the landlord, of the house, is neither his benefactor, his brother, nor his friend; he is simply his upper servant. The gold that he spends at his house entitles him to treat his host as he chooses; he cares about his host's money, not his respect. (IX, 5)

The position of humility adopted by many ancient travellers has given way, in his view, to those who arrive in foreign lands animated principally by the spirit of conquest. The newly institutionalized forms of cross-national commerce, such as the chartering of trading companies that act as quasi-sovereign entities abroad, are among the eighteenth-century travels that Diderot has in mind. The ancient ethic of hospitality, "that sacred virtue", he suggests, has become obsolete with the advent of more modern, and more aggressive, forms of travel, trade, and exchange.[14]

Diderot's anti-imperialist arguments sometimes focus at length on precisely these violent, unchecked passions that are unleashed among crusading voyagers given the peculiar social conditions in which they find themselves, and that lead, in his view, to the modern erasure of ancient norms of hospitality. Under global empires, the weakening of hospitality arises not only from the technological means of European colonists and merchants to create their own habitations abroad, but also from their lack of a set of humanizing characteristics that Diderot views as essential for basic human decency and that he sees at the heart of social life, both European and non-European. Hence, in his efforts to criticize European imperialism, he attempts to craft a moral and political psychology of the imperial mind-set, one key feature of which details the disorientation that occurs when those who cross borders are unmoored from the ethical frameworks—from the general will of humanity—that normally would have grounded their perspectives.

For Diderot, understanding modern, global empires requires an analysis of the character of individuals who regularly cross borders and "are fond of going from one country to another" (V, 9). To be sure, sheer coercion and prejudice—as Diderot notes, a whole panoply of intolerable social and political conditions, from oppressive governments and lack of religious toleration to cruel systems of punishment—could drive people from their lands (V, 19). For those who, in some sense, voluntarily go halfway around the world, it is more difficult, in Diderot's view, to discern the motivating factors behind such decisions. Given his view that people are inclined to be attached to their homelands or at least to more familiar lands because of a fondness for such societies, the ties of blood and friendship, acquaintance with the local climate and languages, and the variety of customary associations that we associate with places in which we have lived and worked, he suspects that very powerful inducements must exist to get people to leave their societies (V, 9).[15] In part, he asserts that states and the proxies of states, such as the Indies companies, play a central role in stirring up interest in global commerce through their efforts to recruit voyagers; as a result, "[i]t is imagined that fortune is more easily acquired in distant regions than near our own home." (V, 19) In addition to the political forces behind this phenomenon, he acknowledges that enterprising individuals exist in every age because of a natural energy and curiosity, and that not only the thirst for gold, but also the thirst for knowledge may impel some to travel (V, 19). Overall, then, Diderot concludes that "tyranny, guilt, ambition, curiosity, a kind of restless spirit, the desire of acquiring knowledge, and of seeing things, [and] tedium" have driven, and will continue to drive, a certain number of humans to the farthest reaches of the earth (IX, 5).

Whatever the reasons for their voyages, imperial voyagers and commercial travellers (who often, in Diderot's view, lay the groundwork for imperial exploits) are potentially dangerous, for they suddenly find themselves outside the network of reciprocal relationships and expectations that had once given them the cultural contexts for their actions, beliefs, and values—for their *moeurs*. For Diderot, while such contexts obviously vary according to time and place, these differentiating national characters are the particular spheres within which more humanitarian, universal moral ideas develop, those that enable connections across the various lines of difference that appear to divide humanity. The general will of humanity itself, then, weakens sufficiently such that the most egregious behaviour characterizes European conduct abroad; it is most likely for this reason that Diderot employs the image of unleashed tigers that were once domesticated by their social contexts and thus animated at least

partly by the bonds of reciprocity, but now run rampant in the subjugated lands of the non-European world. As we have seen in his discussion
of the changing norms of hospitality, crossing borders need not always
produce such destructive and violent results. Indeed, Diderot theorizes
that the ideal relations in the modern world among European and non-
European peoples would not have to be restricted simply to trade, but
could in theory also involve some forms of settlement in already settled
lands. Such settlement, however, would not involve colonization; rather,
Europeans should settle in settled areas of the non-European world only
with the permission of the host society and in the spirit of ancient hospitality that has been so often abrogated by modern travellers. In a discussion of how the French should conduct themselves if they ever get to
reestablish regular contact with India, Diderot writes that all such settlers
should become "naturalized" into their host country (IV, 33). A wise
people, he ultimately recommends, will never encroach upon the liberty
or property of the host country or destroy their places of worship, but
will conform to their customs and laws. Diderot was under no illusions,
however, about the likelihood of such travel, and indeed many of his
contributions to the *Histoire* document in vivid detail how far from this
ideal Europeans have in fact conducted themselves abroad.

On the Cruelties Unleashed by Empire
in the Non-European World

One of the primary methods that Diderot uses to argue against European
imperialism is to detail what he considered to be the catastrophic effects
of empire upon non-European peoples, and to attempt to offer explanations as to why Europeans engage routinely in such barbaric actions in
the non-European world. In a typical passage, he summarizes the devastation of European imperial incursions abroad as the work of an evil
genius.

> Settlements have been formed and subverted; ruins have been heaped on ruins;
> countries that were well peopled have become deserted; ports that were full of
> buildings have been abandoned; vast tracts that had been ill cemented with
> blood have separated, and have brought to view the bones of murderers and
> tyrants confounded with each other. It seems as if from one region to another
> prosperity has been pursued by an evil genius that speaks our [European] sev-
> eral languages, and which diffuses the same disasters in all parts.[16] (IV, 33)

The nineteen books of the *Histoire* describe and judge European contacts
with the non-European world by dividing this history according to the
activities of each imperial power. In the opening book, Diderot considers

at length the British experience in India. He denounces the devastation brought upon India by conquest and trade, and notes that this is particularly tragic given what he deems from a previous analysis to be the natural plenitude and gentle mores of the region. "The rage of conquest, and what is no less destructive an evil, the greediness of traders," writes Diderot, "have, in their turns, ravaged and oppressed the finest country on the face of the globe." (I, 8) From a consideration of the indigenous politics of India as the British began to make contact with Indian rulers, he concludes that internally weak, and thus especially vulnerable, countries eventually fall prey to conquerors, but that this produces an even worse barbarism. The clashing customs, manners, religions, and languages of conquering and conquered peoples, which have not coexisted over a long period of time, produce a kind of chaos whose effects several centuries cannot dispel (I, 8).

In a chapter entitled "Oppressions and cruelties exercised by the English in Bengal", Diderot focuses upon the 1769–70 Bengal famine and attempts to determine whether the English can be held morally accountable for it. After a grim description of the amount of misery and death that the famine brought about, Diderot blames the English for ignoring the desperate needs of starving Bengalis after a drought led to poor harvests. Although noting that it is difficult to determine the merits of the charge that the monopoly of the British East India Company is to blame, "no one", he contends,

> will undertake to defend them [the English] against the reproach of negligence and insensibility. And in what crisis have they merited that reproach? In the very instant of time when the life or death of several million of their fellow creatures was in their power. (III, 38)

While on the surface this appears to be a purely natural disaster, Diderot argues that it was the failure of the British to respond effectively to the miseries of Indians during the drought that yielded the famine. Mere misfortune, then, was greatly compounded by what amounts to a form of passive injustice, the failure to intervene or to act when one has the power to stop or to prevent further disaster.[17] As Diderot concludes, "it is not to be doubted that, if instead of having solely a regard for themselves, and remaining entirely in negligence of everything else, they had initially taken every precaution in their power, then they might have accomplished the preservation of many lives that were lost." (III, 38) While there was no revolt against the British, Diderot argues that the affected Indians would have been justified in doing so and could have made a powerful plea about their oppression under the English. Hence, he provides a speech in the guise of a downtrodden Indian (one of Diderot's many sympathetic rhetorical attempts to give voice to oppressed imperial subjects) in which the English are described as onerous masters who seek only to enrich themselves and who at times seem to deny even that Indians are "human creatures". As Diderot's Indian exhorts,

> Deprived of all authority, stripped of our property, weighed down by the terrible hand of power, we can only lift our hands to you to implore your assistance. You have heard our groans; you have seen famine making very quick advances upon us; and then you attended to your own preservation. You hoarded up the small quantity of provisions that escaped the pestilence; you filled your granaries with them, and distributed them among your soldiers. (III, 38)

All this compares unfavourably to what likely would have been the actions of the Mughal sovereigns. Indians' former rulers, he suggests, were more humane and less grasping; they would have sought assistance from neighbouring realms and opened up their own coffers in the thought that by preserving their subjects they were enriching themselves. In contrast, the English weigh down Indians with tyranny and indifference, offering nothing to help Indians' preservation while taxing them, managing their commerce, exporting their merchandise, and reaping benefits from their industry and soil, which pours resources into English factories and her other colonies. "All these things you regulate, and you carry on solely for your own advantage. But what have you done for our preservation? What steps have you taken to remove from us the scourge that threatened us?" (III, 38) On the supposition that "every sentiment of humanity was extinguished in their [English] hearts", as a result of the corrupting influences of absolute, imperial rule upon the English themselves, Diderot suggests that wrenching descriptions of the humanitarian catastrophes created or deepened by the English are unlikely to have any effect upon them. Only the comparison he made with India's former rulers, he contends, could possibly sway the English, since it appeals to England's reputation and national standing.

For celebrants of the English government and its relative moderation at home, the daily abuses by it (and by its trading company proxy) and "the entire loss of all principle", he notes, are especially curious and disturbing. Diderot suggests that even countries that have achieved a less despotic form of rule at home are virtually guaranteed to act despotically abroad when they amass far-flung imperial realms. The English might have arrived in India as traders, he writes, but they are now absolute rulers, and so it is nearly impossible for them not to do wrong. He argues along these lines that the great distance of India from their country, the different climate and its effects both upon ruler and ruled, and the accompanying unlikelihood of viewing Indians as fellow subjects, are among the causes of English oppression abroad. Whatever the sanctity and moderation of English jurisprudence at home, one could not rea-

sonably expect the British East India Company to restrain itself according
to even some semblance of the rule of law, for, as he argues, the whole
purpose of the company's activities in India was profit. Ultimately, the
English government gave the company "the destiny of 12 million people" in order to increase Great Britain's revenue by "9 million livres per
annum" (III, 38).

In his reflections upon the earliest phases of the Spanish empire, Diderot acknowledges that there is a certain grandeur to imperial exploits,
though, in his view, they are outweighed by the sheer moral blindness of
such enterprises. Hernán Cortés surely possessed great qualities that
stand as shining examples of his distinctive character; yet, the entire enterprise in which he and his countrymen were collectively engaged was at
bottom corrupt, and so his faults, in some sense, are those of his people.
As Diderot concludes, "[t]his Spaniard was despotic and cruel, and his
successes are tarnished by the injustice of his projects. He was an assassin
covered with innocent blood; but his vices were of the times, and of his
nation, and his virtues were his own" (VI, 12). Cortés's impressive personal qualities and skills were put to use, in Diderot's view, in a fundamentally unjust and necessarily violent cause. Founders are, in a sense,
imperious figures, but he argues that one should distinguish imperial
founders, who aim to subjugate and rule a foreign people with whom
there are no or few preexisting bonds, with the "peaceable founder",
who is thoroughly acquainted with a country, its geography, temperament, and genuine needs, and accordingly takes the time to foster the
institutions and practices necessary to develop a stable, lasting, and just
society (VI, 12). Thus, while what so many have viewed as the greatness
of empire understandably inspires some admiration—arising, Diderot
writes, from the sheer atrociousness of such a project—the accompanying horrors also lead one to "freeze with horror." (VI, 24) Thus, in light
of his repeated expressions of astonishment and wonder at the extraordinary military and political successes of the conquistadors, Diderot notes
explicitly that his goal in writing the history of such exploits is bound
up with a moral duty to highlight the evils perpetrated by his fellow
Europeans.

> It has not been my intention to be the celebrant of the conquerors of the other
> hemisphere. I have not allowed my judgement to be so far misled by the bril-
> liance of their successes as to be blind to their crimes and acts of injustice. My
> aim is to write history, and I almost always write it bathed in tears. (VII, 1)

Given his objective, not only to describe the relations between the European and the non-European world, but to make clear the injustices that
have so often marked these relations, he warns his readers at the outset of
Book VII to be prepared for a litany of further atrocities, some of them

to be committed yet again by the Spanish, but many more by the hands of the other European imperial powers.

> We are here going to display scenes that are still more terrible than those that have so often made us shudder. They will be uninterruptedly repeated in those immense regions that remain for us [in the *Histoire*] to go over. The sword will never be blunted, and we will not see it stop until it meets with no more victims to strike. (VII, 1)

By the end, once the spectacle of European empire has run its course, there will be no people left to oppress. The globe itself, he implies, places a geographical limit to the wandering madness begun by the Spanish.

One of the great ironies, in Diderot's view, of modern European imperialism is that the conquests and injustices that once afflicted so many European societies as a result of the barbarian invasions have simply been repeated on a wider scale by those who were once subjugated peoples. "The Spaniards," whom he notes were "the descendents or slaves of the Visigoths, like them, divided among themselves the deserted lands and the men who had escaped their swords. Most of these wretched victims did not survive for long, doomed to a state of slavery worse than death." (VIII, 32) In part, Diderot refers here to the slavery of the soul, to the devastation of indigenous peoples' spirit to govern themselves effectively. Those Peruvians, he notes, who have managed to escape death or the brutal tyranny of the conquerors, have "fallen into the most degraded and brutal state" (VII, 27). Their religion, which once elevated their spirits, and the other institutions that formed the context for their thoughts and actions, have been decimated. What results, suggests Diderot, is the "listless and universal indifference" to which "it is in the power of tyranny to plunge humans." (VII, 27) In light of this, dispensing liquor to such nations, usually for ill purposes to begin with, he notes, has done as much harm to them as the use of arms; we must rank this "among the number of calamities with which we have loaded the other hemisphere." (VIII, 6) It is precisely because of the destruction of Amerindian nations in Peru and elsewhere, and the resulting condition of the "few men who remained there", that Spanish imperialists turned toward another continent, in order to keep their fields and mines in operation. "[B]ut this mode of substitution," writes Diderot, "which was dictated by the refinement of European barbarity, was more prejudicial to Africa than useful to the country of the Incas." (XII, 27) For Diderot, all this suggests that the state itself is a monopoly of brute power that tends to be exercised over ever more spheres of life. Empire only strengthens this power and further creates such opportunities; it should come as no surprise, then, that it would want monopolistic power even over the trade of human beings themselves. "The government, ever intent on laying taxes upon vices and virtues, upon industry and idleness, upon good and bad projects, upon the liberty of exercising oppression, and the permission of being exempted from them, made a monopoly of this base traffic." (XII, 27)

The causes of the ferocity of the Spanish conquest and the reasons why Spain did not simply engage in a mutually dependent trade with an independent Mexico and Peru—ignoring, in this respect, "the true principles of commerce"—are manifold, according to Diderot, and they have much to do with the curious nature of the imperial enterprise itself (VIII, 32). The ease of their early victories over various Amerindian peoples, the natural pride of conquerors, and in general their thirst for riches and the spirit of religious fanaticism, set them on their path toward further imperial activities. He also notes that fear and panic, in addition to the difficulty of stopping the carnage once it began, enabled the brutality brought about by conquest. Furthermore, the increasing power of Spain within Europe that its initial successes yielded provided a further impetus for extending their empire. Finally, Diderot considers the possibility that "the sentiments of humanity grow weaker the more distant we are from our native country", especially when humans become ferocious as a result of being disconnected to any of the social, legal, and political contexts that might otherwise have moderated their behaviour. In light of this, the Spanish failed to recognize in Amerindians the cultural agency that defines humanity itself, "the image of an organization similar to their own (a similarity which is the foundation of all moral duties)", which he calls elsewhere, as we have seen, the general will of humanity (VIII, 32). Diderot counsels against immediately granting liberty to the Spanish colonies, on the ground that a hasty departure would leave newly independent countries barely able to function, given the extent of the Spanish destruction of indigenous societies. While liberation is a moral necessity, Spain has a responsibility, he argues, to renew its lands and peoples—not as an act of civilization, it should be noted, but to avoid the further oppression that would result if the Spanish simply left the Americas in its destroyed condition—after which somewhat regenerated societies could then be run by truly free people. Posterity itself, he intones, in an invocation to Spanish monarchs, will not forgive them until they make productive the lands that they destroyed and return happiness and freedom to indigenous inhabitants. Only after such an effort of careful decolonization, he implies, will a revival of indigenous rule be meaningful (VIII, 35).

Given the development of African slavery to repopulate the Americas, Diderot worries that Africa might become "the scene of our cruelties, as Asia and America have been, and still are". (XI, 9) Rather than learn any lessons from the horrors of the earliest conquests of the Americas, the

imperial powers seem determined, he notes, to repeat their calamitous
practices among the peoples of Africa. Yet again, Diderot believes, the
dehumanization of ever more non-Europeans creates ripe conditions for
the most barbaric cruelties.

> Savage Europeans! You doubted at first whether the inhabitants of the regions
> you had just discovered were not animals which you might slay without re-
> morse because they were black, and you were white. . . . In order to repeople
> one part of the globe that you have laid waste, you corrupt and depopulate
> another. (VIII, 22)

At first, he notes, Europeans viewed their slaves in the Americas and in
Africa as virtually animals, but then over time they could occasionally
accept them as potential fellow Christians, a fact that only "redoubles"
the horror of slavery since, having acknowledged them as human, they
continued to practise slaveholding.

Another form of self-serving blindness, in Diderot's view, which afflicts
Europeans and leads to enormous suffering in the non-European world,
concerns property. Diderot argues that Europeans fail to recognize that
the right to property is universal. In a discussion about the origin of
property, he argues that in the first ages of the world, all humans had a
common right to everything upon the earth. Unfortunately, he notes, this
is the understanding of property that Europeans have used in their dealings with Amerindians. This is the only standard of "public right" with
regard to property that they appeal to during their imperial endeavours,
though in this case entirely erroneously. Such a standard, he contends,
can only be applied legitimately "to the primitive state of nature, which
the European nations considered America to be when it was first discovered." (XIII, 13) Thus, the injustices committed against Amerindians began with the mistaken notion that America constituted an open region,
free of legitimate property claims. The protection that property should
enjoy, Diderot contends, is no less valid when one enters a distant territory than it is in one's own land.

> Isn't the nature of property the same everywhere; isn't it everywhere founded
> upon possession acquired by labour, and upon a long and peaceable enjoy-
> ment? Europeans, can you then inform us at what distance from your residence
> the sacred title becomes abolished? Is it at the distance of a few steps, of one
> league, or of ten leagues? You will answer in the negative, in which case it
> cannot possibly be even at the distance of ten thousand leagues. Do you not
> perceive that while you arrogate to yourselves this imaginary right over a dis-
> tant people, you confer it at the same time to those distant people over your-
> selves? . . . You hold the system of Hobbes in abhorrence among your neigh-
> bouring countries, and yet you practise at a distance this fatal system, which

makes strength the supreme law. After having been thieves and assassins, nothing remains to complete your character, but that you should become, as you really are, a set of execrable sophists. (XIII, 13)

The only form of political rhetoric, or sophistry, in Diderot's view, that European imperialists hold on to consists then of corrupted principles and half-baked theories that are intended merely to provide an excuse for the instigation and perpetuation of mass injustices, such as the expropriation of Amerindians' lands. No genuine understanding of property rights, he asserts, could legitimize such seizures of goods and lands, any more than Amerindians could legitimately claim Spain on behalf of their kings.

At times Diderot steps back from such analyses of specific injustices, such as slavery or violations of property rights, or of particular episodes in the history of European empires, in order to assess the more general pathologies of conquest. He regrets that

> [h]istory entertains us with nothing but the accounts of conquerors who have worked to extend their dominions at the expense of the lives and the happiness of their subjects, but it does not set before our eyes the example of [even] one sovereign who had thought of restraining their limits. (XIII, 1)

The peculiarity of this, in his view, is that a thorough examination of the effects of empire reveal that it is fatal to the construction of a healthy, long-lasting polity. Is it at all proper, he thus asks, to found settlements at so much expense and with so much labour in other hemispheres? A "vast empire" and an immense population, he suggests, are "great evils" (XIII, 1). They both offer the surface impression of greatness, but they cause far more problems than are usually acknowledged. Very small states over time tend to increase in size without violent conquest, Diderot suggests, adding that very large states necessarily break down into smaller units. The efficient and just rule of a body politic depends crucially, he implies, upon a territory and population that are self-sustaining and that can be effectively governed. There are, in this sense, natural limits to a healthy political society, which the creation of empires violates with pernicious results. Accordingly, he asks, "Is not this extension of empire contrary to nature? And must not everything that is contrary to nature have an end?" (XIII, 1) While the increase of European governments' power through conquest might be destined to end, Diderot fears that it may be the fate of states nevertheless to attempt vainly to govern vast realms. At such a great distance, he argues, the effects of laws of the 'mother country' upon imperial subjects can hardly be great, and their obedience will likely be weak. Over time, he predicts, they will cease to be interested in the affairs of the metropole. Moreover, drawing implicitly upon his understanding of the general will of humanity, he argues that the absence of "witnesses and judges of our actions necessarily induce[s] corruption in our manners"; outside of the domestic context of social practices and institutions, then, colonists subvert the very ideas of virtue and justice, even as they are called upon to establish such foundations in order to build colonial societies abroad. Hence, the directors sent to govern colonies, he charges, are tyrants. The administrators and other officials who run the imperial enterprise lack the "spirit of patriotism", roaming as they do from one possession to the next (XIII, 1). By "patriotism", Diderot implies that they lack any attachment to a community of persons and to the rule of law that binds a community, rather than to a dogmatic attachment to a particular country and a corresponding hatred of foreigners. In this sense, then, his use of the general will of humanity and the language of patriotism mutually reinforce one another, for Diderot attacks a kind of profiteering, destructive cosmopolitanism while also viewing a wide array of cultural differences across societies to be the manifestation of a shared, cosmopolitan commitment to the norms of respect and reciprocity.

Diderot expresses astonishment throughout the *Histoire* about the sheer level of cruelty involved in the imperial enterprise. As he moves from the activities of the Spanish and Portuguese in the non-European world, and the widely discussed 'black death' that many of his contemporaries attached to Spanish rule abroad (but withheld from their own governments), Diderot turns his attention to the English, French, Dutch, and Danes. Will they be "less savage" in their activities in the non-European world than the Spanish and Portuguese who have been so roundly condemned by the Europeans of his day? "Is it possible", he asks,

> that civilized men, who have all lived in their country under forms of government, if not wise, at least ancient, who have all been bred in places where they were instructed with the lessons, and sometimes with the example, of virtue, who were all brought up in the midst of polished cities, in which a rigid exercise of justice must have accustomed them to respect their fellow-creatures; is it possible that all such men, without exception, should pursue a line of conduct equally contrary to the principles of humanity, to their interest, to their safety, and to the first dawnings of reason; and that they should continue to become more barbarous than the savage? (X, 1)

The rest of the *Histoire*, of course, is meant to show precisely that the other European states who sought to become imperial powers proceeded in the same destructive, inhumane manner. As Diderot notes, the countries from which imperialists come are by no means the model of wise government and virtue. Yet, one would expect some semblance, he believes, of moderation to have been inculcated in countries that at least on occasion practised the rule of law. That this was obviously not the case led Diderot to determine how such seemingly 'civilized' persons could unleash such furious horrors abroad.

> This change of character in the European who leaves his country is a phenome-
> non of so extraordinary a nature, the imagination is so deeply affected by it,
> that while it attends to it with astonishment, reflection tortures itself in endeav-
> ouring to find out the principle of it, whether it exists in human nature in
> general, or in the peculiar character of the navigators, or in the circumstances
> preceding or posterior to the event. (X, 1)

Diderot then answers at length that all three of these reasons appear to be behind the inhumanity of Europeans' actions in the non-European world. Humans who are free from "the restraint of laws", he argues, tend to be more "wicked". When they are "far from the effects of public re-sentment . . . no longer awed by the presence of their fellow citizens, or restrained by shame and fear", a "spirit of depredation follows" that manifests itself with horrible violence (X, 1). This, he implies, results from the aggression and violence at the heart of human behaviour that is normally conditioned by domestic forms of habituation and restraint. In addition, those who travel tend to be dissatisfied with their lot in life, or they are sufficiently ambitious "to entertain a contempt for life, and to expose themselves to infinite dangers" in the hope of gaining power and riches. The expense of travel, the sufferings involved, and the need to justify such costly voyages all contributed to the rapacious and greedy attitude of voyagers. Hence, the specific character of voyagers themselves led in part to nearly ceaseless violence abroad. For them, the "New World" was thus "a rich prey to be devoured" (X, 1). Finally, in the ruling circles of Europe, divisions and competition among royal houses exacerbated, in Diderot's opinion, the cruel ambitions of imperialists abroad.

Moreover, there was little oversight of imperial administrators and travellers by governing officials in the metropole, who were often indif-ferent to what took place overseas (X, 1). In general, Diderot argues, the very idea of building empires is bound to be inconsistent with construct-ing and maintaining peaceful, just societies.

> Is it possible even in our days to rule nations that are separated by immense
> seas from the mother country in the same manner as subjects who are situated
> immediately under the eye of the sovereign? Since distant posts are never solic-
> ited and filled, unless by indigent, rapacious men, without talents or morals,
> strangers to all sentiment of honour, and to every idea of equity, the refuse of
> the higher ranks of the state, must we not consider the future splendour of the
> colonies as a chimerical notion; and will not the future happiness of these re-

gions be a phenomenon even more astonishing than their first devastation? (X, 1)

Given the litany of bloodthirsty, greedy, and shortsighted European actions abroad that Diderot so often presents in the *Histoire*, he notes his frustration at the unwillingness of those with any power in the capitals of Europe to heed his warnings and to decolonize, even though it would ultimately be not only in the interests of humanity, but also in their own best interests. Given that the lot of both Europeans and non-Europeans is never truly improved by any of the imperial activities overseas, then breaking the chains that tie Europe to such colonies, in his view, is imperative. Such advice, he realized, would continue to be ignored by those who had much to profit in the short term from imperial aggression abroad. "I am much afraid that my voice has only exclaimed, and will only exclaim, in the desert." (X, 1)

Trading Companies and Conquest: On Commerce and Imperial Rule

For Diderot, the phenomenon of modern imperialism was increasingly a commercial affair. While it was clear that religious conversion, European geopolitics, and notions of improving or civilizing other peoples, among others, all continued to play significant roles in the imperial enterprise, Diderot understood that the growing importance of the European trading companies and of the profit-oriented, commercial side of empire demanded an analysis of the role of commerce in the global affairs of his day.[18] Hence, in a discussion of the importance of global commerce in English society, Diderot jokes that

[t]he passion for trade exerts such influence over you [the English] that even your philosophers are governed by it. The celebrated Mr. Boyle used to say that it would be a commendable action to preach Christianity to the savages because, were they to know only as much of it to convince them of their obligation to wear clothes, it would prove of great service to English manufacturers. (X, 13)

While the eighteenth century is often interpreted as an age that celebrated commerce as a way of inducing peace and industry among otherwise aggressive and warlike European states,[19] Diderot's view of commerce was ambivalent. On the one hand, it could indeed bring about relations among distant peoples and promote social ties and productive industry (I, intro.; XII, 24). On the other hand, it was the impetus behind so many of the cruel and destructive practices of the imperial powers, who either misunderstood or chose to ignore the true benefits that a well-arranged global commerce could ideally promote. The whole range of Diderot's positive commentary upon commerce in the *Histoire* makes clear that the beneficial aspects of commerce usually refer to *commerce* understood broadly as communication, interaction, and exchange (not only of goods, but also of ideas). The English and French word *commerce* can mask the ways in which this concept refers both to communication or interaction and to economic barter, trade, and industry. In ancient and medieval writings, the Latin *commercium* was similarly multi-faceted.[20] The idea that 'the Enlightenment' as such ultimately provided the justifications for modern market-oriented commerce masks the rich ambiguity of the concept of commerce that many of the most prominent eighteenth-century thinkers self-consciously exploited as they sought to analyze the emergence of global commerce in its multiple forms. Diderot's ambivalent understanding of commerce in the *Histoire* shapes his discussion of the relationship between travel, trade, profit, and empire, thereby providing another plank for his criticism of empire. His anti-imperialist arguments along these lines focus on the violent, unchecked passions unleashed among commercial voyagers and other imperialists due to their "thirst for gold" (IX, 1).

In a discussion about English traders in India, Diderot argues that the thirst for gold did not take hold at first, as the English usually formed small trading settlements with the consent of local Indian governments. The English numbers were small, and in this period, it seems, they often respected the ancient norms of hospitality. Diderot even goes on to state that the earliest expeditions to the East Indies were "nothing more than the enterprises of humane and fair traders" (III, 2). The escalation toward the blood-soaked frenzy of tigers returning to the forest began very shortly thereafter, and it was instigated, in his view, largely by the competition among European powers in the East Indies. The competition that was sometimes said in eighteenth-century writings to yield "frugality, economy, moderation, work, wisdom, tranquillity, order, and rule" brought instead a fierce desire to build exclusive commercial ties to the non-European world.[21] "They thought that it was difficult to acquire great riches without great injustice, and that, in order to surpass or even equal the nations they had censured, they must pursue the same conduct. This was an error which led them into false measures." (III, 2) Such ambitions released the English from the ties of social norms and instead yielded the imperial mind-set previously described, not only with its rank injustices but also, as Diderot likes to point out, with a precarious hold upon the gains achieved by such violence, fraud, and deceit. While prosperity might come faster with injustice, he notes, the authority and the possessions that follow from it are fragile precisely because of the means used to acquire them. Thus, both out of a concern for indigenous nations and for European nations' own welfare, Diderot asserts that he "can never be convinced that it is a matter of indifference whether we make our appearance before foreign nations in the character of infernal spirits, or in that of celestial beings." (III, 2) Empire had become an increasingly commercial affair—ultimately, "the passion for trade" was the instigating factor behind an increasing number of imperial ventures, and commerce was the "sole object" of the many wars and violent conflicts among imperial powers (X, 13).

The false confidence in a nation's powers that global commerce encourages, in Diderot's view, induces political instability and violence, as European states become increasingly hostile and arrogant toward one another. The idiotic rivalry among European nations, as he describes it, each of which appears to think that its prosperity somehow requires the poverty and weakness of all the others, is sadly not lessened by the painful experience of continual wars and animosities. Far from fostering the co-operative bonds of mutual commerce and practising *le doux commerce*, European nations at most pay lip service to the ideals of peace, while acting in direct contradiction to them. "[W]e hear on every side," he writes,

> nations, especially commercial ones, crying out for peace, while they still continue to conduct themselves toward one another in a way that excludes them from ever obtaining that blessing. They will all aspire to happiness, and each of them would enjoy it alone. They will all equally hold tyranny in contempt, and they will all exercise it upon their neighbours. They will all consider the idea of a universal monarchy as extravagant, and yet most of them will act as if they had either attained it or were threatened by it. (XII, 14)

The battles and tensions over global trade and colonization exacerbate the already fragile relationships among European states, then, which even in the best of times could come apart easily because of the hazards intrinsic to international politics, with its lack of a common "tribunal" to which all nations could submit. After reflecting upon the social, economic, and political damage done to European nations themselves by the growth of commerce, Diderot concludes with a discussion about how commerce and imperial pursuits have ultimately weakened and subverted Dutch republicanism. This makes it more difficult, he regrets, for supporters of republicanism outside of Holland to make their case, and so the zeal for creating and maintaining empires abroad also weakens the chances for democratization in Europe. Diderot darkly concludes that it may be the case that "the destiny of every commercial nation [*nation commerçante*] is to be rich, careless, corrupt, and dominated." (II, 27)

For Diderot, economic monopolies over trading routes abroad and political monopolies over sovereignty within European societies went hand in hand. Absolute authority in one sphere merged easily with tyrannical control in another. Indeed, the political character of his discussions of commerce stems from this connection; his criticisms of the monopolies of quasi-sovereign imperial companies are often only thinly veiled attacks upon the corrupt and unjust political authority of European sovereigns who lord over both the unfortunate inhabitants of European societies and the inhabitants of an increasing number of far-flung, non-European societies. Diderot contends that monarchs, ministers of state, and commercial chieftains, who already collectively exercise an overwhelming sovereign power, now seek to enlarge this power, while disingenuously justifying imperial strength abroad as a means to safeguard domestic security. Addressing European sovereigns, Diderot argues that the jealous and cruel ambition of European powers who seek to monopolize trading privileges and imperial rule is the real

> motive for which you take up arms, and massacre each other! It is to determine which of you shall retain the exclusive privilege of tyranny, and the monopoly of prosperity. I am aware that you colour this atrocious project with the pretence of providing for your own security: but how can you be credited, when it is evident that you set no bounds to your ambition; and that the more powerful you are, the more imperious you become? (V, 4)

Diderot's tone throughout the *Histoire* on such matters is pessimistic; he continually describes European governments as largely unaccountable to the interests of their subjects and increasingly corrupted by wealth. Commenting upon the lively debates in England about whether the East India Company's charter would be renewed in 1780, he notes that everything seems to suggest that a renewal would be enacted by Parliament, despite the dreadful effects that such imperial and commercial power has had upon both the English and the Indian nations. The commercial profits that benefit the political class are large enough, he implies, to rule out any possibility of reforming the East India Company; thus, "[g]overnment, after having secured for itself the major part of the produce of these conquests, will again deliver up these regions to the oppressive yoke of monopoly." (III, 41)

In a 'speech' to the English that Diderot contributed to the *Histoire*, he not only lists a variety of the injustices committed against Indians and highlights the failed efforts of those who plead their case in England, but also prophesies that the English will continue to oppress India and should therefore expect to be avenged.

> The horrid spectacle of so many immense regions pillaged, ravaged, or reduced to the most cruel servitude will be displayed before us again. The earth now covers the carcasses of three million humans who have perished through your

[British] fault or neglect [a reference primarily to the Indian famines in company territories in the 1770s, which Diderot discussed earlier in detail]: they will cry out to Heaven and to the earth for vengeance, and will obtain it. (III, 41)

Diderot balances such appeals to the commercial, imperial classes—arguing that based only on their self-interest, they should understand that they will eventually come to their ruin since they will be forced at some point to answer for their oppression—with the grim reality that, for now, they have bought with gold the silence of legislators and the courts. Diderot's final rhetorical appeal, when he has outlined the depths of injustice, is almost always to the selfishness of the powerful. However, in the case of commercial zealots who build empires abroad for European states, he knows that even this tactic may well be ineffectual, for global trade does not depend necessarily upon protecting commercial gains in any one region. Since new markets and new lands for pillage can always be found, global economic arrangements give powerful interests no incentive to cultivate any one relationship. Accordingly, Diderot characterizes the monopolists' "creed" as a paean to globalizing ventures that lack any rootedness in particular communities:

> Let my country perish, let the region I command also perish; perish the citizen and the foreigner; perish my associates, provided that I can enrich myself with his spoils. All parts of the universe are alike to me. When I have laid waste, exhausted, and impoverished one country, I shall always find another, to which I can carry my gold. . . . (III, 41)

Diderot argues further that the metropole has little concern even for the European inhabitants of its colonies, and that their great distance from the halls of power, both imperial and commercial, mirrors the plight of rural inhabitants within European countries, who remain largely ignored, he notes, by those in cities (XIII, 41). Addressing colonists, he argues that they should "implore the assistance of the mother-country to which you are subject, and if you should experience a denial, break off your connections with it. It is too much to be obliged to support at once misery, indifference, and slavery." (XIII, 41) The absurdity of the situation, in Diderot's view, is that the most profitable colonies receive the fewest liberties and are often the most oppressed, for their masters are "commercial states" that accordingly rule in light of the most cruel spirit of administration; in large part, he contends, it is pure profit of the most short-sighted kind that drives them to heavy-handed rule (XIII, 41). Colonies that become independent, with their mixed populations of indigenous inhabitants, slaves (whom Diderot hoped would be freed or who would more likely free themselves by violence), and the descendants of

Europeans may well be the hope of the future, he suggests, if they can learn the proper lessons from Europe's disastrous commercial and imperial exploits. Thus, in an invocation to the people of North America, Diderot declares,

> [L]et the example of all the nations which have preceded you, and especially that of the mother-country, serve as a lesson to you. Dread the influence of gold, which, with luxury, introduces corruption of manners and contempt of the laws. Dread too an unequal distribution of wealth, which yields a small number of rich citizens, and a multitude of citizens plunged in misery. . . . Keep yourselves free from the spirit of conquest. The tranquillity of an empire diminishes in proportion to its extent. (XVIII, 52)

The eventual independence of colonies, however, was not a solution to the problems associated with global commerce, as Diderot well understood. The manner in which global commerce itself should be reformed after having been steeped in blood, tyranny, and corruption from the discovery of the New World onward was, in some respects, an open question for him, for he never presents a systematic response to this issue in the *Histoire*. Still, he believed that a reform both of European states (to break their absolute sovereignty, and to make them more accountable to their subjects) and of the international order (to create a meaningful tribunal that would oversee the increasingly complex political and commercial disputes among nations) would be necessary first steps. He was, however, under no illusions about the likelihood of such developments. His pessimism about domestic political reform followed from his belief that the citizens of European states were pacified by the influx of commercial goods and were increasingly unaware, or tolerant, of the most egregious social and political injustices both at home and abroad. Europeans have become reconciled, he writes, to a "regular and constant system of oppression", and social and political debate has been reduced ultimately to what amounts to "the various ranks of slaves assassinating each other with their chains, for the amusement of their masters." (VI, 1) Yet Diderot also affirms that the spirit of barter and exchange is not fundamentally inconsistent with peace and tranquillity. In the future, he hopes, governmental sanctions will apply across borders "to the private engagements between subjects of different nations and . . . those bankruptcies, the effects of which are felt at immense distances, will become concerns of government." Although Diderot refers here primarily to commercial bankruptcies, their attendant moral bankruptcies, as we have seen, are also among the effects of a global commercial order; these, too, could perhaps be regulated by a set of transnational practices and institutions. The one certainty for Diderot is that global commerce has become the key framework within which international politics is practised; thus, "the annals of nations must hereafter be written by commercial philosophers, as they were formerly by historical orators." (VI, 1)

Even without thoroughgoing institutional reforms, however, Diderot believes that it could be beneficial simply to transform the way most people conceptualized commerce both as a practice and as an ideal. In a discussion of what the French could hypothetically achieve in their trade with the East Indies, in the unlikely event that they recover the influence they once had there, Diderot explores at some length what nonexploitative commercial relations might look like not only in India, but in general (IV, 33). Diderot describes a relationship in which Europeans might form trading posts, but would do no more politically than to serve as the mediators of local disputes, in contrast to the Indies companies that served as the auxiliaries of some local political powers in their (sometimes manufactured) disputes with others. No trading posts should be fortified, local customs and religions should be respected, and the very idea of conquest should be banished from the minds of those who voyage to the Indies. As Diderot notes, "[t]o conquer, or to plunder with violence, is the same thing." An extensive and flourishing trade would no doubt involve competition with other European powers, but this could occur lawfully if the nature of exchange and trade was itself moderate and just, characterized by a "faithful observance of engagements" with indigenous peoples and other European nations and contentment "with a moderate profit".[22] Settlers must become "naturalized" into their host country, in order to avoid becoming the 'tigers' free of any national character who cross borders with no ambition but wealth and destruction. It is thus absolutely crucial "to keep good terms with the indigenous inhabitants [*les indigènes*]" (IV, 33). In a final appeal to humanitarian norms, he writes, "Let us, therefore, no longer be imposters on our first appearance; servile, when we are received; insolent, when we think ourselves strong; and cruel, when we have become all powerful." (IV, 33)

From Diderot's perspective, however, non-European nations should not wait for the unlikely possibility that European states and their commercial proxies will reform themselves. The only examples of successful resistance to the most corrupting and unjust forms of commerce, in his view, are those of non-European nations that were strong enough to curtail interactions with untrustworthy European merchants and potential imperialists; as diplomatically harmful as this can be, he notes that it is a defensible and sensible strategy, one consistent with the norms of hospitality, as Kant also would later argue as part of his theory of cosmopolitan right. Upon entering an inhabited country, Diderot contends, what is due to one as a matter of justice and hospitality from the indigenous society is limited. The host country can justifiably curtail visitors' attempts to promote commerce and communication if it concludes that a peaceful and moderate commerce is unlikely to result. Writing from the point of view of a European visitor, he writes that

> if I am granted sanctuary, fire, water, bread and salt, then all obligations towards me will have been fulfilled. If I demand more, I become a thief and a murderer. Let us suppose that I have been accepted. I have become acquainted with the country's laws and *moeurs*. They suit me. I want to settle there. If I am allowed to do so, it is a favour done to me, and a refusal cannot offend me. The Chinese may be bad politicians when they shut us out of their empire, but they are not unjust. Their country has sufficient population, and we [Europeans] are too dangerous as guests.[23] (XIII, 1)

Most societies, however, were either decimated or weakened by their encounters with Europe or had already been conquered; shutting down commerce with European states was a strategy that few non-European realms could attempt. Moreover, as Diderot was well aware, less technologically complex nomadic societies, such as hunters and herders, were particularly vulnerable to the juggernaut of commerce and empire, and obviously lacked the military and political power that a nation like China could deploy. In light of this, he writes that tragically "one cannot help imagining that before three centuries have passed they ['primitive'—i.e., nomadic peoples] will have disappeared from the earth." (XV, 4)

The Disastrous Effects of Empire upon Europeans

It is only on rare occasions, according to Diderot, that conquest produces genuine benefits for imperial powers themselves. In what he describes as one of the great ironies of modern European history, various forms of oppression within Europe, including slavery and harsh feudal laws, were eased somewhat at the beginning of the crusades. The vassals of feudal lands were "almost reinstated . . . in the order of human beings" by being sold property by the lords to fund conquests abroad. As a result, a minimal right to property and some rudimentary forms of independence became instituted. Thus, "the first dawnings of liberty in Europe were, however unexpectedly, owed to the crusades; and the rage of conquest for once contributed to the happiness of mankind." (I, 13) Much more often, however, the imperial enterprise further strengthens governmental power, which already tends toward a dangerous expansion of authority (IX, 30). The character of imperial governance is such that the great distance of colonies from the metropole increases the already complex array of matters that governments must take account of, in light of which state power assumes further roles—with yet further opportunities for injustice. As a consequence, Diderot argues, empires lead invariably to abuses at home and abroad (VIII, 23). Along these lines, he presents the administration of the Caribbean colonies as a typical case, for it seems inevitable that they will continue to be administered in a harsh and absolute fashion. Their colonial administrators are either corrupt to begin with or they are made so by being given absolute power. Hence, in overseeing a system of laws that are, by their nature, not attuned to the interests and needs of its subjects, and given that they are rarely given the time to understand any of the local features of their constituency before they return home, disaster tends to follow both for them and for their colonial subjects (XIII, 56).

As we have seen, Diderot concludes that even the descendants of Europeans in colonies are poorly treated by imperial administrators who simply institute programs that are set in the metropole. Much of his criticisms of this kind stem from the view that the sovereigns in Europe are motivated primarily by a spirit of jealousy of other sovereigns' imperial power. Thus, they would be less affected if their colonies were destroyed by the sea, Diderot suggests, than if they were taken over by a rival power (XIII, 41). Now that new communities have been created by the cohabitation and mixing of various peoples, through settlement, slavery, and the remnants of indigenous populations, remarkable new societies might prosper in the future, in a manner that might even eschew the injustices of past imperial practices. But for this to occur, the masters of such societies could no longer be monarchs and royal councils thousands of miles away in Europe (XI, 31). At the moment, he notes, the descendants of Europeans in the Caribbean, for instance, have had their characters thoroughly corrupted by carrying out the most brutal functions of imperial rule, such as slaveholding (XI, 31).

The lack of judgement exercised by the most powerful classes in Europe disturbs Diderot, for a clear-headed assessment of imperial politics would reveal that the possession of colonies creates far greater problems for European countries than what are seen to be the impressive gains in riches and power, which only continue to dupe governments into expanding their imperial exploits. In a discussion about whether the acquisition of Canada has been advantageous or harmful to England, he argues that it is forgotten "that every domain, separated from a state by a vast distance, is precarious, expensive, ill-defended, and ill-governed" (XVI, 23). The politically powerful routinely fail to think about the long-term economic, political, and moral costs of empire in part because of the obsession for national glory that imperial enterprises stoke in the capitals of Europe. Hence, since they never consider "whether a miserable little island will not occasion cares and expenses that cannot be compensated by any advantage, they will suffer themselves to be dazzled with the frivolous glory of having added it to the national dominion." (XVI, 23)

These and many other lessons and dangers are lost upon those who are consumed by "the rage of extending their dominions". The dangers of an ever increasing state power in European countries, which already supported a framework of customs, practices, and institutions that weighed down most of its subjects, should be even more obvious in an age of empire, when the brute force of state administration covers extensive territories across the globe. Such developments further oppress European subjects, and Diderot concludes bleakly in a notable passage that the very idea of settled communities with fixed magistrates and a codified rule of law, indeed with all of the hallmarks of what are considered to be 'civilization', appear only to promote the interests of an increasingly haughty and aggressive elite.

> Such are the effects of national jealousies, and of the rapaciousness of government, to which men, as well as their property, become prey. What our enemies lose is reckoned an advantage, what they gain is looked upon as a loss. When a town cannot be taken, it is starved; when it cannot be kept, it is burnt to ashes, or its foundations are razed. . . . A despotic government separates its enemies from its slaves by immense deserts to prevent revolts within one, and emigration from another. In such a manner has Spain chosen to make a wilderness of her own country and a grave of America, rather than divide its riches with any of the other European nations. The Dutch have been guilty of every public and private crime to deprive other commercial nations of the spice trade. They have frequently thrown whole cargoes into the sea rather than sell them at a low price. . . . England destroyed the neutral French inhabitants of Acadia to prevent them from returning to France. Can it be said after this that civilization [*la police*] and society were made for the happiness of mankind? Yes, for the powerful man; yes, for the evil man. (XVII, 16)

When Diderot wrote his contributions to the *Histoire* in the 1770s, France had lost most of its colonial possessions as a result of the Seven Years' War, and was reduced largely to its Caribbean plantations. Yet, his anti-imperialism by no means assumed the historical demise of the imperial project, for he clearly believed that while the balance of imperial power might shift among European states, imperial rule itself appeared to be firmly entrenched, largely because it served a variety of governmental, commercial, and clerical interests. Ultimately, however, empire came at a high cost not only to subjugated non-Europeans, but to Europeans as well, whose prospects for peace, economic stability, and freedom were under even greater threat, he maintained, than before the advent of modern imperialism.

While Diderot's concerns about the impact of empire upon European societies, and in particular upon European governments, fostered a deep pessimism about the nature of political rule itself, he also writes in the

Histoire of some positive lessons about politics that might be gleaned from the experience of imperialism. In a more hopeful vein, he writes that "[n]o society was ever founded on injustice", that is, as a matter of principle (XVIII, 1). Such a polity would either be destroyed by what would naturally be its many enemies or by its own immorality. A society that is virtuous, in contrast, would do no injury to anyone, and it would be founded upon an impartial equity, stable laws, and an exercise of political power that would protect every group and all ranks. For such a peaceful and productive society, neighbours would rush to its defence. The unreal quality of such a polity, as far removed from reality as a society founded thoroughly upon injustice, should hence be considered as a kind of "imaginary excellence in politics." (XVIII, 1) Politics, then, is inevitably imperfect, for it never truly occupies either of these extreme or idealized images; nonetheless, some societies may well be closer to one end of the spectrum than another. "These two sorts of government", Diderot explains, "are equally unknown in the annals of the world, which presents us with nothing but imperfect sketches more or less resembling the atrocious sublimity or the affecting beauty of one or the other of these great portraits." (XVIII, 1) While numerous factors influence where along this idealized spectrum any one society sits, the possession of imperial realms is a feature that virtually guarantees, according to Diderot, a condition of injustice for the society in question. Often the nations that are the most astonishing in their achievements—not simply within what could plausibly be described as their realm, but also (in light of conquest and the building of empires) in "the theatre of the world, [and thus] impelled by destructive ambition"—display "a greater resemblance to the former [societies founded upon injustice]." The nations, in contrast, that fail to achieve such grand proportions and spectacles are nevertheless, precisely because of their more modest goals and the vast injustices they have forsaken in concentrating upon local matters of social import, more likely to achieve at least some modicum of political justice. "Others, more wise in their constitution, simpler in their manners, more limited in their views, and enveloped, if we may use the expression, with a kind of secret happiness", Diderot explains, "seem to be more conformable to the second [to the societies founded upon justice]." (XVIII, 1) Still, while historical experience, in Diderot's opinion, demonstrates that the metropolitan societies of imperial powers corrode and move closer to pure conditions of injustice as a result of empire, ruling elites are unlikely to be swayed from conquest in light of this, since they are motivated primarily by the sheer possession of power.

The most powerful nations, Diderot suggests, are often insignificant in their origins. In a chapter on the early history of Denmark, which describes the variety of forest-dwelling peoples who eventually plundered the Gauls in the quest of glory and a milder climate, he argues that such conquest is the single most important factor in determining the sheer power of states. "It would be difficult to produce one single instance of a nation, since the creation of the world", he notes, "that has either extended or enriched itself during a long interval of tranquillity, by the progress of industry alone, or by the mere resources of its population." (V, intro.) Because the brute force that a state, or a state in league with other religious and feudal institutions, can marshal over its own subjects and against other states appears to be the paramount goal of sovereigns, states engage in imperial exploits whenever the best opportunities of this kind arise. Given that arguments premised upon the welfare of Europeans would fail to stir the interests of the governing elites who sought, in Diderot's view, to solidify and expand their power, he turns not infrequently to arguments about the destruction and death that will inevitably befall European imperialists themselves. "Nations that are subdued long for a deliverer; nations that are oppressed, for an avenger; and they will soon find one", he warns (IV, 33). The prospect of Europeans—not only lowly soldiers and colonists, but a number of the most powerful among them—being massacred, he hopes, might help to establish, from selfish motives, the view that fostering a good character and reputation abroad best secures European interests. Both in his discussions of slavery and imperialism, Diderot turns to the violence that will overcome Europeans if they persist in their colonial efforts.

Diderot makes an appeal to European sovereigns to abolish slavery, only to chastise himself: "But what am I saying? Let the ineffectual calls of humanity be no longer pleaded with the people and their masters: perhaps, they have never been attended to in any public transactions." (XI, 22) Accordingly, he switches rhetorical tactics, aiming instead at Europeans' self-interest. In part, Diderot believes that arguments about the perils that empire create within European societies, let alone humanitarian arguments, are most likely ineffective because of the arrogance and cruelty of absolute monarchs and their corrupt courts. Moreover, the increasing importance of luxury goods that imperial activities and the slave trade furnishes also damages, he notes, the ability of the people to empathize with the plight of oppressed non-Europeans. The evisceration of human sympathy inherent in the emerging commercial practices of his day affects consumers, then, and not only, as one would expect, the manufacturers, traders, agriculturalists, and other producers and middlemen of the imperial economy. The zeal for profiteering abroad is matched by the consumption of steadily multiplying goods at home, most of which serves little social purpose, as Diderot notes often, and only fuels further corrupt and rapacious activities in the metropole and in the colonies. Thus, he finds that the kind of rhetorical tactics employed by his fellow *philosophes* to rally readers to the cause of African slaves, for instance, would likely fail. The intermingling of cruelty and imperial commerce depicted in Voltaire's *Candide*—recall Candide's encounter with a dying fugitive slave, bleeding heavily and with of his two limbs hacked off in punishment for having escaped from a local plantation, who tells him that "this is the price of the sugar you eat in Europe"—may well make for a powerful image. In Diderot's judgement, however, the goods brought to Europe from the non-European world generally deadened any sympathetic response to suffering that such stories might otherwise stoke.

Before describing the traditional defences of slavery and repudiating each one, Diderot notes that arguments alone will fail to end the slave trade. In an age, he contends, in which human equality is constantly affirmed, Europeans appear nevertheless only to take pity and to become outraged at the treatment of fellow Europeans—for instance, those who have been taken captive in the notorious raids off the coast of Barbary.

> Writings, which will become immortal, have established in the most moving ways that all humans are brothers. We are filled with indignation at the cruelties, either civil or religious, of our ferocious ancestors, and we turn away our eyes from those ages of horror and blood. Those of our neighbours whom the inhabitants of Barbary have weighed down with irons obtain our pity and assistance. Even imaginary distress draws tears from our eyes . . . especially at the theatre. It is only the fatal destiny of the Negroes that does not concern us. They are tyrannized, mutilated, burnt, and put to death, and yet we listen to these accounts coolly and without emotion. The torments of a people to whom we owe our luxuries are never able to reach our hearts.[24] (XI, 22)

In light of this phenomenon and what he took to be the deafness of all political powers to any arguments based upon moral considerations, Diderot concludes that slaves will most likely have to liberate themselves by violence. He predicts that this will eventually be achieved by a "great man", a "Black Spartacus", in a passage of the *Histoire* that would famously inspire the Haitian revolutionary, Toussaint L'Ouverture, who would later be described by others, and would then describe himself, as precisely this foretold avenger.[25] (XI, 24) Given Diderot's theory of the deadening effect of imperial commerce upon human sympathies, he replaces Voltaire's strategy of fostering pity for suffering slaves with the more searing image of blood vengeance, appealing to Europeans' wholly self-interested desire not to have their throats slashed open, a prospect that Diderot not only believes is just, but that he describes gleefully in some of his most provocative contributions to the *Histoire*.[26]

In addition to resistance against slavery, Diderot also calls for and justifies the use of violence against Europeans engaged more broadly in imperial enterprises. One of the most vivid instances of an appeal to force, once again in light of what he assumes will be the failure of all arguments and negotiations to deter imperial powers in their ventures, occurs toward the end of his analysis of Dutch colonial ambitions in southern Africa. After discussing the distinctive customs and practices of Hottentot society, Diderot bemoans the fact that they were being steadily overtaken, beginning in the seventeenth century, by the forces led by Jan van Riebeeck, the Dutch East India Company official who founded Cape Town. Given the many other interactions between European and non-European peoples that are surveyed in the *Histoire*, Diderot feared that peoples like the Hottentots would not use force against European visitors. Yet, only in violently resisting the Dutch would the Hottentots have any chance of preserving their society. Their lives might be beset with dangers in the African wilderness, but the Dutch will almost certainly deprive them of their liberty. Diderot argues that the "wild beasts that inhabit" the forests surrounding the Hottentots "are less formidable than the monsters under whose empire you are going to fall. The tiger may perhaps tear you to pieces, but he will take nothing but your life away." (II, 8) The Dutch arrive, he notes, in the manner of so many modern conquerors, portraying themselves peacefully as faithful allies, but concealing their true intentions. Their outlook is based entirely upon the benefits that they can procure for themselves, without any sense of even the most basic norms of decency and respect; these they will continue to deny the Hottentots, Diderot suggests, just as Europeans have denied all rights to non-Europeans in other continents. In addition to the greed for power and commercial benefits, the Dutch are inspired by the same grossly inegalitarian disposition as that of other Europeans who have ventured into non-Europeans' territories: the different climate, geography, physical attributes, customs, and institutions of the Hottentots will thus inspire not wonder and reflection, but rather the most base inhumanity and dogmatic prejudices. "Their attitude will be that of benevolence; their look, that of humanity: but cruelty and treachery reign in the bottom of their hearts. . . . You must either agree with their extravagant opinions," Diderot warns, "or they will massacre you without mercy, for they believe that the man who does not think like them is unfit to live." (II, 18)

One option for non-European peoples who are nomadic and likely to be subjected to imperial rule might be to flee—"Fly, Hottentots, fly!" Diderot exclaims at one point—but such strategies in the end will fail, for European explorers and conquerors will reach them eventually. The ideal response is to confront incoming Europeans directly with brute force, the only language they appear to understand. "Do not address them with representations of justice, which they will not listen to," he insists, "but speak to them with your arrows." (II, 18) Diderot even hopes that the Dutch colonialists will all be killed, if only the Hottentots can see through Dutch false promises and accordingly steel their resolve for the battles that might save their liberty. "[T]ake up your axes," he counsels, "bend your bows, and send a shower of poisoned darts against these strangers. May there not be one of them remaining to convey to his countrymen the news of their disaster!" (II, 18) Knowing that such advice would disturb many of his European readers, Diderot nonetheless notes that his arguments are made not only in the guise of historical judgements against Riebeeck and other past imperialists, but toward those who seek to undertake and to defend such ventures currently and in the future. To those readers offended by his words, he remarks that such a reaction deserves a similar condemnation, for it arises from a sympathy toward murderous Europeans. "[Y]ou perceive in the hatred I have vowed against them [the Dutch imperial incursions into the Hottentots' territory] that which I entertain against you." The contemptuous attitude that Diderot holds against those who express some sympathy toward Europeans suffering abroad in the midst of their imperial activities seems only to reinforce his pessimism, for it fosters his belief that the work of writers alone will fall upon deaf ears. Thus, as a last resort, he routinely turns to violence, in the hope that Europeans' desire to live and to flourish might lead to behaviour that humanitarian arguments alone should ideally inspire. Even after colonization takes place, if violent resistance by indigenous peoples does not occur initially, it is inevitable that Europeans will be attacked and ultimately destroyed by the violent forces that they themselves unleash in such territories. If for no other reason than self-interest, he implies, Europeans should decolonize and rescind their imperial holdings; they can do so now, with the hope of forging peaceful and respectful ties of commerce and communication, or they will be made to leave by a series of bloody revolts against their imperial governance. "This is the decree pronounced by fate upon your colonies: you must either renounce your colonies or they will renounce you." (XIII, 1)

Europe: Not a Civilization Fit for Export

Some of Diderot's arguments that undercut the standard justifications of European imperialism concern not so much the activities of empire itself, but more generally the corruption of European civilization. Accordingly, he challenges European pretensions of civilizing others by criticizing many of Europe's religious and political institutions and practices as fundamentally unjust, and thus as unfit to be exported abroad. Diderot views "the fanaticism of religion and the spirit of conquest, those two disturbers of the universe" as equally problematic features of global relations. Some of his arguments about Europe's own woes are directed toward the

Catholic church specifically, but also more generally toward the power of religious elites. In this respect, he notes, the abuse of power that the Catholic priesthood engages in is indicative of the problems associated with religious clergy indigenous to the non-European world as well. The "sacred dialect" of Sanskrit in India, he argues, serves a familiar purpose: the laity is thereby deprived of the resources with which they might question the prerogatives of clerical power, which in this case is housed among the Brahmins. Thus, "the spirit of the priesthood is everywhere the same; and that at all times the priest, either from motives of interest or pride is desirous of keeping the people in ignorance." (I, 8) Still, Diderot notes that many individuals of great talent and virtue enter such professions and do not directly engage in deceiving and tyrannizing their "fellow creatures". (I, 8) It is not religious doctrine as such, but the abuse of the enormous social and political power that religious elites wield that Diderot most often attacks in the *Histoire*. Hence, at the end of a critical discussion of church policy during which Diderot calls for the end of the sale of indulgences and, more broadly, for a broad reform of church policy, he argues that the tenets of the faith, however absurd from his own standpoint, would not bother anyone if the church were in fact a positive influence upon society. As he writes, "[y]our spirit of intolerance, and the odious means by which you have acquired, and still continue to heap, riches upon riches have done more injury to your opinions than all the arguments of incredulity." (VIII, 28) Given that Diderot's quarrel with the church in the *Histoire* is primarily social and political, rather than about theological doctrine, his criticisms focus not upon ideas that missionaries propagate abroad, but upon the significant ideological and material support that religious institutions provide to the imperial enterprise. In this respect, his analysis of religious power differs somewhat from his satire of church doctrines on the liberty of women, marriage, and sexuality in the *Supplément*. Commenting upon the Pope's grant of Peru to Spain, Diderot notes that the papacy does not have legitimate control over such matters in the first place; he concludes that the choice between "submission to the European monarch, or slavery; baptism, or death" amounts to a contract that should horrify anyone with any sense of morality and justice (VII, 2). The establishment of European religious power in the non-European world, he finds, simply replicates abroad the injustices that it has sown and continues to sow in the Old World. Diderot argues that the church forces indigenous peoples to be impious by demanding that they give up their gods, and encourages them to break their bonds with their own "legitimate sovereign". The indigenous king who voluntarily accedes to such papal injustices abandons his country, political power, and religion "to the mercy of an ambitious despot . . . and [to] the most dangerous system of Machiavellism." (VII, 2)

Challenging such abuses of religious power is difficult for the same reason that reforming governmental power is ineffective. Toward the end of a brief history of asylum, including houses of worship, for alleged criminals and outcasts, Diderot notes that such safe havens are sometimes abused. "The most dangerous of asylums, however, is not that into which a man may make his escape," he asserts, "but that which he carries about with him, that which accompanies and invests the guilty person, which serves him as a shield. . . . Such are the ecclesiastical habit and character." (VI, 13) For Diderot, the use of privileged power to hide oneself from laws and judgements that ought to be made equally without regard to rank is the common thread that binds clerical and sovereign institutions. The ideal that "justice is equally and without distinction due to every citizen" cannot easily be put into practice, given the corrupt advantages that the powerful hold in order to distance themselves from reform and critical scrutiny (VI, 13). Religious power in particular is perhaps the most difficult to challenge when it is synonymous with state power. Drawing upon the English travel literature about India, Diderot notes that Brahmins in Calicut unusually possess sovereign power directly. Such forms of theocratic rule, he argues, tend to become "the worst of all governments, because the hand of the gods adds to the weight of the sceptre of tyrants. . . . The orders of the despot are changed into oracles, and the disobedience of the subjects incurs the stigma of a revolt against Heaven." (III, 15) But even when clerical institutions are not formally conjoined with sovereign power, the close relationships among the two in European societies create an enormously complex and domineering set of institutions that can easily thwart attempts at change. When state power and religious power are in league with one another, he contends, humans are oppressed, and when they conflict, even the most minimal norms of justice are set aside in order to settle their differences. Religious powers, he argues, are only satisfied with state power if the government uses the "axe" that they have sanctified against practices, people, and all that they have deemed sinful or heretical. As he writes, "when the latter [state, or sovereign power] has conquered and enslaved the world, the former [religious authority] interposes and prescribes laws in its turn: they enter into a league with each other, humanity falls prostrate, and submits to its chains" (III, 15). These two parties, one under the banner of the sovereign and the other under the standard of superstition, as Diderot describes them, fight against decent social and political norms and against each other until the blood of innocent persons streams in the streets. The dynamics that result both from the conjoined and from the riven powers of states and churches play themselves out in the non-European world. Imperial rule in the non-European world, from this perspective, is simply an extension of this seemingly omnipotent coalition of secular and divine power. The spread of European civilization amounts, then, to the spread of a particularly corrupt and unjust constellation of sovereign and religious powers; having sown injustice within Europe for hundreds of years, their combined strength now brutally dominates the rest of the globe.

Most of Diderot's arguments about the inadequacy of European societies, and hence the absurdity of asserting that an ideal of the European way of life should be actively promoted by force abroad, concerns the injustice of European political institutions, rather than its religious activities and powers. Indeed, as we have just seen, it is the political dimension of religious power, and especially those moments when clerical force and governmental authority reinforce one another, that most disturb him. Thus, first and foremost, he maintains that Europe's social and political degradation in particular should not be exported abroad. It would be understandable, he writes, and there "might" even be "some excuse" to be made on behalf of Europeans (though he is careful to avoid claiming that they would be wholly excusable), if Europeans had arrived in southern Africa with the intention of leading Hottentots into a "more civilized kind of life" or encouraging *moeurs* "preferable" to those in Europe (II, 18). Such an enterprise might well have been well intentioned, however morally dubious ultimately, but Europeans have done worse by either attempting to spread their own highly imperfect, and by no means superior, mores and practices abroad or even engaging in outright brutality simply to satisfy their avarice. With regard to the Hottentots, for instance, he asserts that the Dutch arrived in their territory merely to drive them out of their homeland and, when possible, to use the Hottentots "in the place of the animal who ploughs the ground under the lash of the farmer's whip" (II, 18).

Many of Diderot's moral arguments about the Hottentots are a response to a common question that underlay imperialist ventures: could such a wandering lifestyle of herders, so remote from the sedentary, fixed, and refined institutions and practices of European societies, give the Hottentots any real happiness, and, if not, would not their condition be improved by the introduction of a 'civilized' life? He responds in part by asserting that Europe's own ills do not place it in the position to judge the Hottentots as fundamentally 'unhappy'. One would have to be not only thoroughly "prejudiced in favour of the advantages of our social institutions", but also a total "stranger" to the sufferings in Europe to make such comparative judgements about nomadic and sedentary lifestyles (II, 18). In response to Europeans who view the rustic lives of the nomadic Hottentots as animalistic, focusing upon elements of their lives that were seen to be especially distasteful—that they clothed themselves, for instance, in animal entrails—Diderot asserts that the hatred, evil, and duplicity of Europeans abroad, in addition to the general corruption that pervades their polities, disgusts his reason more than the Hottentots' "uncleanliness" disgusts his fellow Europeans. He argues at length that Europeans tend to overlook their own similar, or even worse, problems when they condemn others' faults. Thus, referring to Europeans' criticisms of the Hottentots' supposedly vulgar religious practices and simple-minded beliefs, he writes,

> You [Europeans] smile with contempt upon the superstitions of the Hottentots. But do not your priests poison your minds in your infancy with prejudices that torment you during life, which sow divisions in your families, and arm your countries against each other? Have not your ancestors destroyed each other several times in defence of incomprehensible questions? (II, 18)

Encounters with non-European peoples, he implies, ought to be an occasion for sustained and critical self-reflection about the shared problems and injustices that face diverse peoples. Instead, he contends that Europeans' blindness toward their own faults leads to an arrogance that fuels their aggression in the non-European world. In order to deflate such pride, he contends that the advanced knowledge of the arts and the fixed system of laws that instills pride in many Europeans often create problems at least as great as their benefits; moreover, much of this would be of no use to the Hottentots, given the type of life that they choose to lead. Diderot criticizes imperialists for speaking the language of virtue abroad and asserting that they are the agents for spreading such virtues despite the fact that their societies fail to practise them or to live by them in the course of satisfying their colonial ambitions. Their hypocrisy stems not only from the injustices that imperial ventures unleash, but crucially also from the deep flaws in the institutions and practices of European societies, which many Europeans fail to recognize.

Hence, Diderot often engages in a blistering assessment of European societies themselves in a work that is otherwise largely focused upon the activities of Europeans in the non-European world, for this approach undercuts imperial arrogance. Some of Diderot's criticisms along these lines target royal absolutism and, more broadly, state power as such, and on these occasions non-European societies are at times taken equally to task; his other criticisms focus on the particular ills of European polities or upon the precarious role that Europe has come to occupy in global politics. Commenting upon the monuments that sovereigns commission to celebrate their own glory, he argues that very few of them would exist if only truly public-spirited monarchs were so honoured. Indeed, he suggests, if all the inscriptions on such monuments were truthful, they would consist mainly of a litany of oppressions, murders, and injustices (V, 3). Frederick the Great of Prussia, he notes, has often been celebrated for his

strong rule and patronage of the arts, winning praise from German philosophers, who at times overlook his bloody exploits, but he is overall a
rare breed, a ruler who is, in many respects, a "patriot king" (V, 10).
Most rulers, however, make "no distinction between truth and error, justice and partiality, good and evil, consider the principles of morality
merely as metaphysical speculations, and imagine that human reason is
swayed entirely by interest." (V, 10) The monarchs of France, in particular, he implies, are no exception to this general assessment. In a lengthy
address to Louis XVI, Diderot complains of the great problems facing
France and the lack of any political will to confront such issues. From
oppressed and destitute farmers who are routinely extorted by feudal and
governmental taxes, to desperate poverty in the cities and the unnecessary
luxuries of the military class, the nobles, and the royal house, he attacks
the corruption and the excessive wealth of a tiny and powerful few (IV,
18). Such contributions to the *Histoire* serve to repudiate the view that
Europe represents a higher, more just, and happier existence. While it
also, of course, provides him with an opportunity to further a number of
his criticisms of European social and political life that he had undertaken
in earlier writings (such as his observations on Catherine II's proposed
reforms in Russia), given his view that imperial activities abroad are, in
some respects, extensions of pathologies at home, such judgements about
European life and politics are part of his broader anti-imperialist agenda.

Diderot suggests that many of the roots of Europe's domestic injustices derive from once understandable (and, in some cases, perhaps even
justifiable) rules and institutions that outlasted their original social purposes. In this sense, he appears to believe that an appreciation of injustices in the non-European world illustrates the sources of inequality and
misery that all societies share in some form. Thus, in a discussion about
the beleaguered lives of the lowest, pariah castes of India, Diderot offers
a conjecture about how such indignities may have arisen. In contrast to
the "half barbarous governments" of Europe, he argues that Indians'
more moderate system of legislation spared the lives and did not shed the
blood of "malefactors", but instead banished them from respectable
community (I, 8). This unjustly applied to the children of such individuals as well, and thus over time their outcast status became institutionalized, ultimately bearing no relationship to the injustices that provided
at least some justification for the initial banishment. Such a speculative
account is characteristic of Diderot's intellectual disposition in the *Histoire*, and thus alive to the apparent paradoxes of history and to the possible sociological origins of contemporary practices and institutions. It also
underscores the extent to which he engages non-European societies in a
sympathetic, but critical spirit; thus, his anti-imperialist arguments in the
Histoire usually do not rest upon a naïve veneration or idealization of

non-European peoples. With regard to the caste system more generally, then, Diderot argues that in a land rich with resources and a people with an otherwise compassionate moral system (which, in his view, makes Indians "averse to persecution [from each other] and the spirit of conquest"), it is a particular tragedy that there exists at the heart of Indian society such a "barbarous inequality". In attempting to determine how such a moral order could have formed, Diderot notes that the answer is most likely rooted in the same principle that has been the source "of all of the calamities that have befallen the inhabitants of this globe." (I, 8) In this case, he argues that the original hierarchical distinctions constituted a moral "error" that over time became generalized to encompass every station of Indian life; it became the basis of "an entire system of politics and morality". In such a condition, humans' innocent propensities begin to contradict their sympathetic inclinations toward each other; thus, only "perpetual violence" can enforce the moral order, which itself creates resentment and discord.

As a matter of moral psychology, Diderot contends that people, even the lowliest victims, tend to blame nature rather than humans themselves for the miseries of life. People begin to believe that a number of social injustices are built into the fabric of social and political life itself, or are somehow preordained or natural, rather than viewing them as thoroughly conventional and thus subject to reform; "such is the picture of all the people of the earth, excepting, perhaps, a few societies of savages." (I, 8) Diderot's cautious qualification stems from his belief that there could be a few, less complex societies that order their social practices almost seamlessly with the most basic needs and desires of human communities such that rank injustices and pervasive conflicts between natural needs and social resources are minimal. Such is the picture of Tahiti that Diderot knowingly constructs in the *Supplément*; even there, as we have seen, such a society is by no means natural in any stereotypically utopian sense, but is rather made up of creative, cultural beings who consciously form and maintain such collective lives. Still, Diderot appears to believe that some peoples who practise relatively simple and well-ordered lifestyles *might* not suffer from the tragic slavishness that characterizes the vast majority of human societies. In a passage marked by Rousseau's influence, Diderot regrets that "[a]bsurd prejudices have perverted human reason, and even stifled that instinct that teaches animals to resist oppression and tyranny. Multitudes of the human race actually believe themselves to be the property of a small number of men who oppress them." (I, 8)

The injustices that mark European societies and that inculcate the belief that oppression is a sorry fate that is somehow inevitable or even justifiable led Diderot to bouts of pessimism. Throughout his contributions to the *Histoire*, moments of dark cynicism recur that call into question whether Europe could reform itself in the future. At times, he fears that the great revolutions that brought spectacular periods of change in the ancient world will become less common over time because the "several nations of the earth, after repeated shocks . . . seem at length totally content with the wretched tranquillity of servitude." (VI, 1) An increasing number have become reconciled with the abuses of political authority at home and with rampant injustice abroad. Diderot suggests that overthrowing or establishing governments, or avenging the natural rights of humanity, are no longer—even rhetorically—the goals of great struggles and battles; rather, political projects now only gratify the caprices of a few powerful men who want to further their realms by adding another few towns. European political elites, he argues, never seek the happiness of their people, but instead desire to augment their riches and security by raising large armies, fortifying frontiers, and encouraging increasingly violent forms of trade. Hence, he regrets that "Europe, that part of the globe that has the most influence over the rest seems to have fixed itself on a solid and durable basis. . . . The period of founding and subverting empires is past." (VI, 1) Such pessimism about the strength and durability of injustice practised both at home and abroad by European powers, and consequently the seeming intractability of imperial governance as a form of political rule, never leads Diderot to suggest that European empires should be seen as inevitable, nor does he ever relent from his searing criticism of the imperial enterprise. In part, the moments of tragic despair about the plight of European societies in the *Histoire* help to explain the scepticism that Diderot held for any claim that Europe was in a position to educate or to improve the world through imperial rule. Ultimately, however, his frustrations about the cruelties of European politics do not fully represent his analysis of the strength of the imperial order, for in less pessimistic moments, he discusses the fragility of anything humanly made, even the seemingly permanent institutional bases of entire civilizations.

Diderot argues that the process of "civilization"—the construction, maintenance, and development of social and political institutions and processes in a sedentary, agriculturally based society—tends to make peoples lose their virtue, courage, and love of independence. As we have seen, much of his criticism along these lines concerns the growing power of the state and the abuse of public, or publicly sanctioned, forms of legal, social, and clerical power. Diderot contends that the oldest civilized societies are those of Asia, which were thus the first to undergo despotism (V, 34). In contrast with the tradition of theorizing oriental despotism as a fixed category that resulted either from climate or the despotic character of the peoples of Asia, Diderot's argument that despotic gov-

ernments and societies are never destined to last follows from his belief
that no form of political rule can entrench itself permanently. All arbitrary
power, he argues, hastens its own destruction; revolutions are bound to
occur under such conditions, and they eventually restore at least some
modicum of liberty (V, 34).[27] In addition, seemingly powerful civilizations will one day unravel and end up in ruins. Reflecting upon the destitute condition of modern Peru, and its fall from grandeur to a debased
and impoverished colony, Diderot contends that even the greatest civilizations are powerless against the unforeseen, contingent character of historical change. Europe too, he asserts, will see upon its soil, arising
"upon the ruin of our kingdoms and our altars", new peoples and new
religions (VII, 28). Europe's reign over the world will not be permanent,
as if it were the crowning glory, or the end, of history:

> But as commotions and revolutions are so natural to mankind, there is only
> wanting some glowing genius, some enthusiast, to set the world again in
> flames. The people of the East, or of the North, are still ready to enslave and
> plunge Europe into its former darkness. . . . A city that took two centuries to
> decorate is burnt and ravaged in a single day. . . . You nations, whether artisans
> or soldiers, what are you in the hands of nature, but the sport of her laws,
> destined by turns to set dust in motion, and to reduce the work again to dust?
> (XIX, 12)

The apparent fatalism of such comments about the cycles and flux of
history, and the delusion of believing that any human institution or practice could last throughout the ages, never led Diderot to doubt that
humans themselves are responsible for altering their social and political
conditions for the better.

Hence, Diderot exclaims that writers should attempt to "revive those
rights of reasonable beings, which to be recovered need only to be felt!"
(I, 8) Philosophers are key to this task, he argues, for they can publicize
the sources of injustice and appeal to government officials, the "slaves"
who act as agents of royal, clerical, and commercial masters. By perform-
ing this function, Diderot proclaims that the people can then over time
"reassume the use of their faculties, and vindicate the honour of the human race." (I, 8) Diderot often acknowledges, however, the unlikelihood
that such results would follow from the writings of the *philosophes*, in
large part because powerful elites shelter themselves from any critical
commentary. Thus, it often seems like "folly", he finds, to address "our
discourse to deaf persons, whom we cannot convince of anything, and
whom we may offend" (VI, 25). Diderot's hopes appear to have focused
instead on the new societies being formed outside of Europe, those that
brought various peoples together into thoroughly new national communities. He notes, for instance, that the intermixture of peoples that results

from trade, travel, and empire, make it impossible to try to keep the blood of a nation or even a family "pure": "The purity of blood among nations, if we may be allowed the expression, as well as the purity of blood among families, cannot be more than temporary, unless kept up by whimsical or religious institutions." (V, intro.) The inevitable mixture creates a new people with a distinctive character. If ever the new peoples outside of Europe attain independence, they could, Diderot asserts, form societies that might learn the right lessons from Europe. Thus, he calls upon young "Creoles" to come to Europe to collect information about ancient mores and to take note of the productive spirit that Europeans had lost. They should "study our weakness, and draw from our follies themselves those lessons of wisdom that produce great events." (XI, 31) Strikingly, for Diderot, it is primarily Europe's mistakes from which the non-European world could profit. Pointing to the damage done both to the Americas and to European societies as a result of European imperialism in the New World, he asserts that "America has poured all of the sources of corruption on to Europe. To complete its vengeance, it [America] must draw from it [Europe] all the instruments of its prosperity. As it [America] has been destroyed by our crimes, it must be renewed by our vices." (XI, 31) Perhaps the only real hope that Diderot ultimately held was for the non-European world to seize independence themselves, and in a future post-imperial age to foster societies and transnational relationships that would avoid the brutality of Europe's modern imperial practices.

> Since the bold attempts of Columbus and of Gama, a spirit of fanaticism, until then unknown, has been established in our countries, which is that of making discoveries. We have traversed, and still continue to traverse, all the climates from one pole to another, in order to discover some continents to invade, some islands to ravage, and some people to spoil, to subdue, and to massacre. Wouldn't the person who put an end to this frenzy deserve to be reckoned among the benefactors of humanity? (XIX, 15)

Diderot's anti-imperialist arguments range from criticisms about the injustices of profit-oriented commercial enterprises abroad, and attacks upon the role of the church and missionaries, to arguments based upon the damage done to European societies by constructing and maintaining empires abroad and the impossibility of fairly and efficiently governing far-flung imperial realms, as well as claims that Europe's half-barbarous societies are hardly the model for any other country to adopt. In addition, Diderot's arguments often proceed by describing at length what he viewed to be the horrific devastation visited upon non-European peoples, and by attacking what he took to be the error of judging foreign practices and institutions, such as those of hunting and pastoral peoples, only by the standards of one's own society. The basic elements behind the various arguments of Diderot's anti-imperialist political theory include the idea of a basic human dignity that all humans share, in part because of their individual freedom, sociability, and ability to reason and communicate about justice. Along these lines, I have argued that his concept of a general will of humanity is the ethical touchstone of a number of his political arguments. The second key component concerns the idea that humans are fundamentally cultural agents—that is, that they are social creatures who craft, maintain, and reform social and political practices and institutions. As we have seen, Diderot develops this understanding with regard to Tahitian society in the *Supplément* as well; in the *Histoire*, this contextualized and pluralistic understanding of humanity plays a key role in his characterizations of non-European peoples and in his arguments against European empires. A third key feature of Diderot's anti-imperialism balances his commitment to cross-cultural moral norms with the view that whole peoples, as well as many of their practices and institutions, are morally incommensurable; that is, they cannot be rank ordered as definitively inferior or superior. Each of these elements alone undercuts imperialist conceits, but taken together they form a philosophically powerful response to defenders of European empire. Diderot's anti-slavery and anti-imperialist political thought was widely read and discussed by his contemporaries, for Raynal's *Histoire* became one of most popular underground books of the eighteenth century. It is not surprising, then, that Kant and Herder appear to have read it; as we will see, their anti-imperialist political philosophies are, to a remarkable degree, cut from the same cloth. They too treat humans as cultural agents and interweave commitments to moral universalism and moral incommensurability in the course of their arguments against European imperialism.

Four

Humanity and Culture in Kant's Politics

THE eighteenth century marks a crucial moment in the development of humanitarian intellectual thought, by which institutions and practices such as slavery and imperialism, along with their underlying ideologies and various justifications, begin finally to undergo critical scrutiny from a legion of European political thinkers. In the preceding chapters, I have argued that the philosophically most robust, and historically most innovative, forms of early humanitarianism theorize the category of the human being as fundamentally social, cultural, and plural. In contrast, we have seen that other Enlightenment-era thinkers like Baron Lahontan and Rousseau, who present stripped-down accounts of a coherent, underlying natural humanity (an undifferentiated essence shorn of all 'artifice', of all cultural and social attributes) are more likely to dehumanize (not in intent, but in effect) at least some non-European peoples. In part, these philosophical anthropologies failed to yield a sustained and thoroughgoing criticism of the imperial activities of European states because they were conceived in light of a recurring anthropological image of New World peoples as mechanized and instinct-driven creatures, beings whose destruction, enslavement, and abuse were thus unlikely to elicit the sympathy and moral outrage necessary for the development of a more inclusive, anti-imperialist political theory. Hence, mutually reinforcing philosophical and anthropological assumptions and arguments stood in the way of a more genuinely inclusive politics, one that in distinct yet broadly similar respects Diderot, Kant, and Herder began to theorize.

There is an ironic and paradoxical character to the story that I have told thus far. Prima facie, it would seem that a stable bedrock of universal qualities (however thin) would best ground a humanitarian ethic, for it would seem that such an ethic would require a fairly stable delineation of a human essence that we share as humans and that we could appeal to in our conviction that we are all, at bottom, similar beings with an equal moral worth. But, in fact, the more that political thinkers treated the universal category of humanity as socially embedded at a fundamental level and as necessarily marked by (what we would now call) cultural difference—that is, the more that differences among humans were viewed as integral to the very meaning of humanity—the more likely it became that foreign, and in particular non-European, humans were accorded moral respect *as humans*. Hence, the more the universal category of the human was particularized, the more meaningful and robust it became in moral practice. Put somewhat differently, the acknowledgement of others as social and cultural beings helped to foster respect for actual, concrete others as human beings. In addition to this understanding of human nature and human diversity, a further idea that enabled not only humanitarian perspectives, but also an anti-imperialist politics, was sometimes developed: entire peoples and a number of their practices and institutions are incommensurable and, thus, cannot be ranked in a hierarchy or judged as inferior or superior. We saw in the last chapter that Diderot offered one version of these views. In this and the next two chapters, we will encounter two other variations of such arguments in the writings of Kant and Herder.

In this chapter, I turn to the late eighteenth-century writings of Immanuel Kant, a figure who, in many respects, represents well the spirit (and perhaps even some of the letter) of Diderot's anti-imperialism. Kant probes more deeply, however, into the distinctively *human* character of reason and freedom through which cultural differentiation is itself produced and transformed. In the *Critique of Pure Reason*, Kant famously lists what he takes to be the three most fundamental philosophic questions that concern speculative and practical reason: what can I know? what ought I to do? what may I hope?[1] (A805/B833) Kant qualifies this claim in the *Logic* by proclaiming a fourth question, "what is the human being?", which, he explains, simply encompasses the former three questions under a larger heading (9:25). In one respect, then, according to his own understanding, the question of humanity encompasses Kant's entire philosophic worldview. Yet, in a more specific sense, the conceptualization of humanity in Kant's practical philosophy details specific aptitudes and characteristics that shape his diagnoses of the ills of modern society, his responses to these in terms of how we ought to reform our unjust social conditions, and his assessment of what oppressed humans may be able to hope for in a distant political future. It is this specifically moral and political sense of 'humanity' that I discuss in this chapter, and that returns us again to the constellation of concepts that surrounds the eighteenth-century discourse on human unity and diversity: human nature, culture, sociability, moral psychology, progress, and imperialism. In considering these issues, I offer a portrait of Kant's view of the human 'self'—that is, of the human subject or of what fundamentally constitutes the human being—as well as Kant's understanding of the sources of human diversity, which I relate to his broader moral and political thought. Against the widespread view that Kant conceptualizes humans as fundamentally disembodied, metaphysical beings, who are free of social and cultural attachments, I argue that he understands humans as constitutively social and cultural agents who diversely reflect upon, make choices according to, and transform the concrete and plural worlds of experience into which they are born. In the next chapter, I delineate in more detail the political effects of this philosophical theory of humanity, freedom, anti-paternalism, and incommensurability, especially with regard to European imperialism. Kant's understanding of human unity and diversity forms the basis upon which he condemns imperialism and articulates a cosmopolitan conception of global diversity, which defends, against the paternalism of European imperial powers, non-European peoples' freedom to organize their societies and to practise their collective lifestyles in the manner that they see fit.

This chapter focuses on the variety of meanings of, and roles performed by, the concept of 'humanity' in Kant's thought in general, with special emphasis placed on his moral and political theory. I begin with an interpretation of the *Conjectures on the Beginning of Human History* and argue that, for Kant, human beings are fundamentally cultural beings, creatures who constitutively possess what I have called "cultural agency". In the second section, I contend that Kant views *distinctively human* activities as necessarily plural, contextualized by social experience, and, from the standpoint of happiness or satisfaction, incommensurable. One of my key interpretive claims is that Kant moves away from his earlier contention in the *Groundwork of the Metaphysics of Morals* that all non-moral, nonautonomous willing is simply heteronomous. Thus, instead of simply contrasting heteronomy and autonomy, Kant begins to develop an understanding of 'humanity', or cultural agency, that fills the conceptual space between them. In particular, I show how cultural agency presupposes a particular doctrine of practical reason and freedom that I specify with reference to *The Metaphysics of Morals*. Further developing this theme in the third section, I interpret crucial passages in *Religion within the Boundaries of Mere Reason* and compare Kant's accounts of 'humanity' and 'personality', along with their respective accounts of freedom and reason. In the section on Kant's social criticism, I argue that Kant's more rarefied understanding of freedom and controversial account of practical reason (those associated with 'personality') are motivated by his moral concerns about social inequality and the vulnerability of cultural agency. Kant's most abstract presentation of universalism is thus theorized as fundamentally an expression of moral egalitarianism and social criticism, rather than simply an attachment to rationalism per se. I interpret Rousseau's influence on Kant in this context.

In the fifth section, I elucidate the concept of 'dignity' and show how it is related to a second understanding of humanity: personality conceptualized as an 'intellectual' or 'noumenal' humanity. I then turn in the next section to the concept of noumenon by examining how and why it is deployed in the *Critique of Pure Reason*. I show that it represents one of Kant's conceptual weapons *against* metaphysics. Human dignity is thus revealed as both a representation of the finitude of human reason and a bulwark against social and political injustice, rather than an affirmation of metaphysical essences or a nonexperiential 'world'. In the following section, I examine Kant's understanding of an 'aesthetic humanity' and its relationship to the cultural activities of modern societies, as well as to his social and political concerns. In particular, I examine what Kant sees as the sociable qualities of taste, beauty, and the communicability of aesthetic judgements, and their political import in cultivating a cosmopolitan disposition of moral reciprocity. I then explore in the eighth section how Kant's understanding of humanity as cultural agency structures his political theory and philosophy of history. This provides a means of responding to the classic, vexed question about the relationship between Kant's contractarian (positivist) justification of the rule of law as such and the moral (normative) picture of republicanism and an international federation of states. I argue that, for Kant, European states are minimally legitimate because they secure agreements and contracts that constitute the realm of 'acquired rights', and that this can be theorized from a social contract doctrine, but that they should also be roundly criticized for often failing to respect the one 'innate right' of humanity: freedom, specifically the cultural agency that constitutes humanity itself. Turning to his philosophy of history, I contend that Kant's understanding of progress is meant to work precisely at the level of cultural humanity, not at the level of moral principle or of historical prognosis. By drawing upon and attending to human imagination and experience, his philosophy of history constitutes a narrative that seeks to foster the hope necessary for future political action and reform. This stands in sharp contrast, I will argue, to philosophical histories and theories of progress that justify European rule over non-European peoples in the course of presenting triumphalist accounts of the rise and ultimate superiority of European civilization.

This detailed view of Kant's concept of humanity and its various roles in his moral and political thought provides the conceptual background for an intensive examination in the next chapter of his account of global diversity and anti-imperialism.

Humanity as Cultural Agency

The starting point of this chapter consists of a deceptively simple question. What precisely is Kant referring to when he uses the term "humanity" (*Humanität, Menschheit*)? More specifically, when Kant contends that we should never treat the humanity in our persons simply as a means, but always also as an end in itself, what is it that we are being asked never to abuse and always to respect morally? Understanding Kant's distinctive senses of the concept of humanity enables us to appreciate better his ethical injunction, and in ways that reveal insightfully his concept of culture, his appropriation of and response to Rousseau, the connection between his aesthetics and morality, and the cosmopolitan political theory that weaves these various strands together into a unified and open-ended moral vision.

Kant's first significant published discussion of humanity's most salient and distinctive features takes place in a lively historical essay, *The Conjectures on the Beginning of Human History* (1786). Kant explicitly proclaims the almost wholly conjectural nature of his enterprise. Conjectures, he argues,

> should not present themselves as a serious activity but merely as an exercise in which the imagination, supported by reason, may be allowed to indulge as a healthy mental recreation. Consequently, they cannot stand comparison with a historical account which is put forward and accepted as a genuine record of the same event. . . . (8:109)

A "journey" taken "on the wings of imagination", however, would seem to require an orientation of some kind in order to avoid becoming an entirely random or frivolous excursion. Kant's use of the book of Genesis as a "map" underscores the hypothetical nature of this work; it also illustrates a speculative mode of thinking that he elaborates and defends at the opening of the essay and that he deploys similarly in his reflections about historical progress.[2]

Given Kant's frequent references to Scripture, it is important to underscore the metaphorical usage of Genesis, which otherwise could be misleading. In this context, it is worth noting that one of Kant's contemporaries, Georg Forster, believed that one of the key aims of the *Conjectures* was to defend the story of human origins in Genesis as the literal truth.[3] In fact, in using Genesis, Kant was following, but also criticizing, Herder, who also drew upon Genesis in the course of his own philosophy of history in the *Ideas Toward a Philosophy of History of Humankind*. As John Zammito has argued, the *Conjectures* as a whole is, in large measure, a polemic against Herder's popular *Ideas*, a work that Kant believed represented at times the kind of wild metaphysical flights of fancy that he had done his best to seal off from philosophical discourse in the *Critique of Pure Reason* and whose first two installments he had recently criticized in two book reviews in 1785.[4] Kant's use of Genesis, then, appears to be partly a satirical attack on Herder's more spiritual use of Scripture.[5]

Before describing some of the distinctive features of humanity, Kant explains that humans are to be understood at the outset of his conjectural history as already having developed significant physical and social skills. Drawing upon Genesis, he hypothesizes an original human pair in order to unfold his arguments. Kant notes that he "imagine[s] them not in their wholly primitive natural state, but only after they have made significant advances in the skilful use of their powers." Thus, "the first human being" could stand, walk, speak, talk ("speak with the help of coherent concepts"), and "consequently *think*." Kant demurs from speculating about how humans could possibly have reached this physical and cognitive level. He contends that "the reader might find too many conjectures and too few probabilities if I were to try to fill this gap, which presumably occupied a considerable interval of time." (8:110) As we will see, Kant's method relies upon a conjectural ability to create a story of origin and development that can be discerned from current evidence—"the guidance of experience as mediated by reason"—and so the hypotheses made, while by their very nature always hypothetical, can at least, in Kant's view, avoid amounting to thoroughly unfounded speculations. It becomes clear at this point, therefore, that while Genesis might provide a "map", it is the work of our minds (informed both by experience and imagination) that will do the travelling; the reader can judge, Kant notes, "whether the route which philosophy follows with the help of concepts accords with that which the Bible story describes." (8:110) In addition to avoiding hypotheses wholly unconnected to what can be at least partly justified according to our experiences of human life, Kant also notes briefly that a wholly primitive description of humanity simply *cannot* be a guide for ethical thinking. "I wish merely", Kant declares, "to consider the development of human behaviour from the ethical point of view, and this necessarily presupposes that the skills in question are already present." (8:111) From this claim emerges a key difference between Kant's and Rousseau's approach toward the theorization of human nature, one that, as I will later discuss, explains much of their political divergences. There may indeed be an interesting story to tell about the development of humans' basic cognitive, physical, and social skills (of the kind Rousseau attempts to describe in the early portions of his *Discourse on Inequality*), Kant thinks, but such a narrative would have no bearing on our ethical self-understanding. In what appears to be a consideration of the state of knowledge in his day, Kant suspects that such stories, like those attempting to explain the very existence of human beings, would amount to "wild conjectures" that "cannot be deduce[d] from prior natural causes". (8:110) The fundamental point, however, is that they would be entirely irrelevant to an ethical understanding of humanity. Ethical reflection, for Kant, takes as its *starting* point a particular set of shared aptitudes that lie well beyond Rousseau's portrait of primitive or original humanity. Rousseau's classic complaint against earlier social contractarians and their states of nature in the *Discourse on Inequality* is that previous thinkers had not gone back far enough to discern humans' true nature. But to venture speculatively *so* far back, Kant implies, is to leave the human world entirely, and in a manner that could generate nothing of ethical value for humans today.

Kant delineates four hypothetical moments of human development that allow him to model what he takes to be the most distinctive and ethically salient characteristics of humanity. The animal creature he sets up as a foil to the human being is instinctively driven. The movement from animality to humanity is one toward freedom and culture. First, Kant draws metaphorically upon Genesis to describe the human power to create desires, to imbue a particular thing or activity with value. At first, Kant writes, one can imagine creatures guided solely by instincts that, among other things, allow them "to sense in advance whether a given food is suitable for consumption or not." (8:111) Eventually, however, humans begin to engage in comparisons that lead them to foods that only resemble those that they are drawn to by instinct; or, their curiosity may have been piqued by noticing another animal eating such unfamiliar foods. Kant notes that "it is a peculiarity of reason that it is able, with the help of the imagination, to invent desires which not only *lack* any corresponding natural impulse, but which are even *at variance* with the latter." (8:111) Basic instincts that help us to survive continue to exist, but alongside a rational and imaginative ability that opens up "an infinite range of [desirable or valuable] objects". (8:112) In treating humans as the creator of values, Kant emphasizes the dangers involved in such "experiments". The ignorance of the possibly harmful "hidden properties" of newly desirable objects, the "remote effects" (the contingent, unintended consequences) of acting in ways not brought about immediately by instinct, and—following Rousseau—the generation of "superfluous" (and potentially enslaving) needs, yield a sense of "anxiety and fear". Humans, as creative beings, stand "on the edge of an abyss." Still, whatever the actual or potential harms, this development was "enough to open man's eyes": "He discovered in himself an ability to choose his own way of life without being tied to any single one like the other animals."

The second feature of human distinctiveness also concerns the creative use of imagination and reason. Using the symbol of the apple, Kant moves from instincts of preservation, most notably for food, to sexual instincts "by which nature ensures the survival of each species". The fig leaf metaphorically represents reason and imagination moulding a given instinct such that it is "withdrawn from the senses". While the "sexual stimulus" for animals is sharp, transient, and satisfied quickly, humans have imaginatively transformed sexual desire into a more moderate but also a more "prolonged and even increased" desire. Kant argues that rendering "an inclination more intense and lasting by withdrawing its object from the senses already displays a consciousness of some rational control over the impulses" (8:113). By proscribing the immediate arousal of sexual instinct, humans transform it creatively into a complex, aestheticized desire. "*Refusal*", Kant writes, "was the device which invested purely sensuous stimuli with an ideal quality", and hence marks the transformation of sexual appetite "from a feeling for the merely agreeable to a taste for beauty". Related to this transformation are the dynamics of social relationships that Kant views as central for ethical life. The increasing interaction among individuals who confer value not only upon nonhuman objects, but also upon each other, fosters a "sense of decency", a concern about being able to inspire respect from others and avoiding others' contempt. What Rousseau had castigated as the development of *amour propre*, the vanity that corrupts the inherently good nature of asocial, natural individuals, is described by Kant as "the first incentive for man's development as a moral being". Kant's discussion in the *Conjectures* makes clear that humans' creative powers and sociability are by no means necessarily productive of ethical ends. Rather, as I later show, Kant appropriates much of Rousseau's pessimism about modern society while maintaining concomitantly that the human potential for more freedom and less injustice lies in the very sociability that has tended to enslave us. It is the sense of decency that is found among social beings, even if only fleetingly and for vain ends, that constitutes "the proper foundation of all true sociability". Accordingly, Kant concludes that, from an ethical perspective, in spite of the social ills and the harm to individuals that this development unleashes, it "is more important than the whole endless series of subsequent cultural developments."[6]

Anticipation of the future constitutes the third differentiating aspect of humanity. On the one hand, this allows humans to plan for the future, "for remote objectives", but it also serves as "the most inexhaustible source of cares and worries which an uncertain future evokes, and from which all animals are exempt". Though Kant here goes on to discuss the fear of death itself, his more general concern (later in the *Conjectures* and in his other philosophical-historical writings) is that the use of our powers of memory and imagination can lead to a withdrawal from active, public life. In moments of despair arising from thoughts of continued hardship and the ills of modern life in particular, Kant feared that individuals would often grudgingly accept a future of living under oppressive social and political conditions and view them as unchangeable or natural features that are intrinsic to human life. As I later argue, the primary aim of Kant's philosophy of history is to present another conjectural story in order to foster the hope—and, from the standpoint of moral psychology, the empowerment—needed for individuals themselves to bring about social and political reform.

The fourth development describes the "obscure" realization that since human beings are constitutively cultural beings, each human can then "claim to be an end in himself, to be accepted as such by all others, and not to be used by anyone else simply as a means to other ends." (8:114) Morality, as properly understood in Kant's view, arises from the gradual understanding of this basic anthropological fact. Kant speculates that the moral egalitarianism of viewing not only oneself, but all humans, as equally endowed with the capacity for cultural agency may have originally arisen because of a sense of difference from, and superiority over, other animals (8:114). In any case, it is the awareness of our "equality with all rational beings, whatever their rank" that engenders what we might now call a humanitarian moral sensibility.

As we have seen, a being with culture is one who can create desires, values, and ideals, a being who can inscribe meanings and idealizations of beauty on to the world, and one who can anticipate the future. The *Conjectures* models a fundamental idea in Kant's thought that is not often appreciated: that "humanity", as a set of distinguishing and constitutive capabilities and powers, consists of *cultural agency*. In Kant's view, human beings are fundamentally cultural beings. But what underlies these distinctively human features? What about them imbues humanity with a worth that, as a matter of moral principle, should never be abrogated? Answering this requires a precise delineation of the particular kinds of freedom and reason that Kant associates with cultural agency.

Cultural Freedom and Embedded Reason

In the *Groundwork of the Metaphysics of Morals*, the second of Kant's three descriptions of the categorical imperative runs as follows: "So act that you use humanity, whether in your own person or in the person of any other, always at the same time as an end, never merely as a means." (4:429) Kant specifies what an end in itself refers to—that is, what constitutes humanity—only very briefly: "rational nature exists as an end in itself." (4:428–29) So in respecting the humanity in a person we are respecting "rational nature", and, by implication, the kind of freedom that is linked to rational nature. This, of course, is not much help in specifying more precisely what it is that should be respected, and, in addition, why we ought to respect it. In an introductory section of *The Metaphysics of Morals* (1797) entitled "On the Relation of the Faculties of the Human Mind to Moral Laws", Kant finally disaggregates the concept of freedom (and, accordingly, the concept of practical reason) that he had defined in the *Groundwork* (1785) and the *Critique of Practical Reason* (1788) in the most general terms.

Under the overarching concept of the faculty of desire, Kant elaborates the specific kind of freedom of which cultural activity is the manifestation. The faculty of desire itself is simply "the faculty to be, by means of one's representations, the cause of the objects of these representations." (6:211) To the extent that our desires can be understood as related to human *faculties*—and not simply, for instance, to physiological impulses—we ourselves are the sources of such desires.[7] In very general terms, then, what Kant refers to as culture (as a constitutive trait or condition) is possible because humans possess the faculty of desire. Kant then analyzes this faculty more closely in a manner that specifies the particular aspect of this faculty, and the accompanying understanding of freedom, that gives rise to culture:

> The faculty of desire in accordance with concepts, insofar as the ground determining it to action lies within itself and not in its object, is called a faculty to *do or to refrain from doing as one pleases* [*nach Belieben*]. Insofar as it is joined with one's consciousness of the ability [or capacity, *des Vermögens*] to bring about its object by one's action it is called *choice* [*Willkür*]; if it is not joined with this consciousness its act is called a *wish*. (6:213)

In wishing or in choosing to do or to have something, we engage in a form of practical reasoning that determines the objects of our actions (or wishes), of what we think will please us. As with the *Conjectures*, Kant describes a purely determined animal and the character of its choices against which he conceptualizes *human* choice: "[t]hat which can be determined only by inclination (sensible impulse, *stimulus*) would be animal choice (*arbitrium brutum*). Human choice, however, is a choice that can indeed be *affected* but not *determined* by impulses" (6:213). This is a crucial point, for it indicates a form of freedom—distinctively human freedom—that is neither wholly heteronomous nor autonomous.[8] Rather, human choice is influenced by instinct and one's surroundings, but given our *human* freedom not entirely so. Kant then notes that "[f]reedom of choice is this independence from being determined by sensible impulses; this is the negative concept of freedom." (6:213) Again, the kind of freedom that issues in cultural values and activities is thus influenced by our basic instincts and impulses without being guided entirely by them. Moreover, as I discuss below, it is a freedom that is *necessarily* influenced (though not wholly determined) by our particular experiences. It is thus a social and cultural freedom, one that is, by implication, also socially and culturally embedded in the sense that our experiential surroundings provide the resources for these decisions.

Given that the freedom underlying cultural activity is negative in character (that is, it consists of the open space, as it were, that otherwise would be determined largely by our biological instincts), with what materials do we make such decisions as to how to live, what to desire, and how to achieve particular ends or goals? Kant provides a contextualized and pluralistic account of the sources from which humans make decisions of value that is worth quoting at length:

> Only experience can teach us what brings us joy. Only the natural drives for food, sex, rest, and movement, and (as our natural predispositions develop) for honor, for enlarging our cognition and so forth, can tell each of us, and each only in his particular way, in what he will *find* those joys; and, in the same way, only experience can teach him the means by which to *seek* them. All apparently a priori reasoning about this comes down to nothing but experience raised by induction to generality, a generality (*secundum principia generalis, non universalis*) still so tenuous that everyone must be allowed countless exceptions in order to adapt his choice [*Wahl*] of a way of life to his particular inclinations and his susceptibility to satisfaction and still, in the end, to become prudent only from his own or others' misfortunes. (6:215–16)

Experience, not practical reason itself, Kant argues, furnishes the materials from which we reflect about our possible choices, reject or accept such choices, or fashion new alternatives. In part, humanity consists in consciously reflecting upon the experience that is given to us through our most basic instincts, from which we can determine how in particular we will control, transform, and satisfy such natural drives. Moreover, as our predispositions to social life and culture develop in the course of our lives, we draw upon the enlarged experiences of our surrounding worlds, including the humanly transformed worlds into which we are born.[9] Even in the stark world that Kant describes in the *Conjectures*, where we cannot draw upon the experience of a human world rich with values and desires of our making and remaking (since all desires that are not wholly instinctual in this hypothetical world must be created from scratch), the examples that Kant provides are those of experience that the original couple draws from their natural surroundings: drawing analogies to what they have seen other creatures doing, or noting the similarity of mysterious items to foods that they are drawn to by instinct. As *cultural agents*, our practical reason itself prescribes no specific values, desires, or ways of living, let alone those that might guarantee happiness or satisfaction.

> For however plausible it may sound to say that reason, even before experience, could see the means for achieving a lasting enjoyment of the true joys of life, yet everything that is taught a priori on this subject is either tautological or assumed without any [objective] basis. (6:215)

The most fundamental sense of Kant's concept of humanity, then, denotes cultural agency, and bound up with this is a form of a posteriori (experientially based) practical reason—which he delineates in *The Metaphysics of Morals*—an aspect of volition that enables humans to make choices about their values and ways of life based upon the subjective understanding of their varied experiences. The role of practical reason in its cultural mode is to choose (or to wish) among materials that are given in the world of experience, but that are understood, imagined, and valued differently by each individual, thereby engendering new combinations of materials, or as it were, new cultural possibilities for wishing and acting, as Kant's discussion of the conscious development of desires in the *Conjectures* makes clear.[10]

From Humanity to Personality

The distinctive qualities of humanity, as well as its relationship to our capacity to be moral (to treat each other with the respect we deserve as persons with humanity), can be explained further by examining Kant's discussion of such issues in *Religion within the Boundaries of Mere Reason* (1793). In the *Religion*, Kant discusses some key predispositions that characterize "the human being". These predispositions are "original", he explains, because "they belong to the possibility of human nature" as such; that is, "they belong with necessity to the possibility of this being". Kant also notes that while these predispositions can be isolated for conceptual purposes, humans are constituted by the various combinations and interrelationships among these features. Moreover, Kant asserts that his discussion is not meant to be exhaustive, but rather he attempts to identify only those predispositions that "relate immediately to the faculty of desire and the exercise of the power of choice [*Willkür*]." (6:28)

Kant outlines predispositions to animality, humanity, and personality, which refer respectively to our status as living beings, living *and* rational beings, and responsible beings. By living beings, Kant refers to the physical and mechanical drives of humans: "self-preservation", "the propagation of the species, through the sexual drive" (including the care of the resulting offspring), and "community with other human beings, i.e., the social drive" (6:26). Kant makes explicit in the *Religion*, therefore, what was assumed in the *Conjectures*, that social relations among humans are related to very idea of human beings.[11] Humanity is both living and rational in that it involves a form of practical reasoning that is bound up with the values, desires, and ideas of satisfaction and happiness of our lived experience. Thus, from this perspective, Kant believes that humans are situated in particular worlds and are made up of internal physiological drives, which inform humans' practical reasoning about their desires, values, and goals.

The predisposition to personality "is the susceptibility to respect for the moral law as of itself a sufficient incentive to the power of choice

[*Willkür*]." (6:27) We are predisposed to personality because we are capable of acting morally, of treating each other as ends in ourselves and
not merely as means; we are capable, that is, of having a "good character,
and this character, as in general every character of the free power of
choice, is something that can only be acquired" (6:27). Humans are not,
therefore, naturally moral, but are constituted fundamentally with an
ability to develop a character that will strive to act morally. Truly moral
action, for Kant, consists of treating humans as ends in themselves simply
for duty's sake; that is, for no other reason than that one ought to act in
such a manner toward oneself and every other human, rather than for
personal advantage or gain.

Here I return again to Kant's theory of freedom and practical reason in
order this time to distinguish more precisely humanity from personality.
In the *Metaphysics of Morals*, Kant argued that negative freedom, the
freedom created from not being wholly determined by one's internal
drives and impulses, consisted of a power of choice (*Willkür*). This is the
freedom of humanity (as cultural agency) and, as Kant writes in the *Religion*, it "is rooted in a reason which is indeed practical, but only as subservient to other incentives", incentives drawn, that is, from experience
(6:28). A political metaphor that accords with some of Kant's own moral
language, one used by the Kant scholar Henry Allison, illuminates most
clearly the differences between the conceptions of reason and freedom in
humanity and personality.[12] Kant's theory of volition can be understood
as involving legislative and executive functions. For both humanity and
personality, the executive function is *Willkür* (the power of choice). But
if our power of choosing executes a "law", from where does the law itself
originate? As we have seen for the conception of humanity as cultural
agency, experience furnishes our power of choice with the materials necessary for a practical choice; this constitutes a form of practical reason (an
executive) whose legislative materials, we might say, are provided by experience. But in the case of personality, *Wille* itself (simply reason, or
'pure reason') legislates to our executive power, our power of choice. As
Kant explains in the *Religion*, personality (our capability to know and to
act—for duty's sake, to the best of our ability—upon the principle that
we should never treat humanity merely as a means, but also always as an
end in itself) "is rooted in reason practical of itself, i.e. in reason legislat-
ing unconditionally."[13] (6:28)

Our cultural character or identity, that is, the anthropological fact of
our cultural strivings and activities, gives rise, though obscurely, to the
idea of the moral respect owed to all humans simply as a result of their
being human. But Kant's discussion of personality brings out another
aspect of this ethic: the explanation of *why* all humans *should* respect one
another does not issue from our social reality, but from practical reason

itself. Many ideas arise from the fact that we, in part, live in social and cultural worlds of our own making and remaking; this does not, in and of itself, Kant appears to suggest, make any of them binding upon all humans in spite of our varied inclinations, life-choices, traditions, and so forth. A moral norm of such generality, according to Kant, can arise only from practical reason itself, not from our necessarily plural and partly incommensurable experience. We can attain at least a vague *understanding* of such equality from reflecting upon ourselves as *humans*, as the *Conjectures* suggests, but such a norm of equal moral worth is *authoritative*, in Kant's view, not because of our sentiments, our psychological self-analysis, or our empirical study of others, but because of practical reason itself. In short, to use Kant's language, the idea that we should respect humanity in our persons is an a priori (reason-based), not an a posteriori (experientially-based), judgement.

Regardless of the justifications given for the validity of this argument— issues that, in this context, would take us far afield—it is crucial to understand for what reasons Kant would support such a view (of autonomy and of moral practical reason) in the first place. Recall that in *The Metaphysics of Morals* he suggests that a certain kind of practical reason and freedom exists short of presupposing that humans can be fully autonomous; we are not faced, then, with a stark choice between a heteronomous will that is wholly determined by our inclinations and a purely autonomous will, as the *Groundwork* had earlier (at least seemingly) implied. Why, then, could not a morally egalitarian view be based on this less rarefied and more common-sensical view of reason and freedom? Coming to terms with this question reveals Kant's concerns about the unequal social dynamics of cultural activity and his deep indebtedness to Rousseau. It also shows us that the idea of humanity as cultural agency, and the modest conception of practical reason and freedom that are bound up with it, remains a central component of Kant's ethical theory— it is not, in other words, set aside in favour of a more abstract vision of humanity as personality.[14]

Kant's Social Criticism: The Vulnerability and Commodification of Cultural Agency

We saw in the *Conjectures* that Kant describes humanity with reference to a hypothesized original couple's use of reason and freedom in the course of making comparisons with other animals' behaviour and the objects of their desire. In discussing humanity in the *Religion*, Kant focuses as well on comparative judgements about happiness and self-worth, but in the context of social relations in which humans observe and judge one another: "only in comparison with others does one judge oneself happy or unhappy." (6:27) Just as he discusses in the *Conjectures* the rise of honour and some of its benefits (to which I return later), Kant argues in the *Religion* that the "self-love" that arises from the predisposition to humanity engenders "the inclination *to gain worth in the opinion of others*, originally, of course, merely *equal worth*: not allowing anyone superiority over oneself" (6:27). The features that constitute humanity, then, give rise to a sense of worth: self-worth and the equal worth of others. As Kant asserts in the *Conjectures*, our cultural agency is an expression—and psychologically gives rise to the idea—of our fundamental equality, that we are all equally ends in ourselves worthy of respect. The freedom and reason associated with humanity are ennobling: "man's release from the womb of nature . . . [engenders] a change of status [from animality to humanity] which undoubtedly does him honour". But, Kant notes, "it is fraught with danger" (8:114). The danger consists principally in the exploitative social practices and beliefs—what, Kant writes, "can also be named [the] vices of *culture*"—that emerge from the use of memory, imagination, practical reason, and freedom of choice.[15] From the cultural agency that distinguishes us as beings with humanity "arises gradually an unjust desire to acquire superiority for oneself over others." (6:27) The social reality of humanity's equal worth is thereby, at best, jeopardized and, at its all too frequent worst in Kant's view, debased.

Kant's social criticism, especially in connection to the concept of culture, is evident clearly in the second part of the *Critique of Judgement* (1790), the "Critique of Teleological Judgement". In accord with his previous use of the term, Kant describes culture as "man's aptitude and skill for [pursuing] various purposes for which he can use nature (outside or within him)." (5:430) Kant again differentiates humans from animals in light of this capacity, and emphasizes both the reasoning and volitional properties that engender humans' capacity for culture: "Man is indeed the only being on earth that has understanding and hence an ability to set himself purposes of his own choice" (5:431). Kant's understanding of culture is thus bound up with freedom—*Willkür*, the power of choice—when we consider it conceptually, yet in reality, in modern societies at least, it often generates social practices and opinions that disempower humans. To elaborate this criticism, Kant develops the concept of "culture as skill", which appears to refer not to the general disposition toward cultural activities that constitutes humanity as such, but to the highly differentiated needs, desires, and practices within a complex society.[16] For these reasons, Kant sometimes uses the term 'culture' to refer to the cultural activities of settled societies—for the German word *Kultur* refers both to the cultivation of our natural capacities and to the cultivation of lands (agricultural cultivation). As we have seen, however, Kant also describes humanity as constitutively cultural—that is, he holds that all humans per se are cultural agents.[17]

In discussing Kant's understanding of the reason and freedom that make possible cultural agency, I argued that the materials that inform humans' power of choosing as cultural agents (which are themselves transformed through their actions) are humans' natural drives and the social worlds in which they live. One obvious advantage of life in a modern society, from this standpoint, is that there are more materials, as it were, that one could transform and from which one could choose. In modern societies, then, humans would appear to possess the advantage of being more skilful and, thus, of having better developed their human capacities. If humanity refers to the power to set ends in general (not only ethical ends chosen for their own sake)—one might call this the general predisposition to skill itself—then modern societies would presumably offer the best environment within which to develop this in a particularly robust and perhaps advanced sense.[18] Kant writes accordingly that "[t]he culture of *skill* is indeed the foremost subjective condition for an aptitude to promote [*befördern*] purposes generally" (5:431). The freedom related to cultural agency is itself endangered and weakened, however, by the oppression unleashed by modern cultural activities. Most people, Kant argues, are kept in a state of dependence such that they toil without being able to draw upon and develop their agency in any meaningful way. Kant argues that

[i]t is hard to develop skill in the human species except by means of inequality among people. The majority take care, mechanically as it were and without particularly needing art for this, of the necessities of life for others, who thus have the ease and leisure to work in science and art, the less necessary ingredients in culture. These others keep the majority in a state of oppression, hard labor, and little enjoyment. . . . [O]n both sides trouble increases with equal vigor as culture progresses. . . . For the lower class the trouble results from violence from without, for the higher from insatiability within. (5:432)

The majority of people in modern societies are not, of course, animalized, for that would necessitate the very loss of cultural agency itself—their lives become mechanical "as it were" and the more creative aspects, the art, of cultural agency is not "particularly" needed in their arduous lives. By being forced "from violence without" to lead lives that can strive and desire for little beyond their appointed, menial tasks, the 'majority' of people, then, are used simply as means to others' ends. Members of the leisured class, on the other hand, have only themselves to blame for their selfish and arrogant attachment to the putatively refined activities and objects of modern life. "I cannot dispute", Kant admits ruefully, "the preponderance of evils that the refinement of our taste to the point of its idealization, and even the luxury of sciences as food for our vanity, shower on us by producing in us so many insatiable inclinations." (5:433) Rousseau's strong influence on Kant becomes obvious in such passages, and it is worthwhile to consider the egalitarian impulse it fostered in Kant's thought by his own admission.

Kant first read Rousseau intensively in the early to mid-1760s, roughly two decades before he would publish the *Critique of Pure Reason*. In a now well-known passage from his handwritten notes of this period, he proclaimed that his previously vain attachment to the life of the mind had been tempered by reading Rousseau, thereby inspiring an egalitarian commitment to the equal worth of humanity.

> I am an inquirer by inclination. I feel a consuming thirst for knowledge, the unrest which goes with the desire to progress in it, and satisfaction at every advance in it. There was a time when I believed this constituted the honor of humanity, and I despised the people, who know nothing. Rousseau set me right about this. This binding prejudice disappeared. I learned to honor humanity, and I would find myself more useless than the common laborer if I did not believe that this attitude of mine can give worth to all others in establishing the rights of humanity.[19] (20:44)

As a number of scholars have argued recently, the profound impact of Kant's reading of Rousseau can be measured by examining the resulting transformations in his moral thought and the early development of his critical philosophy and political theory.[20] Underlying all of these elements in Kant's philosophy as a whole, in part because of his reading of Rousseau, is a fundamental commitment to egalitarianism and human freedom. But the nature of this commitment—in particular, the manner in which Kant seeks to defend human dignity, on the one hand, and the precise meaning of his call for the moral respect of our shared humanity, on the other—requires further examination. In short, how do Kant's two rather distinct understandings of humanity that we surveyed thus far (humanity as cultural agency and also as personality) relate to one another?

Humanity as Dignity

Kant's various discussions of the term "dignity" (*Würde*) illustrate his concern about our humanity becoming instrumentalized solely for others' ends. For while it might seem that the duty to respect others' (and one's own) humanity is equivalent to claiming that we should respect human dignity, he uses the term humanity in two distinct senses. As we have seen, Kant distinguishes humanity from animality and personality (all three of which together constitute the human being); as I have called it, this is humanity understood as cultural agency. But when he discusses dignity, he employs a different understanding of humanity, one that corresponds solely to "personality".[21]

Kant's uses of the term 'dignity' often arise in the context of discussing self-worth. The notion of self-esteem, of properly valuing oneself, appears partly to motivate his concern about identifying humanity as something with an absolute worth. One of the key legacies of Kant's intensive engagement with Rousseau's thought is the attempt to explain how all humans are *equally* of absolute worth, for, following Rousseau, the oppressive social practices and beliefs that seem to reign in modern societies puts this equality at risk. People do not value themselves as intrinsically worthy beings, who are both capable of respecting others and who can demand such moral respect from others, because the social dynamics of modern life appear to reduce their value to one of exchange.

In the *Groundwork*, Kant discusses dignity by contrasting it with mere things that can have a price and can be exchanged, the two examples of which are items with a "market price" that appeal to our presumed needs and those with a "fancy price" [*Affectionspreis*] that appeal to our sense of taste. Kant then introduces the concept of dignity: "but that which constitutes the condition under which alone something can be an end in itself has not merely a relative worth, that is, a price, but an inner worth, that is, dignity." (4:434–35) The problem with market-oriented and aesthetically based judgements of peoples' worth consists in the inequalities, oppression, and instrumentalized relationships they foster. As we have seen, Kant argues in the *Religion* that the predispositions to humanity involve a form of 'self-love' that necessarily rests upon comparisons with others; such comparisons, which generate ideas and social practices that inculcate a view of humans' inequality, rest upon pricing humans according to the various ways in which they can be used for our purposes. In particular, "[s]kill and diligence in work have a market price; wit, lively imagination and humor have a fancy price" (4:435). Our dignity, Kant asserts, rests in our capacity to be moral, which itself, as we have seen, depends upon a conception of autonomy: "Hence morality, and humanity insofar as it is capable of morality, is that which alone has dignity. . . . Autonomy is therefore the ground of the dignity of human nature and of every rational nature." (4:435–36)

"Humanity insofar as it capable of morality" is not the same as the concept of humanity understood as cultural agency, then, but rather is simply personality. Along these lines, it should be noted that in the *Religion*, Kant describes personality as "the idea of humanity considered wholly intellectually", that is, humanity as an autonomous subject, as *homo noumenon* (6:28). Looking upon human beings as intrinsically— and equally—worthy beings in light of their personality, the condition of being subject to the dictates of practical reason (that we should regard each other as ends in ourselves) and thus their ability to be positively free (autonomous) itself is an acknowledgment of a dignified, even a holy, status. "This estimation therefore lets the worth of such a cast of mind be cognized as dignity and puts it infinitely above all price, with which it cannot be brought into comparison or competition at all without, as it were, assaulting its holiness [*Heiligkeit*]." (4:435) Humanity, considered as personality, cannot be commodified or judged inferior—it lies beyond the pale of social inequalities and oppression and, thus, Kant seems to hope, reaffirms our status as beings who should never be treated solely as means but always also regarded as ends in ourselves. Kant's rarefied conception of human dignity, therefore, derives not from a penchant for abstract, metaphysical essences—a view that itself misunderstands the very concept of noumenon, as I later argue—but arises instead from concrete social and political concerns. The concept of dignity is meant to serve as a bulwark against the commodification and brutalization of humans.[22]

But what, then, is to be protected? What does Kant want morally respected when he states that it is a categorical imperative that we should treat the humanity in our persons as an end in itself? In this context, he cannot mean by "humanity" the idea of dignity or what it is rooted in (namely personality), for personality (our capacity to be conscious of and act upon the imperative that we morally respect ourselves and others) is not what is being used merely as a means. Rather, it is our cultural agency that is abused and so it would seem that *that* is what ought to be the object of respect—yet Kant argues that is not our capacity for cultural agency that provides humans with an inner, absolute worth. Kant's discussion of servility in the "Doctrine of Virtue" of *The Metaphysics of Morals* clarifies this crucial issue, the consequences of which are important for Kant's political thought and anti-imperialist arguments.

Kant asserts that humans considered as animals, that is purely as physical beings with no practical reason, are of "an ordinary value". Even in the distinctive sense of a being with understanding—one "who can set himself ends" (humanity as cultural agency)—our capacities give us "only an extrinsic value" that is calculated in terms of our "usefulness" to others.[23] In elaborating this assertion, Kant's concerns about injustice and his egalitarianism come to the fore again: our distinctive qualities as human beings, what sets us apart from other animals, "gives one man a higher value than another, that is, a *price* as of a commodity in exchange with these animals as things". Such a system of valuation renders the worth of human beings even less than the "universal medium of exchange", since humanity's extrinsic value becomes measured solely in terms of "money" (6:434). Kant's response to this grim situation deserves to be quoted at length, for it illuminates most clearly the nuances of his ethical account of humanity:

> But a human being regarded as a *person*, that is, <u>as the subject of a morally practical reason</u>, is exalted above any price; for as a person (*homo noumenon*) he is not to be valued merely as a means to the ends of others or even to his own ends, but as an end in itself, that is, he possesses a *dignity* (an absolute inner worth) by which he exacts *respect* for himself from all other rational beings in the world. He can measure himself on a footing of equality with them.
>
> Humanity in his person is <u>the object of the respect</u> which he can demand from every other human being, but which he must also not forfeit. (6:434–35, underscoring added)

The object of our moral respect is our humanity, understood as our cultural agency. This is the aspect of ourselves that is in need of protection for it is so often, as Kant argues, abused and treated as a mere thing, as a commodity with a price. But in respecting the humanity in our person, we claim ourselves as autonomous beings who can freely give norms to ourselves. We put into practice, in Kant's view, our positive freedom and the dignity that it provides equally to every human being.[24] Put differently, the humanity that Kant asks us to respect in his categorical imperative is humanity as cultural agency; our capacity to understand and to act upon such an ethical imperative reveals our fundamental equality with all other humans as *persons*, or *homo noumena*.

On the one hand, the *object* of this moral respect is a figure amenable to current understandings of the 'self'—the socially situated, imaginative, and value-inscribing cultural agent who lives in a necessarily pluralistic world. On the other hand, with regard to the *subject* of the moral law, Kant's thought uses language that now often strikes many commentators as peculiarly rarefied, for it seemingly posits an abstractly metaphysical view of the human being. A brief examination of Kant's introduction of the term "noumenon" will help us to ascertain whether Kant's conception of humanity as personality promotes the idea of an other-worldly human essence that is detached from our social and cultural worlds.

Noumenon as the Curtailment of Metaphysics

For many who are familiar with the basic terms of Kant's thought, the concept of noumenon invariably conjures up vistas of other-worldly Platonic realms or free-floating, unencumbered apparitions. Accordingly, the noumenal character of Kant's epistemological and ethical thought is often described pejoratively as metaphysical.[25] In order to discern whether such concerns are justified, especially in light of Kant's second sense of 'humanity' as a *homo noumenon*, we need to understand why and how Kant himself uses the term. Although it is out of the question in this chapter to rehearse the epistemological framework within which Kant makes the phenomenon/noumenon distinction, a brief look at the epistemological context within which he first uses the term helps to clarify his strategy. In the *Critique of Pure Reason*, Kant argues at length that human understanding is limited cognitively to what can be known empirically, as possible objects of experience, although we are far from being simply passive receptors of what 'objectively' lies outside us. Rather, in a move that Kant himself famously described as his Copernican revolution, the human mind, through what he describes as its "categories" and "forms of intuition" (such as space and time), moulds such empirical sensory perception into a form that we then cognize as being (for example) spatial and temporal.[26] For Kant, the great benefit of such a view is that it dispelled the entire tradition of metaphysics that attempted to identify and claimed to know the essences of objects and spiritual worlds.

The problem remains, however, that we can abstractly think of the possibility of an objective knowledge of the world, of how it might 'actually' be or what its properties 'really' are behind what we can discern from our experience; we might also begin to think that we have knowledge (or could have knowledge) about what we have never experienced. From the standpoint of a "critical" philosophy, Kant argues, one should learn that we can never have any such knowledge.[27] Nevertheless, the yearning to move beyond the range of experience, the impetus for metaphysical speculation and its ostensible knowledge, is part of humans' basic desire to know themselves and their surrounding world. The problem is clearly stated at the very outset of the first edition of the *Critique*:

> Human reason has a peculiar fate in one kind of its cognitions [*Erkenntnisse*]: it is troubled by questions that it cannot dismiss, because they are posed to it by the nature of reason itself, but that it also cannot answer, because they surpass human reason's every ability.
>
> Our reason falls into this perplexity through no fault of its own. Reason starts from principles [*Grundsätze*] that it cannot avoid using in the course of experience, and that this experience at the same time sufficiently justifies it in using. By means of these principles our reason (as indeed its nature requires it to do) ascends even higher, to more remote conditions. . . . By doing this, however, human reason plunges into darkness and contradictions; and although it can indeed gather from these that they must be based on errors lying hidden somewhere, it is unable to discover these errors. For the principles that it employs go beyond the boundary of all experience and hence no longer acknowledge any touchstone of experience. The combat arena of these endless conflicts is what we call *metaphysics*. (A vii–viii)

Kant introduces the concepts of phenomena and noumena in order (1) to explain this process by which we are led beyond what we can possibly know and (2) to attempt to *contain* this process—that is, to eliminate the traditional practice of metaphysics itself.

This striving for knowledge that we can never have (but about which we are capable of speculating) is best represented for Kant by "the concept of a noumenon, i.e., of a thing that is not to be thought at all as an object of the senses but is to be thought (solely through a pure understanding) as a thing in itself" (A 254/B 310). Kant stresses repeatedly that although we can speculate about such alleged knowledge,

> in the end, we can have no insight at all into the possibility of such noumena, and the range outside the sphere of appearances is (for us) empty. I.e., we have an understanding that problematically extends further than this sphere; but we have no intuition—indeed, not even the concept of a possible intuition— through which objects can be given to us outside the realm of sensibility. . . .
> The concept of noumenon is, therefore, only a *boundary concept* serving to limit the pretension of sensibility, and hence is only of negative use. But it is nonetheless not arbitrarily invented; rather, it coheres with the limitation of sensibility, yet without being able to posit anything positive outside sensibility's range. (A 255/B 310–11)

The idea that noumenon is a "boundary concept" is often undermined by Kant's own language in describing noumena; in part, the difficulty arises in discussing noumena (which are outside the bounds of space and time) in terms that are not themselves spatial and temporal. This, of course, is impossible, so Kant tends to rely upon metaphors (e.g., that we may want to think of noumena and phenomena as two different "worlds"), which are often deeply misleading because they appear to imply that "noumenon" is a metaphysical realm or essence when, in fact, the concept of noumenon is itself introduced in order to *deny* our knowledge of anything metaphysical.[28] This is emphasized most lucidly and succinctly by Kant himself: through the concept of a noumenon, one "acknowledges not cognizing things in themselves through any categories, and hence only thinking them under *the name of an unknown something.*" (A 256/B 312)

The 'dignified' view of humanity—one defended by Kant, as I have argued, because of his egalitarian social and political concerns—is based on the finitude of our self-understanding and our knowledge of the surrounding world, not on a positive affirmation and cognition of anything outside the realm of experience. When we think of ourselves as moral persons, persons who equally possess an absolute worth that demands (categorically, without exception) our moral respect (that is, as *homo noumenon*), we are therefore only thinking of ourselves "under the name

of an unknown something." According to Kant, we cannot know precisely how it is that we are conscious of this demand and no purely empirical explanation can be given as to how it motivates our actions. Kant
defends the idea that we are intrinsically worthy beings, then, not by
theorizing a fundamental essence that underlies our experienced selves
and surroundings, but by *presuming* that an aspect of ourselves that we
cannot understand resists all attempts to turn us into mere things or
commodities.[29] Oddly, Kant's affirmation of reason's ignorance and limited power is used as the 'name' (noumenon) by which the 'unknown'
feature of ourselves, the power to know and act upon moral duty, is
presumed. In other words, despite its central importance to Kant's ethical
thought, the very basis of human dignity, the idea of a *homo noumenon*,
rests upon that which we cannot know. Many of Kant's contemporaries
recognized the modesty of this defence of the concept of human dignity,
and accordingly of practical reason. Kant's sceptically minded critique of
theoretical knowledge and his somewhat meagre vindication of practical
reason led a number of his most influential, self-described followers, such
as Karl Leonard Reinhold and J. G. Fichte, to revive the metaphysical
theorizing that Kant had done his best to destroy.[30]

Aesthetic Humanity: The Opportunities and Injustices of 'Civilized' Sociability

As we saw in the first section, "Humanity as Cultural Agency", Kant
describes humans' cultural agency as partly aesthetic in character, for it
involves inscribing the world with value and transforming humans' natural drives and the objects of their surrounding worlds not only for purposes related to survival, but also to create and to transform a plurality of
increasingly complex idealizations of beauty. Humanity as cultural agency
involves some conception of taste and beauty. But in settled agrarian
societies, in Kant's view, only a small segment of society partakes of well-
developed aesthetic lifestyles. These lifestyles, values, and practices constitute a narrower use of *Kultur* in Kant's thought, one that refers to the
aesthetic features of complex, modern societies. In these contexts, 'culture' refers to sociable practices that are partly aesthetic (they are the
source of "sensible feelings of pleasure or displeasure" about matters of
beauty and taste [6:456]) and that also occur among individuals of settled societies—this, of course, is in keeping with the etymological source
of the term 'culture' itself.[31] Thus, Kant writes about the social transformations that occur with the early development of agriculture, especially
the "rise" of "culture" (*Kultur*) and the "beginnings of art" that go
beyond the most basic "cultural developments" that characterize human-

ity as such (8:119). It is important to keep in mind, then, that just as Kant moves back and forth between two senses of humanity, he also uses *Kultur* in two distinct senses: to denote, first, cultural agency ("culture in general"), the general ability of humans to set ends for themselves in a manner that draws upon their imagination, memory, values (including aesthetic values), and surrounding experiences, and, second, the social practices of the leisured classes in what we might now call 'modern' societies, which for Kant involve, among other things, judgements of taste.

In the *Critique of Judgement*, Kant's theory of judgements of taste depend on two crucial claims, one sociological and the other anthropological and ethical. Kant argues that conceptions of charm and beauty that arouse "great interest" are possible in what (in the *Conjectures*) he describes as hunting or pastoral societies, but that "judgements of taste" depend crucially upon a sustained network of communication within which matters of decorum, beauty, and other considerations of taste can be practised, discussed, and debated. This in turn requires the settled life of an agrarian society ("civilization", the sedentary, civil life of the polis) as well as at least a somewhat leisured existence.[32] As we will see in the next section, Kant bemoans the fact that only a fraction of the individuals living in civil societies partake in the refined communicative activities of a civil society, and that such practices seem to flourish as a result of the hard labour of a majority of individuals in any state. The crucial point here, however, is that communicable judgements of taste, according to Kant, depend upon social dynamics that only a sedentary life affords. Thus, Kant contends that

> we judge someone refined if he has the inclination and the skill to communicate his pleasure to others, and if he is not satisfied with an object unless he can feel his liking for it in community with others. . . . Initially, it is true, only charms thus become important in society and become connected with great interest, e.g., the dyes people use to paint themselves (roucou among the Caribs and cinnabar among the Iroquois), or the flowers, sea shells, beautifully colored feathers, but eventually also beautiful forms (as in canoes, clothes, etc.) that involve no gratification whatsoever, i.e., no liking of enjoyment. But in the end, when civilization has reached its peak, it makes this communication almost the principal activity of refined inclination, and sensations are valued only to the extent that they are universally communicable. (5:297)

Kant maintains an ambivalent view about such "civilization" for it involves, in his view, no genuine moral progress, but a great deal of social refinement, much of which (as Rousseau also thought) is hypocritical and vain. Moreover, again like Rousseau, Kant is deeply concerned about the enormous inequality and oppression on which refined or civilized activities rest, as I discuss further in the next section. Thus, the aesthetic features of 'civilized' life in a settled society are not necessarily superior to those of nonsettled societies. Rather, Kant's contention is that the kinds of aesthetic experiences and judgements made in such societies are qualitatively distinct. Kant's opinion, then, is that hunting and pastoral peoples aestheticize aspects of the world around them (for they are humans, and thus cultural agents, who necessarily inscribe values on to the world), but that they do not lead the sedentary and leisured existence that is socially necessary for fixed spheres of communication, and thus for judgements of taste, to be at the centre of their aesthetic experience. For Kant, judgements of taste involve not simply communication, but the pleasure we feel from having such views validated, in some sense, by others; thus, settled patterns of intersubjective communication are crucial, on his view, for the practice of judgements of taste.[33] The kind of environment that he has in mind is what has come to be known as the bourgeois public sphere: salons, coffeehouses, sociable dinner parties, and other locales where 'polite', interactive discussions (those which Rousseau came to detest) could occur relatively freely, even in absolutist states like eighteenth-century Prussia and prerevolutionary France.

The eighteenth century often gave rise to many writings about such a social sphere. As Daniel Gordon has shown in his study of the language of sociability in late-seventeenth- and eighteenth-century French thought, these attempts at identifying and celebrating a 'public sphere' or 'civil society' provided a means of encouraging a society of equals under conditions of absolutist rule.[34] Located within the extreme poles of revolutionary change, on the one hand, and withdrawal from social life altogether, on the other, the conceptualization of social life as a distinct phenomenon was a preoccupation of many philosophers of the eighteenth century. As Gordon has suggested, this new mode of intellectual discourse identified and legitimized a relatively free and egalitarian space in an otherwise authoritarian and unequal society; thus, during the eighteenth century, terms like 'society', 'social', 'sociability', and 'sociable' proliferated in French intellectual and literary writings.[35] Kant was profoundly influenced by such thinking and sought to integrate it into his thought. But rather than use it as a *substitute* for an anti-absolutist politics (as was often the case in the French discourse on sociability), Kant *supplemented* his explicit support of republicanism with a social and aesthetic theory that emphasized that conditions of moral reciprocity could be cultivated through such social activities.

As Kant's second book review of Herder's *Ideas* makes clear, Europeans cannot look to their ultimate ends as humans by imitating the ostensibly natural lives of indigenous peoples. Kant criticizes Herder for appearing to hold—from the premise that Tahitians achieve their happiness more easily than Europeans, given the latter's oppressive and complex social and political institutions—that happiness is extremely difficult or even impossible to attain in civilized societies. The life that Kant believed Herder was valourizing, of "happy human beings merely enjoying themselves", amounts not to a description of the ends to which the members of sedentary, agrarian societies should work, but rather resembles the lives of "happy sheep and cattle".[36] Kant thus aimed to counter those who presented the ills of European life as so great that only the simplest pleasures of faraway lands could give humans true happiness. Such ethnographic portraits, in Kant's view, carried with them the risk that the social interactions of polite society, which were at the heart of aesthetic humanity, would no longer be valued and nurtured, even though this was necessary, in his opinion, for any moral and political progress in civilized societies to take place.[37] Kant's concern was that an increasing number of individuals, overcome with the "falsehood, ingratitude, [and] injustice" of their sedentary, agrarian societies and the fact that the social relations in such societies often led humans to do "every conceivable evil to each other", tended to celebrate seemingly magical and utopic distant lands on which one could lead a life free of the cares and injustices of civilized life (5:276). Kant's fear, then, is that writings like Herder's treatment of Tahiti would further encourage, as he writes in the *Critique of Judgement*,

> the tendency to withdraw from society, the fantastic wish for an isolated country seat, or even (in young people) the dream of happiness in being able to pass their life on an island unknown to the rest of the world with a small family, which the novelists or poets who write Robinsonades [writings in the style of Daniel Defoe's *Robinson Crusoe*] know so well how to exploit. (5:276)

Such dreams, however, take individuals away from the aesthetic activities in social settings that could at their best develop the dispositions of reciprocity and sympathy, and indirectly help to combat the very injustices of civilized societies. Like Diderot, then, Kant did not believe that versions of what Diderot satirized as the "myth of Tahiti" could be used to solve Europe's grave injustices. As we will see in the following chapter, Kant defends the right of peoples to order their collective lives as they see fit, and thus he explicitly defends the rationality and freedom (the cultural agency, and thus the fundamental humanity) of nomadic and pastoral peoples in the course of attacking European imperialism, but he also believes that the means of civilized societies could be used to alleviate their tremendous injustices. Ultimately, Kant's defence of aesthetic humanity and sociability, I will now argue, was a response to Rousseau's second *Discourse* and the pessimistic conclusion that might follow from it: that civilized societies and the forms of sociability within them were irremediably unjust and, hence, could not serve as the basis for the eventual creation of a less unjust society.

Kant connects aesthetic determinations of taste with one fundamental aspect of what it means to be a human being: social living. He asserts that since the urge toward social living is a natural propensity of all human beings, the sociability that is engendered by judgements of taste relate to this constitutive feature of humankind. The sociability and communicative practices of the leisured classes of Kant's day develop what he describes as "aesthetic humanity". These practices, in other words, pertain to "culture" as understood in a narrow sense, in distinction to "culture in general", which characterizes humanity as such. In addition to increased sociability, the refined practices of leisured townspeople foster bonds of sympathy and moral reciprocity. In part, as I have said, Kant held these views because of the French tradition of theorizing sociability, which he inherited and appropriated, but he framed this understanding in a unique manner, I argue, to provide a defence against Rousseau's objections of some of the benefits of sociably aesthetic practices.

Determinations of taste in modern societies, according to Kant, are intrinsically social in character for they involve the communication of our ideas of beauty and taste to others, as well as the nurturing of sympathy as individuals attempt to understand the aesthetic judgements of their interlocutors. In the *Critique of Judgement*, therefore, Kant argues that, from an aesthetic viewpoint,

> humanity [*Humanität*] means both the universal feeling of sympathy, and the ability to engage universally in very intimate communication. When these two qualities are combined, they constitute the sociability that befits [our] humanity [*Menschheit*] and distinguishes it from the limitation [characteristic] of animals. (5:355)

In stark contrast to such a view is Rousseau's passionately argued contention that the social aspects of life in 'civilized' societies are thoroughly vain and hypocritical. I have argued in this chapter that the egalitarian impulse that lies behind such a view influenced Kant enormously. But Kant did not appropriate wholesale Rousseau's dark assessments of the depravities and fundamental artificiality of social life itself. Given that Rousseau saw humans' sociability as thoroughly unnatural, his attempts to remedy the corruption engendered by social life either seek to remake human nature (the work of a great legislator) and to situate humans in a utopic society that appears communal (given the ideal of the 'general will') but that oddly eschews any reciprocal social deliberation, or places a more select group or individual in the hands of a wise educator (Rousseau himself) who, for instance, raises Emile by sheltering him from the ravages of social life. In the *Anthropology*, Kant writes,

> [A]s for Rousseau's hypochondriac (gloomy) portrayal of the human species when it ventures out of the state of nature, we need not take this as a recommendation to re-enter the state of nature and return to the woods. What he really wants to do is to show the difficulty that reaching our destiny by way of continually approximating to it involves for our species. . . . Rousseau did not really want man to *go* back to the state of nature, but rather to *look* back at it from the step where he now stands.[38] (7:326)

Kant interprets Rousseau, therefore, as being acutely aware of the challenges of improving humanity's moral situation. But the condition that we are to look back upon for Kant is rather different than the original state of nature that Rousseau describes. As I have discussed, Kant asserts that a social drive, a predisposition toward communal relations, is constitutive of humanity. And in the *Doctrine of Right*, Kant's hypothetical description of a state of nature (a condition without the public rule of law) is *not* asocial: "a state of nature is not opposed to a social but to a civil condition, since there can certainly be society in a state of nature, but no civil society (which secures what is mine or yours by public laws)."[39] (6:242) Since the social aspects of human life are not, for Kant, at bottom unnatural, he is willing to craft a more sympathetic view of the potential benefits of the social dynamics within modern societies than Rousseau could have theorized.

Although Kant does not criticize Rousseau explicitly on this issue (perhaps, one suspects, because he held him in such high regard), his argument in the *Anthropology* against Swift's caustic remarks about human virtues could well apply to Rousseau:

> All the human virtue in circulation is small change: one would have to be a child to take it for real gold.—But we are better off having small change in circulation than no money at all; and it can eventually be converted into genuine gold, though at a considerable loss [i.e., with much extra effort]. It is high treason against humanity to issue these coins as *mere counters* having no value at all, to say with the sarcastic Swift: "Honor is a pair of shoes that have been worn out in the mud. . . ." (7:152–53)

The "small change" that might not compensate for the oppression unleashed by modern societies, but that at least provides some productive energies that could coalesce into genuine social and moral reform, rests in part upon conceptions of honour and decency, beauty and taste, and in general upon the sociability that accompanies these social practices, norms, and judgements.[40] For instance, conceptions of taste (in music, painting, sculpture, architecture, horticulture, rhetoric, poetry, and so forth) rely upon social communication and so foster interconnections among individuals that encourage at the very least relatively humane, if not intentionally moral, behaviour.[41] Kant argues accordingly that "[m]aking a man well-mannered as a social being falls short of forming a morally good man, but it still prepares him for it by the effort he makes, in society, to please others (to make them love or admire him).—In this way we could call taste morality in one's outward appearance" (7:244). Rousseau's *amour propre* is thus transformed by Kant into a potentially beneficial characteristic.[42]

Kant believes that the vocation of humanity itself is to work toward, however slowly and hesitantly (and, thus, in a manner that gradually approximates), an ideal form of sociability, a cosmopolitan condition in which humans can interact with one another peacefully and nonexploitatively both within and among their respective societies.[43] The refined activities and norms of social life in civilized societies, Kant hopes, might contribute modestly to this long-term cosmopolitan goal. In *The Metaphysics of Morals*, Kant describes such social interaction as a "duty of virtue" in a remarkable passage that encapsulates the recurring theme of "aesthetic humanity" in his writings:

> [O]ne ought to regard . . . [the] circle drawn around one as also forming part of an all-inclusive circle of those who, in their disposition, are citizens of the world—not exactly in order to promote as the end what is best for the world [*das Weltbeste*] but only to cultivate what leads indirectly to this end: to cultivate a disposition of reciprocity—agreeableness, tolerance, mutual love and respect (affability and propriety, *humanitas aesthetica et decorum*) and so to associate the graces with virtue. . . .
>
> These are, indeed, only externals or by-products (*parerga*), which give a beautiful illusion resembling virtue that is also not deceptive since everyone knows how it must be taken . . . [they] are, indeed, only tokens; yet they promote the feeling for virtue itself by a striving to bring this illusion as near as possible to the truth. By all of these, which are merely the manners one is obliged to show in social intercourse, one binds others too; and so they still promote a virtuous disposition by at least making virtue fashionable. (6:473–74, underscoring added)

Kant's consideration of sociability and its moral dimension should, along with so many other aspects of his thought, dispel the still common view that he ignores or slights the role of emotions, passion, and feeling in moral judgement and activity. In fact, although he clearly believes that engaging in behaviour that is undertaken simply out of principle is alone worthy of any real moral merit, he also contends that it is both impossible to tell when this is done and, in any case, unlikely to occur given the complexity of humans' moral psychology. Thus, the bonds of love, sympathy, sociability, the moral dimensions of beauty, and the impact of narratives (see the final section) upon the human imagination all play significant roles in his understanding of ethical life. Kant attempts to identify a variety of nonmoral motivations and contexts that help humans to lead a life that at least *conforms* outwardly to attitudes and actions that respect others as ends in themselves, even if not from principled motives. Thus, one must work with, and not wholly against (as with Rousseau), aesthetic humanity (by cultivating sociability and a compassionate character) to create a "disposition of reciprocity" and a concern for others that, at least on the surface, accords with moral behaviour.

It is important to note that all of these efforts are on the level of cultural humanity, of cultural agency, for they depend, in varying degrees, upon the powers of memory, imagination, and beauty and thus attend to the experiences that contextualize and inform human practices and judgements, not simply upon rational calculations. Elaborating his earlier claims about aesthetic humanity, Kant argues in the *Doctrine of Virtue* that there is a duty—of a conditional or indirect kind, given that it is not a duty from moral principle—to attempt to make oneself susceptible to the emotional (or "aesthetic") feelings that help bring about outwardly moral judgements and acts.[44] Kant explains that this works at the level of humanity because it concerns humans as reasonable beings who are also structured by the stirrings of care and affection that one can find in animals as well, rather than referring to humans as purely rational beings (or persons).

> *Sympathetic joy* and *sadness* (*sympathia moralis*) are sensible feelings of pleasure or displeasure (which are therefore to be called "aesthetic") at another's state of joy or pain (shared feeling, sympathetic feeling). Nature has already implanted in human beings receptivity to these feelings. But to use this as a means to promoting active and rational benevolence is still a particular, though only a conditional, duty. It is called the duty of *humanity* (*humanitas*) because a human being is regarded here not merely as a rational being but also as an animal endowed with reason. Now, humanity can be located either in the *capacity* [*Vermögen*] and the *will* to *share in others' feelings* (*humanitas practica*) or merely in the *receptivity*, given by nature itself, to the feeling of joy and sadness in common with others (*humanitas aesthetica*). (6:456)

We have a duty, according to Kant, to help engender active sympathy by making ourselves open to the emotional receptivity to the pain or joy of others—an indirect duty, in Kant's terms, to help realize our practical humanity by cultivating our aesthetic humanity. As we have seen in this section, one way to satisfy this duty, for those who can, is to enter the sociable world of communicative sites to develop, in a parochial fashion, a character that can resemble a humane citizen of the world. Kant further elaborates the moral psychology presupposed by such duties in the following significant passage:

> [W]hile it is not in itself a duty to share the sufferings (as well as the joys) of others, it is a duty to sympathize actively in their fate; and to this end it is therefore an indirect duty to cultivate the compassionate natural (aesthetic [*äs-thetische*]) feelings in us, and to make use of them as so many means to sympathy based on moral principles and the feeling appropriate to them.—It is therefore a duty not to avoid the places where the poor who lack the most basic necessities are to be found but rather to seek them out, and not to shun sickrooms or debtors' prisons and so forth in order to avoid sharing painful feelings one may not be able to resist. *For this is still one of the impulses that nature has implanted in us to do what the representation of duty alone might not accomplish.* (6:457, emphasis added)

Aesthetic humanity, then, is a particular instantiation of humanity as cultural agency, one that could produce inequalities and injustices, but which could also, at its best, foster the social conditions for moral reciprocity.

The idea that duty itself might not accomplish much on its own leads Kant to question both the efficacy of moral principle alone and of a cosmopolitan disposition. While Kant is frequently portrayed as slighting the role of emotions and local commitments in building a moral life, passages like the one above and, in general, his defence of some forms of polite or sociable activity, suggest that he was sceptical that humans *would* (even though they *could*) act upon humanitarian moral principles alone. In a late essay, *The End Of All Things* (1794), Kant argues that love, despite its potentially parochial and prejudicial character, is nevertheless indispensable for a moral life, even though such a life can ultimately be defended morally according to how much respect is given to human beings as such (whether or not they are "one's own"). As a matter of moral psychology and of moral practice, Kant argues that there must be a mutually reinforcing sense of local and universal affections.

> Respect is without doubt what is primary, because without it no true love can occur, even though one can harbor great respect for a person without love. But if it is a matter not merely of the representation of duty but also of following duty, if one asks about the *subjective* ground of actions from which, if one may presuppose it, the first thing we may expect is what a person *will do*—and not a matter merely of the *objective* ground of *what he ought to do*—then love, as a free assumption of the will of another into one's maxims, is an indispensable complement to the imperfection of human nature (of having to be necessitated to that which reason prescribes through the law). For what one does not do

with liking [*gern*] he does in such a niggardly fashion—also probably with sophistical evasions from the command of duty—that the latter [moral duty] as an incentive, without the contribution of the former [love], is not very much to be counted on. (8:337–38)

In contemporary debates about patriotism versus cosmopolitanism, Kant is often viewed understandably as the historical standard bearer of the cosmopolitan camp.[45] What many have failed to note, however, is that Kant himself believed that while every individual should be a "friend of human beings as such (i.e., of the whole race)" (6:472), such cosmopolitan sentiments in his view are usually too thin to motivate humane behaviour. As he notes in the *Doctrine of Virtue*,

> Now the benevolence present in love for all human beings is indeed the greatest in its extent, but the smallest in its degree; and when I say that I take an interest in this human being's well-being only out of my love for all human beings, the interest I take is as slight as an interest can be. I am only not indifferent with regard to him. (6:451)

In his lectures on ethics from 1793, Kant expresses similar concerns in a discussion about "patriotism", "love for a particular group", and "cosmopolitanism".[46] He argues that group loyalty ("love for a particular group, or common obligation under a particular rule, to which there arises by custom a distinctive appearance") and cosmopolitanism ("a general love . . . for the entire human race") are both fraught with dangers. In considering "the love for societies, for orders of freemasonry, for the station one belongs to, and for sects such as the Herrenhuter [the Moravian brotherhood who in North America became known as the Hutterites]", Kant worries that such attachments "could be detrimental to the propensity for a general love of mankind" because, from the standpoint of any one member, "the class of men with whom he stands in no connection seems to become indifferent". Given the cosmopolitan understanding that many have of Kant's ethics, this should come as no surprise, but he then turns his sceptical eye toward the cosmopolitan: "the friend of humanity, on the other hand, seems equally open to censure, since he cannot fail to dissipate his inclination through its excessive generality, and quite loses any adherence to individual persons". (27:673) As in the *Doctrine of Virtue*, Kant's concern is that in loving everyone generally, the cosmopolitan loves no one in particular. Kant suggests that the kind of loyalty that might avoid such pitfalls would be that of the "cosmopolite" who possesses "a moral sense with dutiful global and local patriotism" and who "in fealty to his country must have an inclination to promote the well-being of the entire world." (27:673–74) This would stand in contrast, Kant argues, with the "error that the Greeks displayed, in that they evinced no goodwill towards *extranei* [outsiders], but included them all, rather, *sub voce hostes = barbari* [under the name of enemies, or barbarians]" (27:674). Although in his lectures on ethics Kant does not go on to elaborate the nuanced disposition he favours (to show more precisely how one might conceptualize loving humanity as such in addition to fostering local, particular ethical concerns and commitments), it should be noted that in contemplating the need for, and the possibility of, such a middle ground between the parochialism of local attachments and an empty cosmopolitanism, Kant evinces precisely the moral psychology that he had already theorized in his portrayal of sociability and aesthetic humanity in the *Critique of Judgement* and that he would later elaborate in the *Doctrine of Virtue*.

A wide variety of human behaviour and dispositions, then, that are not animated by purely moral, universal intentions—those toward which humans are drawn passionately, which generate aesthetic enjoyment and satisfaction, and which focus on local concerns (as opposed to more universal and abstract aims)—can foster humane, reciprocal, and egalitarian conditions among individuals. There are a wide variety of motivations, practices, and ideals that are not moral from the standpoint of a categorical morality, but that, from an understanding of humans' moral psychology, nevertheless further the universal goal of loving humanity much more effectively than subscribing to universal duties. Kant's approach to the possible connections between local and universal bonds is, in many respects, not unlike that of Edmund Burke (whose *Philosophical Inquiry into the Origin of our Ideas on the Sublime and the Beautiful* [1757] Kant admired greatly). Burke wrote famously in *Reflections on the Revolution in France* that

> [t]o be attached to the subdivision, to love the little platoon we belong to in society, is the first principle (the germ, as it were) of public affections. It is the first link in the series by which we proceed toward a love to our country and to mankind. . . .[47]

Kant was aware of the problems facing those who strive to love humanity as an abstraction; his understanding of concrete human beings and their complex moral psychology led him to provide an account of the actual human feelings of care, love, and respect that operated on a plane of behaviour and motivation distinct from that on which categorical moral judgements are made. To be sure, Kant did not endorse passion, inclination, emotions, and the love of 'one's own' *as such*, for he thought that such a blanket endorsement would sanction the most prejudicial and violent commitments, those that he associated with the ancient Greek enmity toward the *barbaroi* and that he would later identify at the heart of European imperialism. Instead, he believed that a passion for the local spheres of life, for the love of one's own, and for the ties of sociability *could* further humanitarian ends if they strengthened the bonds of moral reciprocity and equality and, thus, counteracted humans' proclivity toward using others as mere means. Thus, Kant articulates an approach that attends to the local spheres of life, with care for particular persons and groups, to bring about conditions or practices that accord with, and can be justified in light of, broader humanitarian principles and goals.

Humanity as Cultural Agency in Political Context: Combating State Paternalism

In this section, I begin by considering briefly why Kant believes that the aesthetic practices and sociability of modern life that I just discussed are not enough to combat deep structural injustices. In part, Kant argues that many of these oppressive inequalities are maintained by the abusive power of the state. This brings us to his explicitly political writings. To understand the political perspective from which Kant engages in a critique of modern society and politics, I examine the role that humanity as cultural agency plays in his analysis of politics within a single state. I focus on the following question: what role does anti-paternalism play in Kant's politics and how is it related to his understanding of freedom and cultural humanity? Kant identifies one innate right of humanity: the freedom that is the source of "culture in general", that is, the distinctively human freedom that is at the heart of humanity as cultural agency. He contends that states not only often fail to protect this core freedom, but they also willfully abuse it by treating individuals paternalistically. The idea of 'enlightenment' and the importance of communication in tempering and slowly reducing the power of the state underpin Kant's commitment to individual and collective self-determination. As we will see in the following chapter, Kant applies such arguments against the paternalism of modern European states in his criticisms of European imperialism.

Notwithstanding Kant's social analysis and aesthetic understanding of modern European societies, he remained suspicious of attempts to let the social interactions of (as it is now often called) civil society do the sole work, as it were, of combating the oppressions of modern life. One particularly striking example of this consists of his treatment of the duty of beneficence. The duty itself is quite straightforward: "[t]o be beneficent, that is, to promote according to one's means the happiness of others in need, without hoping for something in return, is everyone's duty." (6:453) As with many of Kant's duties of virtue, however, the duty of beneficence creates an imperfect (or wide) obligation—who one assists, how generously one provides, and how often one helps are the kinds of

questions to be answered differently by individuals according to their socially informed and ultimately diverse judgements. Immediately after having defined and defended this duty, Kant expresses reservations about
according any moral merit to the wealthy who help others in need.

> Someone who is rich . . . should hardly even regard beneficence as a mer-
> itorious duty on his part. . . . The satisfaction he derives from his beneficence,
> which costs him no sacrifice, is a way of reveling in moral feelings. (6:453)

Kant's underlying concern is not the self-congratulatory delusions of
wealthy philanthropes, but the structural injustice that lies beneath the
very need for such informal acts of charity at all. In particular, he complains that most of the societal inequality that makes the practice of beneficence such a pressing humanitarian necessity is *politically* maintained.

> Having the resources to practice such beneficence as depends on the goods of
> fortune is, for the most part, a result of certain human beings being favored
> through the injustice of the government, which introduces an inequality of
> wealth that makes others need their beneficence. Under such circumstances,
> does a rich man's help to the needy, on which he so readily prides himself as
> something meritorious, really deserve to be called beneficence at all?[48] (6:454)

Kant called for institutional reforms that might mitigate this injustice—
most notably, the abolishment of hereditary nobility and serfdom, an institution that he viewed as morally equivalent to slavery.[49] But even if
some of the most unequal and despotic state-sanctioned institutions were
eliminated, Kant believed that the power of European states would continue to be a problem to reckon with both domestically and interna-
tionally.

Any nuanced understanding of Kant's politics must come to terms
with his deeply ambivalent view of state power. On the positive side, it
secured the public rule of law, which he viewed as essential for guarantee-
ing the basic security and minimally just conditions for individuals and
their social relations, such as those involving contractual and property
relations (i.e., the protection of what Kant calls our 'acquired rights',
rights that arise because of our actions).[50] One of Kant's most basic anthropological assumptions is that humans are fundamentally conflict-rid-
den beings. As we have seen, Kant believes that humans are constituted
by a natural drive toward communal relations; nevertheless, as he asserts
in *Idea for a Universal History*, the human being is also characterized by
"a great tendency *to live as an individual*, to isolate himself, since he also
encounters in himself the unsocial characteristic of wanting to direct everything in accordance with his own ideas." (8:21) The worst forms of
brutality and the ominous sense of insecurity that our social tensions foster can be held in check, Kant asserts, by a nondespotic public power.

Given that humans are not naturally peaceable and that they at least occasionally abuse their freedom, he contends that "man is an animal who needs a master." (8:23) Yet Kant was also perfectly aware that the state was by no means a morally unproblematic arbiter in practice. He conceptualizes the basic problem as follows: while "man is an animal who needs a master",

> this master will also be an animal who needs a master. Thus while man may try as he will, it is hard to see how he can obtain for public justice a supreme authority which would itself be just, whether he seeks this authority in a single person or in a group of many persons selected for this purpose. . . . This is therefore the most difficult of all tasks, and a perfect solution is impossible. Nothing straight can be constructed from such warped wood as that which man is made of. Nature only requires that we approximate to this idea. (8:23)

Both the tone and substance of Kant's political writings seem to indicate that the modern state works reasonably well in providing the security that is necessary for protecting humans' acquired rights, most notably property and contractual rights. But not all of our rights are created externally through our actions and then secured by public power. There is, Kant argues, one innate right, "that which belongs to everyone by nature, independently of any act that would establish a right":

> *Freedom* (independence from being constrained by another's choice), insofar as it can coexist with the freedom of every other in accordance with a universal law, is the only original right belonging to every man by virtue of his humanity. (6:237)

This is precisely the kind of freedom, as we have seen, that underlies Kant's understanding of humanity as cultural agency. In Kant's political theory, the innate right of humanity rests similarly upon the protection of negative freedom, the freedom of constitutively human choice and the equality and independence that are linked to it. The rule of law and the framework of rights secured by the state ideally protect the social domain of external freedom within which our cultural agency is exercised and can flourish. A public recognition of our innate right of freedom, therefore, can safeguard the external social space and the egalitarian conditions within which the capacities and powers of humanity can develop diversely.[51] The inner motivations of actions (the ideal of persons acting morally simply for the sake of morality) is not the concern of politics, as Kant makes clear in his distinction between "right" and "virtue".[52] Politics concerns most fundamentally an ethical respect for humanity as cultural agency, and a respect for the pluralism and the conflicts that such human freedom inevitably engenders.

Consequently, political freedom does not entail the elimination of conflict. Our political goal, Kant argues, should be to construct

> a society which has not only the greatest freedom, and therefore a continual antagonism among its members, but also the precise specification and preservation of the limits of this freedom in order that it can co-exist with the freedom of others. (8:22)

Antagonism and conflict are essential components, Kant believes, of freedom itself, and politics ideally seeks not to diminish these social tensions but to foster free, lawful, and nonviolent conditions of mutual antagonism.

While acquired rights might be at least minimally safeguarded in many states, including the absolutist states with which Kant was familiar, the innate right of freedom is much more likely to be violated, *and often by the state itself.* This is a fundamental paradox in human politics, according to Kant, for humans need a public power to secure their freedom, yet this very freedom is often violated (and, at times, quite brutally) by the exercise of public power. In the second part of *The Conflict of the Faculties*, after contending that we cannot necessarily count the forces of nature on our side since humans might all be destroyed by a future global natural disaster (such as another ice age), Kant writes that natural (i.e., environmental) processes care nothing about humans:

> [f]or in the face of the omnipotence of nature, or rather its supreme first cause which is inaccessible to us, the human being is, in his turn, but a trifle. But for the sovereigns of his own species also to consider and treat him as such, whether by burdening him as an animal, regarding him as a mere tool of their designs, or exposing him in their conflicts with one another in order to have him massacred—that is no trifle, but a subversion of the ultimate purpose of creation itself. (7:89)

Attempts to discipline such abusive acts of state power, Kant fears in the *Critique of Judgement,* will be "hindered by people's ambition, lust for power, and greed, *especially on the part of those in authority*" (5:433, emphasis added). And for those hoping for reform from above, Kant notes pointedly in *Toward Perpetual Peace* that the "possession of power unavoidably corrupts the free judgement of reason." (8:369) Kant's anti-paternalism and commitment to the concept of 'enlightenment' stem principally from a concern that paternalistic and oppressive governments seek to weaken and pacify their subjects to control them, and not infrequently to abuse them, more easily. Clearly, in Kant's view, states themselves have no interest in generating "a continual antagonism" within their societies, however much humans' social and cultural lives would flourish as a result of such conditions. Instead, governments prefer "domesticated animals" for subjects, as Kant suggests in "What is Enlightenment?" Similarly, in the *Critique of Judgement*, after contending that the elaborate images and rituals of religion tend to obscure whatever worthy moral norms might be at the heart of such faith, Kant argues,

> [T]hat is . . . why governments have gladly permitted religion to be amply furnished with such accessories: they were trying to relieve every subject of the trouble, yet also of the ability, to expand his soul's forces beyond the barriers that one can choose to set for him *so as to reduce him to mere passivity and so make him more pliable.*[53] (5:274–75, emphasis added)

To counter this, Kant asserts that individuals must take action into their own hands and attempt to think and to act for themselves—to become adults and not the infants that states want them to be—for they clearly cannot simply rely upon the hope that the government will of itself promote human development, battle societal injustices, and curb its own vicious power.[54]

The cynicism about governmental power that underlies such views is often underappreciated. Indeed, Kant's political thought is built in large part upon the necessarily uneasy tension that arises from a hatred of the paternalistic, war-mongering, and imperializing states of his day, on the one hand, *and* a social contractarian affirmation of the legitimacy of the public rule of law (including that of absolutist states), on the other. Kant's conception of political affairs is clearly open-ended; he did not believe that modern European states represented or approximated a concrete and historical flowering of a hitherto unrealized rationality. This leaves open, however, the question of how one might proceed from, for instance, Prussian absolutism to a republican (a representative democratic) state. It is a little-known fact that in his *Reflexionen* (unpublished reflections) of the late 1780s, Kant supported the right to rebellion under certain conditions: when the sovereign breaks a fundamental, constitutional agreement with his people, the relationship between the sovereign and the people is no longer rightful, but rather breaks down into a state of nature, out of which a new political power must be constituted.[55] His enthusiasm for the French Revolution and what he hoped would be the birth of a large and powerful republic in Europe should come as no surprise, then, despite his late, published injunctions against revolution. Kant even defended the legitimacy of the radical political changes in France by arguing in *The Metaphysics of Morals* (1797) that King Louis XVI had given away his sovereignty to the people (and thus had transformed the French state from a monarchy to a republic) by calling the Estates-General.[56] Thus, while Kant criticized the right to revolution, he viewed the transfer of power from the French monarch to the people as legitimate, and was careful in his late political essays to criticize only one incident of the French Revolution itself: the execution of the king, a point that a number of supporters of the revolution, including Condorcet and even honorary revolutionary citizens like Tom Paine, made unsuccessfully in the heated Convention debates about the fate of the king.[57]

Despite all of this, given Kant's ultimate rejection of a right to revolution (first articulated in his 1793 essay "Theory and Practice"), the remaining political options for subjects in absolutist states became more complicated.[58] Any politics of peaceful reform, as opposed to a politics of violent rebellion, required the use of basic freedoms; however, with the death of Friedrich II (Frederick the Great) in 1786, and the much more conservative rule of his nephew Friedrich Wilhelm II and his notorious Minister of Education and Religious Affairs, Johann Christoph Wöllner, Kant viewed the situation of Prussians as increasingly restrictive, given that many of the most basic freedoms of expression and dissent became foreclosed. As Allen Wood notes,

> Wöllner's aim was to halt the spread of undisciplined apostasy among the clergy and to compel both spiritual and secular teachers to return to orthodoxy at least in their public instruction, if not in their private beliefs. On July 9, 1788, less than a week after his appointment, Wöllner promulgated an edict in the king's name covering the conduct of educators and ecclesiastics and the education of theological candidates. The edict was explicitly directed against "enlightenment" thought and pledged the removal from their offices, both ecclesiastical and professorial, of those who propagated it.[59]

Thus, set against the repressive political climate of his day, one might be able to appreciate better the vigour of Kant's defence of "freedom of the pen" and "public reason", as limited and intellectual as it might seem from a contemporary standpoint, for it appeared to Kant that these were the last precious shreds ("the single gem remaining to us") of freedom that allowed at least some criticism of state power, and without which the chances of any reform were slight. In 1786, shortly after the death of the relatively liberal Friedrich II, Kant had suspected an imminent decline in the already limited freedom of expression afforded to clergy and professors in Prussia. He defended the concept of enlightenment, as thinking for oneself, and chastised others for using their freedoms to propagate ideas that would be deemed harmful to civil life (and that could then be used as a pretext to limit further freedoms of expression). One can note the sense of desperation in the following passage from *What Does It Mean to Orient Oneself in Thinking?* in which Kant warns that not only the freedom to communicate, but also the freedom to think is capable of being crushed by the state, for free thinking crucially depends upon free communication.

> The freedom to think is opposed first of all to *civil compulsion*. Of course it is said that the freedom to *speak* or to *write* could be taken from us by a superior

power, but the freedom to *think* cannot be. Yet how much and how correctly would we *think* if we did not think as it were in community with others to whom we *communicate* our thoughts, and who communicate theirs with us! Thus one can very well say that this external power which wrenches away people's freedom publicly to *communicate* their thoughts also takes from them the freedom to *think*—that single gem remaining to us in the midst of all the burdens of civil life, through which alone we can devise means of overcoming the evils of our condition. (8:144, underscoring added)

Kant himself was eventually censured in a 1794 letter issued by the king (and signed by Wöllner) that resulted in Kant's 'choice', under pressure, to terminate lecturing and writing about religion. In language that must have been particularly loathsome to him, Kant was criticized for not furthering the state's "paternal purpose" and was ordered to begin to do so, rather than suffer "unpleasant measures".[60] Given that others had been imprisoned or exiled under Wöllner's campaign against heterodox opinions, this was far from being an idle threat.

Kant is by no means a political strategist, and it would be peculiar to judge him in that light, in terms, that is, of how much specific guidance he provides citizens to "overcome" the evils of their condition. Frederick Beiser has noted rightly that Kant

> had little or no conception of concerted or organized political activity. Trade unions, political parties, and pressure groups were unknown in eighteenth-century Prussia, and Kant could not approve of secret societies, such as the Freemasons, whose clandestine activities violated his demand for publicity and openness.[61]

Nevertheless, while theoretical work of this kind may have been foreclosed by Kant's political environment, Kant himself suggests reasons as to why providing specific strategies or theories of political action is not the work of philosophers, but rather of citizens. For a thinker as devoted to freedom and anti-paternalism as Kant, it would be odd indeed to expect anything resembling a political programme from on high. In order to understand the animating features of his politics, it is more productive to illuminate the *form* or the *kind* of political thinking, judgement, and action (and dissent) that Kant favours. The idea of individuals thinking for themselves (in contrast to what he sees as the prevalent practice in which individuals' lives are thoroughly ordered and disciplined by the state) forms his understanding of enlightenment and public reason, and is supported philosophically by his account of cultural agency, which constitutes anthropologically what it means to be a human being and which defines politically the one innate right that all humans possess simply as a result of their humanity. Kant's anti-paternalism and commitment to freedom lead, not surprisingly, and increasingly throughout his life, to a politics of self-determination at both the individual and collective levels. Collectively, Kant's defence of republicanism—or of what we would now call a representative democracy—is one realization of this commitment, as is his defence of individuals engaging in discussion and nonviolent dissent ultimately to create and then to improve a republic. Moreover, it is also clear, though it is less often studied, that his attack on European imperialism (another form of paternalizing European state power) and his defence of non-European peoples' freedom to determine their own affairs is yet another result of his distinctive understanding of, and commitment to, enlightenment and freedom. Humans themselves, and not philosophy in general or any particular philosopher, need to do the work of reform in order to make political progress a reality. Unlike Moses Mendelssohn's arguments about the meaning of enlightenment (in an essay that was published shortly before Kant's own essay on the subject), Kant believed that enlightenment is practical, not theoretical.[62] It consists *not* of propagating a body of "objective rational knowledge" (Mendelssohn), but of *practices* that engender independence and freedom and that, consequently, resist the infantilization and passivity that oppressive states want to breed in their subjects. Kant hoped that the practice of enlightenment will gradually develop a robust society of communication and dissent, one that, as he argues in "What is Enlightenment?", can transform both the character of a people as a whole and ultimately even the state, which might find itself compelled gradually over time to treat humans in accord with their dignity.

Humanity as Cultural Agency in a Philosophy of History: Kant's Narrative of Hope

Is the concept of progress or a philosophy of history necessarily imperializing and unappreciative of human diversity? It is a commonplace that one goal of the so-called 'Enlightenment project' was to herald a linear progression toward a reason-based society, an account of progress that, most powerfully in the nineteenth century, often justified European imperialism in light of its supposedly progressive role in disseminating reason and law to barbaric realms. Thus, in light of the history of political thought and contemporary claims about Enlightenment philosophies of history, the role that history and progress play in Kant's politics deserves careful attention. I will argue that Kant's philosophy of history can best be understood, and indeed he himself characterizes it, as a narrative of hope that appeals to the imagination, the intent of which is to energize passive individuals who would otherwise take the injustice of the modern world as an inevitable necessity. Thus, Kant's theory of progress and philosophy of history constitute an attempt to convince people of the contingency and historicity of social practices and political institutions, at least some of which can be (and ought to be) transformed through social and political activity. The goal toward which humans should work is cosmopolitan, a goal that is premissed on the idea that peoples characterized by different languages, religions, and land-use practices should be able to live freely and unhindered by the violence of others, including especially European imperialists.

Kant took it as a given that the officials and rulers of states would be unlikely to initiate reforms without being pushed in that direction by their subjects. If it did nothing else, the rule of Friedrich Wilhelm II taught this lesson to the *Aufklärer* quite clearly—enlightened despotism thus became an increasingly unpopular political sentiment.[63] As we have seen, the passivity of most individuals concerned Kant and partly engendered his antipathy toward state paternalism and his call to individuals to take responsibility for their own affairs, to dissent peacefully and communicatively in order to discipline state power. But there were also understandable reasons, Kant thought, for what he considered to be the disempowering malaise of modern individuals. In the face of political oppression and injustice, he feared that most individuals would accept their grim and cruel fate, and perhaps even view their situation as somehow natural (built permanently into the structure of social life itself) or even as providential (punishment by higher powers). Kant also wanted to respond to political realists who viewed as utopian those who used ideals to promote ideas of reform. Kant responded to such pessimism and conservatism by crafting a narrative of possible progress that employed their very assumptions. He needed, then, to describe a realistic scenario whereby humans, with all their faults and without having their natures miraculously transformed, could improve their social and political condition, partly through their own efforts and partly through good fortune. Only by such a narrative could (1) hard-headed realists be convinced that the deployment of political ideals is not chimerical and (2) those numbed by the tragedies of modern life feel empowered that their attempts at reform, however small and seemingly insignificant, could indeed bring about positive change. These are the central goals of Kant's philosophy of history.

I use the word narrative deliberately, for many interpreters have been led astray by Kant's metaphorical use of the term 'nature'. As George Armstrong Kelly notes,

> A fair amount of nonsense has been written about Kant's 'ruse of nature', according to which nature wills, urges or grants this or that, leading men in ways they do not suspect and toward goals which, ultimately, will prove to be compatible with a voluntary moral destiny.[64]

Kant's theory of progress and history lie fully within his critical strictures, and he deploys terms like 'nature' and 'providence' not to indicate cosmic and animistic forces at work in history (one should be careful indeed of reading Hegel into Kant), but to structure the complex flow of human events in a coherent manner. In the "Critique of Teleological Judgement", Kant argues at length that the idea of ends or purposes in organisms or in nature (in our surrounding world) is not something that is found or wisely discerned by wise philosophical investigations; rather, such concepts mould an otherwise confusing network of biological organisms, natural processes, and human practices into a reality that is coherent precisely to the extent that it is *made to seem* purposive.[65] As Kant writes,

> when we apply teleology [the concepts and language of purposes and ends] to physics [mechanistic explanations of the world], we do rightly speak of nature's wisdom, parsimony, foresight, or beneficence. But in speaking this way we do not turn nature into an intelligent [*verständig*] being (since that would be absurd), nor are we so bold as to posit a different, intelligent being above nature as its architect, since that would be presumptuous. (5:383)

Teleological judgements, of the kind that Kant makes in proposing his narrative of historical progress (that is, in ascribing purposes to human history), are "reflective", not "determinative". They constitute an attempt to portray the world by "analogy" to the idea of purposes "without [if one is being critically minded] presuming to *explain* it in terms of that causality." (5:360) Kant's critical analysis of the concept of purposiveness indicates that "nature" should not be viewed as an actual guiding force of a spiritual or mystical kind. The agency that he seemingly ascribes to nature in the historical essays is quite obviously metaphorical and is meant to indicate a feasible goal toward which humans themselves should work.

In his *Idea for a Universal History with a Cosmopolitan Intent* (1784), Kant argues that the free exercise of human wills, and thus the whole series of human events, if viewed "on a large scale" seems to exhibit certain patterns, just as meteorological phenomena and annual statistics of marriages, births, and deaths exhibit patterns, despite the seeming randomness of any single event or small groups of events (8:17). But humans pursue their goals neither purely by instinct (such as animals) nor in accordance with a prearranged rational plan (as hypothetical "rational cosmopolitans" on other planets might). So, strictly speaking, a "law-governed history of mankind" is not possible, as it would be for bees, beavers, or perfectly rational beings. On the whole, despite some exceptions and the fact that we are "so proud" of our "supposed superiority", human behaviour is characterized by "folly and childish vanity, and often of childish malice and destructiveness." Kant concludes,

The only way out for the philosopher, since he cannot assume that mankind follows any rational purpose of its own in its collective actions, is for him to attempt to discover a purpose in nature behind this senseless course of human events. . . . (8:18)

Kant's aim, therefore, is to *construct* a "guiding principle" of human history. In one sense, it is guiding because it helps to motivate ourselves to bring about a worthy political goal; it instills within us a hope from which we will guide ourselves. Kant admits that it is a peculiar kind of history that seeks to explain how we might get from our present political condition to one that is based upon goals that are presumed, from the outset, to be valuable. In a telling passage, Kant notes,

It is admittedly a strange and at first sight absurd proposition to write a *history* according to an Idea of how world events must develop if they are to conform to certain rational ends; it would seem that only a *novel* could result from such premises. (8:29)

Kant does not go on to dispute such a characterization, noting only that "this idea might nevertheless prove useful." His philosophy of history is indeed a novel, or a fictional narrative, that is deployed specifically to try to bring about the ends toward which he assumes we should work. Thus, the last "proposition" of his universal history is that

a philosophical attempt to work out a universal history of the world in accordance with a plan of nature aimed at a perfect civil union of mankind, must be regarded as possible and even as *capable of furthering the purpose of nature itself.* (8:29, italics added)

In discussing the role of narrativity in Locke, Hegel, and Nietzsche, Joshua Dienstag has identified precisely the manner in which, I believe, Kant's philosophy of history is best understood. He argues that

political theory, rather than relying [exclusively] on concepts of abstract right and duty, often attempts to guide by giving its readers a particular sense of time. That sense of time persuades not only by logic but also by giving readers a more convincing account of history and of the particular roles they are to play.[66]

As we have already seen, Kant's understanding of humanity as cultural agency highlights the role of imagination, memory, experience, and beauty in our judgements and actions. With his philosophy of history, Kant works at the level of humanity to persuade his readers that they must not give up hope for a better future.

Kant understood well (as his theory of humanity, aesthetics, sociability, and morality, especially in the *Doctrine of Virtue*, all make clear) the importance of nonmoral motivations for human actions. In the *Conjectures,* he explains what role a narrative of progress can play in encouraging social and political reform, especially among those who are understandably numbed by the injustices of the world.

> Thinking people are subject to a malaise which may even turn into moral corruption, a malaise of which the unthinking are ignorant—namely discontent with that providence by which the course of the world as a whole is governed. They feel this sentiment when they contemplate the evils which so greatly oppress the human race, with no hope (as it seems) of any improvement. (8:120–21)

Kant's critique in *Theory and Practice* of what he saw as Moses Mendelssohn's pessimism about human progress rests in part on the following view of moral psychology: individuals will not attempt to make the world a better place if they also believe that progress itself is a chimerical, unrealistic, or impossible ideal. Kant argues that Mendelssohn's efforts toward furthering the toleration of Jews and working to win civil rights for them must have rested upon such a view.

> This hope for better times, without which an earnest desire to do something profitable for the general well-being [*Wohl*] would never have warmed the human heart, has moreover always influenced the work of well-disposed people; and even the good Mendelssohn must have counted on it when he exerted himself so zealously for the enlightenment and welfare of the nation to which he belonged. For he could not reasonably hope to bring this about all by himself, without others after him continuing along the same path. (8:309)

Kant believed, however, that, unlike Mendelssohn, most individuals who meditate upon injustice and oppression become debilitated as a result; their depression about the human condition leads to passivity or to misanthropy.

Kant even interpreted the popularity in his day of apocalyptic visions of humanity's ultimate demise as an indication of such pessimism. In his bitterly satirical essay, *The End of All Things* (1794), Kant argues that "our opinion about the corrupt nature [*Beschaffenheit*] of the human race, which . . . is great to the point of hopelessness" leads a number of people to prophesy the end of the world and to attempt to decipher "the omens of the last day". Regarding such omens, he notes,

> Some see them in increasing injustice, oppression of the poor by the arrogant indulgence of the rich, and general loss of fidelity and faith; or in bloody wars igniting all over the earth, and so forth; in a word, in the moral fall and the rapid advance of all vices together with their accompanying ills, such as earlier times—they think—have never seen. Others, by contrast, [find them] in unusual alterations in nature—in earthquakes, storms and floods, or comets and

atmospheric signs. In fact it is not without cause that human beings feel their existence a burden, even if they themselves are the cause.[67] (8:331–332)

Kant is sympathetic to the concerns that motivated such fears, but he remains concerned that humans were increasingly responding to social and political injustices by extinguishing all hope for a better future. If we let ourselves be numbed by always having in mind the many injustices of social and political life and hence never contemplating the chances for progress, the resulting "spectacle", he writes,

> would force us to turn away in revulsion, and, by making us despair of ever finding any completed rational aim behind it, would reduce us to hoping for it only in some other world. (8:30)

Thus, a philosophy of history or a theory of progress, for Kant, was a means of inculcating hope among people who increasingly were turning away from the task of reforming their societies and governments. The progress that he theorizes, in his view, is speculative, but by using the language of nature, such a narrative may be enough to show that genuine progress is possible, and with this renewed hope, individuals might work toward such an end.[68]

Kant's notion of "progress" does not lead to imperializing results, as it so often does in other (especially later nineteenth-century) thinkers because the role of progress for him is to historicize contemporary injustices and to motivate individuals to confront them.[69] Thus, progress and a universal history are not part of a descriptive account that engages in the *legitimation* of extant societies, states, or political practices (such as imperialism); rather, his narrative of progress and universal history constitutes a *delegitimation* of practices and institutions that might otherwise be taken for granted. Thus, in the *Conjectures*, Kant suggests that the role of conjectural history is to show that humans are themselves responsible for what are ultimately *human* injustices, not injustices that are built naturally into social and political life. Kant argues that

> it is of the utmost importance *that we should be content with providence*, even if the path it has laid out for us on earth is an arduous one. We should be content with it partly in order that we may take courage even in the midst of hardships, and partly in order that we should not blame all such evils on fate and fail to notice that we may ourselves be entirely responsible for them, thereby losing the chance to remedy them by improving ourselves. (8:121, underscoring added)

The hope that is instilled by a narrative that proclaims that we are heading toward, however slowly and haltingly, a cosmopolitan future of peace and freedom should embolden human beings to attempt to work toward this goal. Thus, after arguing that we should be content with providence, Kant concludes the *Conjectures* not by asserting that we should relax and simply let nature do its mystical work, but rather that "each individual is for his own part called upon by nature itself to contribute towards this progress to the best of his ability." (8:123)

The goals of history that Kant formulates are *political* in substance— that all human beings and all human peoples should live in freedom and in peace—and *cosmopolitan* in character. The goals are cosmopolitan both in terms of space and time: they must involve all the peoples of the globe and, as he argues often, they must span many generations. It is both an international and an intergenerational effort. Kant attends to the complexity of this task not only by trying to instill human hope to get individuals to take action (to become *agents*), but also to indicate the *limits* to human agency. Yirmiyahu Yovel has noted perceptively that the conscious and unconscious aspects of Kant's philosophy of history are ultimately complementary.[70] Thus, while it is at first a paradoxical feature of Kant's theory that it proclaims both the importance of conscious human action toward political reform *and* the unintentional workings of political progress (at times by selfish acts and even as the result of wars and misery), the point of crafting a narrative of hope would be lost if it had to rest upon the unrealistic view that humans across the globe could act together in some uniform way toward political progress. Thus, from his theory of unsocial sociability in the *Idea for a Universal History* to his view in *Toward Perpetual Peace* that the conflicts of the world might contain within them the seeds for our future peace, Kant attempts to craft a narrative of progress that rests upon the assumption that human nature would not have to be transformed to the condition of moral purity for positive political change to take place. In part, it seems, he is responding to political cynics for whom any talk of historical progress and political ideals seem wildly utopian. Accordingly, in the *Conflict of the Faculties*, after arguing that political progress is possible "without the moral foundation in humanity having to be enlarged in the least", Kant warns that "we must also not hope for too much from human beings in their progress toward the better lest we fall prey with good reason to the mockery of the politician who would willingly take the hope of the human being as the dreaming of an overstressed mind." (7:92) In addition, the complexity of cosmopolitan progress would have to rest, Kant assumes, *in part* upon social dynamics that lie beyond the agency of any one individual or group of individuals.[71] In particular, for global progress to occur over time, there must be a fortunate conjunction of a variety of disparate conscious attempts at progress *and* unconsciously and unintentionally beneficial actions and practices. Accordingly, Kant argues that it is only from "nature" or "providence" that we can

> expect an outcome that is directed to the whole and from it to the parts, whereas people in their schemes set out only from the parts and may well

remain with them, and may be able to reach the whole, as something too great for them, in their ideas but not in their influence, especially since, with their mutually adverse schemes, they would hardly unite for it by their own free resolution. (8:310)

For Kant, the ultimate point of highlighting such nonintentional, larger social forces, however, is that it might convince humans that "nature" (i.e., luck, or fortune, or chance—any of the aspects of history that are beyond our conscious and intentional control) is at least partly on their side.

The reason one ought to reflect about "nature" or "providence" in history, then, is not to convince ourselves of a guarantee of any particular social and political outcome, but to generate hope from the fact that humans control at least *some* part of their destiny. Kant's narrative is meant to excite human passions and imaginations in order ultimately to spark the agency of his readers—to stir them from their complacency and malaise, so that they work toward improving their social and political lives. At the same time, in order to create a realistic portrayal of positive change (and thereby to engender the hope not simply of those who are numbed by human injustice, but those who are political cynics), Kant resorts frequently to language that emphasizes the *limits* to human agency and the fact that a transformation of human nature is not necessary for political progress. The feebleness and cross-purposes of well-meaning human efforts, in addition to human selfishness and antagonism, might plausibly lead, by good fortune, to an improved social and political reality. From the perspective of moral psychology, Kant contends that humans need at least that much hope in order to be able to *act* in the face of oppression and injustice toward a cosmopolitan future of peace and freedom. The "assurance" that progress will occur "is admittedly not adequate for *predicting* its future (theoretically) but that is still enough for practical purposes and makes it a duty to work toward this (not merely chimerical) end." (8:368)

THE CONCEPT of humanity plays a robust and multifaceted role in Kant's thought: understood as cultural humanity (or cultural agency), the most foundational of the senses in which he uses the term 'humanity' and the one that I have elaborated most fully, it identifies the constitutive aspects of the human condition. As aesthetic humanity, a specific variant of humanity as cultural agency, the concept suggests the moral character of sociability in complex modern societies (and, thus, the narrower understanding of "culture"). As dignity or *homo noumenon*, it refers to an egalitarian idea (which can be postulated, but not proven) that all humans possess the ability to reason about and to act upon moral principles for their own sake, the most important of which is to respect others' humanity (i.e., their cultural agency). Finally, Kant's political thought denotes the freedom (the one "innate right" of humanity) that makes cultural agency possible and that any just political order should protect, which has important implications (as we will see in the following chapter) for his understanding of international and cosmopolitan justice.

Ultimately, for Kant, humanity (*Humanität, Menschheit*) and culture (*Kultur*) are fundamentally linked concepts. Notwithstanding the other meanings of these concepts, 'humanity' refers most fundamentally to what Kant views as the basic anthropological fact that humans are beings who create and/or sustain and transform desires, values, and ideals, inscribe their own meanings and idealizations of beauty on to the world, and draw upon memory, imagination, and skill to orient themselves and transform their surroundings. Given Kant's emphasis on culture and freedom as integral to the very idea of humanity, I have called his view 'humanity as cultural agency'. We saw earlier that Diderot's political thought is animated by a similar understanding of humanity. As Kant makes clear in *Conjectures on the Beginning of Human History, Religion within the Boundaries of Mere Reason,* and *The Metaphysics of Morals,* the uses of reason and freedom that humanity as cultural agency presupposes are embedded within and partly shaped by humans' social contexts. In sharp contrast to the typical (ostensibly Kantian) view of the rarefied human subject who stands free of all social and cultural attachments, Kant asserts that 'humanity' refers fundamentally to the idea that human beings are situated within, and also have the powers to transform, their concrete, empirical surroundings. In our capacity as beings with humanity, we use our practical reason, not alone and free from all worldly influences, "but only as subservient to other incentives" (6:28), incentives that are informed by reflections upon our environmental and social surroundings. Kant writes that the contextual reasoning and freedom that animates cultural agency makes possible "human choice", a "freedom of choice" (or "negative freedom") that we possess as beings with humanity (as opposed to an "animal choice" that is driven by instinct alone, or enactments of our "positive freedom" that we make as moral persons when we act out of our commitment to moral duty alone) (6:213). This sphere of constitutively human activity is simply "culture in general" (6:392). All humans, simply because of their humanity, use their reason, freedom, memory, imagination, skill, and other powers to extend and transform their cultural lives. Thus, when Kant discusses what differentiates humanity (*Humanität*) from animality, the concept of *Kultur* is almost always present. Kant describes the capacities that allow us to draw upon our surroundings and alter our environments as the "incentives to culture" that all humans have as beings with humanity (6:27); the social injustices, such as inequality, that often arise from the plural uses of our distinctively human powers are deemed to be "the vices of culture" (6:27); and the increasingly complicated practices and institutional arrangements that the uses of our distinctively human powers yield and transform are all "cultural developments" (8:113). Kant's universal moral injunction, therefore, is an appeal to all humans to respect their fellow humans' cultural agency. Accordingly, Kant's political thought also places this understanding of humanity at its core, identifying the one innate right of humanity, which citizens and states should protect, as the distinctively human freedom that underlies humanity as cultural agency. As we will see in the next chapter, Kant's anti-imperialism builds upon precisely these understandings of humanity, culture, and freedom.

Five

Kant's Anti-imperialism: Cultural Agency and Cosmopolitan Right

KANT's hatred of paternalism plays an important role in his political understanding of civil societies, as we saw in the last chapter. I begin this chapter with a section that investigates the relationship between human flourishing and freedom in the *Doctrine of Virtue* (the second part of *The Metaphysics of Morals*), in particular the latitude that Kant prescribes to *individuals* in determining their cultural activities, and thus the anti-paternalistic arguments that he makes about self-development. This will show how Kant's understanding of humanity as cultural agency helps to produce a moral philosophy that is both universal and pluralistic, and it makes clear the wide diversity of ways of life and understandings of happiness that Kant affords to individuals to order their lives as they see fit. This lays the basis for investigating how Kant applies this understanding of human flourishing and freedom to whole societies, as part of his defence of non-European peoples' resistance against European imperial power. Before doing so, I examine in the next section the languages of human diversity in Kant's political philosophy. Strikingly, despite Kant's earlier theorization of human races, in his late published writings—in particular, precisely the texts in which he theorized the antagonistic relationships between European and non-European peoples and attacked European imperialism as manifestly unjust—he ultimately drew upon an understanding of peoples that emphasized their collective freedoms in light of their subsistence and land-use practices. This is an account of human diversity that stresses the differences among nomadic, pastoral, and agriculturalist peoples, differences that nonetheless point to the equality of all peoples as cultural agents. The core of Kant's anti-imperialist political thought, which is the focus of the third section, can be found in his defence of nomadic and pastoral peoples in *The Metaphysics of Morals* and especially in his writings on 'cosmopolitan right', by which he articulated the conditions of justice that should obtain between states and foreigners and between individuals from different societies. In light of this understanding of cosmopolitan right, Kant criticized European imperialism and defended non-European peoples against what he viewed as the destructive powers that were being exercised by imperial trading companies, explorers, and other imperial travellers whose violent conquests of foreign lands and peoples transgressed the fundamental right to hospitality shared by all humans. Cosmopolitan right emerges as the fullest expression of what Kant identifies as the one 'innate right of humanity', the right to a distinctively human freedom (cultural agency) that all humans possess by virtue of their humanity. Finally, in the fourth section, I examine the unique features of Kant's social contract theory, including his understanding of a state of nature, which help to explain why he did *not* believe that non-agrarian peoples were under a political duty to create their own civil states on the model of those in Europe, China, or in other sedentary societies.

Self-Cultivation, Pluralism, and Cultural Freedom

Kant famously argues that humans ought to strive toward acting morally for the sake of morality itself rather than for personal advantage, social stature, or any other selfish benefit. We have a duty, that is, to perfect ourselves morally, despite what Kant takes as the impossibility to know if we or others have ever actually acted out of principle. Given that we can cognize this ideal of moral self-perfection and that no one can definitively disprove the possibility of acting morally (in Kant's pure sense), we are thus under a duty of virtue to improve our moral characters. Thus, the presumption that we are capable of striving toward making our ethical actions less selfish and more principled is enough to put us under a moral duty to engage in such striving. In distinction to moral perfection, Kant also describes a duty of "natural perfection", an obligation to develop the capacities or powers that we possess simply by being human. This concerns not the incentives or motivations that lie behind our ethical actions, but the use and development of our capacities in order to bring about a wide variety of goals or "pragmatic purposes" (*pragmatishcher Absicht*), not simply moral purposes, that we decide to pursue. As I have been arguing, Kant's view is that these human skills involve the use of reason and freedom in a manner that depends, for their orientation, upon our surrounding experience—a diverse, plural, and often a socially informed experience. The cultural capacities that distinguish the human species, then, are embedded in, and necessarily draw upon, the world of experience. Thus, as I have suggested, the practices that indicate what is constitutively human are not based upon a radical autonomy that abstracts from the contexts of our lives. Our cultural activities, in other words, are neither spontaneously generated de novo nor cognized abstractly from metaphysical realms. Rather, they result simply from the free use of our reason, a particular aspect of our freedom and reason that is constitutively human and, thus, contextualized by experience; as I have shown, this is what Kant calls a distinctively "human choice" in the introduction to *The Metaphysics of Morals*. I have called this particular kind of freedom "cultural agency", for it indicates both the freedom and the context from which such freedom is exercised; moreover, it incorporates Kant's own use of the term *Kultur* in association with the distinctive aspects of reason and freedom that, for him, fundamentally constitute humanity.

Thus, in the *Doctrine of Virtue*, Kant returns to the concept of humanity as cultural agency in the course of describing an ethical duty to perfect one's distinctively human powers. He writes that "*Natural* perfection is the *cultivation* of any *capacities* whatever [*aller Vermögen überhaupt*] for furthering ends set forth by reason." (6:391) "Reason" in this context refers to the cognitive ability whereby we choose a multiplicity of ends, ends that are sometimes antecedently provided by tradition or custom or, at times, creatively fashioned. In other words, Kant is not referring to the moral aim of acting out of duty for duty's sake; he is careful to distinguish in this section between moral and natural perfection. That humans have such cultural capacities or powers and that we make use of them at least minimally is, for Kant, a brute anthropological fact. Yet, as noted earlier, either through indolence (see the *Groundwork*) or, more disturbingly, through the lack of sufficient opportunities because of social inequalities and political oppression (see *The Metaphysics of Morals*), such human powers can remain woefully underdeveloped. Kant argues elsewhere that the latter problems can be mitigated through the abolishment of serfdom and hereditary nobility, governmental funding for education and charitable institutions, and private acts of beneficence. Whatever the prevailing social and political conditions, however, Kant argues in the *Doctrine of Virtue* that we should cultivate such capacities in order to realize, as much as possible, the potential of the humanity (the cultural agency) in our person:

> The capacity to set oneself an end—any end whatsoever—is what characterizes humanity (as distinguished from animality). Hence there is also bound up with the end of humanity in our own person the rational will, and so the duty, to make ourselves worthy of humanity by culture in general, by procuring or promoting the *capacity* to realize all sorts of possible ends, so far as this [capacity] is to be found in the human being himself. In other words, the human being has a duty to cultivate the crude predispositions of his nature, by which the animal is first raised into the human being. (6:392)

As we are now in a position to discern, Kant distills some of his previous treatments of humanity as cultural agency into this passage: the *Conjectures* provides a speculative narrative of an animal raising itself "into the human being" by redescribing Genesis in philosophical anthropological terms, and the *Religion* attempts to survey the most fundamental natural predispositions of animality and humanity. Kant's position on natural perfection suggests that treating the humanity in our person as an end it itself involves, in part, the duty *to oneself* of cultivating this very humanity. Here we find Kant employing a traditional use of the term culture, as he himself recognizes, for its Latin root, *cultura*, means simply to tend, nurture, or cultivate. As he writes in the *Doctrine of Virtue*, a "human being has a duty to himself to cultivate (*cultura*) his natural powers (powers of spirit, mind, and body), as means to all sorts of possible ends." (6:444)

Kant stresses two crucial features of this duty. First, it is a duty only toward oneself, not toward others. As I have noted, Kant was concerned about promoting social and political conditions that would be conducive to human development or flourishing, but the direct ordering of another's life choices would violate the independent freedom and attendant anti-paternalism that are central to his understanding of a dignified, enlightened life. To be sure, this involves difficult questions of where one draws the line between creating conditions for others that are necessary for their agency and determining one's own agency directly, but there does not seem to be any patent inconsistency in being committed both to eradicating slavishness and poverty, or positively stated, to developing both an independent character as well as fruitful and just social conditions from which "culture in general" can develop widely. Second, like many duties of virtue in his thought, the duty of one's own perfection is a 'wide' or 'imperfect' duty. While we are under a general duty to cultivate our constitutively human powers, each individual should decide the kind and the extent of such self-development, for reason itself provides no universal rule that issues categorically any particular cultural goal or even the extent to which any one goal should be realized.

> No rational principle prescribes specifically [*bestimmt*] how far one should go in cultivating one's capacities (in enlarging or correcting one's capacity for understanding, i.e., in acquiring knowledge or skill [*Kunstfähigkeit*]). . . . With regard to natural perfection, accordingly, there is no law of reason for actions. (6:392)

Moreover, the kinds of self-development that individuals pursue will vary widely according to the differing contexts within which they live. As he notes,

> the different situations in which human beings may find themselves make a human being's choice [*Wahl*] of the occupation for which he should cultivate his talents very much a matter for him to decide as he chooses [*sehr willkürlich*]. (6:392)

Here again one finds Kant defending a form of freedom, or self-determination, not as a radical conception of autonomy that abstracts from social contexts, but precisely in light of the situated circumstances of actual human beings. In addition, the diversity of human choice that Kant recommends follows from his recognition of the diversity of contexts within which humans lead their lives. In his view, this is a diversity that must be incorporated, not eviscerated, by any proper account of ethical life.

Kant outlines three broad powers that he takes all humans to have, but that each human will develop in different proportions; the specific balance of developed powers will vary among individuals because of their differing backgrounds and, ideally, their *own* judgements as to whether they are capable of cultivating different balances of these powers to the extent necessary for engaging in various pursuits. "Powers of spirit", Kant writes, refer to the creative rational abilities that are required, for instance, in logic and mathematics. "Powers of soul [*Seelenkräfte*]", which Kant also calls the powers of mind, refer to capabilities that are distinctively human and that he believes are the "highest" of the human faculties, presumably because they best represent what is truly human and enable a wide variety of human thought and action.[1] Such powers are

> those which are at the disposal of understanding and the rule it uses to fulfill whatever purposes one might have, and because of this experience is their guide. They include memory, imagination and the like, on which can be built learning, taste (internal and external embellishment) and so forth, which furnish instruments for a variety of purposes. (6:445)

Finally, Kant writes, "cultivating the powers of the body . . . is looking after the *basic stuff* (the matter) in a human being, without which he could not realize his ends. Hence the continuing and purposive invigoration of the animal in him is an end of a human being that is a duty to himself." (6:445) Kant takes the body to be an integral part of the human being that has great value and should therefore be cultivated. Hence, he argues elsewhere on the topic of ethical asceticism that the body should not be punished by those attempting to lead a pure moral life—morality, in short, should not involve harshly disciplining the body.[2] Rather, a proper understanding of morality, in Kant's view, demands that we cultivate the body, although the kind and extent of such cultivation is a matter for each individual to decide.

Again, the anti-paternalism of Kant's view must be underscored. In discussing ends that are also duties, Kant lists two kinds: promoting one's own (not others') perfection, in the manner that we have discussed, and the happiness of others, for instance, by improving social and political conditions or through individual acts of kindness and beneficence. Importantly, Kant argues that it cannot be a duty either to perfect others or to make oneself happy.

Perfection and happiness cannot be interchanged here, so that *one's own happiness* and *the perfection of others* would be made ends that would be in themselves duties of the same person. For *his own happiness* is an end that every human being has (by virtue of the impulses of his nature), but this end can never without self-contradiction be regarded as a duty. What everyone already wants unavoidably, of his own accord, does not come under the concept of *duty*. . . . So too, it is a contradiction for me to make another's *perfection* my end and consider myself under obligation to promote this. For the *perfection* of another human being, as a person, consists just in this: that he *himself* is able [*vermögen ist*] to set his end in accordance with his own concepts of duty; and it is self-contradictory to require that I do (make it my duty to do) something that only the other himself can do. (6:386)

Thus, it seems clear why Kant's theory of human perfection fits within the category of imperfect duties, duties that allow a wide latitude within which individuals themselves can determine the precise judgements necessary to lead their lives. Kant, then, argues that individuals should balance and perfect the three natural human powers as they see fit.

Which of these natural perfections should take precedence, and in what proportion one against the other it may be a human being's duty to himself to make these natural perfections his end, are matters left for him to choose in accordance with his own rational reflection about what sort of life he would like to lead and whether he has the powers necessary for it. . . . (6:445)

We will see later that, when applied to *groups* of humans, Kant's argument against attempting to perfect others and the wide latitude that he recommends individuals should have to determine their own lives will inform some of his anti-imperialist arguments.

From Kant's perspective, even if humans lead their lives simply within the range that their natural powers themselves afford, and thus only to satisfy their most basic needs, they are still not purely natural or instinctually determined creatures, but rather humans who have decided by means of their free faculties not to engage in any further development of their capacities. "Even supposing", Kant argues, that a human being

could be satisfied with the innate scope of his capacities for his natural needs, his reason must first show him, by principles, that this meagre scope of his capacities is satisfactory; for, as a being capable [*fähig*] of ends (of making objects his ends), he must owe the use of his powers not merely to natural instinct but rather to the freedom by which he determines their scope.[3] (6:444)

Such a hypothetical case suggests not a determined being, stripped of all culture and freedom, but a cultural agent who expresses through his lifestyle a self-conscious desire not to engage in self-cultivation beyond developing the abilities that are necessary to make effectual his most basic, life-sustaining activities. Thus, cultural agency runs to the very core of what it is to be human—it runs, as it were, all the way down and, hence, if stripped away from humans through a Rousseauian counter-factual mental exercise, *nothing* that could be described meaningfully as fundamentally human would remain.

Bound up with Kant's view of humanity and human flourishing is an account of the wide latitude that humans have (and, increasingly, *should* have, given felicitous social and political reforms) in making their determinations of value, beauty, work, and other forms of cultural life. Cultural agency necessarily involves acts of freedom, a freedom that is guided not by categorical or absolute judgements, but by relative or comparative judgements about what will satisfy us or make us happy.[4] This sphere of thought and action involves subjective preferences that are not thoroughly determined by our physiological (or 'animal') impulses, and that are not taken simply because we place ourselves under a moral duty. In light of what, then, are these preferences made? For any human being, judging and choosing in light of experience involves, according to Kant, "instruction . . . from observing himself and his animal nature [our most basic instincts and needs] or from perceiving the ways of the world, what happens and how we behave". As Kant himself notes, his stringent use of the words "moral" or "morality" differs from the common meaning of these terms in his day, which correspond more to the conditions of cultural humanity than to moral personality: "the German word *Sitten*, like the Latin *mores*, means only manners and customs" (6:216). It is the popular understanding of morality that Kant acknowledges with his theorization of humanity, given his emphasis on customs, manners, the ways of the world, and our determinations of how those around us behave. In short, the latitude of human choice contains within it the rich complexity and plurality of human life as well as the relativity and partiality of so many of our judgements.

For Kant, these are the resources, then, that inform *human* choice, choice that is constitutively human in contrast to a more abstract and rational choice (an a priori, nonexperientially based choice). Emphasizing the relativity of such human choices, Kant writes that

> the preference of one state of determination of the will to another is merely [or simply] an act of freedom (*res merae facultatis*, as jurists say), in regard to which no account at all is taken of whether this (determination of the will) is good or evil in itself, and is thus indifferent with respect to both. (8:282)

Such preferences, of course, might be oppressive and cruel; they might, in Kant's terms, use others simply as means for one's own ends. Accordingly, Kant reiterates his argument that our choices need to be checked

by the regulative idea of "a categorically commanding law of free choice
[*der freien Willkür*] (i.e., of [moral] duty)", in order to prohibit actions
in which oneself or others are used as mere things (8:282).[5] Nonetheless,
there is a significant cultural space, as one might call it, that lies outside
the bounds of what is absolutely prohibited and that remains, from the
standpoint of a categorical morality, "morally permissible" or "morally
indifferent". This does not entail that we have no standards at all to
guide us within this cultural space; rather, this domain of action and
deliberation is indeed subject to rules, values, and judgements, although
they vary enormously over time and place (and even for the same individual), and are thus not universal in scope. As we saw in the last chapter, by
induction from one's varied experiences, Kant argues that it might be
possible for an individual to form generalities to make choices within this
wide sphere of morally permissible actions and judgements, but these
generalities would be merely rules of thumb, not universal principles.
Such standards are incommensurable, since there is no shared standard
that exists to adjudicate decisively among them. As cultural agents, then,
humans exercise what Kant describes as acts of freedom that are informed
by our experience: *res merae facultatis.*[6]

> An action that is neither commanded nor prohibited is merely permitted, since
> there is no [universal] law limiting one's freedom (one's authorization) with
> regard to it and so too no [moral] duty. Such an action is called morally indif-
> ferent (*indifferens, adiaphoron, res merae facultatis*). (6:223)

The latitude of morally permissible cultural activity and choice is wide;
the room it affords to make diverse judgements and choices stems from
Kant's limited account of universal morality, one that concerns itself only
with what is good in itself and, especially, what is wrong in itself.[7] Even
moral duties, as we have seen, while categorical in nature (e.g., *every*
human should help others in need, *all* humans should cultivate their own
capacities), often involve crucial judgements of kind and degree (whom
to help and how, which powers to develop and to what extent) that are
not prescribed by reason alone and that amount to much more than the
easy application of a universal norm. Thus, even a *morally* conscientious
human life, in Kant's own account, requires the use of this experientially
informed and pluralistic freedom, or cultural agency. Fundamental questions of value, therefore, arise in our distinctively human (our cultural)
lives, but they are not about universal goods or evils, nor do they necessarily concern the promotion of unselfish incentives, for they are not decisions made simply from duty, but are instead (as Kant calls them) "human choices" that are made according to partial and varying experiences.[8]

Such choices are individual; they may be, and often are, informed by
social experience, but the ultimate judgements ought to be one's own.

This is bound up, in Kant's thought, with the idea of *enlightenment* it-self—*sapere aude*, or 'daring to know', entails a life of thinking and act-ing for oneself, not wholly apart from the world or entirely autonomously (as I have suggested, in Kant's own view, this would be *inhuman*), but in a manner that recognizes and respects the capacities that each of us, as individuals, possesses. For Kant, then, acting and thinking for oneself reciprocally implies respecting others' actions and judgements—an anti-paternalistic concept of enlightenment and a respect for a robust plural-ism of attitudes and practices go hand in hand. Kant's concept of enlight-enment is often understood more narrowly as simply a call for individual freedom, but it is also an invocation for what would follow from a grad-ual liberation of such creative energies: a plurality of life-choices, as op-posed to the stifling uniformity of paternalistic authorities. But does Kant defend this kind of cultural freedom for *groups* of humans as well, in particular for non-European peoples? As I will show, Kant was just as troubled by the paternalism that European imperial powers exhibited to-ward non-European peoples as he was by the paternalism of political and ecclesiastical authorities that disciplined and infantilized individuals within European nations. But before I explore this question in depth, in order to show how Kant's accounts of humanity, pluralism, and anti-paternalism apply to human groups, we must first understand how Kant categorizes the variety of peoples on the earth.

Anthropological Diversity: From Race to Collective Freedom

In his mature or late writings, Kant deploys a tripartite sociological dis-tinction among hunting, pastoral (nomadic herders), and agricultural (sedentary) peoples that had been used in earlier eighteenth-century clas-sifications of peoples to differentiate the wide array of human groups. Montesquieu, for instance, relies upon a similar division of peoples in *The Spirit of the Laws* (1748):

> One difference between savage peoples and barbarian peoples is that the former are small scattered nations which, for certain particular reasons, cannot unite, whereas barbarians are ordinarily small nations that can unite together. The former are usually hunting peoples; the latter, pastoral peoples.[9]

Montesquieu contrasts such peoples to those who cultivate their lands, use money, and are ruled by civil laws: *nations policées*, or civilized na-tions. In addition, while Rousseau often contrasts simply "primitive" and "civilized" peoples in the *Discourse on Inequality*, we know that he in-tended to write a *History of Morals* [*Moeurs* (customary moralities)], the table of contents of which indicates a distinction among savage, barbaric, civilized (*policés*), working, and virtuous peoples; this system of classification in part seems to have been influenced by Montesquieu.[10] As we have seen, Diderot also emphasizes the importance of peoples' differing land-use practices. And perhaps most famously, Scottish Enlightenment writings often employed a similar system of classification—the so-called four-stage theory of social development—that analyzed hunting, pastoral, agricultural, and commercial societies.[11]

As one would expect, Kant's view of humanity as cultural agency influences his conceptualization of human diversity as well. The most salient differences among groups of humans and, more broadly, among nations turn not upon biological or environmental differences, but simply upon the different uses of the situated reason and freedom—the cultural agency—that define us as creatures with humanity. Kant, in his delineation of global human diversity, identifies peoples exclusively by their *activities* as cultural agents. This stands in contrast to two other strategies of coming to terms with the diversity of peoples that eighteenth-century ethnography presented: (1) dividing up the world's peoples according to a theory of biological or intrinsic ability (as race theorists would do en masse in the nineteenth century, building upon the early development of the concept of race in the eighteenth century, to which Kant himself contributed); and (2) focusing on environmentally induced characteristics (sloth, industriousness, and so forth) that were said to be engendered by various climates. Kant's account of humanity as cultural agency leads him to treat the most socially fundamental human activities, those around which entire societies are organized and shaped, as central to an understanding of the diversity of peoples. Accordingly, Kant presents hunting, pastoralist, and agrarian pursuits as rationally chosen or sustained activities, not as biologically (i.e., instinctually or racially) or climatically determined practices. A crucial consequence of this view is that nomadic peoples do not lead the 'natural' lives of noble (or ignoble) savages, as opposed to the 'artificial' lives of the Chinese, the Europeans, or other agriculturalists. Rather, they lead lives as humans, as cultural agents, and thus they consciously continue to lead and to transform their lives as a result of distinctively human judgements, which are often, in his view, incommensurable and, thus, are not often amenable to universal moral censure. Kant's account of human diversity attends to the plurality of distinctively human judgements—"culture in general"—that individuals and groups make differently, and for which there often exists no objectively valid, universal measure of superiority, moral goodness, or excellence.

Although this is not much noted, it is clear that Kant's categorization of the diversity of peoples underwent a transformation in his published writings from the mid-1780s onward. The manner in which he concep-

tualizes the plurality of humankind moves from an almost exclusive reliance upon the biological and hereditary concept of 'race' to the sociological and activity-based concept of how peoples freely use the land on
which they live, which I sketched earlier and which I will later examine in
more detail. In his precritical period, and to a lesser extent in the early
years of his critical period (by convention, the years immediately following the 1781 publication of the *Critique of Pure Reason*), Kant developed a theory of race in order to account for the diversity of mores and,
especially, for differences in skin colour and physiognomy both in published essays and in his lectures on anthropology and physical geography.
While the nineteenth century constitutes the preeminent age of race-
based classifications, during which the language of race gained an explicitly political currency among many European thinkers, it is also the case
that the roots of race theory lie in a number of writings of the eighteenth
century, especially those by natural historians such as Buffon and Blumenbach, but also by late-eighteenth-century philosophers such as Kant.[12]

Kant's intellectual interest in the concept of race seems to have been
motivated by the need to explain biological inheritance, especially what
he viewed as the intriguing fact that skin colour passes from one generation to the next. In addition, as I mentioned in the last chapter, like
Buffon, Kant argues that the great variety of human beings, despite their
remarkable physical differences, all derive from a common source. Thus,
Kant vigorously opposed the multiple-origin theory that some of his contemporaries, such as Georg Forster, had defended and which suggested
that black Africans, for instance, were, strictly speaking, a different species
than white Europeans. Kant relied on the concept of climate to explain
the ultimate origins of physical differences, such as skin colour, among
humans; after many generations, he contends, such differences become
hereditary. In his 1775 essay, *On the Different Races of Man* (*Von den
verschiedenen Racen der Menschen*), Kant concludes that his theories

> at least are substantial enough to be a counterweight to those other commen-
> taries that find the differences in the human genus so impossible to reconcile
> that they prefer to assume discrete local creations. . . . Precisely because of
> Nature's propensity to adapt to the soil everywhere over long generations, the
> human form must now everywhere be supplied with local modifications.[13]

From a humanitarian perspective, the great danger of any race- and
climate-based theory is that *predetermined* characteristics (those arguably
determined by climate and/or by biological inheritance) might include
(and in race theories often do include) not simply physical features but
also intellectual capacities that, in turn, presumably affect the kinds of
mores, social practices, and political organizations of various peoples. Before Kant published any writings on the concept of race, he had already

made such a judgement under the influence of David Hume's notorious suggestion about nonwhite peoples (or in his language, nonwhite "species"). In a footnote to his essay "Of National Characters" (1748), Hume airs the following suspicion:

> I am apt to suspect the Negroes, and in general all the other species of men (for there are four or five different kinds) to be naturally inferior to the whites. There never was a civilized nation of any other complexion than white, nor even any individual eminent either in action or speculations. No ingenious manufactures amongst them, no arts, no sciences. On the other hand, the most rude and barbarous of the whites, such as the ancient GERMANS, the present TARTARS, have still something eminent about them, in their valour, form of government, or some other particular. Such a uniform and constant difference could not happen, in so many countries and ages, if nature had not made an original distinction betwixt these breeds of men. Not to mention our colonies, there are NEGROE slaves dispersed all over EUROPE, of which none ever discovered any symptoms of ingenuity; tho' low people, without education, will start up amongst us, and distinguish themselves in every profession.[14]

Kant may have awakened from his dogmatic slumbers by reading Hume, as the story goes, but in this case, he simply appropriated Hume's prejudicial dogma. In the early work *Observations on the Feeling of the Beautiful and Sublime* (1764), during the course of paraphrasing Hume's contention (though Kant limits his statement to "Negroes"), Kant concludes that the mental capacities of black and white races may be fundamentally different.

> The Negroes of Africa have by nature no feeling that rises above the trifling. Mr Hume challenges anyone to cite a single example in which a Negro has shown talents. . . . So fundamental is the difference between these two races of man, and it appears to be as great in regard to mental capacities as in colour.[15]

Kant asserts that he will not inquire whether the differences among peoples "are contingent and depend upon the times and the type of government, or are bound by a certain necessity to the climate", although in the case above he clearly leans toward the latter.[16] His lectures on physical geography clearly underscore a climate-based account of race and point to the "certain necessity" of differences among humans, most notably of their cognitive abilities.[17] In these early lectures, Kant gave a climatological explanation for what he took to be the greater perfection of those in temperate zones as well as for historical conquests of Europeans and central Asians over the less temperate parts of the world.[18]

In Kant's later years, when he developed his theory of humanity as cultural agency and his anti-imperialist political thought, the hierarchical and biological concept of race disappears in his published writings.[19] Race makes no appearance in the *Critique of Judgement* (1790), not even in its "Critique of Teleological Judgement", and plays no role in his discussions of human diversity and imperialism in the *Conjectures* (1786), *Toward Perpetual Peace* (1795), and *The Metaphysics of Morals* (1797). In his last published discussion of race, within a short essay entitled "Über den Gebrauch teleologischer Principien in der Philosophie" ["Concerning the Use of Teleological Principles in Philosophy"] (1788), Kant makes no arguments about the preeminence of whites or Europeans over other human races. In the *Anthropology from a Pragmatic Point of View* (1798), published late in Kant's life and based upon a revision of anthropology lecture notes, he bypasses a detailed discussion of race by recommending a work by Christoph Girtenner (7:320). Girtenner's *Über das kantische Prinzip für die Naturgeschichte* [*On the Kantian principle for Natural History*] (1796) is an application of Kant's hereditary theories to *nonhuman* species.[20] Notably, in all of the late published writings in which one would expect Kant to use the concept of human races—for instance, in his treatments of the development of human nature, the development of social and cultural history, the relationships between European and non-European peoples, and imperialism—he instead consistently focuses upon subsistence methods and land-use practices to account for human diversity, a method that emphasizes the collective freedoms of diverse peoples.[21] Kant never repudiated the hierarchical claims of his earlier writings on race, and indeed he continued to lecture about the concept of race late into his life. Yet, strikingly, his development of the idea of a distinctively human freedom (i.e., of cultural agency) and concomitantly his sociological account of human diversity displaced both the cognitive and the hierarchical assumptions and arguments of race theory in his late moral and political works, in which he explicitly defended non-European peoples and the equality of varying collective lifestyles (including pastoralism and nomadism) and vehemently attacked European empires and conquest.[22] Thus, I turn now to the other identifiable strand of Kant's theoretical understanding of human diversity, one that dominates his later, considered writings on morality and politics, and that provides the conceptual language with which he both analyzes social and political relationships among European and non-European peoples and denounces European imperialism.

The *Conjectures* provides a speculative account of the early development of agriculturally based, sedentary societies that is clearly inspired by Rousseau's *Discourse on Inequality*, but, unlike Rousseau, Kant also attempts to identify the tensions among nonsedentary and sedentary communities and the tendency of the latter to assimilate or to colonize the former. This latter point is crucial: whereas Rousseau discusses the linear transformation from "primitive" to "civilized" societies, Kant speculates not only about the early development of settled societies but also about the *relationships* between settled and nonsettled societies in the premodern era. As we will see, in a crucial discussion of property in *The Metaphysics of Morals* and in his writings on cosmopolitan right, Kant also suggests how such relationships should (and should not) be developed in his own day of increasingly global commercial relationships and European imperial expansion.

In his discussion of the political consequences of global cultural diversity, Kant focuses on the tensions between pastoral peoples—those whose sustenance and way of life is based primarily upon herding domesticated animals, as well as "sporadic digging for roots or gathering of fruit"— and agrarian peoples (8:118). Like Rousseau, Kant believes that the introduction of agriculture and the early growth of settled communities instigate profound changes in human life, including the rise of a variety of artistic, scientific, and other cultural developments, and, concomitantly, the rise of a disturbing amount of inequality and social and political oppression. Kant also describes the basic differences between entire nations that practise varying collective lifestyles and the resulting social tensions among these *coexisting* peoples:

> *Pastoral life* is not only leisurely, but also the most reliable means of support, for there is no lack of fodder for animals in a largely uninhabited country. *Agriculture* or the planting of crops, on the other hand, is extremely laborious, subject to the vagaries of climate, and consequently insecure; it also requires permanent settlements, ownership of land, and sufficient strength to defend the latter. The herdsman, however, abhors such property because it limits his freedom of pasture. (8:118)

The external conflicts between pastoralists (and hunters), on the one hand, and settled societies, on the other, create a situation virtually identical to that of a Hobbesian state of nature. In this case, however, rather than the pernicious atmosphere of conflict arising from *individuals*, or loosely organized bands of individuals, with different personal understandings of the danger or insecurity of others' behaviour, the *Conjectures* delineates the conflicts between nations (or peoples, *Völker*) that arise because of their differing collective ways of life.

Kant argues that civil constitutions and the public administration of justice arose in part because of the specific internal social needs of settled societies, such as the need for a stable system of property relations and the desire to manage "major acts of violence" through public power rather than through acts of private vengeance (8:119). In addition, however, external relations among settled and nonsettled peoples also provided an impetus to the political organization of agriculturally based societies:

Where people depend for their livelihood on the cultivation of the soil (and on the planting of trees in particular), they require permanent accommodation; and the defence of such property against all encroachment requires a large number of people who are prepared to assist one another. Hence those who adopted this way of life could no longer live in scattered family units, but had to stick together and set up village communities (incorrectly described as *towns*) in order to protect their property against savage hunters or tribes of pastoral nomads. (8:119)

Once such agriculturally based societies gain strength, Kant suggests three alternatives for the ensuing relationship between nonsettled and settled peoples. First, their conflicts might drive some nomadic peoples to the far reaches of the earth in search of safe territories in which they can practise their way of life. In *Toward Perpetual Peace*, Kant speculates that the peoples near the Arctic Ocean, such as "the Ostiaks or Samoyeds" must have been driven to such extreme terrain and climates by war (8:363–65).[23] Similarly, agriculturalists felt compelled to "distance" themselves "as far as possible" from peoples who might undermine "the fruit" of their "long and diligent efforts" (8:119).[24] The second option is a somewhat voluntary assimilation: in short, hunting and pastoral peoples will choose to enter settled societies. The social oppression and injustice of settled societies might be overlooked by nonsettled peoples given "the growing luxury of the town-dwellers" and thus they may "let themselves be drawn into the glittering misery of the towns" (8:120). Third, Kant also mentions briefly the forced assimilation of nonsettled peoples through the colonial activities of settled societies. Population growth, among other factors, impels settled nations to expand by force "like a beehive, [to] send out colonists in all directions from the centre—colonists who were already civilized." (8:119) Kant understood, in the early essay *Idea for a Universal History* (1784), the implications of such activities in his own day, though only later (in his writings from the mid-1790s onward) would he condemn them. The efforts of imperialists in the past and in his own day, he implies, did not and would not spare peoples who lead nonsettled ways of life. Kant anticipates—here without judgement—that "the political constitutions of our continent . . . will probably legislate eventually for all other continents" (8:29).

Anti-imperialism and Cosmopolitan Right

Kant recognized that the ongoing, often antagonistic relationships among diverse peoples constituted the global political reality of his day, one that demanded, in his view, not only a conjectural history of their early development as he had earlier provided, but also an ethical and political analysis. His concept of cosmopolitan right, one of his three categories of political justice, is meant precisely to offer a critique of empire.

Kant's account of differing property regimes raises many of the central imperial issues that he most fully addresses in his theory of cosmopolitan right. In a striking section of *The Metaphysics of Morals*, he ponders some of the moral issues that are raised by conflicts among peoples who practise different collective ways of life, in the context of a discussion about the various uses of property. Kant dismisses John Locke's argument that one must mix one's labour with the land (for instance, through the practice of agriculture) to be able to claim it legitimately as one's own property. As we have seen, this agriculturalist approach to justifying private property was often used by British and French colonialists as a means to deny indigenous peoples any ownership of the land they occupied, on the view that they did not mix their labour with, and thus did not 'improve', the land in any manner.[25] Accordingly, such territory was considered to be *res nullius*, or 'belonging to no one'. It is significant, then, that Kant addresses this theory of property just before discussing conflicts between agrarian and non-settled peoples in general and the moral claims of European imperialists in particular. Kant presents the Lockean view in the form of a question before rejecting it swiftly:

> [I]n order to acquire land is it necessary to develop it (build on it, cultivate it, drain it, and so on)? No. For since these forms (of specification) are only accidents, they make no object of direct possession and can belong to what the subject possesses only insofar as the substance is already recognized as his. When first acquisition is in question, developing land is nothing more than an external sign of taking possession, for which many other signs that cost less effort can be substituted.[26] (6:265)

The clearest aforementioned sign, in Kant's view, is the capability of defending such land; in short, if peoples are capable of actively resisting others' attempts to use or to occupy their lands, this itself constitutes a sign that they are the first possessors, regardless of whether they have cultivated or developed their lands.[27]

Kant then moves to the issue of neighbouring families or peoples who practise different collective ways of life. Can they, he asks,

> resist each other in adopting a certain use of land, for example, can a hunting people resist a pasturing people or a farming people, or the latter resist a people that wants to plant orchards, and so forth? Certainly, since as long as they keep within their own boundaries the way they want to *live* on their land is up to their own discretion (*res merae facultatis*). (6:266)

We saw earlier in this chapter that Kant uses the Latin juristic term *res merae facultatis* to refer to that part of the faculty of desire by which *individuals* exercise their cultural (or 'negative') freedom to make distinctively 'human choices', choices that result from our status as beings with 'humanity' and that necessarily yield a plurality of perspectives and practices. Recall that Kant defends giving individuals a wide latitude to reflect and to act upon their choices about happiness, value, beauty, work, which capacities they will cultivate, and other matters relating, broadly stated, to their cultural activities and judgements. Here Kant applies this anti-paternalistic idea of a pluralistic and experientially situated freedom to *groups*, that is, to the collective ways of life of entire peoples.

Kant continues his argument by moving immediately from the topic of neighbouring peoples, who are adjacent to one another presumably because of much earlier migrations of the kind that he describes in the *Conjectures*, to the more deliberate encounters of European voyages of discovery and imperial activity. Kant notes that

> it can still be asked whether, when neither nature nor chance but just our own will brings us into the neighborhood of a people that holds out no prospect of a civil union with it, we should not be authorized to found colonies, by force if need be, in order to establish a civil union with them and bring these human beings (savages) into a rightful condition (as with the American Indians, the Hottentots [of southern Africa] and the inhabitants of New Holland [Australia]); or (which is not much better), to found colonies by fraudulent purchase of their land, and so become owners of their land, making use of our superiority without regard for their first possession. (6:266)

Kant contemptuously labels such rationalizations of European imperialism as "Jesuitism" and writes that "it is easy to see through this veil of injustice". He concludes bluntly that "[s]uch a way of acquiring land is therefore to be repudiated." (6:266) Hence, Kant defends the freedom of societies, including those of hunting and pastoral peoples, to organize their most basic collective practices in the manner that they see fit and to defend their way of life against imperialists and others who attempt to alter them.

To understand more fully the nature of Kant's opposition to imperialism, one must examine his writings on cosmopolitan right, the primary *critical* purpose of which is to condemn European imperialism. Yet a crucial question immediately presents itself before one can investigate the concept itself: namely, to what domain of human activity does cosmopolitan right refer? Kant insists adamantly that the concept of a right should be theorized at *three* conceptually distinct levels: the domestic, the international (rights pertaining to the law of nations), and the cosmopolitan.[28] His political writings make clear that at each level one can formulate an ideal against which actual political practices can be judged and which we should collectively attempt to realize, however imperfectly. Thus, the idea of civil rights applies to the institutions and practices of individual states. The ideal against which actual regimes are judged is that of a "pure republic" in which public authority flows from the sanctity of freely made laws and not from the arbitrary power of any one group of particular humans, a regime in which "*freedom* [is] the principle and indeed the condition for any exercise of [public] coercion" (6:340).[29] The right of nations (or right of states) applies to the relations among states. At this international level, the regulative ideal against which present actions should be judged and toward which states should strive is a free federation of states eventually encompassing "all the nations of the earth." (8:357) To whom or to what practices, then, does cosmopolitan right apply, if not to relations among individuals or relations among states? And what is the ideal of cosmopolitan right against which the relevant extant practices should be judged?

In recognition of the heightened discovery, travel, and imperial activity of his century, Kant believed that a discussion of justice at only the domestic and interstate levels could not fully capture the newly emerging ethical problems of the modern age. Although his discussions in *Toward Perpetual Peace* of ancient trade routes—such as those that connected Europe to Central Asia, India, and China—exemplify his understanding of the extensive history of commercial relations and activity between Europe and the non-European world, Kant also believed that the world of his day had become integrated to a degree that went far beyond transnational relationships of the past.[30] One can plausibly describe this aspect of Kant's thought, then, as an early attempt to grapple with the globalization of economic, political, and hence moral ties. Kant suggests that since the

> community of nations of the earth has now gone so far that a violation of right on one place of the earth is felt in all, the idea of a cosmopolitan right is no fantastic and exaggerated way of representing right. . . . (8:360)

In formulating this new ethico-political category, Kant stresses that it rests not upon a preposterous and idealistic view of the international community, but rather responds to the actual global relationships that make the idea of cosmopolitan right a moral necessity. Cosmopolitan right is therefore

> a supplement to the unwritten code of the right of a state and the right of nations necessary for the sake of any public rights of human beings and so for perpetual peace; only under this condition can we flatter ourselves that we are constantly approaching perpetual peace. (8:360)

Kant affirms the importance of cosmopolitan right even more starkly in *The Metaphysics of Morals*, where he asserts that if we fail to secure a semblance of justice at any one of the three levels of human interaction (the domestic, international, and cosmopolitan levels), then "the framework of all the others is unavoidably undermined and must finally collapse." (6:311) For Kant, the particular activities that have engendered not only the reality of a community of nations on the earth, but also the issues of justice at this cosmopolitan level, are almost all related to European colonialism. Visiting foreign lands "and still more settling there to connect them with the mother country, provides the occasion for troubles and acts of violence in one place on our globe to be felt all over it." (6:353)

In a discussion of international right in the "Doctrine of Right", Kant argues that the analogy between warring states in the international arena and warring individuals in a state of nature reaches its limit when one fully considers issues of global justice because

> we have to take into consideration not only the relation of one state toward another as a whole, but also *the relation of individual persons of one state toward the individuals of another, as well as toward another state as a whole.* (6:344, emphasis added)

Kant informs his readers that in this section (on the right of nations, that is, on international justice), he will concern himself only with those features of international relations that *are* analogous to a hypothetical state of nature, leaving unanswered the question of when he might consider the nonanalogous relationships that he described briefly above. We later find that he saves his discussion of non-interstate global relationships for his section on cosmopolitan right. It then becomes clear that cosmopolitan right concerns how individuals from one political realm ought to relate to individuals of another (foreign) realm, as well as how states and foreigners should treat one another—i.e., what visitors owe to foreign states, and what states, in turn, owe to such foreign visitors.

Along these lines, Kant explains in a footnote in *Toward Perpetual Peace* that cosmopolitan right refers to

> the *right of citizens of the world*, insofar as individuals and states, standing in the relation of externally affecting one another, are to be regarded as citizens of a universal state of mankind (*ius cosmopoliticum*). (8:349)

Although the emphasis here on being citizens of the world might appear to be a slightly different way of representing the domain of cosmopolitan right, in Kant's German this amounts simply to a description of the word used for "cosmopolitan right" itself, as *Weltbürgerrecht* is literally a compound of "world", "citizen", and "right". While Kant argues against an actual world government and instead for simply a voluntary federation of states, he believes that the complex interrelationships between states and foreigners raise issues of justice that can only be met by a separate category of justice, one that recognizes that the interrelationships among humans bind them together as fellow citizens of the earth, despite the fact that they inhabit different sovereign realms. Thus, as Kant makes a point of emphasizing, humans from different societies owe something to each other *as a matter of justice*, not simply as a matter of philanthropy or generosity, despite the absence of a shared sovereign power that unites them all. The one innate right of humanity—the protection of the distinctively human freedom that underlies humanity as cultural agency—that humans possess simply by being human and not because of any civil agreements or the possession of citizenship hence receives its most robust political expression in Kant's account of cosmopolitan right. In *The Metaphysics of Morals*, the three concepts that are said to follow from the innate right of humanity are equality, freedom, and communication, each of which is central to Kant's understanding of cosmopolitan right.

It should be clear, then, why a discussion only of interstate relations is insufficient for the purposes of discussing political justice at a global level. The language of justice—or, in Kant's terms, the domain of right—extends beyond the borders of any one state and, at a global level, involves more than just interstate relations. Kant's statements about cosmopolitan right suggest that it is not its global scope that distinguishes it from international right. Instead, cosmopolitan right is unique in that it attempts to articulate a normative ideal that attends to the ethical problems raised by increasingly common relationships between "[foreign] individuals and states", in contrast to the traditional purview of the 'law of nations' that pertains mainly to "states in relation to one another (*ius gentium*)" (8:349). Presumably, even if the ideal condition of a voluntary federation of states were met, ethical problems would still be raised by the manner in which (for example) states and foreigners (or individuals from different countries) dealt with one another. Such foreign individuals might act as the agents of a state or they might simply be travellers of the kind who voyaged frequently in Kant's day, with no apparent intention of conquering lands, however much their information might have helped later colonialists. Bougainville, the eighteenth-century French explorer who circumnavigated the globe and whose travel writings inspired Diderot's dialogue about Tahiti and imperialism, seems to fit this latter category. As we saw earlier, in a book review of Bougainville's *Voyage autour du monde*, Diderot criticized Bougainville's travels for, perhaps unwittingly, laying the groundwork for what Diderot assumed would be French colonial activity in the South Pacific. Diderot was, of course, prescient in this regard; indeed, Tahiti remains one of France's last colonial outposts. Yet, unlike Diderot, who proclaimed in his book review that Bougainville and every other European should simply leave Tahiti alone, Kant never, even for rhetorical effect, called for a prohibition of developing transnational ties. Rather, his category of cosmopolitan right attempts to articulate an ideal with which one can both condemn European imperialism *and* encourage nonexploitative and peaceful transnational relations.

Kant understood, of course, that injustices often followed voyages of discovery and the commercial activities of trading companies, such as (to use one of Kant's examples) the British East India Company. Nonetheless, he argues that the "horrifying" abuses that transnational voyages have unleashed "cannot annul the right of citizens of the world *to try to* establish community with all and, to this end, to *visit* all regions of the earth." (6:353) As he explains, cosmopolitan right should be limited to "conditions of universal *hospitality*" (8:357), which include, for instance,

> the right of a foreigner not to be treated with hostility because he has arrived on the land of another. The other can turn him away, if this can be done without destroying him, but as long as he behaves peaceably where he is [*auf seinem Platz*], he cannot be treated with hostility. (8:358)

But why should we try to establish community with others at all? As we have seen, Kant's understanding of the transnational ties that were developing in his day (often unjustly because of 'hostile' Europeans) brought issues of cosmopolitan justice to the fore. In addition to the timeliness of theorizing cosmopolitan right in his day, Kant provides more fundamental reasons that suggest its enduring moral importance.

First, the finitude of humans' geography, that is, the very idea of a "globe", entails that individuals and societies *cannot* avoid interacting with one another. Humans do not live on an infinite plane along which they can spread without having to engage each other. Along these lines, it may be helpful to recall Kant's account of the social effects of war and the forced migrations that, in his view, originally populated much of the earth. At some point, Kant implies, whole peoples cannot continue to flee the injustices of persecution and settle in neutral, unoccupied territories. The globe itself poses intrinsic geographical limits to the strategies of mass exodus and national isolation. Since humans live on a "sphere, they cannot disperse infinitely but must finally put up with being near one another" (8:358). This geographical argument, in combination with the political reality of increasing interconnectedness among peoples, presents the need for an ethical standard by which individuals and states can attempt to relate to one another in a nonexploitative manner. The relationships among far-flung peoples will not only take place at the realm of interstate relations, but will also be fostered as a result of trade, voyages of anthropological and scientific study, and other forms of travel and contact. Kant's concept of cosmopolitan right seeks to attend to this complex global reality.

Second, Kant's account of property serves as the basis for an argument about the legitimacy of humans to voyage in pursuit of community with others. A key tenet of Kant's theory of property is that "[a]ll human beings are originally in *common possession* [*Gesammt-Besitz*] of the land of the entire earth" (6:267). In other words, the territories that peoples possess today have not always been owned, but were originally held in common. Thus, there is a certain arbitrariness as to why certain people live on, and rightfully possess, particular areas of the earth. As Kant suggests in *Toward Perpetual Peace*, "originally no one had more right than another to be on a place on the earth." Hence, Kant's argument is that we should not presume from the simple fact that we legitimately possess a territory that this gives us the authority or the right to exclude others from it entirely. Given the ultimately arbitrary origins and, consequently, the equivocal status of our property, the rightful possessors of territories lack *absolute* authority over it. The individuals and governing authorities of nations, therefore, are under an ethical obligation to visiting foreigners, who themselves possess a certain authority that demands ethical respect.[31] At one point, therefore, Kant refers to one aspect of "the right of hospitality" as "the authorization of a foreign newcomer" (8:358).

In part, the authorization of those who roam from territory to territory derives from humanity's collective ownership of the earth's *surface*, if not its underlying land. There are also vast swaths of the earth's surface that are uninhabitable and that create ideal opportunities for travellers to seek community with other societies. As Kant argues, the "right to visit", or

> to present oneself for society, belongs to all humans beings by virtue of the right of possession in common of the earth's surface. . . . Uninhabitable parts of the earth's surface, seas and deserts, divide this [global human] community, but in such a way that *ships* and *camels* (*ships* of the desert) make it possible to approach one another over these regions belonging to no one [*die keinem angehörten*] and to make use of the right to the *earth's surface*, which belongs to the human race in common, for possible commerce. (8:358)

Kant's understanding of the legitimacy of travel stands in striking contrast to one of the prevalent views of voyaging and seeking out new lands and peoples in the tradition of European thought. Even Diderot, though ultimately a kind of cosmopolitan at heart, as his reveries about cross-cultural learning, interethnic marriage, and transnational community building evince, feared nonetheless that the very act of travel created corrupt and rapacious behaviour, for travellers who were too far removed from the *moeurs* of their homelands at times became ferocious beasts abroad. Of course, Diderot's concerns about travel stemmed almost exclusively from his hatred of imperialism and the cruel domination of foreign peoples that ultimately resulted from travel in the modern age. But

Diderot was simply giving an anti-imperialist spin on a theme with an ancient provenance. As Anthony Pagden has noted, the

> disapproval of travel belongs to an ancient European tradition, one which locates the source of all civility—which is, after all a life lived in cities (*civitates*)—in settled communities, and which looks upon all modes of nomadism as irredeemably savage. . . . Crossing the ocean was an act contrary to nature, for the gods—or God—had filled half the world with water precisely in order to keep humans apart.[32]

Set against this intellectual context, and unlike Diderot who often deploys (and thus seemingly endorses) a classic trope of this kind either to subvert it ultimately or to cast doubt on some other tradition, Kant unambiguously dispels this view of travel. With regard to oceans, for instance, he argues the following:

> Although the seas might seem to remove nations from any community with one another, they are the arrangements of nature most favoring their commerce by means of navigation; and the more *coastlines* these nations have in the vicinity of one another (as in the Mediterranean), the more lively their commerce can be. (6:353–54)

For Kant, nomadism per se, is not evil or depraved. Though one can only speculate about such matters, his fairly generous views of hunting and pastoral peoples in the light of most imperial discourse (for instance, Kant's view that their collective lifestyles are fundamentally human and free and his defence of their legitimacy in resisting imperial subjugation and all coercive efforts to change their societies) may have something to do with his approval of the nonsettled, nomadic voyagers whose travels created and strengthened a kind of global or transnational civil society, related to, but distinct from, the relations of states. His theory of originally communal and traversable property establishes the authority of voyagers and, thus, the right to make contact and communicate with others.[33]

Kant combines these two arguments of geography and property in a passage worth quoting at length. He writes in *The Metaphysics of Morals* that humans are enclosed

> all together within determinate limits (by the spherical shape of the place they live in, a *globus terraqueus* [a globe of earth and water]). And since possession of the land, on which an inhabitant of the earth can live, can be thought only as a possession of a part of a determinate whole, and so as possession of that to which each of them originally has a right, it follows that all nations stand *originally* in a community of land, though not of *rightful* community of possession (*communio*) and so use of it, or of property in it; instead they stand in a community of possible physical *interaction* (*commercium*), that is, in a thoroughgoing relation of each to all the others of offering to engage in commerce with

any other, and each has a right to make this attempt without the other being authorized to behave toward it as an enemy [simply] because it has made this attempt. (6:352)

Kant's use of the Latin *commercium* indicates that although cosmopolitan right seeks *in part* to protect those engaged in market-oriented trade (commerce in the narrow sense), the concept of a right to visit is also intended more widely to refer to any possible interactions among individuals of different peoples. Kant's own language, in which he moves back and forth from *Wechselwirkung* (interaction broadly construed) to *Verkehr* (a term that he sometimes uses to denote contractual, trade or market-based interactions, but that also means, more generically, dealings or contact), both of which are usually translated into English as 'commerce', indicates the wide scope of Kant's understanding of commercial relationships. It would be a mistake, in other words, to treat cosmopolitan right simply as a kind of bourgeois right, to view it as a concept that Kant uses in order to legitimate an early form of global capitalism. Indeed, given the nature of Kant's attack on European imperialism, in many respects he uses the ethical standards of a commercial community (widely construed as cosmopolitan interaction) to attack the injustices wrought by the narrower, market-oriented sense of commerce, such as the exploitative, profit-seeking practices of voyagers and the actions of quasi-sovereign corporations like the imperial Indies companies. The two senses of commerce, however, need not *always* be opposed. The "spirit of [market] commerce" and the related "power of money", both of which Kant marshals famously in defence of the idea of a realistic (non-naïve) belief in political progress, are selfish forces that (Kant wants his readers to hope) might engender a prudentially oriented respect for cosmopolitan right, since the concept itself might not motivate individuals to abide by it (8:368). Here, then, we see Kant attempting to use market-oriented commerce in service of the broader idea of a just and peaceful *commercium* that the concept of cosmopolitan right demands.[34] But when the two are in conflict, Kant's anti-imperialist arguments evince the primacy of the latter, ethical idea of *commercium*.

Kant asserts emphatically that a right to visit is not a right to conquer or a right to settle. Cosmopolitan right "does not extend beyond the conditions which make it possible to seek commerce with the old inhabitants." (8:358) Authorized visitors, too, are under certain obligations to foreign peoples (a visitor's authorization is not absolute, just as a state's authority over its land is not absolute) and, thus, inhospitality can flow in either direction. At one point, Kant criticizes some non-European practices such as those of the inhabitants along the Barbary coast "in robbing ships in adjacent seas or enslaving stranded seafarers, or that of the inhab-

itants of deserts (the Arabian Bedouins) in regarding approach to nomadic tribes as a right to plunder them" (8:359). Nonetheless, he singles
out European "commercial states" as particularly egregious offenders of
cosmopolitan right given their imperial exploits.

> If one compares with this [the idea of cosmopolitan right] the *inhospitable*
> behavior of civilized, especially commercial, states in our part of the world, the
> injustice they show in *visiting* foreign lands and peoples (which with them is
> tantamount to *conquering* them) goes to horrifying lengths. When America,
> the Negro countries, the Spice Islands, the Cape, and so forth were discovered,
> they were, to them, countries belonging to no one [*die keinem angehörten*],
> since they counted the inhabitants as nothing. In the East Indies (Hindustan),
> they brought in foreign soldiers under the pretext of merely proposing to set
> up trading posts, but with them [came] oppression of the inhabitants, incite-
> ment of the various Indians states to widespread wars, famine, rebellions,
> treachery, and the whole litany of troubles that oppress the human race.
> (8:358–59)

In addition to his effort to defend oppressed people's resistance to imperial rule, Kant investigates some other responses to the horrors of European activity in the world. Given their cruel behaviour, Kant praises the
restrictions imposed upon Europeans by China and Japan, much as Diderot had justified China's prohibition of Europeans in the *Histoire des
deux Indes*. Kant writes that "China and Japan (*Nipon*), which had given
such guests a try, have therefore wisely [placed restrictions on them], the
former allowing them access but not entry [*den Zugang, aber nicht den
Eingang*], the latter even allowing access to only a single European people, the Dutch, but excluding them, like prisoners, from community with
the natives."[35] (8:359) In a moment suggestive of his contextualized view
of moral and political judgement, Kant praises the seemingly harsh restrictions because of China and Japan's historical memory and political
circumstances.[36] Europeans had created such a pernicious historical record of foreign exploitation, in Kant's view, that non-European countries
that had the ability to do so, and that were not already dominated from
without, could legitimately curb European activities within their territories. Thus, actions that might prima facie violate the right to hospitality—
in particular, the treatment of foreigners as virtual prisoners—become
permissible in light of judgements of historical experience. Europeans,
Kant implies, had worn out their welcome in much of the world long ago
and, at least in some parts of the globe, were being treated accordingly.

While Kant does not rule out the legitimacy of making contact and
developing reciprocal ties with peoples through travel, he insists that the
right to try to establish community with others "is not, however, a right

to *make a settlement* on the land of another nation (*ius incolatus* [right to inhabit]); for this, a specific contract is required." (6:353) The people itself must genuinely allow foreigners to inhabit their land as guests. As he suggests in *Toward Perpetual Peace*, even a right to be a "guest" requires "a special beneficent pact" that invites foreigners to become "members" of a household or, for that matter, of society in general (8:358). Kant understands, however, that the more pressing question in the context of imperial activity concerns whether diverse peoples, such as hunters or pastoralists, rightly possess the lands that they inhabit and, even if they do, whether their use of such vast swaths of land is defensible. He considers such views by examining a common imperialist argument whereby a number of colonial settlements would be deemed justifiable because colonists simply become the *neighbours* of indigenous peoples; surely for this, the argument runs, no special agreement or pact of beneficence is necessary. Kant puts the question as follows: "in newly discovered lands, may a nation undertake to settle (*accolatus* [dwell near, as a neighbour]) and take possession in the neighbourhood of a people that has already settled in the region, even without its consent?" Kant responds,

> If the settlement is made so far from where that people resides that there is no encroachment on anyone's use of his land, the right to settle is not open to doubt. But if these people are shepherds or hunters (like the Hottentots, the Tungusi, or most of the American Indian nations) who depend for their sustenance on vast open stretches of land [*großen öden Landstrecken*], this settlement may not take place by force but only by contract, and indeed by a contract that does not take advantage of the ignorance of those inhabitants with respect to ceding their lands.[37] (6:353)

As inviting as "discovered" territory may seem to potential colonists, "vast open stretches of land" are not necessarily inhabitable by foreigners without indigenous peoples' real and uncoerced consent, since its very vastness may be necessary for the basic sustenance of hunting or pastoral peoples. One implication of this passage is that individuals from settled societies are deceiving themselves by judging other peoples according to their own ultimately conventional (in this case, agrarian) standards. Lands that appear to serve no purpose, in the European view, may very well be necessary for the collective lifestyles of whole nations. Such judgements, in other words, must be made in a manner that presupposes the rationality and freedom of indigenous peoples' land use, especially when that use relates to their basic survival. With the decline of anti-imperialist political thought in the post-Enlightenment age, Kant's call to respect the freedom of non-European peoples and his arguments against imperialism would later invite scorn from commentators who concluded that such beliefs offered "proof of Kant's incapacity to judge of cultural-historical things", since "primitive peoples", according to this view, "lack concepts of right, [and thus] treaties [with them] cannot be made, as Kant demands."[38]

Given Kant's anthropological assumption that land use is one of the most fundamental social characteristics of a people, his defense of hunting and pastoral uses of land is an endorsement of the humanity (the cultural agency) of such peoples' collective ways of life. We have already seen that Kant does not hold the view that pastoralist and hunting peoples lead lives that are irrational or inhuman and thus that they have no right to their lands. Rather, when peoples engage in such collective practices, he argues, their distinctively human freedom (*res merae facultatis*) must be respected. As we have just seen, the political criticism that such a view makes possible is taken up by Kant in his discussions of cosmopolitan right.

We have already surveyed the principal reasons why Kant finds Europeans' imperializing mission unjust: it violates peoples' freedom to order their collective ways of life and it oversteps the ethical limits imposed upon travellers according to cosmopolitan right, an ethical and political concept that he articulates precisely to scrutinize interactions between foreign peoples and voyaging individuals, including colonialists and members of potentially exploitative trading companies. Underlying all of this philosophically, I have suggested, are Kant's understanding of negative freedom and distinctively human choice (which for him are among the sources of "humanity" and "culture in general"), and his anti-paternalistic commitment to a wide latitude of judgement and self-determination. In addition to his positive defence of non-Europeans against imperial incursions, Kant dismisses two "specious [*scheinbar*] reasons" given to support the colonization of the New World: that "it is to the world's advantage, partly because these crude peoples will become civilized . . . and partly because one's own country will be cleaned of corrupt men, and they or their descendants will, it is hoped, become better in another part of the world (such as New Holland [Australia])." (6:353) Kant's reply is swift and concise: "But all these supposedly good intentions cannot wash away the stain of injustice in the means used for them." (6:353)

But why does Kant believe that the standard justifications of imperialism are "specious" and only "supposedly" good? In particular, why does Kant contend that the mission to civilize others is specious? To be sure, as we have seen, he abhors the coercion involved in such imperializing activities—the *means* of imperialism—as ethically unacceptable because of their intrinsic brutality and because they are a manifest affront to the idea that peoples ought to be allowed to make their own determinations as to how to organize their societies. But what of the *ends* of imperialism, especially the standard imperialist justification that 'civilized' societies ought to civilize 'primitive' peoples? Is the very goal of 'civilizing' other peoples just or unjust? If the questions are put in this manner, then the answer can be drawn straightforwardly from Kant's anti-paternalism: just as individuals (or states) should not directly order others' life choices, groups of colonialists should not restructure the collective life choices of entire peoples. Thus, if the human freedom that underlies humanity as cultural agency itself is given its due, then there cannot be a duty to civilize others, just as there cannot be a duty to develop other individuals.

As discussed earlier, however, Kant justifies a moral duty to develop one's *own* human capacities. Is there, then, a corresponding duty for *peoples* to 'improve' or 'perfect' *themselves?* In the language of the eighteenth century, are hunting and pastoral peoples duty-bound to become "civilized" through their own internal efforts? How far does Kant accept the global diversity of peoples that he identifies? To flesh this out further, we can ask the following: While there is no just way for Europeans or any other nations to bring such changes about by force, should hunting and pastoral peoples *themselves* (through their own actions, and of their own volition) transform their lifestyles and practices into those of agrarian societies and institute the public administration of justice and rule of law, as described, for instance, in the "Doctrine of Right"? The general question, then, is whether these ways of life (hunting, pastoral, and agricultural) are commensurable—whether, that is, they can be ranked or ordered along some universal scale of value, such that an 'inferior' people ought to raise themselves to a 'superior' level of social and political development. Kant did not address this question directly in his political philosophy (incidentally, this itself is astonishing in the light of eighteenth-century developmental accounts of non-European peoples), but it is worthwhile to reflect along these lines upon the broader implications of his theory of cosmopolitan right, as I do briefly below. In the next section, I will examine Kant's political thought in order to determine what light his social contract account might shed on this issue.

We have seen already that in *The Metaphysics of Morals* Kant treats the decision to lead a hunting or pastoral existence as an instance of human choice, i.e., of cultural agency. Kant's use of the language of distinctively human freedom, e.g., *res merae facultatis*, to defend the viability of such differences among peoples indicates that absolute moral judgements about them cannot be made. Consequently, hunting, pastoral, and agrarian societies are neither morally obligatory nor morally wrong. For Kant, as I argued earlier, choices at the cultural level involve relative or comparative judgements that are based upon varying and partial understandings of experience. If one chooses to continue a nonsettled existence, this falls within the range of judgements that a categorical ethics cannot prescribe or deny. Judgements of this kind are morally neutral and thus are judged according to standards of satisfaction and happiness that, for Kant, are inherently plural. There are no universal standards of happiness, he argues, with which one could definitively rank various morally neutral ways of life, whether they are individual lives or the most fundamental collective practices (the most basic issues of land usage) of entire nations. The three forms of group life with which Kant differentiates global peoples are, thus, incommensurable; there is no universal value with which one could rationally judge one against the other. This is the ultimate consequence of Kant's claim about societies and how they should structure their most fundamental collective practices (from hunting or herding animals to farming and the sedentary, urban lives it makes possible): again, "how they want to live on their land is up to their own discretion (*res merae facultatis*)." (6:266) Strikingly, by invoking the language of humanity, in the broad sense of cultural agency, Kant affirms the ultimate incommensurability of these collective ways of life.

An Unusual Social Contract Doctrine

In Kant's thought, the only potential source for making a claim that a nonsettled people is under a categorical duty to become a settled people, and thus that along some objective scale of value, the life of agrarian nations is superior to that of hunting and pastoral nations, rests upon his social contract theory: it is a categorical imperative, Kant argues, that individuals in a state of nature should leave this noncivil condition and institute a collective public power that is based upon the rule of law. For most social contract theorists before Kant, the concept of the state of nature is much more than a metaphor used to legitimate civil power. Amerindians and other New World inhabitants almost always played a prominent role as empirical illustrations of the natural (noncivil) condition of humanity in social contract doctrines. This underscored the argument, as it typically ran, that the social contract was not a hypothetical construct, but rather a sober and incisive description of Europe's own history.[39] New World peoples, in this view, represent empirical examples of the natural and savage Europeans of the distant past, before they became civilized; that is, before they entered civil relations under a contractually created sovereign power. In addition to providing an arguably historical and anthropological foundation for the legitimacy of the modern state, deploying the figure of New World lawless savages sometimes served to legitimate the imperial enterprise—if European savages acted rightly in forming civil societies in ancient times, then contemporary savages should civilize themselves as well, though now with the imperial help of their civilized brethren. The issue of agrarianism is central given that the standard understanding of civil society and civilization—and thus of politics itself—is based upon city life, the sedentary life of the *polis* that agriculture makes possible.

In at least one important way, Kant deviated from the social contract tradition that he inherited and appropriated by jettisoning any reliance upon Amerindians, South Pacific Islanders, or indeed any non-Europeans in theorizing a state of nature. Kant insisted that his social contract doctrine was hypothetical and, in this respect, he is rather unusual, though not unique, for Rousseau also makes a similar claim, though it is largely undermined, as I argued in chapter 2, by his relentlessly naturalistic portrayal of Amerindians and Hottentots in his discussion of the earliest state of nature. Kant describes in the clearest possible terms both the hypothetical nature and the chief purpose of the social contract device in *Theory and Practice*:

> [I]t is by no means necessary that this contract (called *contractus originarius* or *pactum sociale*) . . . be presupposed as a *fact* (as a fact it is indeed not possible)—as if it would first have to be proved from history that a people, into whose rights and obligations we have entered as descendants, once actually carried out such an act, and that it must have left some sure record or instrument of it, orally or in writing, if one is to hold oneself bound to an already existing civil constitution. It is instead *only an idea* of reason, which, however, has its undoubted practical reality, namely to bind every legislator to give his laws in such a way that they *could* have arisen from the united will of a whole people and to regard each subject, insofar as he wants to be a citizen, as if he has joined in voting for such a will. For this is the touchstone of any public law's conformity with right. (8:297)

Kant did, however, rely upon another frequently cited example used by social contractarians to elaborate and defend his views about the law of nations. While Kant seemed to believe that an actual empirical example may be impossible to provide, he also held that one remarkable *analogy* to it could be found in the political world of his day: states in the international order, he argues, lead an existence that is almost identical to the grim and unstable predicament of individuals in a hypothetical, noncivil condition.[40]

The imperializing rhetoric that sometimes follows from a naturalistic representation of New World peoples in social contract theories does not hold in Kant's political thought because of his exclusive use of the international order as an empirical example of a natural state. The one occasion in which Kant uses the classic image of the Amerindian in his political writings consists of a satirical moment in *Toward Perpetual Peace*. Kant plays ironically with the idea of New World individuals as natural savages and cannibals to criticize the violent behaviour of European states,

much as Montaigne drew upon conventional sixteenth-century stereo-
types of Amerindians to decry the cruelty of intra-European religious fanaticism in "Of Cannibals":

> Just as we now regard with profound contempt, as barbarous, crude, and brut-
> ishly degrading to humanity, the attachment of savages to their lawless free-
> dom, by which they would rather struggle unceasingly than subject themselves
> to a lawful coercion to be instituted by themselves, thus preferring a mad free-
> dom to a rational freedom, so, one must think, civilized peoples (each united
> into a state) must hasten to leave such a depraved condition, the sooner the
> better; but instead each state . . . command[s] many thousands to sacrifice
> themselves for a matter that is of no concern to them; and the difference be-
> tween European and the American savages consists mainly in this: that whereas
> many tribes of the latter have been eaten up by their enemies, the former know
> how to make better use of those they have defeated than to make a meal of
> them, and would rather increase the number of their subjects, and so too the
> multitude of their instruments for even more extensive wars, by means of them.
> (8:355)

Kant's ironic use of a predominant image of the Amerindian in order to
attack what he characterizes as European savagery is fraught, like all such
rhetorical strategies, with the danger of reifying the very image that is
meant to be deployed facetiously. Still, we know from his lectures on
physical geography that Kant doubted the existence of cannibalism, and,
accordingly, censured Europeans for using the term "cannibal" as a place-
holder for any people about whom they knew virtually nothing, such as
most of the peoples of Africa.[41] And, as we have seen in *The Metaphysics of
Morals*, non-European peoples, including hunters and pastoralists, in
Kant's view, lead their lives not as a result of "mad freedom", but rather
because of their distinctively human freedom. By conceptualizing the difference between hunting, pastoral, and agrarian peoples as one rooted in
human freedom—the freedom that characterizes "culture in general"—
such collective lives immediately win respect as *equally* legitimate forms
of life that are neutral from the standpoint of a categorical morality.[42]

In addition to all this, it is well worth noting Kant's attitude toward
linguistic and religious diversity on a global scale. Kant supports a plurality of societies that are characterized by various religions and languages. He argues in *Toward Perpetual Peace* that this diversity is a check
against the political despotism of large states or, worse on his view, a
single world state. In an argument that is obviously relevant to empire-
building—though here he does not explicitly make such a link (as
Herder did), focusing instead on the spectre of a world government—
Kant argues that political communities of this vast size are bound to be
despotic and ultimately anarchic: "as the range of government expands

laws progressively lose their vigor, and a soulless despotism, after it has destroyed the seed of good, finally deteriorates into anarchy." (8:367) Sociologically, then, the existence of human differences (especially, for Kant, religious and linguistic differences) is politically advantageous; thus, the fact of difference should be celebrated by any friend of political freedom. But such differences can also "bring with them", Kant concedes, "the propensity to mutual hatred and pretexts for war". Moreover, as he knew, imperialism can undo by force, by stamping out or by subverting religious and linguistic difference, what (we can speculatively presume) "nature" uses to keep human groups from forming a despotic universal state. Kant hoped that a combination of selfish motives (the spirit of commerce and the power of money) and a "gradual approach of human beings to greater agreement in principles", most crucially that of the law of nations and cosmopolitan right, would make imperialism and aggressive state actions ethically unacceptable to a more enlightened global community (8:368). The diversity of languages and religions would then remain and would serve a key purpose in securing political freedom and cosmopolitan justice, while its potentially damaging effects might be mitigated for both selfish and moral reasons.[43] Kant realized that this constituted a *hope*, and (as we saw in the last chapter) he staked this hope not upon a guarantee of political progress but upon a realizable goal toward which individuals could and should work.

It is clear that while Kant views hunting and pastoralist peoples as social groups who live freely chosen, human ways of life, he does not also consider them to be *political* societies. In this respect, he exemplifies much of the history of theorizing civil life, which is, by both linguistic and philosophical tradition, the sedentary life of a polis. As I have argued, there is a strong assumption that runs throughout much of the tradition of European political thought that fundamentally links agrarianism and the political (or civil) life. The social contract tradition often reinforced this link by treating nonsettled peoples as perfect examples of individuals in a state of nature who ought to leave their condition to create a civil (and presumably a settled, agrarian) life. In Kant's understanding, many New World peoples are social but noncivil humans. This would seem to indicate that they are identical to the individuals of Kant's state of nature, for, in his social contract account, the state of nature can be, and often is, social; what ultimately defines this condition is that it is not civil. Kant did not believe, however, that the hunters and pastoralists of his day were identical to the noncivil, natural humans of his social contract narrative, as I later argue for three reasons. In this respect, in the tradition of modern political thought, Kant was a most unusual social contract theorist. What follows from this is that hunting and pastoralist peoples are *not* under a categorical duty to transform their societies on the model of

Kant's understanding of the public law, and thus to change themselves into agricultural, sedentary states. Kant's social contract doctrine accords, therefore, with his humanitarian and pluralistic defence of peoples' freedom to lead their collective ways of life as they see fit.

First, as I have argued, it is crucial that we comprehend Kant's intention in using the peculiar narrative of a social contract. Kant seems to construct the metaphor of a state of nature not as a basis from which to urge New World peoples to enter into a settled, civil condition, but rather to demand that already established states enter into a voluntary congress to secure, however tenuously, international peace.

Second, Kant does not believe that the actual, historical origins of European civil societies were contractual. Indeed, Kant responded to a common objection to social contract theory simply by accepting it. Hume and Kant both agree that no voluntary contracts were ever drawn up historically, and that this is especially clear in light of evidence provided by the power politics of modern imperialism. The creation of civil societies in the New World, they contend, is rooted in violence, not voluntary consensus. In his 1748 essay "Of the Original Contract", Hume argues:

> Almost all the governments, which exist at present, or of which there remains any record in story, have been founded originally, either on usurpation or conquest, or both, without any pretence of a fair consent, or voluntary subjection of the people. . . . The face of the earth is continually changing, by the encrease of small kingdoms into great empires, by the dissolution of great empires into smaller kingdoms, by the planting of colonies, by the migration of tribes. Is there any thing discoverable in all these events, but force and violence? Where is the mutual agreement or voluntary association so much talked of?[44]

In a different context, Kant argues against potential revolutionaries who might try to research the actual origins of society in order to expose it, in a Rousseauian fashion, as a sham or a confidence trick by the rich and powerful.[45] Engaging in such historical research with the practical intent of delegitimizing a current regime is pointless, Kant argues, since either the origins themselves are opaque or, to the extent that they can be discovered, they no doubt will have unscrupulous beginnings. If *that* is the standard of contemporary legitimacy, Kant implies, no current political order would be even marginally legitimate.

> It is *futile* to inquire into the *historical documentation* [*Geschichtsurkunde*] of the mechanism of government, that is, one cannot reach back to the time at which civil society began (for savages [*Wilden*] draw up no record of their submission to law; besides, we can already gather from the nature of uncivilized [*roher*] human beings that they were originally subjected to it by force). (6:339)

Kant appears to be making a point identical to Hume's: the hunting and pastoralists of the eighteenth century are not voluntarily forming civil societies, but rather are having sedentary, civil life *imposed* coercively upon them.

Kant's language implies that hunters and pastoralists do not often form agrarian civil societies of their own volition, unless they are unjustly forced to by others. Indeed, in the *Anthropology*, Kant suggests that it is unusual for peoples to move from a nonsettled to a settled condition. In this sense, it is possible that he differs from Diderot who, in the *Histoire des deux Indes*, makes the sociological claim that an internal logic of "primitive" societies leads them, if left to themselves, to evolve into a civilized condition (and that civilized states eventually collapse and lead to a primitive condition). In contrast, Kant argues,

> Since nomadic peoples (pastoral tribes, such as the Arabs) are not bound down to any land, their attachment to their way of life—though this is not altogether free of constraint—is so strong, and their haughtiness about it, which makes them look down with contempt on settled peoples, so great that the hardship inseparable from it has not been able to divert them from this way of life in thousands of years. Peoples who are purely hunters (like the Olenni-Tungusi) have really ennobled themselves by this feeling for freedom (which has separated them from other tribes related to them). (7:269)

This fits well with passages that we have already seen from the *Conjectures* about nonsettled and settled peoples who look down upon one another and who each believe their lives to be superior. We saw then that at least some nonsettled individuals would be attracted to what Kant called the "glittering misery" of the towns, and would thus voluntarily assimilate into civil societies; but others, he implied, would be colonized by agriculturalists who would spread out like "bees" radiating outward from their civilized hive (8:119). In short, Kant believes that many of the social transformations from a nonsettled to a settled condition both historically and in his time were engendered by an externally imposed brute force, rather than an evolutionary, internal social transformation. At the same time, in the *Critique of Judgement*, Kant argues that certain aspects of the natural world can be viewed by humans as having purposive powers, even though we cannot state that such purposes are at all intentional ends of nature; along these lines, he argues that

> the vermin that plague humans in their clothes, hair, or bedding are, in accordance with a wise dispensation of nature, an incentive for cleanliness, which is in itself already an important means for the preservation of health. Or the mosquitoes and other stinging insects that make the wilds of America so trying for the savages are so many goads to spur these primitive people to drain the swamps and let light into the thick, airless forests and thereby as well as by the cultivation of the soil to make their abode more salubrious. (5:379)

Such statements in Kant's thought indicate that there may in fact be universal features of human life that could impel nomadic societies to become agrarian and sedentary over time by the volition of such peoples themselves. For Kant, this would be a mixed blessing, for as his writings make clear, civilized societies offer both greater opportunities (at least for the privileged in such societies, as he notes) for the development of a wide range of human capacities and the development of aesthetic humanity, which he very much values, while they also create and perpetuate massive injustices not only to themselves but very often to other peoples. It remains an open question, then, whether Kant believed, like Diderot, that sedentary, civilized societies, without conquests and imperial rule, would have developed in all areas of the world. Still, the upshot of all these considerations is that Kant's social contract doctrine in particular is not meant to suggest that the peoples of the New World *should* (it is an open question whether they freely *will* at some point) eventually form sedentary societies. The social contract doctrine for Kant is a hypothetical theory—an "Idea" in his terminology, just like his philosophy of historical progress—that he admits has little or no historical or empirical basis, but that serves as an ideal with which especially European states and the international relations of his day could be assessed.[46]

A third aspect of Kant's understanding of a social contract is that such a contract is meant to provide a normative orientation for the political practices of "states", that is, of settled, agricultural societies that are characterized by the public administration of justice (a *Rechtstaat*). Kant's social contractarianism obligates individuals in such societies to strive perpetually toward freer, more just, and less violent political conditions. A limitation of Kant's political theory, insofar as it constrains his ability to come to terms with human diversity, is a common assumption of much eighteenth-century political thought: civil life, in its fullest sense, requires a sedentary, agriculturally based society. Thus, Kant describes nonsedentary groups, including New World peoples, as tribes, societies, or peoples, but never as constituting states. In this respect, the most humanitarian sixteenth-century Spanish theologians, especially Las Casas, had a much broader and more flexible understanding of the kinds of societies that one might consider to be political. Since he was writing within a Christian Aristotelian tradition, for Las Casas to prove that Amerindians were fully human beings, he needed to show that they were political beings, given Aristotle's fundamental claim that "man is by nature a political animal". But if politics and political life are viewed more narrowly and artificially, if they refer to a centralized, public power that is constructed either by consent or by force, then a defence of others as human beings need not show that other peoples are law-governed and civil. Thus, for Kant, the assumption that Africans, Amerindians, South Pacific Islanders, and Australian aboriginal groups are human and that they live their collective lives in a human manner consists simply of theorizing their group behaviour as humanly and freely chosen. From this perspective, freedom, and not politics per se, becomes central to a justification of others as truly human; and, for Kant, as we have seen, it is specifically a concept of cultural freedom, a plural and experientially situated and informed freedom, that characterizes all human groups and all individual humans. It is a freedom that makes humans distinctively similar and yet incommensurably different.

What follows from this is that New World peoples do not seem to be under a political obligation, in Kant's view, to enter civil relations. Although Kant does not make such a claim explicitly, we know that he finds hunting and pastoralist lives defensible on the grounds of cultural freedom and that he does not proclaim in his political writings that such peoples ought to transform their ways of life to form agriculturalist, settled states. The general issue then becomes how Kant's social contract narrative is broadly consistent with his defence of non-European peoples given his contractarian argument that all savages (all noncivil beings) are under a moral duty to enter civil relations with one another. One can reconstruct a number of passages from Kant's writings to suggest that the hypothetical inhabitants of a state of nature are agrarian, settled individuals. Thus, it is a *moot question* to ask whether hunters and pastoralists should become civil beings: the problems that the state is created for, according to Kant's social contract story, are those of settled peoples. Thus, while Kant considers many New World peoples to be noncivil and nonagrarian, they are *not* examples of the hypothetical natural humans in a social contract narrative who are under a categorical duty to leave their condition and to create a coercive public power.

Although the duty to join a civil society is mandatory, from a moral viewpoint, Kant always makes a curious exception to it in his descriptions of it. Consider the following two examples, from *Theory and Practice* (1793) and *The Metaphysics of Morals* (1797) respectively:

> The union of many for some (common) end (that all of them have) is to be found in any social contract; but that union which is in itself an end (that each ought to have) and which is therefore the unconditional and first duty in any external relation of people in general, *who cannot help mutually affecting one another*, is to be found in a society only insofar as it is in the civil condition [*Zustand*], that is, constitutes a commonwealth. (8:289, emphasis added)

> From private right in the state of nature there proceeds the postulate of public right: *when you cannot avoid living side by side with all others*, you ought to leave the state of nature and proceed with them into a rightful condition, that is, a condition of distributive justice. (6:307, emphasis added)

Why would Kant make such qualifications? The *Conjectures* (1786) offers some valuable clues. Kant argues there that nonsettled peoples are not subject to civil authorities, in his full sense of the term "civil", because their lack of fixed property allows them a much greater opportunity of exit that agrarian-based citizens possess. Using pastoralists as his example, he claims,

> The *Bedouins* of Arabia still describe themselves as children of a former *sheik*, the founder of their tribe (such as *Beni Haled* and others). But the sheik is by no means their *master*, and he cannot force his will upon them as he chooses. For in a nation of herdsmen, no one has fixed property which he cannot take with him, so that any family which is discontented with its tribe can easily leave it and join forces with another. (8:120)

Apparently, Kant believes that individuals in nonsettled societies are in a position in which they *can*, without enormous effort, "avoid living side by side with all others". (6:307) Whatever one might think about the anthropological accuracy of such a view, Kant's account of the character of social relationships in societies that lack any fixed property differs from his hypothetical description of a state of nature. This is made clear by Kant in a transitional sentence of the *Conjectures* in which he begins his discussion of the original formation of civil societies:

> The following period began with man's transition from the age of leisure and peace to the age of *labour and discord* as the prelude to a social union. Here, we must make another major leap and suddenly put him in possession of domestic animals and of crops which he can propagate himself for his own consumption by sowing and planting.[47] (8:118)

The necessary precursor to the creation of a civil authority is sedentary, agricultural life. This is the condition that creates most of the problems to which the formation of the state is meant to mitigate: securing fixed property, defending permanent settlements, and punishing by public law (rather than by private vengeance) major acts of violence that occur among people who have settled close to one another; in short, a state is created to make (at least somewhat) secure the inherently insecure sedentary lifestyle.[48]

Due to these three features of Kant's social contract doctrine—its international intent, hypothetical nature, and agriculturalist character—the contractarian model of a *Rechtstaat* does not lead to the view that nonsedentary peoples are under a duty of justice to form a public administration of justice in the manner of civilized states. In this sense, Kant's distinctive uses of the social contract and the metaphor of the state of nature do not carry with them the usual developmental implications of social contractarianism for nonsedentary peoples. Kant hypothesizes a social contract in rather narrow terms such that it models not humanity per se, but a peculiar form of noncivil social relations that he believes never existed historically and that, in any case, does not resemble conditions in the New World.[49]

All social contract doctrines are also narratives that present an evolutionary or developmental story about how societies and polities form and reform themselves over time. Kant accordingly presents such a developmental account in his political philosophy, but it is important to note that the end toward which it works, as Kant's writings on cosmopolitan right make clear, is a world in which agriculturalist, pastoral, and nomadic peoples respect one another's independence and collective freedoms. As we saw in the last chapter, Kant's philosophy of history is meant to instill hope in his readers that such a future is possible and, thus, to make it more likely that they will work toward bringing about such civil, international, and cosmopolitan justice. What Europeans and other agrarian, sedentary societies have achieved thus far, Kant notes in the seventh proposition to the *Idea for a Universal History*, "amounts merely to civilization" and so "we are still a long way from the point where we could consider ourselves morally mature." In large part, what held Europeans back from moral maturity, in Kant's view, was that their "states apply all their resources to vain and violent schemes of expansion". Whether or not Kant, like Diderot, held the opinion that all nonagrarian peoples would eventually by their own volition develop sedentary societies (in which case they would then be morally obliged to work toward fostering systems of rights and republican governments), this was *not* in any way, for Kant, a prerequisite for such peoples' individual and collective rights and independence to be respected. Nor, as Kant argues repeatedly, was this an end toward which European states could legitimately coerce them, either directly by imperial and military force or indirectly by commercial means.

KANT'S NUANCED account of humanity and his accompanying understanding of moral and political judgement—one that comprises a commitment both to moral universalism and to a doctrine of moral incommensurability—animates his account of cosmopolitan justice among European and non-European peoples in a variety of intriguing ways. Kant defends the lives, the freedom, and the independence of peoples remarkably different from his own *both* as incommensurably diverse and as similarly human. Kant, like Diderot and Herder, views the universal and particular features of humanity as deeply interwoven. What makes us different, in many respects incommensurably different, relates fundamentally to what defines us as *human*—this, Kant implies, is what defenders of empire, in their quest to justify the profitable destruction and conquest of foreign societies, actively deny. For Kant, to respect the incommensurable pluralism of both individual and collective lives, either at home or abroad, is to respect our shared humanity.

Six

Pluralism, Humanity, and Empire in Herder's Political Thought

IN THE MOST stereotypical, but still widely articulated, contentions about eighteenth-century political thought, Johann Gottfried Herder's writings are said to be a counterpoint to Enlightenment thinking. In these accounts, Herder is a nationalist in contrast to the Enlightenment's cosmopolitanism, a romantic to the Enlightenment's faith in reason, and a cultural pluralist to the Enlightenment's monistic penchant for universal, cross-cultural truths.[1] The problems with such characterizations lie partly in their assumptions about Enlightenment thinking, as I will discuss further in the following chapter: first, that there is such a thing as 'the' Enlightenment; second, that its core features are easily categorized; and, third, that terms like 'cosmopolitanism', 'nationalism', 'reason', and so forth are straightforwardly precise and helpful concepts that can accurately describe the attitudes and arguments of eighteenth-century thinkers. If, as I will suggest in the next chapter, Enlightenment or eighteenth-century political thought should be pluralized so as to come to terms with its actual complexity—that is, to appreciate its otherwise underemphasized or even occluded nuances—then we should also consider rethinking its supposed antithesis: the category of 'the Counter-Enlightenment' and, hence, reconsider whether Herder is an (or even the paramount) example of 'Counter-Enlightenment' thought.

To be sure, Herder himself believed that his writings were at odds with what he thought was the 'spirit' of his age. Such self-understandings are crucial for an appreciation of how Herder understood his own intellectual projects, but we should not be misled by such assertions to think that he was largely outside of, and not much influenced by (or only negatively influenced by), a variety of eighteenth-century discourses that are commonly associated with 'enlightened' thinking. One of the many philosophical benefits of revising widely held characterizations of Herder's thought is that we begin to appreciate the complex manner in which he sought to balance humanistic and particularistic ideas. Viewed from this perspective, Herder appears in a new light, as one of many eighteenth-century thinkers who aimed to relate the cross-cultural and culturally particular values, ways of life, practices, and institutions into a coherent whole. The particular balance that Herder creates is distinctive, but it is

not fundamentally distinct—that is, radically different in kind—from
what we can find among thinkers who are usually taken to be among the
paragons of Enlightened thinking (and, importantly, whose writings influenced Herder), such as Denis Diderot and Immanuel Kant.[2] In this
chapter, I argue that a study of his most important political writings—
especially his magnum opus, the *Ideas Toward a Philosophy of History of
Humankind*—reveals a nuanced relationship between his cosmopolitan,
cross-cultural understanding of 'humanity' and his arguments for distinct
national communities. In presenting this interpretation of 'nation' and
'humanity' in Herder's thought, I suggest that his seemingly peculiar
synthesis of universalism and particularism is, in fact, part of a constellation of discourses in eighteenth-century political thought that integrates
such perspectives. The key political topic that can help illuminate the
manner in which he relates these universal and particular languages concerns European imperialism; for, in attacking the enterprise of building
and maintaining European empires abroad, Herder balances a commitment to national self-determination with the idea of a single, shared 'humanity', understood both anthropologically as that in which all individuals and peoples partake equally and, as a moral ideal, that toward which
we all ought to strive, notwithstanding the various (and, for Herder, the
ethically valuable) diversities that seem to divide us.

Herder articulates his social and political thinking largely through his
attempts at reconceptualizing human history.[3] His critical stance toward
historical thinking is most thoroughly and eloquently presented in a remarkable, anonymously published work, *Auch eine Philosophie der Geschichte der Menschheit* [*Yet Another Philosophy of History of Humankind*]
(1774; hereafter *YPH*). In hindsight, a number of the central historical
and political themes that characterize Herder's later writings can be
found, in a distilled form, in this early work, although *YPH* is largely
critical in tone, whereas his later writings are more constructive.[4] While
science and technology per se do not come under attack in *YPH*, as they
do in Rousseau's *Discourse on the Sciences and Arts*, Herder seeks to identify and to probe the symptoms of a variety of social ills through a self-
consciously iconoclastic assault upon prevailing intellectual dispositions.
Dissatisfied with the state of academic knowledge and the conventions of
political life, Herder calls for a new universal history to begin to grasp the
outlines of the human condition in all its variety, a task that he himself
would eventually undertake in the *Ideas* (1784–91), to which I will turn
later.

I detail in the opening sections of this chapter Herder's philosophical
approaches toward the study of history and society in *YPH*, especially as
they relate to first, the limits of generalizations and the contingency
of human lives; second, the perpetual flux that characterizes human

history and all societies; third, the limited horizons of any one individual's knowledge, and the lack of a universal standard by which we can rank peoples or conceptions of happiness; and fourth, the concept of the 'nation'. Herder's arguments in *YPH* already give some indication of the manner in which he would later develop his own anthropological and political study of the world's peoples and histories in the *Ideas*. My analysis of the *Ideas* focuses in the fifth section upon Herder's anthropological understanding of humanity; in the sixth, upon his conceptualization of human diversity; and finally upon his doctrine of moral incommensurability and his ethical understanding of *Humanität*, by which Herder theorizes international justice and a world beyond empire. The languages of moral universalism and humanity are far stronger in Herder's political thought than is usually assumed. Moreover, his commitment to cultural pluralism and his doctrine of incommensurability (and concomitantly his attacks on ethnocentrism) are closely related to his complex understanding of 'humanity'. Stated most abstractly, then, Herder's political thought does not choose between the universal and particular aspects of human life and moral judgement, but presents them as closely interrelated. Hence, his anti-imperialism reflects not simply a defence of cultural particularity and national independence, but also a humanistic affirmation of the universal dignity that he identifies in the diverse flourishing of human reason and freedom from individual to individual, and from people to people.

Generalizations, Contingency, and Historical Judgement

Throughout *Yet Another Philosophy of History*, Herder mocks those who too easily generalize about the social and political features of human societies. "No one in the world", Herder exclaims, "feels the weakness of general characterization more than I do."[5] (*SC* 181) Indicating the fragility and arbitrariness of language itself, topics that he investigated at length in his earlier study on the origin of languages, he concludes that the ultimate result of such facile conclusions is a series of chimerical words that fail to signify any of the particularities that actually constitute social life. Such generalized language must often be articulated and applied in the most arbitrary fashion and, thus, imposes on history and societies a set of characteristics that obfuscates the rich diversity of human life. As Herder notes, it is a difficult enough task to appreciate the nuances of a single individual, let alone the distinctive qualities of a particular people. Yet, he asks,

> If this is so, how then can one survey an ocean of entire peoples, times and countries, comprehend them in one glance, one sentiment or one word, a weak incomplete silhouette of a word? A whole *tableau vivant* of manners, customs, necessities, particularities of earth and heaven must be added to it, or precede

it; you must enter the spirit of a nation before you can share even one of its thoughts and deeds. You would indeed have to discover that single word which would contain everything that it is to express; else one simply reads—*a word*. (*SC* 181)

It is important to note that Herder does not rule out the very possibility of making general claims about humans as such or about specific peoples. His primary concern stems from the oversights and distortions that occur when one acts on the presumption that the primary, or even exclusive, goal of social and historical analysis is to identify and catalogue generalizations.

For Herder, one of the misfortunes that result in adopting such approaches is that foreign peoples remain poorly understood and undervalued. When one applies only "general textbook concepts about the advantages, virtues, and happiness of nations so distant and varied", the consequences are usually "miserable" and reveal, more than anything else, only the "fashionable prejudices of our century" (*SC* 184). Herder's arguments often target the arrogance and parochialism of those who judge other times and places in light of a present age that all too often is assumed to be a pinnacle of wisdom or virtue. Herder implies that correcting this intellectual myopia requires acknowledging not only our own finitude but also the contingency of every situation, of every time and place. Ideally, the recognition of our difference from others should engender an appreciation of the local and circumscribed nature of every situation. In light of this, he contends that the common delusions of superiority and certainty that instead guide the most prevalent understandings of the world and its past leave us with pejorative, insincere, and asinine characterizations of others, from which nothing profitable could possibly be derived. Herder resorts to a series of biting questions to underscore his point:

Why do we not realize that if we do not have all the vices and virtues of bygone ages it is surely because we are not in their position . . . [and] have [neither] their strength and savour, nor breathe the same air. To be sure, this is not a fault, but why fabricate false praise and absurd pretensions? Why delude ourselves about our means of education as if they had achieved something? Why deceive ourselves about our own trifling importance? Why, finally, drag into every century the story of a partial, derisory lie which ridicules and belittles the customs of all peoples and epochs, so that a healthy, modest, unprejudiced man finally comes to read nothing more into all the so-called pragmatic histories of the world than the nauseating rubbish of 'the loftiest ideals of his time'. (*SC* 212)

The tone with which historical and social study is often conducted, a disposition that fails to appreciate the full consequences of the fact that we don't breathe the "same air" as others, leads us to impose our own, parochial set of values on to others.

> The general, philosophical tone of our century wishes to extend 'our own ideal' of virtue and happiness to each distant nation, to even the remotest age in history. But can one such single ideal act as an arbiter praising or condemning other nations or periods, their customs and laws; can it remake them after its own image? (*SC* 187)

As I detail later, Herder theorizes some of the potentially radical implications of such questions on the nature of moral judgement itself, especially to what extent, if at all, one can judge others or compare the values of distinct times and places. Much of his early critique, however, consists of a series of sarcastic denunciations of "philosophy", that is the philosophy of his age or, at times, of his century, though he rarely targets individual figures.

The upshot of such pronouncements is that any philosophical history that is written from what is either taken to be a golden age or from a truly enlightened perspective is simply a crude transformation of one's view of happiness into a universal good or a grand historical realization. In a particularly caustic and telling passage, Herder himself crystallizes his indictment of generalized viewpoints and universal judgements in the study of others:

> As a rule, the philosopher is never more of an ass than when he most confidently wishes to play God; when with remarkable assurance, he pronounces on the perfection of the world, wholly convinced that everything moves just so, in a nice, straight line, that every succeeding generation reaches perfection in a completely linear progression, according to *his* ideals of virtue and happiness. It so happens that he is always the *ratio ultima*, the last, the highest, link in the chain of being, the very culmination of it all. 'Just see to what enlightenment, virtue, and happiness the world has swung! And here, behold, am I at the top of the pendulum, the gilded tongue of the world's scales!' (*SC* 214)

While the concept of progress itself, then, appears to be one of the intended victims of such attacks, we will later see that Herder begins to transform what he takes to be the conventional understanding of progressive change so as to incorporate humans' self-making and transformative freedom—their perpetual striving. He views the tendency to place oneself above others and viewing oneself as the culmination of historical progress as often linked; thus, he derides the pretension that can guide historical inquiry, broadly understood. History, then, is the category under which Herder theorizes both the study of past ages and the diversity of peoples in his own day, and the arrogance that fuels generalizations about vast swaths of human experience.

Herder's criticisms of simplifying and generalizing historical knowledge spring not only from his annoyance at the arrogant intellectual disposition that often guides historical inquiry, but also (and perhaps especially) from his awareness of the particularly dire consequences that result for our comprehension of politics and our ability to reform social and political practices. The legal and political processes by which one examines specific cases, with all of their eccentricities and complications, have given way to a set of indiscriminately applied standardized rules. Linked to this, Herder argues, is a rush to judgement, and a flawed diagnosis of social needs and ills.

> Old traditions, prejudices in favour of painstaking scholarship, slow maturing, searching inquiry, and cautious judging have been thrown off like a yoke from the neck! At the bars of our courts, in place of minute, detailed, dusty learning and the individual treatment and examination of each case, we now have that elegant, free-and-easy fashion of judging all cases from a couple of precedents, leaving aside everything which is individual and unique in favour of facile or grandiose generalities. . . . In our political economy and political science philosophy has offered us a bird's eye view in place of an arduously acquired knowledge of the real needs and conditions of the country; an overall picture, as on a map or a philosophical chart. (*SC* 198)

Herder's attacks upon generalities constitute, in part, an appreciation for local forms of knowledge as crucial for understanding ourselves and others, but they should not be construed as defences of tradition as such. Many of his criticisms are, in fact, made in the name of future reform, challenges to tradition (though not in the sweeping manner that he finds is all too common in many philosophical writings), and the strengthening of liberty against political despotism.[6] The following passage is especially clear on this point, and deserves to be quoted at length:

> This is a time when the art of legislation is considered the sole method of civilizing nations. Yet this method has been employed in the strangest fashion to produce mostly general philosophies of the human race, rational axioms of human behaviour and what-have-you! Doubtless the undertaking was more dazzling than useful. Admittedly, we could derive from it all the commonplaces about the right and the good, maxims of philanthropy and wisdom, views of all times and peoples for all times and peoples. For all times and peoples? That means, alas, precisely *not* for the very people whom the particular code of law was meant to fit like clothing. . . .
>
> What an abyss there is between even the finest general truth and the least of its applications to a given sphere, to a particular purpose and in any one specific manner! The village Solon who abolishes just one bad custom, who initiates just one current of human sentiment and activity, has done a thousand times

more in the way of legislation than all our great rationalists who believe in the
miserable illusion that everything is either true or false. (*SC* 203)

Thus, Herder contends that universal claims about the truth or falsehood
of ideas in the political sphere establishes a mode of thinking that makes
difficult, if not impossible, the task of determining judiciously which
practices and institutions ought to be reformed and in what manner. The
more universal the claim, the more ill-suited it becomes, he suggests,
when we are faced with the specifics of a given political problem. Moreover, Herder contends that a whole array of pernicious consequences result from a homogenizing impulse behind the generalities of historical
inquiry. As we will see later, the generalized judgement Herder condemns, which proclaims simply truths or falsehoods and which impedes
most prospects for genuine reform, is precisely the logic that lies behind
the characterization of whole peoples as simply inferior or superior, as
barbarous or enlightened.

Herder notes that, to some extent, the comprehension of vast amounts
of information, of the kind that was available about the world's peoples,
requires one to make certain classifications and generalities—"[c]an there
be a general picture without grouping and arrangement?" While the impulse to generalize might in part, then, be a result of necessity, Herder
also presents a brief sociology of knowledge which suggests that uniformity and generality are hallmarks of philosophical thinking in his day
because political life itself has become homogenized and centralized.
Thus, the historical scholarship and political theory that he targets are, in
his view, partly reflections of broader social changes that are in the process of effacing local idiosyncrasies and regional differences. It is for this
reason, he contends, that one can now theorize plausibly about Europe
as such, for Europe itself is becoming less differentiated, more identifiable
as an integral whole. Accordingly, in a particularly sarcastic passage,
Herder writes of the social and political changes that are remaking Europe and that enable the scholarship to which he gives biting praise:

> To depict the growth of these circumstances is the sole privilege of our political
> historians and of our historical eulogists of monarchy! How sad were the times
> when people acted according to needs and their innermost feelings; sadder still,
> when the power of rulers was still curbed, but saddest of all, when their reve-
> nues were not yet wholly arbitrary. For it provided the philosophical and histor-
> ical epicist with little scope for generalizing rationalizations and scant oppor-
> tunity for painting the whole of Europe on one vast canvas! (*SC* 207–8)

Not only the understanding of Europe's present, however, is affected by
such changes. When thinkers glorify the present, Europe's past becomes

denigrated and its nuances, contradictions, and contributions are lost. Commenting on the histories and historical reflections of, among others, Voltaire, Hume, and William Robertson, Herder asserts that the presumed superstition and barbarity of past ages is both true and untrue— true because in relative terms one can plausibly contrast certain features of the past and current ages, but untrue "if one considers the earlier epoch according to its intrinsic nature and aims, its pastimes and mores, and especially as the instrument of the historical process."[7] (*SC* 192) The historical process that Herder refers to is only later developed as a theory of social change and progress, intimations of which can be found in *Yet Another Philosophy of History*, as I discuss later. At this point, it should be clear that he has already established the idea of contextual and relative analysis and judgement.

From the outset, Herder resists the obvious counter-argument that such an approach obscures or even legitimizes the injustices of other ages (or other peoples). With regard to the Middle Ages, he writes,

> I am by no means disposed to defend the perpetual migrations and devastations, the feudal wars and attacks, the armies of monks, the pilgrimages, the crusades. I only want to explain them; to show the spirit which breathed through it all, the fermentation of human forces. (*SC* 193)

Thus, to attend to the spirit of temporal or geographic foreignness is to set aside facile judgement in favour of more subtle and complicated accounts, which, Herder insists, does not require legitimating every facet of the object under study. Indeed, he suggests that the very methodology that freely and easily judges others according to its own values is precisely the most stultifying when wants to approach one's *own* society or time in a critical manner.

At the heart of such self-centred viewpoints lies an incomplete and dogmatic appraisal of one's own values, practices, and institutions. Our "political histories and our histories of commerce and trade", Herder complains, offer optimistic praise about extant governments, ideas, and industry (*SC* 214). But the celebration of one's own surroundings and times narrows one's scope and makes it less likely that one can critically assess the present. To transform one's condition, meditating upon a variety of circumstances is crucial for gaining fresh perspectives on all things familiar. "Indeed," Herder writes, "our very enjoyment of the things we boast of may cut us off from experiences which might have proved superior." (*SC* 213–14) The rosy portraits of the modern world that political theoreticians and historians offer their contemporaries are offered sincerely, but they serve a largely social, not an educative, function, for they calm the spirit that might have agitated for change. Such works emerge from an intellectual disposition that ultimately breeds passivity and the most lazy forms of conservatism. Belittling the complacency that results from such self-understandings, Herder casts European polities as dying patients in need of comforting tales of their ostensibly salubrious condition:

> the consumptive invalid lies peacefully in bed, whimpers and—gives thanks! But is he really grateful? And if he is, could not this very gratitude be considered a symptom of his decline, his despondency and extreme timidity? . . . We are faced here with a disease which precludes remedy. Since opium dreams help to ease the agony of death, should I disturb the ailing patient if I cannot hope to cure him? (SC 213–14)

Thus, the enthusiasm with which self-serving political histories are consumed, Herder suggests, indicates precisely the sickness that afflicts the political and social situation of modern Europe, a malady that in other passages he begins to diagnose. For now, it should be noted again that he seeks not an affirmation of present realities, as one might suspect from his attacks upon the easy judgements of moralists, but rather an *immanent* criticism of reformist thinking. For Herder, the prevalent view of his age is one that celebrates reform, but that too often dogmatically accepts present changes as progressive. To be sure, one can plausibly dispute such a characterization of eighteenth-century thought, although the heavily sarcastic tone of *Yet Another Philosophy of History* suggests that he intentionally makes blanket generalizations about his contemporaries for rhetorical effect. Ultimately, Herder was not a reactionary who sought to militate against reform as such. Rather, it was precisely the easy celebration of the language of reform in his age, he believed, that most chilled prospects for actual reform.

The Flux of History

For Herder, one crucial problem with such judgements and generalizations about Europe's condition is that it assumes that a particular set of social and political achievements can be won and preserved. Moreover, it presumes that we can identify fairly stable characteristics of different peoples and ages. As we have seen, Herder argues against such assumptions by noting that historical changes often spring, in part, from contingent circumstances. The questions that "history should pose" should suppose "that things could have been quite different—given another place, another time, and taking into account different cultural developments and circumstances" (SC 182). In part, the task of relativizing our present situation is based upon the recognition of the intrinsic flux of social and

political life. From this, we ought to grasp the futility of assigning relatively fixed characters for each people. Even if the greatness of the cultural and political achievements of a particular people is widely acknowledged, Herder asserts that such developments arose partly by chance
configurations of social factors and, moreover, will undergo further
changes—likely deleterious ones—due to similarly obscure and often un-
predictable causes. Accordingly, he asserts that

> no people long remained, or could remain, what it was, that each, like the arts
> and sciences and everything else in the world, has its period of growth, flower-
> ing and decay; that each of these modifications has lasted only the minimum of
> time which could be given to it on the wheel of human destiny; that, finally, no
> two moments in the world were ever identical and that therefore the Egyptians,
> the Romans and the Greeks have not stayed the same through all time. . . .
> (SC 182–83)

In addition to his obvious distaste of linear conceptions of historical
change and progress, such passages indicate the depth of Herder's antipathy toward easy comparisons among peoples. The particularity of different times and places, in conjunction with the constant movement and
transformation of ideas, practices, and institutions, he argues, should caution us against assigning intrinsic characteristics to specific peoples and
ages. Moreover, Herder notes that even the most common references to
nations obscure internal differences and tensions. Referring to those who
extol ancient Greece in the broadest possible terms, he responds that
"Greece was composed of many peoples: were Athenians and Boetians,
Spartans and Corinthians, nothing less than identical?" (SC 183) In addition to identifying the various strands that make up a larger, and more
commonly portrayed, group, Herder asserts that however precisely a people is defined, it will be marked nonetheless by significant tensions. Not
only are such inconsistencies and clashing differences intrinsic to human
life, but, at times, he argues, they can be socially productive. Thus, he
writes that

> [a] nation may have the most sublime virtues in some respects and blemishes in
> others, show irregularities and reveal the most astonishing contradictions and
> incongruities. . . . [F]or him who wants to understand the human heart within
> the living elements of its circumstances, such irregularities and contradictions
> are perfectly human. Powers and tendencies proportionally related to given
> purposes do not constitute exceptions but are the rule, for these purposes
> could scarcely be attained without them. . . . (SC 184)

Herder contends that only those striving for an inhuman, absurdly understood, singular perfection could be astonished at the conflicts and

complexity within any one people, let alone within humanity as a whole. All of this makes the characterization and inevitable assessments of various peoples a particularly challenging task, if one wants to do justice to the diversity of human life—a goal toward which, for Herder, too few thinkers apply themselves.

Herder insists that his emphasis on contingency and change does not bury human agency under so many blind forces that we should be seen as powerless in the face of our social circumstances. Yet, he is careful to note that even in those instances in which individuals act against the dominant institutions and ideas of their time, they often change little themselves and are capable of inspiring more significant acts only when the social conditions happen to be ripe for reform. "How often before had such Luthers risen and fallen," Herder writes, "silenced by smoke and flame or else by the lack of a free atmosphere in which their words could resound." (*SC* 195) Thus, he argues that the most elaborately wrought schemes of reform often fail, while seemingly minor proposals and acts ultimately lay the groundwork in the future for radical social and political transformations. Herder is particularly interested in the chance events that engender the most significant historical movements. Presaging his future work on empire and its often brutal consequences, his most detailed example is of the extraordinary consequences that followed the invention and refinement of the compass.

> Who can count the revolutions in every part of the world which have come about because of the little needle at sea? Lands, larger than Europe, have been discovered. Coasts have been conquered, full of gold, silver, precious stones, spices—and death. Human beings have been forced, through a process of conversion or civilization, into mines, treadmills and depravity. Europe has been depopulated, her innermost resources consumed by diseases and opulence. Who can count these revolutions, or describe them? Who can count or describe the new manners, the dispositions, virtues and vices? The cycle in which, after three centuries, the world moves, is infinite—and on what does it depend? What gives it its impulse? The point of a needle and two or three other mechanical inventions? (*SC* 196)

Herder understood, of course, that the causes and full significance of European imperialism merit more than a simple technological explanation. And it would be Herder himself who would "count" the effects that European empires wrought—the multiple causes, and especially the complex consequences, of modern imperialism occupy a central place in the *Ideas*. Still, the flux of history, even with phenomena as large-scale as the discovery of continents and the building of empires, turns partly upon chance, unintended consequences, and overlapping (and sometimes contradictory) practices and events.

On the Horizons of Knowledge and
Universal Standards

In Herder's historical writings, the epistemological limits that humans face in grasping the outlines of our condition, our history, and the potential for our future are usually signified by God. It is crucial to note that Herder does not suggest that divine power actually controls human actions, or that our freedom is merely chimerical in light of divine omnipotence, though at times he speaks of history as the workings of God in nature, and also chastises those who naïvely view freedom as complete mastery over one's destiny (e.g., *SC* 223).[8] In his historical writings, the language of divinity usually plays two roles. First, it signifies the limits of human actions and the contingency of human life. Second, God represents the infinite knowledge about the tremendous diversity, and yet ultimate unity, of humanity that will always elude humans' cognitive powers and that indicates the arrogance of humans' ceaseless striving for complete knowledge. Herder is adamant in asserting that "only the Creator can conceive the immense variety within one nation or all nations without losing sight of their essential unity." (*SC* 183) Thus, his use of religious language in *YPH* and later in the *Ideas* injects a tone of epistemological scepticism into his thought, one that largely seeks to curb the pretensions of his contemporaries and indicates the tentative and partial quality of his own arguments about human unity and diversity, rather than primarily undergirding a theological conception of the universe and humans' place within it.[9]

For Herder, the extent to which our knowledge of ourselves and our surroundings is rooted in local circumstances and understandings is significant. The frustration that we feel, or ought to feel, when we aim for too comprehensive a knowledge of the human condition reveals the limitations of our time and place.

> The very limitation of my little corner of the globe, the blinding of my vision, the failure of my aims, the enigma of my dispositions and my desires, the defeat of my energies: these can only be measured in terms of one day, one year, one nation, one century. (*SC* 222)

But Herder does not counsel others to forsake intellectual pursuits that strive to move beyond one's domain. This is obvious in his later writings, especially the *Ideas*, which aims to present a global history; but even earlier it becomes clear that the intellectual disposition with which one engages in such ambitious projects is his central concern. We should temper not only our arrogant dogmatism, but also our cowardice about embarking upon projects that seek to grasp the vast diversity of human life. As Herder argues,

Our short span is infinitely minute in relation to the pride which claims to be everything, to know everything, achieve everything and develop everything, but infinitely great in relation to the pusillanimity which does not dare to be anything. (*SC* 223)

Still, in *YPH*, Herder emphasizes primarily the limitations of our perspectives, and offers an intriguing analysis of how our "horizons" become shaped.

Mother Nature . . . placed in men's hearts inclinations towards diversity, but made each of them so little pressing in itself that if only some of them are satisfied the soul soon makes a concert out of the awakened notes and only senses the unawakened ones as if they mutely and obscurely supported the sounded melody. She has put tendencies towards diversity in our hearts; she has placed part of the diversity in a close circle around us; she has restricted man's view so that by force of habit the circle became a horizon, beyond which he could not see nor scarcely speculate. (*SC* 186)

For Herder, then, the manner in which we are socially acclimatized into particular surroundings explains at least some part of our limited horizons. Since Herder does not use the metaphor of local horizons as simply a representation of intrinsic cognitive limitations, but rather partly of habituation to local circumstances, he therefore leaves open the possibility that we can survey broader horizons, and incorporate more "notes" into the diversely composed melody that makes up our limited spheres. It is crucial to note that for Herder even one's local circumstances are diverse. Thus, rather than contrasting the immense diversity of the globe as a whole with clusters of relatively homogenous units (be they families, small communities, cities, or nations), he points to a variety of diverse practices, institutions, and beliefs, some of which we inhabit and others of which we view obscurely, if at all.

All of this, of course, raises crucial questions of moral judgement, which Herder takes up in the *Ideas*, though at times only indirectly. If our viewpoints are constrained by and limited to specific horizons, then is it possible to judge aspects of societies that are arranged around and formed by different beliefs, histories, and self-understandings? Throughout *YPH*, Herder sharply criticizes the nearly instinctive tendency to make generalizations, and argues instead that a more reflective and cautious historical understanding must incorporate the particularities and contingencies of our varied situations. Only then, he writes,

will you be in a position to understand; then only will you give up the idea of comparing everything, in general or in particular, with yourself. For it would be manifest stupidity to consider yourself to be the quintessence of all times and all peoples. (*SC* 182)

Herder explores some of the ethical consequences of such a view by discussing competing conceptions of happiness.

Judging among various senses of happiness is often impossible, Herder argues, because comparisons often cannot be made, for the simple reason that the tremendous diversity of intellectual temperaments and beliefs belie most attempts to identify normative criteria that span a variety of peoples and times. When such cross-national or cross-temporal efforts at moral judgement are made, they amount, in Herder's view, to celebrations of local goods in the guise of universal goods. Accordingly, he suggests that the "general, philosophical, philanthropical tone of our century wishes to extend 'our own ideal' of virtue and happiness to each distant nation, to even the remotest age in history." (*SC* 187) The problem with such judgements is not simply the arrogance with which they are often made (though this aspect of what is now often called ethnocentrism clearly enrages Herder), but also the mistake in thinking that any one set of human experiences can furnish the material with which one could judge human experience *as such*. In *YPH*, Herder's arguments about moral incommensurability rest upon at least three distinct kinds of claims about human life: psychological, empirical, and normative.

The *psychological* or cognitive claim that supports his argument is that our senses of happiness are shaped so powerfully by the beliefs and practices that surround us that it is difficult, if not impossible at times, to comprehend the aesthetic and intellectual dispositions of other times and ages. In a crucial passage, Herder relates the manner in which standards of judgement are multiplied and details the resultant effects upon our ability to compare and assess different practices.

> When the inner sense of happiness has altered, this or that attitude has changed; when the external circumstances and needs fashion and fortify this new sentiment: who can then compare the different forms of satisfaction perceived by different senses in different worlds? Who can compare the shepherd and the Oriental patriarch, the ploughman and the artist, the sailor, the runner, the conqueror of the world? Happiness lies not in the laurel wreath or in the sight of the blessed herd, in the cargo ship or in the captured field-trophy, but in the soul which needs this, aspires to that, has attained this and claims no more—each nation has its centre of happiness within itself, just as every sphere has its centre of gravity. (*SC* 186)

I will return to the last claim that Herder makes above in a moment. For now, it should be noted that the *empirical* claim that gives force to his arguments and intimations about moral incommensurability is simply the fact that the diversity that characterizes human life is much greater than most thinkers have imagined. Combined with this is the *normative* claim that varying practices and beliefs, which embody distinct conceptions of goodness and value, are ultimately expressions of the diversity that is constitutive of the human condition, rather than pathological deviations from a (putatively) cross-cultural norm that, as Herder often points out, all too often bears a striking resemblance to the dominant presuppositions of a particular age or place. Herder stresses both the empirical reality of an extensive diversity and the idea that this diversity embodies a wide range of human *goods*. Whether or not one believes that each of these goods contributes toward "greater virtue and individual happiness", none of them can be characterized as simply inhuman.

> Is good not dispersed over the earth? Since one form of mankind and one region could not encompass it, it has been distributed in a thousand forms, changing shape like an eternal Proteus throughout continents and centuries. (*SC* 187)

Rather than a cause for moral concern—a source for prejudicial judgements about, and hostile practices against, differing forms of life— Herder presents this immense diversity, therefore, as the plural and unceasing proliferation of humanity itself.

Early Thoughts on National Communities

The diversity that Herder sees as complicating moral judgement and understanding appears to characterize individuals (not simply peoples and ages), yet nations are said to have relatively distinct "centres" around which ethical, aesthetic, and other standards could cohere. Thus, in *YPH*, Herder appears to vacillate between, on the one hand, theorizing diversity and incommensurability at virtually every level of human life (including the variety of characteristics that animate each individual), and, on the other, portraying a coherent and identifiable character or set of characteristics at the level of the nation or people (*Volk*).[10] The political implications of where one situates Herder's theorization of diversity along this spectrum is crucial, for it indicates whether or to what extent his political thought can be characterized as nationalist or proto-nationalist. How much diversity—with all the resultant limits that incommensurability places upon moral judgement—does Herder proclaim? Does Herder champion only a global diversity among nations or a more thoroughgoing diversity within nations as well?

In *YPH*, one can sense how he often manages to maintain this seemingly paradoxical set of arguments because he presents national character as a constantly evolving artifice, rather than as a pregiven or intrinsic quality of a people. Herder argues that peoples will often borrow ideas and practices from one another, but usually only to the extent that what is understood to be the most salient features of a people is thereby invigorated. Other aspects of foreign peoples remain not only poorly understood, but are often shunned. Such prejudices can arise when attitudes toward happiness and conventional practices among different peoples grow apart over time; hence, the "Egyptian detests the shepherd and the nomad and despises the frivolous Greek." It is also the case, of course, that the physical proximity and increasing interaction among peoples can serve as the catalyst for "prejudices, mob judgement and narrow nationalism". Herder sets aside the latter two reactions (no doubt because he believed them to be disturbing and uncompelling), but defends prejudices of particular kinds and in certain contexts as valuable, for they can draw a people together around collective goals, thereby (possibly) enhancing their ability to determine their own future. As he contends,

> prejudice is good, in its time and place, for happiness may spring from it. It urges nations to converge upon their centre, attaches them more firmly to their roots, causes them to flourish after their kind, and makes them more ardent and therefore happier in their inclinations and purposes. (*SC* 186–87)

Presaging an argument later made at greater length by Edmund Burke in the *Reflections on the Revolution in France*, Herder contends that it is possible, therefore, that some prejudices can enhance or safeguard a people's liberty. Precisely like Burke, Herder makes his argument not on the grounds of preserving traditional practices and institutions, but on the view that genuine reform and social change can best take place when a sense of shared purpose animates the body politic.

The "roots" and "centre" of a people are sufficiently plastic, in Herder's view, that they are continually subject to transformation. Moreover, his arguments reveal that he is clearly most interested in the social and psychological effects that the presumption of a common identity has upon a political community. Whether or not, in other words, such a "centre" actually exists, a sense, however inchoate, that it animates the polity and binds the collectivity strengthens a people's ability to transform itself in its own distinct manner. It is this distinctiveness that, for Herder, is crucial, for it serves as a bulwark against the homogenization that characterizes too many of the social and political changes in his day both within Europe and because of European imperial activities in the non-European world. All of this suggests that Herder is not interested in portraying national communities as relatively homogenous units. Rather, each nation's distinctive characteristics are a result of an ever-changing mosaic of practices, beliefs, and literatures. What is crucial for Herder is that, however national character is understood, it must be in some sense one's own, rather than a servile facsimile of another ostensibly superior or civilized nation. For Herder, the sway that French language, literature, philosophy, and customs exert over much of Europe and Russia, as well as European imperial powers' imposition of their institutions and values on to the non-European world, are equally good examples of how the effacement of diversity can undermine the local preconditions for human freedom.

Herder's attacks upon what he describes as cosmopolitanism are best understood in this light. A cosmopolitan worldview, according to Herder, is too often either a pretext for exporting one's one values abroad or a justification for slavishly imitating other nations, at the cost of one's freedom and independence. In part, the hypocrisy of cosmopolitan sentiments rankles Herder, for the idea of "universal love for humanity, for all nations, and even enemies" often coexists, he argues, with injustice toward one's own (*SC* 200). Moreover, he argues that the blind love of the foreign that sometimes animates cosmopolitan yearnings debilitates individuals from carrying out reforms that are suited to their own time and place. Rather than engage in "wishful dreams" (*SC* 187), Herder implies that one should instead foster local sources of liberty to counter the growing and increasingly despotic power of centralized European states. Nonetheless, Herder would go on to theorize the concept of humanity in the *Ideas* in order to reflect upon the ties that bind humankind. In this later work, Herder most fully elaborates the relationship between humanity and human diversity.

'Humanity' as Philosophical Anthropology

Herder published his magnum opus, the *Ideen zur Philosophie der Geschichte der Menschheit* [*Ideas Toward a Philosophy of History of Humankind*] in four parts (1784, 1785, 1787, and 1791), each of which consists of five books. Despite the massive size of the work (nearly one thousand pages in the standard German edition of Herder's writings), he intended to publish another installment of five books, which was never written.[11] Nonetheless, the *Ideas* forms a comprehensive whole that manages to elaborate a political analysis of state power, a theory of human development, an account of moral incommensurability, a doctrine of progress, and a philosophical anthropology, while also surveying a broad range of ethnographic writings and presenting an overview of world history from prehistorical times to the European Renaissance. Despite the ambition of his work, Herder states explicitly at the outset that he intends to provide not a grand metaphysical account of humanity, but a searching empirical study that is guided by normative questions (ix). He notes his luck in engaging in such a study at a time when empirical studies of the vast range of human experience are readily available; the *Ideas*, accordingly, draws upon a wide array of anthropological studies and travel literature. The central questions that guide Herder, in his own view, concern the variety of humankind and whether happiness can be found in all realms. In addition, he poses the crucial question of whether there are any cross-cultural criteria that could be used to judge the happiness of various peoples.

> What is human happiness? How far does it exist in this world? Considering the great diversity of all the beings upon Earth, and especially of human beings, how far is it to be found in every form of government, in every climate, in every change of circumstances, of age, and of the times? Is there any standard of these various states? (vi)

From the beginning of the *Ideas*, then, Herder indicates that the relationship between human nature, moral standards, and cultural difference will constitute his central themes.

Already in the preface to the *Ideas*, however, Herder makes a claim that will presage the crucial normative arguments that run throughout his study. Responding to those who interpreted his previous writings, especially *Yet Another Philosophy of History*, as indicating stages through which all peoples must pass from an uncultivated to ultimately a fully cultured state, Herder proclaims that such comparative distinctions among peoples and the implication that some peoples are uncultured are absurd.

> It had never entered my mind, by employing the few figurative expressions, the *childhood, infancy, manhood,* and *old age* of our species, the chain of which was applied, as it was applicable only to a few nations, to point out a highway, on which the history of culture [*Kultur*], to say nothing of the philosophy of history at large, could be traced with certainty. Is there a people upon Earth totally uncultured? And how contracted must the scheme of Providence be, if every individual of the human species were to be formed to what *we* call culture, for which refined weakness would often be a more appropriate term? (v)

As we will see, the ideas that all humans possess culture and that one cannot judge one set of cultural practices by the standards of another—an account, that is, of humans as cultural agents and of moral incommensurability that one can find in Diderot and Kant—take a distinctive form in Herder's thought. Herder's reflections upon the idea of humanity (understood both anthropologically and as a moral ideal) and of human diversity are the philosophical resources that ground his antipathy toward European imperialism, and they demonstrate the manner in which he views the languages of universal humanitarianism and cultural pluralism as interrelated, rather than antithetical.

In a clear indication of his indebtedness to Rousseau (though importantly, as we shall see, he also contradicts some of the core elements of

Rousseau's philosophical anthropology), Herder contends that humans are distinct from other animals by their ability to perfect themselves.[12] Most animals, he writes, act according to inborn instincts. Apes, on the other hand, are not characterized by a determinate instinct; their actions are more likely to result from noninstinctual choices. Yet, the ape stands on the "brink of reason", for although it can almost "perfect [*vervollkommnen*] itself", it remains incapable of doing so (71). Perfectibility, therefore, is solely a trait of human beings. For Herder, the attempt to perfect oneself involves combining others' ideas with one's own and, rather than simply imitating others (which, Herder notes, apes are able to do according to the most recent natural histories), making the imitation of others a part of one's own identity. Humans, then, are uniquely capable, in his view, of transforming themselves through an intersubjective process of (at least partially) adopting the characteristics of other humans, other animals, and features of their surrounding environments. Herder devotes considerable effort to arguing that humans' erect posture provides the physiological basis for the qualities that are necessary for possessing perfectibility. Whatever its ultimate physical cause, however, the constitutively human, interactive, and transformative capacity of perfectibility depends crucially, for Herder, upon humans' "freedom and rationality" (80). Humans are, in effect, a "living art" with an "art-exercising mind" (86). As he would succinctly assert in the *Briefe*, "the nature of the human being is *art* [*Kunst*]"; humans are by their very nature, then, cultural agents (WH 101, Letter 25).

Central to the artfulness of human activity is language. The consequences of this view for Herder's thought are immense, for (as we will see) distinctively human life is, consequently, fundamentally social and plural. While our ability to reason is a core feature of human nature, Herder argues that speech is the catalyst of reasoning. As Herder writes, the power and freedom of humans' artfulness, senses, and physical nature (such as their "free and skilful hands" [86])

> would have remained ineffective . . . if the Creator had not given us a spring to set them all in motion, *the divine gift of speech*. Speech alone awakens slumbering reason: or rather, the bare capacity of reason, which of itself would have remained eternally dead, acquires through speech vital power and efficacy. (87)

By theorizing speech as a heavenly gift, Herder is able to fold language into the very meaning of humanity; thus, every human on the globe, Herder argues, possesses language and (since it is always linked to language) the faculty of reason, though a reason that is always shaped by the contingencies of the particular speech that forms one's social background. The contextual and intersubjective quality of human knowledge is evident, Herder argues, from the role that hearing plays in the formation of ideas and the development of our cognitive abilities. Rather than the direct perception of reality, he contends that our knowledge of the world is mediated through speech. The voice of another shapes our perception of the diversity in the world and allows humans over time to make such linguistic determinations more freely and with less assistance from (and less dependence upon) others. Thus, Herder writes that there may be

> superior creatures, whose reason looks through the eye, a visible character be-ing sufficient for them to form and discriminate ideas: but the human being of this world is a pupil of the ear, which first teaches him gradually to understand the language of the eye. *The difference of things must be imprinted on his mind by the voice of another*, and then he learns to impart his own thoughts. . . . (89, emphasis added)

Accordingly, "the faculty of human reason" is not ready-made to understand the world and to act within it. Rather, it is "formed in us; and . . . though we come into the World with a capacity for it, we are not capable of possessing or acquiring it by our own power." (111) For Herder, the contexts within which one develops the artfulness that constitutes human life are crucial for determining one's perceptions, beliefs, and the range of one's actions. It is this background that sets reasoning into motion and that partly shapes its various activities.

In part, it is Herder's nominalism with regard to language—developed initially in his *Abhandlung über den Ursprung der Sprache* [*Essay on the Origin of Language*] (1772)—that underscores the embeddedness of particular human experiences.[13] In the *Ideas*, he argues explicitly that "[n]o language expresses things, but names: accordingly no human reason perceives things, but only marks of them, which it depicts by words." (234) Herder contends that the metaphysicians of his day should be aware of this humbling fact. Our speculative reason, he writes, "affords not a single perfect and essential idea, not a single intrinsic truth." (234) Moreover, the languages that are used to denote seemingly similar phenomena are so varied that human reasoning can result less in illumination than in the satisfaction received from a "magic lantern of an arbitrary connection." The consequence of all this is "melancholy", he notes, for it indicates the fragility and narrowness of human knowledge and reasoning. A plurality of opinions and a rash of sheer errors are bound to characterize human thought as such because of its fundamentally linguistic and manifold character.

> Opinions and errors, therefore, are inevitable from our nature; not from any fault of the observer, but from the very mode in which our ideas are generated, and in which they are propagated by reason and language. If we thought in things instead of abstract characters, and expressed the nature of things instead

of arbitrary signs: farewell error and opinion; we should live in the land of truth. (235)

Moreover, since "the reason and humanity of humankind depends upon education, language, and tradition: and in this respect the human being differs totally from the animal, which brings its infallible instinct into the World with it" (263), a blind adherence to a particular tradition or set of customs can enslave humans and rob them of the liberty that language and reason would have provided to them under less dogmatic and oppressive conditions.

In one of his many attacks upon following tradition for tradition's sake and against superstition, Herder notes that while the gifts of reason and liberty allow humans flexibility in their determinations and choice, all too often they cling uncritically to received practices and ideas. In another passage that exhibits Rousseau's influence, Herder argues that

> man . . . can gloss over the most delusive errors, and be voluntarily deceived: he can learn in time to love the chains with which he is unnaturally fettered, and adorn them with flowers. As it is with deceived reason, so it is with abused or shackled liberty: in most humans it is a proportion of powers and propensities that habit or convenience has established. (92)

In addition to these hindrances, Herder also suggests that there are more basic environmental factors that can debilitate human development. He sometimes suggests that the lives of those who appear to live from a bare subsistence are virtually animalistic. Throughout books IV and V of the *Ideas*, for instance, Herder makes numerous references to the pathetic situation of isolated "wild men" and indeed even whole nations who live in the most desperate climates—such as the Pesherays, the indigenous peoples of the southernmost tip of South America, whose environment is a favourite example of early anthropologists of the harshest possible conditions in which a people can live. At one point, he even suggests that "there is evidently a progressive scale, from the human who borders on the brute to the purest genius in human form." (93)

Yet, despite these impediments to the creative use and transformation of language, and thus to the flourishing of distinctively human capacities, he argues that it is only through the combination of a situated reason and language that any change and improvement occurs in human life. To try to move beyond it and seek reform by a more rarefied, speculative reason will result in certain failure. "Manifest are the imperfections in the sole means of propagating human thoughts", writes Herder, "yet to this our improvement is enchained, and we cannot emancipate ourselves from it." (235) All humans ultimately remain free creatures, who despite their environmental, tradition-based, or entirely self-imposed impediments, exercise their reason, language, and freedom in a multiplicity of ways. Herder demands that we assume that each variety of human life is meant to exist and is fulfilling some human purpose:

> It appears that every thing possible to be on our Earth was actually to exist on it: and then only shall we be able sufficiently to explain the order and wisdom of this copious plenitude. . . . (93)

Herder admits that initially he finds it difficult to account for why nations such as the Pesherays exist, given their seemingly dire conditions and the difficulty with which they meet their most basic needs. Thus, in a remark similar to one that Kant would make six years later in the *Critique of Judgement*, Herder writes that

> the whole earth was to be inhabited, even in its most remote wilderness; and only He, who stretched it out so far, knows the reasons why He left on this, His world, both Pesherays and New Zealanders. (93; cf. Kant, 5:378)

Nonetheless, he asserts that while human beings, for the many reasons he provides, are often impeded from freely cultivating their reason, humans are "if not yet rational, yet capable of superior reason; if not yet formed to humanity, yet endued with the power of attaining it." And so, Herder concludes that the "New Zealand cannibal and a Fénelon, a Newton and the wretched Pesheray, are all creatures of one and the same species." (93)

The consequences that Herder draws from this assertion are significant. He challenges those who, in claming the superiority of speculative knowledge, deem inferior those peoples and individuals who do not cognize in this manner or who do not share the same speculative conceptions and arguments. A more embedded account of human reasoning, one that sees it as bound up with language, reveals this is "sufficient . . . for the enjoyment of nature, the application of our powers, the sound employment of life, the improvement of our humanity." (236) Herder proclaims adamantly that all peoples improve their humanity, that is, all humans draw upon, transform, and apply their constitutively human capacities, in every situation and in every corner of the globe. In a crucial passage, he writes,

> can humans be as distant from one another in the sphere of true and useful ideas as proud speculation supposes? Both the history of nations, and the nature of reason and language, forbid me to think so. The poor savage, who has seen but few things, and combined very few ideas, proceeds in combining them after the same manner as the first of philosophers. *He has language like them; and by means of it exercises his understanding and memory, his imagination and recollection, a thousand ways. Whether this be in a wider or narrower circle is*

little to the purpose; he still exercises them after the manner of humankind. (236, emphasis added)

Given that Herder theorizes language to be inherently differentiated and that it involves the use of signs that are, at bottom, arbitrary, the fact that New World peoples are fully human indicates also that they are fundamentally distinct from other humans. As we have seen with Diderot and Kant, Herder also treats humans as constitutively cultural agents, whose very humanity is an indication both of sameness and of difference. To some extent, then, the respect for humans as humans will entail some kind of respect for the variety of beliefs, practices, and languages.

Herder believes that there is a core humanity, although it consists not of a particular set of practices, beliefs, or intellectual refinements, against which some individuals or peoples can be judged more or less human, but a set of open-ended universal capacities that are developed, understood, and used diversely. In contrasting humans with highly developed animals (especially primates), he argues that many of these animals, like humans, have spread throughout the world and have changed in their various climes, but that only nonhuman animals, such as apes and dogs, have differentiated themselves to the extent that one can classify them as essentially distinct beings. Herder asserts that

humankind alone has little varied, and indeed in no essential sense. It is astonishing how uniformly humans have retained their nature, when we contemplate the variations that have taken place in other migrating animals. (96)

From this, Herder argues that there exists a moral community of human beings, and urges Europeans to enter into fraternal relations with humans of other continents. Again, he contrasts humans with animals in this context.

For each genus Nature has done enough, and to each has given its proper progeny. The ape she has divided into as many species and varieties as possible, and extended these as far as she could, but you, O man, honour yourself. Neither the pongo nor the gibbon is your brother: the American and the Negro are. These [beings] therefore you should not oppress, or murder, or steal, for they are humans, like you; with the ape, you cannot enter into fraternity. (166)

Thus, although Herder pushes his arguments concerning incommensurability and cultural difference to such an extent that some have doubted the ability of his political thought to theorize the possibility of sympathetic relations among humans, the core humanity that Herder identifies is interwoven with both his defence of a wide plurality of life-worlds and a significant commitment to moral incommensurability.[14] There is indeed in Herder a sense in which humans can view each other as similarly human, but (as I later elaborate) they do so in part by recognizing each other as necessarily differentiated as a result of the plurality of uses of universally shared capacities.

When Herder refers generically to all human beings considered as a group, he almost always uses *Menschheit*. Humanity (*Humanität*), however, is reserved for a more specific, and generally, in his view, a more exalted set of meanings. As I discuss in the final section of this chapter, for Herder, humanity can represent the moral ends toward which humans ideally ought to strive and the moral balance that ought to exist between human unity and diversity. For now, I examine Herder's use of the term 'humanity' as it denotes the constitutive aspects of human beings. We have seen already that a theory of language and a situated account of reason are crucial for his understanding of human beings as such. Herder states that he intends to use the term 'humanity' to refer precisely to these aspects of the human condition and the sensibilities that they engender; considered together, he argues, such characteristics are dignifying.[15] Beyond this, however, he discusses a variety of social characteristics that are related to reason and language and that are also, in his view, fundamental to morality. Herder describes humans as generally peaceable; this, he says, "constitutes the first characteristic of humanity." (99) Intimate, loving relationships that go well beyond simply a desire to procreate are also a central aspect of a truly human life, and they show that human reason shapes powerful underlying desires and channels them toward forging meaningful bonds among individuals. The habituation that one undergoes within a family inculcates varying degrees and kinds of sociability within children and consequently tends to form yet another "tie of humanity" (101). Despite their varied forms, these bonds of sociability are intrinsic to the human condition:

> Here lies the ground of a necessary human society, without which no human could grow up, and the species could not multiply. Humans therefore are *born* for society. . . . (101)

Entering the lively eighteenth-century debates on sympathy and its relationship to human nature and moral judgement, Herder argues that this natural sociability lays the groundwork, as it were, for the sympathetic disposition that is present in humans and, indeed, at least to an extent, in all sociable animals. Herder's writings on sympathy have been influential, and not only for their linguistic legacies. (As Meinecke has noted, Herder invented the term *Einfühlung* in order to represent his understanding of sympathetic identification; the word "empathy" first entered English by way of a translation of *Einfühlung*.[16]) Significantly, given his defence of non-European peoples against imperialism, Herder argues that sympathy is a constitutive feature of humankind and that, while a full understanding of another's situation is impossible, humans' extensive ability to commiserate with each other across various lines of difference reveals the depth of this sensibility in the social and moral character of humankind. He even argues that sound and language as such are capable of engendering human sympathy, rather than only a language with which one is familiar.

But sympathy, Herder insists, is not sufficient for the purpose of organizing formal social relations and distributing justice. Thus, despite sympathy's powerful hold upon humankind in certain circumstances, on the whole, it tends to become weak when humans interact with those who are presumed to be different. He argues that

> as the sympathy of man is incapable of being universally extended, and could be but an obscure and frequently impotent conductor to him, a limited and complex being, in everything remote; his guiding mother [Nature] has subjected its numerous and lightly interwoven branches to her more unerring standard: this is *the rule of truth and justice*. (102)

Herder develops this idea further when he investigates his more normative understanding of humanity in Book XV of the *Ideas*. For now, he confines himself to stating that some form of the Golden Rule approximates the sense of reciprocity, equity, and respect that can be found at work in a variety of social circumstances. In some sense, the "rule of truth and justice" derives from a similar disposition toward being treated fairly and from the norms that develop from increasing interactions among those with distinct approaches toward social life. Herder implies that the content of various social rules and norms will vary, but that they have a broadly similar character, one that underlies many of them and that indicates a deep universal truth behind the diversity of social relationships and practices. In this sense, his idea of a "rule of truth and justice" is similar to Diderot's partly sociological and partly philosophical concept of the "general will of humanity". Herder contends that

> the laws of humankind, of nations, and of animals, are founded on similarity of sentiment, unity of design among different persons, and equal truth in an alliance: for even animals that live in society obey the laws of justice; and humans, who avoid their ties by force and fraud, are the most inhuman of all creatures, even if they are kings and monarchs of the Earth. (102)

European monarchs and the centralized political power that they represent pose, for Herder, one of the greatest threats to fostering and maintaining the delicate equilibrium that justice requires. Since "[n]o reason, no humanity, is conceivable without strict justice and truth" (102), the oppressive political powers of Europe in both their domestic and imperial guises confirm their own brutal inhumanity, a point that Diderot had also argued forcefully in the *Histoire des deux Indes*.

Indicating a theme that runs throughout the *Ideas*, Herder asserts that there exists a universal impulse to religion, not to any specific religion or theological doctrine, but to a sense of the mystery of our existence and the limits of our own understanding. He criticizes those who reduce religion to fear, yet he also gives a speculative account of the origins of religion by arguing that human curiosity about ultimate causes and the deep connections among beings and actions leads to spiritual reflection. In this respect, he asserts, "the first and last philosophy has ever been religion." (103) Herder emphasizes the universality of such contemplation, and of investing a variety of symbols or invisible realms with meaning, by reiterating the constitutive features of humankind.[17] As he writes,

> Even the most savage nations have practised it [religion]: for no people upon Earth have been found entirely destitute of it, any more than of a capacity for reason and the human form, language and the connubial union, or some of the manners and customs that are characteristic of human beings. (103)

All peoples, therefore, strive to find meaning in their lives and exercise artful and creative capacities, though their languages, customs, intimate relationships, and spiritual pursuits, all of which take on an almost infinite variety. Hence, "we know no creature above the human being [who is] organized with more diversity and art." (107) In part, this is the case because humans are fundamentally cultural and plural beings: "Education [or self-development, upbringing, *Erziehung*], art, culture were all indispensable to him [i.e., to man] from the first moment of his existence". Thus, they comprise the "specific character of humankind itself" (286).

Beyond a set of capacities or powers, however, Herder emphasizes repeatedly that it is the incessant striving and flux of human life that best characterizes humanity; in part, this follows from the characteristics he emphasizes, for they all imply a degree of activity, reflection, and creativity. In this sense, he notes, all humans move toward what might be considered an ideal humanity by cultivating and exercising their powers in manifold ways. Humanity is not a definable goal and it clearly does not represent a singular purpose or end. For Herder, it represents the sum total, and the ever changing uses, of our active powers in different ages and places. He notes that the traditions that one inherits are often restrictive (the "chains" of "prejudices and evil manners") and that the claims of necessity and the influence of environmental factors (such as climate) can impose limits upon human activity and striving, but that everywhere this striving toward humanity occurs in its own distinctive manner. Hence, he argues that

> [t]he design of plastic Providence must have taken in all these steps, these zones, these varieties, at one view, and known how to advance human beings in all of them. . . . (123)

Although Herder uses the language of providence, humans themselves create, sustain, and transform their diverse cultural beliefs, practices, and ideas. Like Kant, Herder calls upon all humans to continue to work toward their self-cultivation by this perpetual and diverse striving, in order for each individual "to become a nobler, freer creature, by his own exertions" (124). Thus, humans possess freedom both as a constitutive characteristic and as an open-ended capacity that is exercised in diverse ways in order to become actual.

It is important to note that Herder himself presents his view of the shared features of humanity to indicate that there is, indeed, something that is identifiably human within the immense diversity of human life. Thus, after having surveyed a number of ethnographic accounts of non-European peoples, Herder writes the following:

> Weary and tired of all these changes of climates, times, and nations, can we find on the globe no standard of the common property and excellence of our fraternity? Yes: the disposition to *reason*, *humanity*, and *religion*, the three graces of human life. . . . Languages vary with every people, in every climate; but in all languages one and the same type of searching human reason is conspicuous. (251)

Underlying the manifold variety of languages, practices, institutions, and beliefs, therefore, there exists a set of capacities that makes such diversity possible and that suggests a common character which animates our various pursuits.[18] Herder argues explicitly (partly, perhaps, against Rousseau, who had suggested that orangutans might be purely natural humans, free of the artifice of society and conventional mores) that humans as such use language, reason, and strive for spiritual meaning. The ethnography of the non-European world, for Herder, confirms what should also be clear simply from a proper self-understanding. As he argues,

> Had humans been dispersed over the Earth like brutes to invent the internal form of humanity for themselves, we would then find nations without language, without reason, without religion, and without morals: for as humans have been, so humans are still. But no history, no experience, informs us of any place where human orangutans dwell; and the fables, which the late Diodorus, or still later Pliny, relates of men without feeling and other inhuman men have the marks of falsehood on the very face of them; or at least are not to be credited on the testimony of such writers. (255)

Again, Herder relates two of his favourite examples, the New Zealanders and the Pesherays, as humans who live in such extreme climates that they appear to lead the most "savage" lives possible; yet even they "possess humanity, reason, and language." (255)

Herder moves, however, from a more anthropological and descriptive sense of humanity to a normative conception of humanity in Book IX of the *Ideas*. As we will see in the final section of this chapter, it is the synthesis of the two that eventually forms his considered view of the concept of humanity. In Book IX, we see already this move toward relating what might be termed human nature with the natural tendency toward respect and reciprocity. Herder begins to discuss the *disposition* to humanity, which consists of the tendency to judge others and oneself by standards of fairness and justice. He argues that New World peoples, despite some practices that might offend Europeans, when considered more carefully, also display this distinctive disposition toward ethical life; moreover, he notes repeatedly (much as Montaigne had) that Europeans themselves have at least as strong a tendency to weaken and subvert this disposition as non-Europeans. Commenting on reports of cannibalism (and, unlike Kant, assuming that to some extent such reports are credible), Herder argues forcefully that

> [n]o cannibals devour their children or brothers: their inhuman practice is a savage right of war to nourish their valour, and terrify their enemies. It is, therefore, nothing more or less than the work of a gross political reason, which in those nations has overpowered [the disposition to] humanity with regard to these few sacrifices to their country, as it is overpowered by us Europeans, even in the present day, in some other respects. Before strangers they are ashamed of this barbarous practice, although we Europeans do not blush at killing men; indeed, they behave nobly and like brothers to every prisoner of war, on whom the fatal lot does not fall. (255)

Following this line of argument, Herder also notes that other practices that are often described to support the claim that many New World peoples lack the capacity to be moral beings—"when the Hottentot buries his child alive" or when "the Eskimo abridges the days of his aged parent"—are the "consequences of lamentable necessity, which at the same time are not inconsistent with the original feeling of humanity." Indeed, he argues that "misguided reason or unbridled luxury has engendered many more singular abominations among us [Europeans]." (255) The upshot of Herder's arguments is to demonstrate not only the hypocrisy of Europeans' pejorative judgements about New World peoples, but also the universality of a moral disposition that takes on many forms. Despite their great variety, Herder believes that they can all be described, in formal terms, as including dispositions of "affection toward children", "gratitude toward friends", the "rule of justice", and "principles of social rights"; thus, the various forms of sociability and the balance achieved in humans' social relations through norms and institutions all point to the constitutive features of humankind.

In a crucial passage, Herder blends his descriptive and normative understandings of humanity and contends that this disposition to humanity is itself human nature:

permit me, after all I have read and examined concerning the nations of the Earth, to consider this internal disposition to humanity to be as universal as human nature, or rather to be properly speaking human nature itself. (255)

Herder ends Book IX with a metaphorical description of the relationship between human unity and human diversity, one that is best to keep in mind as we move toward his ideas about how one ought to conceptualize human diversity. Speaking of the internal disposition to humanity and how it lies within humans simply because of their humanity, he contends that "benevolent God" gave instincts to animals, but impressed upon humans his "image, religion and humanity". He argues that "the outline of the statue lies there, deep in the block, but it cannot hew itself out, it cannot fashion itself. Tradition and learning, reason and experience, must do this. . . ." (256) Herder's own understanding of humanity as the anthropological core of what it means fundamentally to be human is itself "deep in the block" of the *Ideas*. The shared characteristics of humanity, which also include an impulse toward just relations of respect and reciprocity, are not enough to constitute any living human. Like the material from which a statue is made, "humanity" is the essential and important, but ultimately also the somewhat amorphous, material that is shaped and moulded *diversely* by free and active human powers. Hence, for Herder, respecting humanity necessarily entails respecting human diversity.

Conceptualizing Human Diversity: Sedentary versus Nomadic Societies

Herder makes clear, at the beginning of Book VI, that his study of humanity will attempt to integrate an account of humans as such with a theory of human diversity; thus, as he explains, having formed an idea of humans' "general nature", one should then proceed "to contemplate the various appearances" that humans assume on the "global stage." (132) In the *Ideas*, of course, Herder switches back and forth quite rapidly between anthropological statements about the nature of humanity to arguments about what differentiates humanity and how far these differences run. Hence, there is not a clear textual division between his theorization of human nature and cultural difference. In this section, I weave together his various contentions about diversity to elucidate the key concepts and categories that he draws upon and those that he rejects. Moreover, I show how his philosophical anthropology informs, and is informed by, his conceptualization of the multiplicity that permeates human life.

Herder argues that one should be wary of relying uncritically upon the standard division among hunters, pastoralists, and agriculturalists, which was so often used to categorize peoples into distinctive groups (and which was employed, as we have seen, by Rousseau, Diderot, and Kant, among many others). Accordingly, he contends,

> It has been customary to divide the nations of the Earth into hunters, fishermen, shepherds, and agriculturalists; and not only to determine their rank in civilization from this division, but even to consider civilization itself as a necessary consequence of this or that way of life. This would be very excellent if these modes of life were determined themselves in the first place, but they vary with almost every region, and for the most part run into each other in such a manner that this mode of classification is very difficult to apply with accuracy. (202)

Thus, throughout the *Ideas*, Herder makes an effort to distinguish, for example, the specific mores, customs, arts, and traditions of one pastoral people from another; as he notes, the "Bedouin and the Mongol, the Laplander and the Peruvian, are shepherds, but how greatly do they differ from each other. . . ." (202, cf. 199) Nonetheless, despite the importance of such local differences, Herder makes a number of cautious generalizations about the primary differences between nomadic and sedentary peoples, differences that (as we will see) are crucial for his understanding of human development and imperialism.

Herder's discussion of nonagriculturalists centres on the causes of their nomadic lifestyle, the unlikelihood that they will change their lifestyle, and an explanation of the kinds of arts and traditions that this way of life tends to create and nurture. The climate within which a people live, Herder argues, affects its level of artful activity. Those who can live primarily on roots, herbs, and fruits (as Tahitians, for example, were often understood to do) tend to foster "arts and inventions" that attend only to their "daily wants." Not all peoples, however, are fortunate enough to enjoy such naturally bountiful environments; thus, where the climate is "less temperate", the pressures of necessity make humans live "more hardily and with less simplicity." (203) The arts, practices, and customs that are required simply to maintain the sustenance of a people is itself significant, in Herder's view, for it involves the "active powers of the mind". With regard to aboriginal Australians, he explains that the combination of activities that are required to sustain a people's very existence forms a distinctive way of life with its own standards of pleasure and satisfaction (203).[19] Moving to other regions, he argues that the kinds of understanding that are employed by a people are always suited to its specific, local needs. Herder contends, for instance, that the

> [indigenous] Californian displays as much understanding as his country and way of life afford or require. So does the native of Labrador, and of every country on the most barren verge of the earth. Everywhere humans have recon-

ciled themselves to necessity, and from hereditary habit live happily in the labours to which they are compelled. (203, cf. 135)

The mode of transmission from one generation to the next, Herder implies, indicates the cultural knowledge, social narratives, and artful practices that are required for what might erroneously appear to be a 'natural'
life. Accordingly, he hypothesizes the kind of education that a young boy
might receive from the elders of a nomadic people.

> The [Amerindian] boy is educated to aspire to the fame of a hunter; [or] as the
> son of a Greenlander, to seek renown by catching seals: this forms the subject
> of discourse, the songs, the tales of famous deeds that meet his ears; this is
> represented to his eyes in expressive actions, and animating dances. (203)

Songs, Herder later argues, convey much of the essence of a people, for it
is through such artistic modes of expression that the key symbolic meanings, traditions, and propensities of a people are bequeathed to younger
generations (216). The very fact that a people continues to lead its hunting or pastoral life indicates that it has accepted and is willing to continue
and to transform a set of social practices and norms; the members of such
a people show a "rooted esteem for that way of life which they have
received as an inheritance." In contrast to common imperialist arguments, Herder portrays such lifestyles as well-ordered and maintained by
the active powers of the human mind, rather than by instinct or by wild
irrationality.

In all of these respects, therefore, non-Europeans are similar to European peoples—while customs, languages, practices and so forth differ
significantly, each people is artful, creative, and adjusts to the specific
qualities of its geography and climate. Still, as Herder notes, European
societies were considerably more complex and technologically more sophisticated than many of the societies that they encountered in the Americas—what, he asks, can explain this? Herder's query is in part an attempt
to answer the related question of how one can explain the ability of Europeans to conquer the Americas so rapidly, in a manner such that "Europeans could treat . . . [Amerindians] like a flock of defenceless sheep?"
(205) He asserts that differences in physical strength and in "understanding" cannot account for the relative ease of European imperialists' successes. He mentions as obvious contributing factors Europeans' arts and
weapons, but "principally", he argues, the crucial element that guaranteed such swift victories consists of Amerindians' lack of domesticated
animals. Herder explains this curious judgement at first by indicating the
military prowess that Europeans possessed because of their use of horses
and dogs. In addition, he writes that since horses have been introduced
among some Amerindian nations, the "[t]he horse, which the [Euro-
pean] oppressors of their brethren employed as an unconscious instru-

ment of fate, may perhaps at some future period be the deliverer of the whole land" (205). But the ultimate reason that the domestication of animals is of paramount importance, in his view, concerns the consequent psychological and social transformations, which often lead to the establishment of more powerful, and more destructive and imperializing, societies.

As long as humans are kind toward animals, Herder argues, they tend to improve one another. Thus, animals develop "capacities and inclinations" that cannot be found "in the wild animal". Moreover, the domestication of animals and the activities that it enables promote "the active mind of humans"; "the practical understanding on the part of humans", he writes, "has been strengthened and extended by the [domesticated] beast". (206) Herder argues that the lack of many domesticated animals in the New World did not result from a lack of creativity or understanding on the part of New World peoples. Rather, there were simply fewer domesticable animals in the Americas. As he argues,

> [The Americas] had fewer kinds of quadrupeds. . . . The alpaca and llama, the camel-sheep of Mexico, Peru, and Chile, were the only tameable and domesticated beasts: for even the Europeans, with all their understanding [of domestication], have been unable to add any to these, or to render the . . . puma, the sloth or tapir, an animal of domestic utility. (206)

Through this quirk of fate, he argues, much of the global differentiation of lifestyles, institutions, and social practices followed.[20] Herder argues that an inclination toward liberty is linked with the domestication of animals because the use of animals increases humans' ability to fashion themselves and their surrounding environments. In addition, most crucially, it increases humans' inclinations toward "acquisition and permanent property" (135–36).

Hence, in many cases, he suggests, agriculturalism tends to follow from the domestication of animals. Like Rousseau, Diderot, and Kant, Herder argues that "generally speaking, no mode of life has effected so much alteration in the minds of humans as agriculture, combined with the enclosure of land." (207) The sedentary, agricultural life, he contends, lays the foundation for government and laws, although in other passages he also suggests that a form of political rule (if not "civil" rule, the political rule of a town or city) exists among nonsedentary peoples. The establishment of civil life, however, comes at a steep cost, in particular a loss of human freedom because of the *paternalism* of governmental power. As Herder argues, agriculture

> necessarily paved the way for that frightful despotism, which, from confining each human to his field, gradually proceeded to prescribe to him what alone he should do on it, what alone he should be. (207)

Herder makes a number of impassioned attacks against the social evils that are propagated by cities and towns, and argues that the restraints placed upon citizens by states are a result of the problems that sedentary living itself has caused. Following Rousseau, he contends that social oppression does not result from human nature, but rather from humanly constructed and maintained institutions and practices. Political rule, at least in the manner in which it existed in Europe in his day, was for Herder an artificial and unnecessary burden; the quasi-anarchistic moments of his political theory becomes clearest in such passages.[21] As Herder writes,

> He who maintains that laws are necessary because otherwise humans would live lawlessly takes for granted what is incumbent upon them to prove. If humans were not thronged together in [the] close prisons [of cities], they would need no ventilators to purify the air; were their minds not inflamed by artificial madness, they would not require the restraining hand of correlative [of the corresponding political] art. (210)

In addition to the variety of domestic problems that agriculture unleashes, it also leads to an imperializing and crusading mentality, whereby the supposed benefits of such life are spread coercively throughout the globe. Herder often stops short of criticizing arts and sciences per se; moreover, he often celebrates their contribution to human knowledge and even to human prosperity and comfort. Herder even argues that Europe is indebted to Asia, for it was because of the "beneficent" spread of cultivated ideas and practices from Asia that Europe was able to develop beyond a relatively simple life. (145)

But Europeans, in Herder's view, cannot claim any superiority simply because their settled lifestyles have over time produced artistic, scientific, and technological achievements. He attacks the vanity of "so many Europeans, when they set themselves above the people of all the other quarters of the globe with respect to what they call arts, sciences, and cultivation" (241). Those who claim greatness are almost always the individuals who had nothing themselves to do with the invention and improvement of such arts and sciences. In an attempt to undercut some of the standard arguments in favour of European superiority, Herder writes sarcastically that simply learning to use inventions and traditions that one has inherited "is the work of a machine" and that those who merely imbibe "the waters of science", without contributing to it themselves, possess all the merit of "a sponge that has grown on humid soil" (241).[22] On the whole, he argues that one cannot simply be 'for' or 'against' the development of advanced arts and sciences: "I do not think the question is to be answered with a simple affirmative or negative, since here, as in everything else, all depends on what use is made of that which has been invented." (242) Still, Herder finds it difficult to contemplate such refinements without acknowledging that the inequalities upon which they have been developed have "converted many towns and countries into poorhouses" (243).

In a similar vein, Herder argues that the mere possession of books signifies nothing about the value of a people as such; the merits of written documents consist in how well they are understood and appropriated by thoughtful individuals. The practice of writing, in Herder's view, is a mixed blessing, for it tends to homogenize human thought and experience and to stifle creativity. Local variations become erased as the written word makes uniform the diverse understandings of a people so as to record them. As he contends,

> although this way of perpetuating our thoughts fixes both the spirit and the letter, it in various ways fetters and restrains them [as well]. Not only are the living accents and gestures, which formerly gave language such power to penetrate the heart, gradually extinguished by writing; not only are dialects, and consequently the characteristic idioms of particular tribes and nations, rendered less numerous; but humans' memories and the spirit of their mental powers are enfeebled by this artificial assistance of prescribed forms of thought. (239)

At the same time, he notes, writing can promote fraternity and may one day become a universal feature of human societies, in which case fertile cross-national exchanges of ideas and perspectives could check the internal homogenization of expressions, dialects, and perspectives that tends to occur within any written culture. It is perhaps this ambivalent view of writing that leads Herder to reject implicitly the imperial logic of missionaries and others who justify colonization on the grounds of spreading the Gospel. For Herder argues that peoples who do not read and write can win eternal salvation simply by believing in a higher power and immortality, beliefs that, as we have seen, he takes to be nearly universal. Thus, not only for Diderot and Kant, but also for the more religious (though in many respects highly unorthodox) Herder, the religious dimension of imperialist politics is empty and uncompelling.

Given all of this, it comes as no surprise, then, that Herder is unwilling to recommend the sedentary, agricultural lifestyle as a universal end toward which all peoples should either voluntarily progress or coercively be pushed. He protects himself from the charge of hypocrisy—"imagine not that I wish to derogate from the mode of life which Providence has employed as a principal instrument for leading humans to civil society: for I myself eat the bread it has produced." (207–8) But, while admitting that there are numerous benefits to an agriculturally based, sedentary society, he also calls upon his fellow Europeans to give equal respect to different forms of social organization. As Herder exhorts,

[L]et justice be done to other ways of life, which, from the constitution of the Earth, have been destined, equally with agriculture, to contribute to the development of humankind. . . . If Nature has anywhere attained her end, she has attained it everywhere. The practical understanding of human beings was intended to blossom and bear fruit in all its varieties: and hence such a diversified Earth was ordained for so diversified a species. (208)

For Herder, the purpose of human life is manifold and, thus, an appreciation of the diversity of modes of life is fundamentally an acknowledgement of the value of humanity itself.

Let us turn now from the differences between sedentary and nonsedentary peoples to climate, a differentiating feature of human existence that plays some role in nearly every eighteenth-century social and political theory. As Herder acknowledges, there is a long-running debate between, to note the extremes, those who "build so much upon" the concept of climate and others who "deny its influence altogether" (172). Climate certainly plays a significant role in Herder's thought, although the relationship between human agency and environmental factors that he presents is complex. While at times he restricts himself to understanding climate as simply the natural environment within which one lives, he often discusses climate "in the most extensive signification of the word, so as to include the manner of life, and kind of food" (149). In addition to "unchangeable" elements of climate (e.g., heat and cold), Herder argues that climate itself is often variable. Thus, a region's

[natural] products, the food and drink that humans enjoy in it, the mode of life they pursue, the labours in which they are employed, their clothing, even their ordinary attitudes, their arts and pleasures, with a multitude of other circumstances that considerably influence their lives all belong to the picture of changeable climate. (174)

With such a diverse conception of climate, it comes as no surprise, then, to learn that each climatic factor does not produce perfectly uniform results; in fact, each *individual* is shaped by climate differently (179). On the whole, then, climate tends "to operate" most palpably "on the mass, rather than on the individual" (176). He argues that it is accordingly in large-scale social phenomena where we can best view climatic effects, although even at this level, it is "very difficult to be delineated distinctly." (177) In order to get a better sense of how climate may or may not influence human practices and self-understandings, Herder suggests that in the future the most profitable subject of study will probably be colonial populations, from whom one can study the interactions of their modes of life, the climate of their home country and that of their new country, the peoples with whom it interacts and intermixes, and so forth (184–85).

Herder argues that, on the one hand, humans are powerfully shaped by climate, but, on the other hand, that humans themselves can alter their climate, which in turn continues to mould them. Even if humans lacked the ability to transform their surroundings and inheritance, similar environmental factors will still produce diverse outcomes. As he argues, "It is true that we are ductile clay in the hand of climate, but her fingers mould so variously, and the laws that counteract them are so numerous" (172). But, of course, for Herder, humans do indeed possess the freedom that allows them to change their climate within bounds. Even the elements of climate that seem fixed, such as the vegetation of the land, can be altered. Europe, Herder argues, used to be a vast stretch of "dank forest", but now through cultivation it is "exposed to the rays of the Sun, and the inhabitants themselves have changed with the climate." But this symbiosis between human agency and the surrounding environment can also be destructive. As Herder argues, the cultivation of lands forced by European imperialists and the introduction of new ways of life have debilitated many of the indigenous inhabitants, including those who led sedentary lives before the arrival of the Europeans (186). The ability to thrive in an environment takes a significant amount of time to develop, as a result of which sudden changes often yield tragic consequences; for the "nature" of a people that has been habituated to a particular set of practices and institutions will no longer cohere in any manner with their transformed environments. As Herder writes,

> May we not . . . attribute the debility of the civilized Americans, as they are called, in Mexico, Peru, Paraguay, and Brazil, to this among other things, that we have changed their country and manner of living without the power or the will of giving them a European nature? (186)

Given Herder's view that all of the climates on earth blend together and are interconnected, he is opposed to empire-building in part because of his belief that diverse peoples must develop in accord with their specific climates. Sudden, profound shifts in lifestyles, the abrupt introduction of foreign dispositions and institutions into a region, and the massive migration of peoples are bound to generate disastrous results. Even the ecological balance among animals and plants can be disrupted, for America has seen a decrease, Herder argues, in edible birds and the stock of fish, and consequently in the "health and longevity of its inhabitants", because of rapid deforestation and cultivation (186). Thus, while humans can shape their climate, this is a power that is often abused, and in light of humans' symbiotic relationship with climate, such despotic uses of power come back to haunt them.

In the same manner that climates are difficult to identify and to delineate, the category of race, according to Herder, is also diffuse and problematic, although he believes that there are legitimate uses of the term.

Herder does *not* reject all uses of the concept of race, as is commonly claimed. Rather, he opposes the idea that there are a fixed number of exclusive races among the Earth's peoples. He notes briefly that if race is understood in such a rigidly demarcated fashion, then "I see no reason for this appellation." He argues that because skin colour varies so greatly, and in a manner such that any fixed grouping would be arbitrary, complexion cannot be an accurate method of conceptualizing human diversity (166). Herder argues, therefore, that

> there are neither four or five races nor exclusive varieties on this Earth. Complexions run into each other: forms follow the genetic character, and upon the whole all are but shades of the same great picture, extending through all ages, and over all parts of the Earth. (166)

The manner in which he further criticizes this account of race sheds some light on his understanding of the nation. For Herder, race properly signifies a difference in origin. Thus, in discussing conjectures about the earliest migrations in human history, he refers to Mongols, for instance, as a distinctive race. Indeed, in the early books of the *Ideas*, Herder spends considerable time discussing the physiognomic differences among human groups and offers various conjectures as to their ultimate racial origin. But such groups mixed with others over time and settled in diverse climates, which themselves over thousands of years shaped humans diversely. In this respect, then, even if scholars were to agree about the earliest known 'races', no current country or complexion would be synonymous with a particular race. For, as Herder contends,

> every nation is one people, having its own national form, as well as its own language: the climate it is true stamps on each its mark, or spreads over it a slight veil, but not sufficient to destroy the original national character. (166)

For Herder, the concept of the nation provides a grounding that no other category of diversity in his thought (such as climate, agriculturalism, nomadism, or race) offers. While Herder theorizes diversity at the level of the individual to a considerable degree in the *Ideas*, it would be a mistake to believe that this undercuts any appeal to a unitary, communal identity. As we have seen, for Herder, nationality is more a state of mind or a sense of distinctiveness (and a rather flexible one at that) than a collection of objective, essential characteristics.[23] Herder's simultaneous faith in human unity and insistence on deep differentiation and the value of national communities come together most vividly in his thoughts on humanity as a moral ideal. It is in light of this elevated conception of humanity that Herder theorizes moral incommensurability and international justice most fully.

Beyond Empire and toward International Justice: 'Humanity' as a Moral Ideal

We saw earlier that Herder at times begins to blend his descriptive account of humanity, that is, his philosophical anthropology, with a vision of humanity that embodies a moral ideal. From this perspective, the end toward which we should strive is, in some sense, part of our very being, rather an external end. Since the constitutive features that he theorizes are themselves situated in cultural contexts and yield a plurality of practices, beliefs, and dispositions, this suggests that humans' fundamental moral purpose is diverse. In Book XV of the *Ideas*, he elaborates his ethical concept of humanity and relates it to his account of human nature in more detail. The title of the first chapter of the book proclaims that "Humanity is the end [or purpose, *Zweck*] of humankind" (438). As Herder reiterates, humanity itself consists of a variety of capacities that humans exercise diversely, among which are "finer senses and instincts . . . reason and liberty . . . [and] language, art, and religion" (439). From these constitutive qualities, a wide array of social practices and traditions can be, and have been, created, from the societies of hunters and pastoralists to the more complicated institutions of the settled inhabitants of cities. After viewing the broad range of human life, Herder argues that we are in a position to discern what he calls "the grand law of nature: let man be man; let him mould his condition according to what he himself shall view as best." (440) By conjoining self-determination, freedom, and anti-paternalism, Herder crafts a universal law based upon humans' plural nature in order to protect that very plurality. As with so many of Herder's ethical claims, the 'law of nature' appears to be both a social fact and a moral norm, for it refers to the fact that humans have developed themselves diversely, while it also calls upon all humans to let each other cultivate themselves in the manner in which they see fit. The value that Herder places upon human freedom and the ability to reason in a relatively free environment provide the foundation for his ethical concerns. To respect human freedom and reason, one must respect plural forms of life, for the exercise of such capacities necessarily yields practices and beliefs that are moulded variously by climate, language, tradition, and one's own creativity.

Many of these arguments are targeted at the level of the individual; that is, even individuals in similar environments will engage in distinct practices and believe in different standards of happiness. For Herder, at the most general level, the very nature of happiness is somewhat arbitrary because it depends upon the contingencies that structure the life of each individual. Happiness, he writes, is the child of Accident, who has placed him on this spot, or on that, and determined his capacity of enjoyment, and the kind and measure of his joys and sorrows, according to the country, time, organization, and circumstances in which he lives. It would be the most stupid vanity to imagine that all the inhabitants of the world must be Europeans to be happy. (219)

In a crucial passage, Herder stresses that differences of opinion exist among individuals, and that they indicate distinct sets of assumptions and self-understandings. As he argues,

> Happiness is an internal state; and therefore its standard is not seated without us, but in the breast of every individual, where alone it can be determined. Another has as little right to impart to me his mode of perception, and convert his identity into mine. (219)

One's standards of satisfaction, pleasure, and happiness, from the stand-point of each individual, constitute in some respects one's identity. To deny individuals such internal standards by appealing to a form of ethnocentrism or paternalism is to deny them part of their very being. At bottom, these passages suggest powerfully that the individual is the fundamental unit of Herder's claims about incommensurability and self-perfection.

Each individual, however, is also a social being and each set of social institutions, activities, territory, language, and practices constitutes, for Herder, a "nation" which has its own "centre of gravity" that cannot be compared to any other (*SC* 186). Herder's arguments make clear that, for him, the nation is not simply a loose agglomeration of the kinds of practices and characteristics listed earlier. Rather, he explicitly models the nation upon the family. It should be noted that Herder claims that "Nature extended the bonds of society only to families: beyond that, she left humankind at liberty to knit them, and to frame their most delicate work of art, bodies politic, as they thought proper." (248) Nevertheless, he also argues that what is truly "proper" is to follow the social bonds that nature creates:

> Nature educates families: the most natural state therefore is one nation, with one national character. This it retains for ages, and this is most naturally formed when it is the object of its native princes; for a nation is as much a natural plant as a family, only with more branches. Nothing therefore appears so directly opposite to the end of government as the unnatural enlargement of states, the wild mixture of various kinds of humans [*Menschen-Gattungen*] and nations under one sceptre. (249)

This much quoted passage is one of a few moments in the *Ideas* in which Herder could be advocating a political nationalism based on blood ties. Since *Menschen-Gattungen* has often been mistranslated as "races", the overtones become even more troubling. Herder's comments about the nation are related to his anti-imperialism because an idea of incommensurability also applies to nations, with each nation exhibiting its own specific excellence. As Herder writes,

> [N]ations modify themselves according to time, place, and their internal character: each bears in itself the standard of its perfection, totally independent of all comparison with that of others. (452)

Does Herder's commitment to incommensurability, and consequently his anti-ethnocentrism and anti-imperialism, come then at the price of an exclusive ethnic nationalism? Does he favour pluralism globally, while also recommending homogeneity within each nation?

Herder's use of organic metaphors (soil, rootedness, and so forth) and his occasional references to what he calls the "genetic" traditions of a people are, for good reason, sources of much confusion, and they indicate that there are tensions in his writings that no interpretation can or should overcome.[24] At the same time, when one works through each of his arguments about nationality and the distinguishing features of peoples in the *Ideas*, it becomes clear that there is one aspect of a people that, at bottom, constitutes it as a nation: language. We have seen already that language is a key element of Herder's epistemology and of his conceptualization of human diversity. It is also, for Herder, the most crucial component of a nation; his arguments about how the music, songs, and popular literature of a people reveal its innermost desires and distinctive qualities are themselves rooted in his dedication to language as the unique embodiment of traditions, beliefs, and practices. Accordingly, he contends that

> [a] *philosophical comparison of languages* would form the best essay on the history and diversified character of the human heart and understanding; for every language bears the stamp of the mind and character of a people. . . . not only are there certain sounds and letters peculiar to almost every nation, but the giving of names, even in denoting audible things, indeed in the immediate expressions of the passions, in interjections, varies all over the Earth. . . . [T]he genius of a people is nowhere more displayed than in the physiognomy of their language. (237–38)

Herder is indeed a monist, not a pluralist, on the relationship of language to the body politic, for he asserts that multilingual states are often unmanageable and tend to dissolve over time. In part, this contributes to his animus against European imperial projects: large multilingual states, in his view, are almost always the products of violent conquests. It should be noted that Herder's commitment to unilingual states does not seem to undermine his commitment to a flourishing pluralism. Language is the only feature that Herder believes should be shared by an entire people. From Herder's perspective, however, each language is itself malleable and multifaceted; that a nation is unilingual does not, therefore, impede the existence of a wide diversity of practices, beliefs, and norms within any one polity. And, as we have seen with his arguments about the concept of race, each nation necessarily includes much ethnic diversity. In addition, of course, there are many other differentiating features that are not precluded by Herder's preference for unilingual states. In the final analysis, his strident defence of the independence of nations and the safeguarding of their distinctiveness does not betray a desire to create homogenous national communities, but rather underscores his concerns about cultural and political homogenization in the modern world—the main agents of which, for Herder, are European imperial states.

Reflecting upon the immense variety of societies, practices, customs, and religions comprised by the *Ideas*, Herder notes that it is possible to draw a "chain of cultivation" that links all peoples together. But he quickly notes that it cannot be a linear chain on which one could place peoples hierarchically. Rather, the chain would fly off, as he puts it, "in extremely divergent curves." (453) Each curve would contain distinctive strengths and weaknesses and thus would be noticeably dissimilar and, in many respects, incommensurable. As Herder adds, many of these curves would

> exclude or limit one another, until at length *a symmetry takes place in the whole*, so that were we to reason from one perfection of any nation concerning another, we should form very treacherous conclusions. (453, emphasis added)

It is such a symmetry that grounds Herder's claims about the equality of all peoples, for peoples are by no means equal with respect to political liberty, scientific development, and many other practices and institutions. At times, he finds that it is difficult to argue that one people is freer than another, especially in those cases in which foreign conceptions of liberty are not given any weight in deliberating about the nature of freedom itself. Mostly, however, Herder is quite often willing to assert that some peoples are politically less oppressed than others or are more advanced in the arts than others. It is incorrect to assert, therefore, that Herder is simply an incommensurabilist in all matters of judgement; rather, like Diderot and Kant, he attempts to strike a balance between making cross-cultural judgements and limiting their scope. One of the key constraints upon universal moral judgements in Herder's thought is that societies can achieve greatness in one sphere, but can also be sorely lacking in others—thus, he is unwilling to make the claim that any one society is simply better than another. Moreover, social life and institutions are in such flux, in his view, that many of the comparative judgements that one makes must necessarily be of the most provisional nature.

Ultimately, Herder believes that the variety of beliefs, practices, and institutions found around the globe form part of a larger pattern that balances the various strengths and weaknesses of each nation. Considered in this sense, "humanity" as a whole is simply "reason and equity in all conditions, and in all occupations of men." (453) The equality of humans as cultural agents is in part what constitutes humanity. For, behind the immense diversity of human activities and beliefs, one can almost always find "reason, plan, and purpose." The active, artful minds and wills of humans who strive toward change constitutes the momentum that Herder characterizes as progress, and that sustains the symmetry of diverse lifestyles. Strikingly, Herder discusses the nature of both reason and justice by emphasizing the sense of balance that each attempts to seek:

> both reason and justice hinge on one and the same law of nature. . . . Reason weighs and compares the relations of things, so that she can dispose them in durable symmetry. Justice is nothing else than a moral symmetry of reason, the formula of the equilibrium of contending powers. . . . (456)

For Herder, then, the very substance and principles of justice shift as societies seek a balance between diverse and competing claims. Still, the core values of justice are related to reason, which for Herder has a strongly transnational quality. Each society configures its institutions differently, but the basic 'law of equity' can be found among any people. As he contends in the *Letters on the Advancement of Humanity*,

> The power of reason, of course, is manifold, depending on the sensibility that moves it in keeping with the distinct character of various peoples; nevertheless, it is and remains in all human manifestations *one and the same*. The *law of equity* [*Gesetz der Billigkeit*] is not alien to any nation; all have suffered for violating it, each in his own way. (WH 46, Letter 122)

His implicit assumption in such passages is that the struggle for individuals to achieve and maintain such a balance among competing claims according to relatively equitable standards requires the freedom to reflect critically upon one's own set of traditions and practices; yet, in his view, it is precisely this freedom that is increasingly rare in the modern world.

While the form of justice might vary across times and places, then, the proper end of politics always concerns individual freedom, in light of which Herder criticizes the paternalism that European states show toward their subjects and that the European imperial powers exercise toward the indigenous peoples of the non-European world. This is perhaps the most important mark that Kant's political thought appears to have made upon Herder. In the *Letters*, Herder asserts,

> To provide for and to facilitate in each individual case the mutually most bene-
> ficial impact of one human being upon the other, that, and that alone, can be
> purpose of all human community. Whatever interferes with, hinders, or voids
> this purpose is inhuman. Whether the human being lives briefly or for a long
> time, in this estate or that, he is meant to enjoy his existence and to convey the
> best of that existence to others; to that end, the society that he has joined is
> meant to assist him. (WH 100, Letter 25)

In addition, like that of Kant, the goal of Herder's political thought is
thus to bring politics and morality closer together so that humans can
govern their own affairs and live their diverse lives freely. The purpose of
politics is to learn from past errors in order to craft political institutions
and practices that treat humans morally, and hence more often as ends
rather than simply as means to the state's own ends.

> For politics, the human being is a means; for morality, he is the end; both
> sciences must become one, or they will both be harmful to one another. All
> disparities appearing in the process, in the meanwhile, must instruct human
> beings, so that they, at the very least, learn from their own mistakes. (WH 103,
> Letter 25)

The politics that Herder recommends consists of an equilibrium among
competing perspectives that can best be achieved when politics and morality are not fundamentally at odds.

Such symmetry and balance, when it is achieved, is always fragile, and
it is most easily destroyed, in Herder's opinion, by the power of the
centralized and bureaucratic modern state, or as he sometimes calls it to
underline its impersonality, the "machine-state" (217–18). In this respect, the imperial power that is exercised by European states is especially
disruptive to the moral balance that constitutes justice. In Herder's view,
modern empires are repeating tragically the premodern imperial pattern
of destruction, imbalance, and, ultimately, implosion. As he notes,

> Thus Alexander destroyed the equilibrium of the world; and it was long after
> his death before the storm subdued. Thus Rome disturbed the peace of the
> globe for more than a thousand years; and half a world of savage nations was
> requisite for the slow restoration of its quiet. (456)

But what could restore the equilibrium in Herder's day? In an optimistic
moment, he hopes that navigation, rather than supporting conquests
abroad, will provide the means for a new trade, and with it, reciprocal
justice and courtesy, "in short . . . humanity and its eternal laws." (446)
He also reflects briefly upon the increasing ties among individuals and
peoples from throughout the globe and how this might encourage the view
that "they are but one family, on one planet of no great extent." (459)

Like Diderot, however, more typical in the *Ideas* are his speculations of the cross-cultural dialogue that might have been, of opportunities lost.

> All newcomers from a foreign land, who have submitted to naturalize them-
> selves with the inhabitants, have not only enjoyed their love and friendship, but
> have ultimately found that their mode of life was not altogether unsuitable to
> the climate: but how few of such newcomers there are! How seldom does a
> European hear from the native of any country the praise, "He is a rational man
> like us!" (187)

As Herder well knew, not only was imperialism firmly entrenched, but the "grand European sponging enterprise" and the "devastation of three continents" was proceeding full speed ahead. (*SC* 209)

Herder provides the most hopeful articulation of the humanity toward which all peoples and individuals should work, one that would help to ensure that the injustices committed by European imperial powers would never again be repeated, in some of his *Letters on the Advancement of Humanity*. He reiterates in letter 116 that the importance of nationality in forming self-sustaining and free political communities should not be taken to sanction nationalistic and chauvinistic ventures abroad so as to further states' power and territories. "No nation", he writes, "should be allowed to wield the sceptre over other nations by virtue of its 'innate superiority' [*'angebohrner Vornehmigkeit'*], let alone by the power of the sword and the slave-driver's whip." (18:248) To counteract the spirit of conquest, Herder contends that the crossing of borders and the exchange of ideas and goods among peoples could bring about the sympathetic understandings and the rule of equity that he favoured. Yet he under-stood that commerce was also the agent of imperial aggression.

Herder's political thought, then, reflects the same ambivalence toward commerce (understood broadly, as it often was in the eighteenth century, as comprising not only market-oriented trade, but also communication, interaction, and dialogue among diverse peoples) that we have seen in Diderot and Kant. Herder notes in his *Scattered Leaves* [*Zerstrevte Blät-ter*] (1792) that the history of such "connectedness and commerce" has a far longer history than is commonly supposed; even the ostensibly bar-baric Middle Ages, he writes, "did not entirely suspend the extensive communication that was carried on between the peoples of Asia, Africa, and Europe" (WH 67). The great artistic monuments of the globe, he writes, are often situated "immediately along the trade routes of peoples, [and] . . . reflect wealth, trade, and therefore connectedness among peo-ples." (WH 68) Herder wants to harness the potential of commerce for fostering international justice, while also fearing the violent political and economic forces that commerce tends to produce. In the *Adrastea*, the short-lived periodical that Herder launched in 1801, Herder published a fictional conversation between a Briton and an Asian, whom the European attempts to convert. In response to the European's goal of spreading Christianity and European civilization, the Asian intones, "But don't forget that this exalted mission has nothing at all to do with the [British] East India Company or the propaganda from London." (23:505) For Herder, behind many imperial ventures, even some of those carried on in the name of spreading European civilization, lay the ultimate goal of commercial gain. Nevertheless, Herder argues that a nonimperial commerce can produce ties among diverse peoples and encourage the development of an equitable and moral humanity. The great legacy of the late Middle Ages, Herder maintained in the *Ideas*, was the rise of cities and the development of the "title of common liberty: citizenship." (627) Through the struggles between aristocratic and democratic orders in emerging political bodies, liberty increased and trade among regions prospered. The de jure and de facto commercial alliances formed among the city-states and regions of the Mediterranean, the Atlantic ocean, and the North Sea ultimately, in his view,

> contributed more to give Europe the form of a commonwealth than all the crusades and Roman rites, for it transcended religious or national distinctions, and founded the interconnectedness of states upon mutual advantage, emulative industry, probity, and order. Cities accomplished what was beyond the power of princes, priests, and nobles: they formed out of Europe *one common* cooperative body. (628)

The absolutist states (along with the fierce rivalries among them that were often spurred by imperial ambitions) that eventually emerged in Europe extinguished, according to Herder, the transnational ties that the early development of cities and commerce helped to produce.[25] At the global level, however, Herder holds out the hope that what commerce has already brought about under violent conditions could increasingly produce in the future a more just conjoining of diverse peoples from different continents.

In letter 119, Herder briefly articulates seven principles of international relations that would have to be internalized by humans for them to realize a spirit of transnational unity and global justice, two of which concern transnational commerce. In addition to fostering a greater antipathy toward war, encouraging citizens to free themselves from the blind veneration of war heroes, and rejecting the use of deliberate, state-sponsored falsehoods about foreign relations and diplomacy, Herder also recommends a reformed, more self-critical understanding of patriotism that would reinforce, rather than work against, the spirit of international unity

(18:268–71). Such changes in the manner in which citizens would hold accountable state-to-state relations could bring about, he argues, greater empathy toward vulnerable nations, which, when attacked, would then be defended as if one's own country were invaded. The final two principles stress the benefits of encouraging an increasingly interconnected world. Notably, Herder wishes to promote the development of international trade to counter the isolation that nations might otherwise encourage, though such trade should be conducted on equitable, not imperialistic, terms. Perhaps most importantly, the last principle articulates the importance of furthering as many peaceful and genuinely noncoercive contacts across nations and borders as possible. While Herder clearly advocated the extension of international communication and interactions, he rejected the idea that states should eventually merge into larger federations. Like Kant, Herder was opposed to the creation of a world state, but he also did not endorse nonsovereign international institutions, such as Kant's voluntary congress of independent states, preferring instead a more loose-knit understanding of mutual support in those cases when particular states were being threatened or violated.

Such an account of international justice, in Herder's view, made clear Europe's moral obligations toward the non-European world in light of the history of violent conquest and imperial rule. "Europe *must* replace what it has wrongly taken", he writes, "it must compensate for its wrongs, not as a matter of preference, but in keeping with the nature of things as they are." (WH 47, Letter 122) As Herder understood, however, no theory of international justice would likely convince self-interested Europeans to turn away from the power and profits of empire. Thus, like Diderot and Kant, he sanctions the violent resistance of non-European peoples against European imperial forces. Rhetorically, Herder appeals both to European pride and to the self-interested motives of Europeans not to be brutally avenged by non-Europeans, in the belief that if justice will not move imperialists, then perhaps the spectre of violent revolt will make them reconsider their exploits abroad. Hence, he asks in letter 114:

> What are we to say of the culture that the Spaniards, the Portuguese, the English and the Dutch brought to the East and West Indies and among the Negroes of Africa? Are such countries not crying out for revenge since they find themselves plunged for an indefinite time into an escalating disaster? If there were such a thing as a European collective spirit [*Europäischer Gesammtgeist*] . . . it must feel ashamed of the crimes committed by us, after having insulted humankind in a way that hardly any other group of nations had done. (18:222)

In addition to appealing to Europeans' pride and self-interest, Herder also attempts to deflate such pride by noting the contingency of European achievements and civilization. Ultimately, even Europe will decline in its importance and it will collapse, as all civilizations expire.

> Let no one augur the decline and death of our entire species because of the graying of Europe! What harm would it be to our species if a degenerate part of it were to perish? If a few withered branches and leaves fell from the tree that flows with sap? Others take the place of those that withered and flourish ever more freshly. Why should the western extremity of our Northern Hemisphere alone be the home of civilization? And is that really so? (WH 47, Letter 122)

Ultimately, Herder argues, Europeans' animalistic fury in the non-European world will be matched with a similarly ferocious spectacle when Europe itself becomes ravaged by conquest. "If they [Europeans] act impotently, in furious passion, out of cold greed, in meanly-exalted pride", he judges, "then *they* are the animals, the *demons* opposing their fellow humans. And who will guarantee to the Europeans that, some day, the same may not happen to them[?]" (WH 46, Letter 122) Reforming European behaviour now, Herder warns, could save European peoples from the cruel fate that will likely await them when the tables have turned, for "owing to several causes many an inhabited country may become uninhabitable, many a colony may become a mother country." (WH 47, Letter 122) Like Diderot, then, Herder's final appeals are to Europeans' selfish interests. Even here, however, the real note of hope that Herder offers lies not in what he expects imperial states to do either out of more enlightened or self-interested motives, but rather the prospect that European empires will eventually collapse from within because of the grim premise that all civilizations must at some point die.

The very concept of humanity, according to Herder, is rooted historically in the moral disposition that the most egalitarian Romans would afford to all individuals, regardless of origin or rank. "It was among the Romans", he writes,

> to whom the word *humanity* actually belongs, that the concept [of humanity] found occasion to be more specifically developed. Rome had rigid laws concerning servants, children, strangers, enemies; the upper classes had rights vis-à-vis the people, and so forth. Whoever observed the laws with utmost rigidity could be *just*, but not thereby also *humane*. The man of nobility, who on his own did not make use of these rights when they were not fair, who did not act toward children, slaves, the lowly, strangers, and enemies as the Roman citizen or patrician, but as a human being, was *humanus, humanissimus*, not only in conversation and social discourse [*in Gesprächen nur und in der Gesellschaft*], but also in matters of business, in domestic customs, in the entire sphere of conduct. . . . We are in need of this word as much as the Romans were." (WH 108–9, Letter 28)

For Herder, the nations of his day were in need of this moral sense of humanity precisely because of the distinctions of superiority and inferiority that wreaked havoc both within the European world and in the imperial realms outside of Europe. As the hierarchical social relations of Rome's empire curiously produced the ideal of humanity, so too, Herder hoped, European thinkers in modern imperial times, moved by the inequalities of their era, might return to and reinvigorate the concept of humanity. Ultimately, then, Herder offers his exalted understanding of humanity to undercut the categories that help to justify violence and unfreedom abroad, for the proper spirit of human history is the "*sensus humanitatis*, sensibility and empathy for all humankind." (WH 48, Letter 122)

THE DEEP commitment to freedom and the workings of reason as well as the hatred of paternalism that run throughout Herder's writings signal quite clearly the impression left upon him by Kant. Other features, especially the religious tone of Herder's historical and political writings and the centrality of language in his social thought bear the influence of his other teacher in Königsberg, J. G. Hamann.[26] Frederick Beiser has suggested an even-handed route through the issue of contrasting influences and allegiances by noting that even Herder's shrillest criticisms of what the took to be the *Aufklärung* were made generally to affirm the freedom of individuals to order their own lives, rather than to defend religion or tradition as such.[27] What has been overlooked, however, are the family resemblances between Herder's and the later Kant's attacks upon imperialism and the similarity of their accounts of humans as cultural agents— that is, as beings who, by their nature, diversely exercise their reason, memory and imagination, and who are necessarily embedded within and yet are also able to transform social practices and institutions. By focusing on such issues in Kant and Herder, one can point to the unacknowledged (and perhaps unwitting) influence that Herder may have had on Kant's later political thought, given that Herder's criticisms of empire predate the development of Kant's own anti-imperialism. Although it is only possible to speculate about the actual influence that Herder's writings may have had on the later Kant, their conceptualizations of "humanity" and the details of their anti-imperialist arguments are more consonant than is usually noted.[28] This suggests that the contrast between conventional understandings of 'the Enlightenment' and 'Counter-Enlightenment' in approaching the famed Kant-Herder debate should be greeted with some scepticism. Rather than redescribe Herder as a kind of *Aufklärer*, however, it may be more productive, and certainly more accurate historically, to interpret his thought as part of a larger series of eighteenth-century attempts at relating human unity and human diversity. Viewed in this light, Herder's political thought reflects both the opportunities and the difficulties faced by political thinkers who sought to theorize the complicated interrelationships between the universal and particular aspects of human identity and moral judgement.

As we have seen, Herder's commitment to the idea of the 'nation' is instrumental, for it is invoked largely to check the homogenizing and oppressive power of increasingly centralized and imperializing 'state-machines'. His conception of nationality is not necessarily or exclusively based upon climate, territory, or blood ties, each of which can contribute to a people's sense of distinctiveness, but none of which is a crucial component of national communities. As with Kant and Diderot, communication among individuals and peoples is a central feature of Herder's understanding of humanity. He differs from them, however, in his emphasis upon the importance of particular languages (and not only of speech or communication in whatever form it happens to take), each of which, in his view, contains a world of thought and expression that allows liberty and reason to flourish distinctively. Herder's defence of a constructed and ever-changing nationality seeks to safeguard individual and collective liberties and is thus one of the key bases of his anti-imperialism.

The larger framework within which Herder criticizes European imperial power, however, follows a philosophical pattern that one can also find in Diderot and Kant: a commitment to human dignity, rooted in the humanity of each individual; the idea that humans are constitutively cultural agents; and the incommensurability of peoples and of certain practices and institutions (such as nomadism and pastoralism). Since the plurality of languages and nations in the world result from shared human capacities, which Herder also associates with bonds of sympathy and the predispositions to spirituality and reason, his commitment to equality and international justice are universal in scope and they point to a fraternity of humankind, an ethical link among diverse individuals and peoples. While Herder's philosophical arguments grow out of, and are oriented toward, the specific political and social circumstances of his day, they are also indicative of a recognizable intellectual disposition that seeks to balance humanism with pluralism. In this respect, the interrelationship between 'nation' and 'humanity' in Herder's thought has much in common with the balance drawn among analogous languages of human diversity and unity in the political philosophies of some of his fellow eighteenth-century anti-imperialists—between, for instance, Diderot's national character and the general will of humanity and between Kant's conception of cultural agency and cosmopolitan justice.

Seven

Conclusion: The Philosophical Sources and Legacies of Enlightenment Anti-imperialism

THE LATTER half of the eighteenth century is an anomalous period in modern European political thought, for it is only then that a group of significant thinkers attacked the very foundations of imperialism. In contrast, throughout the nineteenth century, virtually all prominent European political philosophers were either agnostic on the issue of imperialism or, like John Stuart Mill, Tocqueville, Hegel, and Marx, explicitly defended European rule over non-European peoples. What explains, then, this curiously short-lived antagonism toward empire during the Enlightenment era? What constellation of philosophical assumptions, concepts, arguments, and temperaments enabled anti-imperialist political theories in the late eighteenth century? Prevalent understandings of 'the' Enlightenment or 'the Enlightenment project', a movement or a project that is demonized by some and extolled by others, cannot do justice to the strand of eighteenth-century writings that I have examined in this book. In part, then, this study of Enlightenment anti-imperialism serves as an occasion to rethink such prevalent historical and philosophical categories in political theory. In addition, the standard oppositions that explicitly or tacitly structure many of the debates about humanity and cultural difference today fail to convey the symbiotic relationship between the universal and particular features of humanity and moral judgement that Diderot, Kant, and Herder theorize. While the specific arguments and philosophical languages they offer are rooted in the distinctive intellectual contexts within which they wrote and that they sought to transform, the distinctive and counter-intuitive outlook that guides their thinking—on issues of empire, universal morality, moral incommensurability, and the relationship between humanity and cultural diversity—represents an underappreciated philosophical legacy of Enlightenment political thought.

I begin this chapter with the historical and methodological issues that are raised by typical characterizations of 'the Enlightenment' and 'the Enlightenment project', which often hold that 'the Enlightenment' and 'Enlightenment universalism' are imperializing ideologies that are fundamentally antagonistic toward cultural diversity. I then turn to an analysis of the philosophical sources of Enlightenment anti-imperialist political thought both to determine the key elements that constitute this form of late eighteenth-century political thinking and to consider its philosophical legacies, which a pluralized understanding of Enlightenment political theory helps bring into view.

Pluralizing 'the' Enlightenment

An appreciation of Enlightenment-era anti-imperialism unsettles a number of unproductive, yet pervasive, historical and theoretical assumptions and arguments. A variety of ethical distinctions that continue to inform a wide range of debates in moral, political, and social theory fail to capture the subtle strategies, arguments, and underlying assumptions that are at work in Enlightenment anti-imperialist writings. Broadly speaking, the idea of a deep tension between what might be called the universal and particular elements of human life, society, and thought informs a variety of contemporary philosophical debates and, accordingly, a number of the key historiographical arguments about the meaning, distinctiveness, and significance of 'the Enlightenment'. The conceptual dichotomies—not always proposed as a stark choice but often present in at least tacit forms—include those between a purely rational and a contextual morality; a fundamental human nature or essence and a differentiated and ever-changing human subject; universally valid moral principles and the relativity of local or customary traditions, practices, and values; the concept of rights or justice and that of the good or of virtue; essential psychological or cognitive attributes and dispositions and socially constructed narratives of identity. These are all often underpinned by a historical claim that 'the' Enlightenment's legacy consists chiefly of being firmly committed to the former component of these binary opposites.

The idea that 'the Enlightenment' or an 'Enlightenment project' can be identified and that contemporary moral and political thought should seek either to defend or subvert this project are prevalent assumptions that steer scholars away from more productive engagements with the manifold variety of Enlightenment-era philosophical arguments about cross-cultural moral judgements and international justice. With regard to empire and questions about cultural diversity, the most relevant aspects of Enlightenment moral, social, and political thought, as commonly conceived, are its commitments to (1) an ahistorical and universalist agenda that eschews any interest in, or at the very least gives little value to, the particularities of human life and cultural difference; and (2) a civilizing and imperializing mission (both in the literal and metaphorical senses of the term 'imperialize'), which uses a doctrine of progress to justify the subjugation of (among others) non-European peoples. In many respects, those who view themselves as defending 'the Enlightenment' offer a similar portrait, though of course with an opposite valence. That is, a standard response to pejorative characterizations of Enlightenment thought is to affirm its commitment to universal values, and to defend this by arguing that celebrations of cultural diversity can solidify the traditions and prejudices that the *philosophes* rightly attacked. Thus, even the most perceptive scholars of Enlightenment-era writings who are fully aware of its diverse sets of arguments and dispositions, and hence the difficulty of identifying a core Enlightenment project, have responded to critical interpretations by concluding, for instance, that "[t]he moral chaos of the modern world stems not from the failure of the Enlightenment Project but from its neglect and abandonment."[1] The persistent identification of eighteenth-century thought with the complex set of evolving social, economic, and political practices, beliefs, and institutions that are gathered under the banner of 'modernity'—and the nearly unanimous agreement that 'the Enlightenment' championed universal values in a manner that was, rightly or wrongly, at the expense of a number of particular identities, beliefs, and practice—have either distorted or hidden from view a number of innovative arguments about cultural difference, humanity, and imperial politics in the Enlightenment era.

Consider, for instance, one of the most common assertions about Enlightenment thought: its penchant for universal moral principles. For the moment, although this understanding involves a wide variety of claims, I want to signal two key assertions that are especially significant in light of the issues under study in this book. First, universalism at times refers to the justification of universal moral judgements to which all human beings are subject by abstracting from the particularities of social and cultural life. Second, and closely connected to this, 'the Enlightenment' is often portrayed as universalist because it is said to support the view that there is such a thing as a universal human nature or ontological essence, which is fixed, permanent, and readily identifiable, since what are taken to be ephemeral social and cultural elements can (at least hypothetically) be stripped away. Bringing these two assertions together, Alasdair MacIntyre argues that "[i]t was a central aspiration of the Enlightenment. . . . to appeal to principles undeniable by any rational person and therefore independent of all those social and cultural particularities which the Enlightenment thinkers took to be the mere accidental clothing of reason in particular times and places".[2] In this view, the most damning feature of 'the Enlightenment' consists of its failure to appreciate the plural and diverse forms of human life.[3] This emphasis on cultural diversity and moral pluralism, the idea that we must begin to take such particularities seriously in any cogent moral and political philosophy by viewing them as integral and meaningful to human life, is often presented, then, as an indictment of modern thinking or as a repudiation of either modernity as such or, more specifically, of 'the Enlightenment project'.[4]

In a particularly blunt version of this perspective—one that is nonetheless symptomatic of popular and largely internalized, unspoken assumptions about Enlightenment thought—John Gray argues that

> [j]ust as the category of *civilization* is a central element in the Enlightenment project, so . . . the idea of *barbarism* is integral . . . since it encapsulates the Enlightenment repudiation of the irreducible plurality of cultures in favor of the assertion that all civilizations are, or will be exemplars of a single model.[5]

Gray's assertion that 'the Enlightenment project' is oriented toward a unitary civilization that lies at the end of progressive historical evolution rests upon a more fundamental philosophical claim that 'the Enlightenment' failed to recognize the connection between human nature and cultural diversity. Gray, for instance, asserts that

> [a]ccording to the philosophical anthropology of the Enlightenment, the diverse and often rivalrous cultural identities manifest throughout human history are not expressive of any primordial human disposition to cultural difference. They are ephemeral, or at least developmental, phases in the history of the species.[6]

From this perspective, then, 'the Enlightenment project' maintains that cultural difference is not integral to the human condition, and so it comes as no surprise that such diversity plays no part in its ideal political and ethical objectives. Cultural difference consists of deviations from a narrowly defined and purportedly rational ideal—known as civilization—and are therefore categorized pejoratively as barbaric. The organizing principle of social development, in this account of 'the Enlightenment project', is "the idea of universal convergence on a single form of social life", that is, "the Enlightenment idea of civilization."[7] The other central features of Enlightenment thought that Gray describes—such as its commitment to a rational morality that all human beings can know and should follow, its theory of progress, and its belief in the "indefinite improvability" of humankind—all reinforce what he views as the core Enlightenment belief in a singular, universal goal of civilization.

The anti-imperialist political philosophies of Diderot, Kant, and Herder cast doubt upon the accuracy and the helpfulness of the philosophical and historical categories by which eighteenth-century political thought is usually interpreted, particularly upon the kinds of constructions sketched above, such as 'the' Enlightenment and 'the Enlightenment project'. In the next section, I will examine how the core elements of eighteenth-century anti-imperialist political thought interweave universal and pluralistic philosophical sensibilities and arguments in ways that call into question such prevalent understandings. To be sure, broad categories and labels like 'the Enlightenment' can serve to orient our thinking productively by grouping together texts, arguments, historical figures, practices, and institutions, all of which may gain through such categories a certain coherence that they might otherwise lack. At times, such groupings and the identification of particular family resemblances may be historically defensible; at other times, and indeed no doubt more frequently, they are anachronistic or simply inaccurate in describing even the broad contours of a particular intellectual age or presumed school of thought. Even in the latter cases, however, they may be defensible if the rhetorical object of such devices is to craft arguments toward some contemporary debate or issue, rather than to illuminate the utterances and the contexts of historical periods, although scholars do not often make such intentions explicit. Labels such as 'the Enlightenment' may not be, in and of themselves, dogmatic, distorting, or otherwise problematic; rather, the manner in which they are used and the intellectual temperament that (tacitly or wittingly) guides the use of such categories determines to what extent they are productive and the extent to which they obfuscate far more than they illuminate. It is incumbent upon political theorists and historians of political thought, scholars who presumably are alive to the power and craft of language, to examine as critically as we can the ways in which we ourselves limit and expand our intellectual horizons through the use of such categories.

Prevalent accounts of what is called 'the Enlightenment' or 'the Enlightenment project' make a series of generalizations that very often egregiously misrepresent, blur, or hide from view entire strands of thought, some of which (were it not for the distorting lenses through which they are viewed) might have been understood to be nuanced and intellectually productive contributions not only to the debates of the long eighteenth century, but also to a range of still debated principles, intellectual tendencies, and institutions. Other strands may not make such positive contributions, but may instead provide us with a more sophisticated intellectual genealogy of problematic tendencies or arguments. The term 'Enlightenment' itself, of course, may still serve a useful function in contemplating eighteenth-century political thought, for there was a sense among many of the most perceptive thinkers of the eighteenth century that they were contemplating social and political affairs in a manner that was historically and philosophically distinctive, and in a way that constituted (at least in part) a break from some of their predecessors. It may be, then, that a set of background social and political conditions, and perhaps even a kind of intellectual temperament, could be plausibly identified, one that could orient us toward productively studying some set of the political and philosophical debates in the eighteenth century. As J.G.A. Pocock has noted, the participants in many eighteenth-century intellectual enterprises "were aware in their own terms of what they and their colleagues and competitors were doing—

aware even of their historical significance, to a degree itself new in European culture—and the metaphor of light (*lumière, lume, Aufklärung*) is strongly present in their writings."[8] It is for this reason that it may be helpful, without being anachronistic or reifying an entire intellectual era, to write of a variety of 'Enlightenments', but not of 'the' Enlightenment.

The interpretive challenge for any conscientious scholar is to resist the slippage from such a realization (that a certain self-consciousness among some eighteenth-century thinkers may have existed), which itself is amenable to variety of competing interpretations, to a more full-blown narrative of the substance or the key elements or principles of eighteenth-century political thought.[9] Popular versions of 'the Enlightenment' or 'the Enlightenment project' should not be replaced by another, non-pejorative definition of these categories that can be constructed from an analysis of eighteenth-century anti-imperialist political philosophy. Rather, my contention is that 'the Enlightenment' *as such* and the notion of an overarching 'Enlightenment project' simply do not exist.[10] In this book, I have identified one particularly understudied, historically unique, and philosophically robust strand of eighteenth-century political thinking, the substance of which should cast some doubt upon the prevalent understandings of 'the Enlightenment' as a whole, in addition to the claim that virtually the entire tradition of modern European political theory is bereft of the philosophical resources with which we could productively rethink our own assumptions about cultural pluralism and moral judgement.[11] But this anti-imperialist strand, which itself is not without its own internal incongruities, is only one element among many often conflicting arguments, intellectual dispositions, and writings that constitute eighteenth-century moral and political philosophy. As Judith Shklar well noted, "that part of the eighteenth century that we call 'The Enlightenment' was a state of intellectual tension rather than a sequence of simple propositions."[12]

It is high time, then, that we pluralize our understanding of 'the Enlightenment' both for reasons of historical accuracy and because, in doing so, otherwise hidden or understudied moments of Enlightenment-era thinking will come to light. In this respect, the study of anti-imperialist political thought shows quite clearly that the idea of an Enlightenment project that celebrated universal values at the expense of cultural difference has obscured what was, in fact, a genuine and contentious struggle among eighteenth-century thinkers about how to conceptualize humanity, cultural difference, and the political relationships among European and non-European peoples. Indeed, on many topics, a wide range of eighteenth-century thinkers, many of them well known and influential, posit theories that fail to fit the 'project' or the core intellectual dispositions attributed to modernity in general or to 'the Enlightenment' in

particular. For the historical and philosophical writings of the Enlightenment era consist of multiple strands (among others, religious, national,
and philosophical, in addition to the diversity that arises even from within
particular intellectual contexts as a result of the unique approaches of
specific individuals), some of which overlap and others of which are deeply
in tension.[13] When too many of these strands are woven together, the
tapestry that results—the 'project', or the single Enlightenment narrative,
or even the 'dominant tendency' of 'the Enlightenment'—ultimately
masks contributions, such as the anti-imperialist political philosophies
under study in this book, that are viewed as antithetical to common understandings of 'the' Enlightenment. A productive presumption, I argue,
is to begin with a pluralized understanding of the Enlightenment era,
and then, if needed (although here some caution is necessary, since it
often will not be helpful to go any further) to make some more general,
tentative claims for the purposes of attending to a delimited range of
topics, questions, or contexts.

If there are many Enlightenments, then what could the term 'Enlightenment' itself mean as a term of distinction—that is, if one prefers not to
include every text and author of the long eighteenth century under the
label 'Enlightenment'? With the entirety of this period in view, it is difficult to comprehend what positive definition could genuinely capture the
diverse range of what one might take to be 'enlightened' attitudes, discourses, arguments, texts, and thinkers. It may well be the case that only
a negative definition of Enlightenment thought, one based upon what
'enlightened thought' is against, could underlie the extraordinary plurality of texts, arguments, and dispositions that one can find in such Enlightenments, for they all counter, in diverse ways, the most orthodox
understandings of religious doctrine and authority and / or the most traditional understandings of absolutist state power. Thus, while thinkers as
diverse as Burke, Hume, Montesquieu, Herder, and d'Holbach contributed constructively to a variety of enlightened discourses, sometimes by
drawing upon and defending some Enlightenments to attack others, it
would be more difficult (though not necessarily impossible) to make this
claim about, for instance, Joseph de Maistre's writings.[14] It should be
noted that this negative understanding of what might constitute the
broader family of Enlightenments is characterized by tremendous internal
diversity, so much so that the struggles among various Enlightenments
are often far more heated and more signficant for an understanding of
eighteenth-century political thought than what can loosely be seen as the
battles they also wage against a similar (though even here, also a diverse)
set of 'enemies'. Hence, we return again to the benefits of pluralized
understandings of Enlightenment thinking, for every move to pin down a
singular meaning or common project carries with it the risk of hiding or

distorting crucial aspects of the moral and political discourses of the long eighteenth century.

In pluralizing Enlightenment-era political thought, we may indeed find ourselves at a loss, without the convenience of well-worn platitudes and comforting generalizations about intellectual periods that shape so many of the attitudes behind, and debates of, contemporary political theory. Indeed, 'the Enlightenment' is but one example of such obfuscating categories that serve narrow, sometimes pejorative, and often scholarly counter-productive, rhetorical purposes; 'modernity', 'postmodernism', and 'liberalism' surely all require a similar pluralization. But the benefits are abundant, for we may find ourselves occasionally surprised at the texts we read, taken aback by what will now appear to be counter-intuitive or irreducibly complex arguments, and in general astonished at the diverse range of textual interpretations that result. We may even find ourselves in a position where we are better able, as Michel Foucault exhorted, to "free ourselves from the intellectual blackmail of 'being for or against the Enlightenment'" and the philosophical arguments and political commitments that are said to follow from it.[15]

Universal Dignity, Cultural Agency, and Moral Incommensurability

Do commitments to the idea of a shared humanity, to human dignity, to cross-cultural universal moral principles, and to cross-cultural standards of justice rest upon assumptions and values that unavoidably denigrate, or that disturbingly undermine respect for, cultural pluralism, that is, the wide array of human institutions and practices in the world?[16] Are they imperialistic either explicitly, to justify Europe's political, military, and commercial subjugation of the non-European world, or implicitly, by indicating a rank ordering of superior and inferior peoples, which could then be used to justify a more indirect, quasi-imperial 'civilizing' process? The aforementioned commitments are sometimes collectively gathered under the term 'Enlightenment universalism' and, as we have seen, they are sometimes considered to constitute the core of 'the Enlightenment project'. I have suggested already that such assertions mask and distort a complex reality. In this case, they obscure the multiplicity of universalisms across eighteenth-century European political thought, each with distinct foundational claims, varying relationships to conceptualizations of human diversity and to humanity (which themselves differ from thinker to thinker, and even from text to text), and different political orientations toward the nature and limits of state power in theory and in practice. These philosophical sensibilities and approaches can yield remarkably different political arguments toward foreign peoples, international justice, and imperialism. Thus, rather than ask whether 'the Enlightenment project' and 'Enlightenment universalism' are compatible with an appreciation of cultural pluralism or whether they are at bottom imperializing ideologies, it is more constructive to pose more precise and historically accurate versions of such questions with regard to particular texts and thinkers.

In this book, I have studied a distinctive variant of Enlightenment writings against empire, one which includes the philosophical and political arguments of Diderot, Kant, and Herder. While there is no such thing as 'Enlightenment universalism' as such, let alone a larger 'Enlightenment project', there is nonetheless an identifiable set of philosophical and political arguments, assumptions, and tendencies about the relationship between universal and pluralistic concepts that animates the strand of Enlightenment political thought under study here. With this in mind, one can more meaningfully ask what the relationship is between universalism, pluralism, and incommensurability in such political philosophies, and how precisely they yield anti-imperialist political commitments. Answers to these more circumscribed questions can be given by better understanding the core elements of Diderot's, Kant's, and Herder's political philosophies, and how they differ from earlier (and, indeed, from many later) understandings and judgements of empire. Immanuel Kant remarks pointedly in *Toward Perpetual Peace* that the Europeans who landed and eventually settled in the New World often denied indigenous peoples any moral status.

> When America, the Negro countries, the Spice Islands, the Cape, and so forth were discovered, they were, to them [to Europeans], countries belonging to no one [*die keinem angehörten*], since they counted the inhabitants as *nothing*. (8:358, emphasis added)

What philosophical concepts and arguments were necessary for New World peoples to be counted finally as *something* and especially to be considered as equals, as they were eventually in some crucial respects, by anti-imperialist political thinkers in the Enlightenment era? In this section, I focus on what I have taken in this book to be the philosophically most robust strand of Enlightenment anti-imperialist political thought.[17] Despite the many differences in the ethnographic sources that Diderot, Kant, and Herder consulted, the philosophical languages that these thinkers employed, and the particular concepts they drew upon to attack European empires, their anti-imperialist arguments intriguingly overlap in important respects. Thus, in this section, I identify and elucidate the family resemblances that exist among their philosophical arguments and rhetorical strategies, and discuss the underlying assumptions, ideas, and intellectual dispositions that make their version of anti-imperialist political think-ing conceptually possible. In contrast to what is effectively the premiss of the kinds of familiar questions asked at the opening of this section, the commitments of Diderot, Kant, and Herder to moral universalism, cul-tural diversity, partial incommensurability, and the delegitimization of empire are not fundamentally in tension but rather reinforce one another.

Overall, there are three principal philosophical sources of Enlighten-ment anti-imperialism. The *first* and most basic idea is that human beings deserve some modicum of moral and political respect simply because of the fact that they are human. This humanistic moral principle alone, however, was far from sufficient for engendering an anti-imperialist poli-tics. The whole modern tradition of natural right and social contract the-ory held this view in some form. Moreover, Amerindians in particular were explicitly described by such thinkers as the pure, natural humans of the state of nature. Yet much of this tradition of modern political thought, from Grotius onward, was either agnostic about imperialism or lent philosophical support to European empires. Not every understanding of what it means fundamentally to be a human fosters the philosophical materials necessary to build a more inclusive and pluralistic political the-ory that could serve as the basis of anti-imperialist arguments. Indeed, as I will argue, some understandings of humanity that are manifestly egali-tarian can nevertheless impede such a development. *Second*, therefore, these anti-imperialist arguments rested upon the view that human beings are fundamentally cultural beings. Diderot, Kant, and Herder all contend that the category of the human is necessarily marked by cultural differ-ence; in this view, humanity is cultural agency. This thicker, particularized view of the human subject, paradoxically, helped to engender a more inclusive and meaningful moral universalism. *Third*, a fairly robust ac-count of moral incommensurability and relativity was also necessary for the rise of anti-imperialist political thought. The anti-imperialist argu-ments offered by Diderot, Kant, and Herder all partly rest upon the view that peoples as a whole are incommensurable. From this perspective, en-tire peoples cannot be judged as superior or inferior along a universal scale of value. Moreover, in distinct but closely related ways, these thinkers argue that our cultural freedom produces a wide variety of indi-vidual and collective practices and beliefs that are incommensurable, given their view that many practices and beliefs lie outside the bounds of a categorical judgement or universal standard. When these three concep-tual developments were brought together, the strand of Enlightenment anti-imperialist political theory that I have identified became philosophi-cally *possible*. I want to reiterate here that this framework is not meant to elucidate all of the anti-imperialist arguments that one can find in the philosophical writings of the Enlightenment era. Moreover, the distinctive intellectual dispositions, personal idiosyncrasies, and domestic political commitments of Enlightenment-era thinkers significantly shaped their particular arguments on the issue of empire. Still, as I will show, these three philosophical ideas play a crucial role in enabling the development of a rich strand of anti-imperialist political theory in the late eighteenth century. In discussing the development of a more inclusive and anti-imperialist political theory, my focus in this section (as it has been generally in this book) is on Europeans' political attitudes toward non-Europeans. Many thinkers in non-European societies clearly operated with similarly self-centred conceptions, but my emphasis throughout is on Europeans' intellectual responses to the fact of cultural difference and imperial politics, not with non-European peoples' understandings of each other or of their accounts of European peoples. Nor do I examine here the variety of intra-European distinctions between allegedly superior and inferior groups, those, for instance, involving linguistic, geographical, class, religious, and gender differences, which of course historically also legitimated differential treatment within European societies. Thus, I do not intend to argue that Enlightenment anti-imperialist political philosophies are inclusive as such, for their underlying principles do not necessarily (and, in the eighteenth century, they manifestly did not) support egalitarian arguments against every form of exclusion.

As I have noted, the *first* idea that enables Enlightenment anti-imperialism—first both historically and analytically—is that foreigners are human beings and, consequently, that they deserve moral respect, however understood. The development, in other words, of some variant of a humanistic moral universalism ensured that the shared humanity of both Europeans and non-Europeans would be acknowledged and given some due. The philosophical and political legacy with which Enlightenment anti-imperialist thinkers struggled, as they themselves understood, was one of exclusion. As they often noted, ethical principles of respect and reciprocity had been limited almost always to (some) members of one's own tribe, polis, nation, religion, or civilization. Accordingly, the distinction between one's own society, however defined, and the *barbaroi* (others, foreigners), whether justified outright or tacitly assumed, influenced not only the anthropological conceptions of, and popular understandings about, foreign peoples, but also legitimated the often brutally differential treatment of various groups. It is along these lines that Kant expresses dismay, in a lecture on moral philosophy, at what he calls the "error that the [ancient] Greeks displayed, in that they evinced no goodwill towards *extranei* [outsiders, or foreigners], but included them all, rather, *sub voce hostes = barbari* [under the name of enemies, or barbarians]". (27:674) In the long history of imperial exploits, actions that in at least some contexts might have provoked outrage in one's own land not only gained legitimacy on foreign soil but were deemed praiseworthy, noble, and even morally obligatory abroad. While European imperialists in the New World, writes Diderot, "faithfully observe their own laws, they will violate the rights of other nations in order to increase their power. That is what the Romans did."[18] Enlightenment anti-imperialists recognized that such Janus-faced practices constituted the very core of imperial activity from the empires of the ancient world to the imperial conquests and commercial voyages of their day. The fact of difference itself lay at the heart of such inconsistent behaviour from Europeans' initial encounters with Amerindians onward, as Diderot notes: "[t]he Spaniard, the first to be thrown up by the waves onto the shores of the New World, thought he had no duty to people who did not share his colour, customs, or religion."[19] Not wanting to single out the Spanish, Diderot suggests further that the Portuguese, Dutch, English, French, and Danes all followed in precisely the same spirit of exclusion and injustice.

From an anthropological viewpoint, such discoveries of non-European peoples no doubt played a role in Europeans' changing conceptions of humanity. From Herodotus onward, of course, travel narratives played a central role in contemplating what it might mean to be, in some fundamental sense, a human being. Given that theorizations of human nature relate, in complicated ways, to changing understandings of the range and characteristics of human societies, institutions, and practices, the European discovery of 'new' lands and peoples accordingly generated further, and at times more complex, theorizations of humanity.[20] Moreover, from the sixteenth century onward, thinkers were particularly keen to consult and appropriate the latest ethnographic reports. In part, the heightened interest no doubt complemented, and may in part have resulted from, what is often described as the intellectual revolution in 'natural philosophy' and the resulting emphasis on experimentation, empirical study, and inductive reasoning in fields such as astronomy, but also (especially from the mid-seventeenth century onward) in the study of human anatomy, physiology, and psychology. Although many of Hume's contemporaries did not share his hope of introducing "the experimental method" to moral philosophy, there was nonetheless a widespread presumption that an understanding of the human condition needed to take account, in some manner, of the growing anthropological literature that detailed the vast range of human experiences, customs, and practices throughout the globe.[21] This turn toward what Georges Gusdorf has called 'human science', however, requires a stable referent for what counts as 'human' while also upsetting the stability of the term by focusing attention increasingly on human difference.[22] In this sense, the attempt at identifying the most salient features of humanity was often an erratic and inherently conflicted task, as John Locke argued it would have to be, given the very nature of our self-knowledge.

Locke's arguments along these lines, in the *Essay Concerning Human Understanding*, illuminate well the intellectual climate that placed travel literature and cultural pluralism at the centre of disputations about what fundamentally constitutes humanity. In the course of his general assault upon innate ideas, and in the context of a discussion about the boundaries of humanity and of how to determine whether an organism is a human being, Locke declares that humans possess no knowledge of "precise Boundaries set by Nature, whereby it distinguish'd all Substances into certain *Species*."[23] Thus, the term "Man", like many other complex ideas, is "of a loose and wandering signification sometimes standing for one, and sometimes for another *Idea*." (608) For Locke, we necessarily reach our self-understanding as humans "with some liberty". He concludes that one should "quit the common notion of Species and Essences" and, instead, embark upon an empirical inquiry of humans, considering them "as they exist, and not by groundless Fancies, that have been taken up about them". (573) Locke notes, however, that a problem arises if we cast our empirical nets nearby, covering only those who are relatively similar to us in this quest. For if understanding humanity depends upon the empirical study of humans, the conclusions we may draw could be erroneous, indeed even "dangerous", when we look only in our immediate, and relatively homogenous, surroundings. (608) Accordingly, Locke discusses the hypothetical case of an English child who forms his conception of a human by drawing upon the visible appearances of humans around him, "whereof White or Flesh-colour in *England* being one, the Child can demonstrate to you, that *a Negro is not a Man*, because White-colour was one of the constant simple *Ideas* of the complex *Idea* he calls *Man*." (607)

Of course, such instances of dehumanization were by no means hypothetical in Europeans' dealings with New World peoples. Consider, perhaps most notably, the sixteenth-century theological debates about whether Amerindians were examples of Aristotle's not fully human, natural slaves.[24] The crucial point here, however, is that even when the human status of foreign peoples was explicitly affirmed, the manner in which their behaviour and social practices were comprehended, and the languages and concepts used to categorize them, were subject to a similar 'liberty' of significations. Many scholars have overlooked this complex history, however, and have assumed that the rise of more inclusive moral and political theories is a fairly straightforward story that results fundamentally from the idea that humans as such deserve moral respect. In such an account, that idea is where the story both begins and ends, and so the development of what can truly be described as a humanitarian ethic is commonly understood to consist merely of a widening circle that gradually includes more peoples, as prejudices and mistaken anthropological viewpoints are set aside.[25] Hence, in this common view, social contract and natural right theories contained within them a humanitarian core that was inconsistently and hypocritically withheld from many non-European peoples. Philosophically, few if any changes would be needed to render such a political perspective more global and more genuinely humanistic in scope, for such theories themselves possessed the elements of an inclusive moral and political doctrine, even if such notions were not always put fully into practice.

It would be a mistake, however, to think that the affirmation of the equal moral status of European and non-European peoples, in addition to the rise of anti-imperialist politics (and thus the affirmation of an equal status on the stage of international political morality), consisted simply of a steadily expanding application of preestablished universal norms. Both the Christian underpinnings of many early modern European writings as well as the universal language of natural right not only coexisted with the exclusion of (among others) New World peoples from such norms, but such prima facie egalitarian and universal philosophies were deployed explicitly to justify the various forms of imperial activity, from the institution of chattel slavery and the mass appropriation of foreign goods and lands to outright genocide.

In one sense, the distinction between ethics at the imperial core and those at the periphery is related to the distinction between the kinds of ethical principles that are invoked during conditions of peace versus those that are applied (or conveniently set aside) during war (when what would normally be understood as patently unjust is legitimized as morally necessitated by the norms of international justice or state security). Not surprisingly, the language of just war was one of the most common means of justifying imperial aggression toward indigenous peoples, and the precise manner in which this language was deployed demonstrates the centrality of cultural difference in justifying domineering behaviour. Some of the standard strategies for justifying war, such as self-defence or the security of the nation, were not particularly effective in an imperial context, given that Europeans were not frequently under unprovoked direct attacks by aboriginal groups nor was the metropole itself in any immediate danger—the Castilian and French crowns, that is, were hardly in jeopardy of being ravaged by the Inca or the Iroquois. Among those who eventually conceded that New World inhabitants were (at least at some minimal level) human beings, as opposed to being examples of Aristotle's subhuman natural slaves, it was nonetheless frequently argued that Amerindians, though formally equals with Europeans, had forfeited both their individual natural rights and collective sovereignties. No sooner had they been granted the status of human beings than the privileges and protections of such a classification were abrogated.[26] Such claims usually rested upon the view that Amerindians' practices were debased to such a degree that they had lost the right to ethical treatment that would normally be afforded to human beings, or more precisely to morally adequate, civilized human beings. The specific practices that were cited varied, though they often included human sacrifice and cannibalism, two recurring favourites of imperial apologists and mainstays in the European popular imagination despite the efforts of sixteenth-century Salamancan theologians like Vitoria and Las Casas, among others, to delegitimize the relevant ethnography—by doubting the existence of such practices, emphasizing their rarity, or indicating morally equivalent practices in the European world that exposed such pejorative cross-cultural judgements as hypocritical.

In addition to such purported moral inferiority, by drawing upon the legacy of the Roman jurisprudential concept of property or lands 'belonging to no one', *res nullius*, as well as the natural law (as Emmerich de Vattel, the eighteenth-century theorist of international law, conceptualized it) that obliged humans to cultivate their lands, some defenders of empire concluded that if non-European peoples failed to till their soil, then this in itself constituted a debased condition that, at minimum, justified the appropriation of their purportedly wasted natural resources. Moreover, slaughtering aboriginals who allegedly failed to exploit their lands was sometimes defended as just on the remarkable grounds that the very existence of such deformed lifestyles constituted a threat to the moral sanctity and health of European civilization.[27] The central idea was that the distinguishing features of New World peoples, however defined, did not partly constitute their humanity, but rather represented the relatively unimportant, and often undignifying, cultural ephemera that they ought to eschew in favour of civilized practices, beliefs, and institutions. Thus, even among those who rejected the idea of non-Europeans' inherent inferiority, a plethora of arguments could still be marshalled to justify their status as beings who did not merit the same moral status as Europeans; moreover, many of these arguments were made from the assumption that because of their very humanity, New World and other non-European peoples should be held accountable to 'civilized' norms.[28] For a variety of reasons, then, the egalitarian assumption of a shared humanity, or of a universal human subject, lay at the heart of a number of manifestly inegalitarian imperialist arguments.

Thus, while modern natural right theories were indeed based upon an egalitarian understanding of humanity, the being that was identified as equal to any other—the idea, that is, of a natural human that can be theoretically identified once the many layers of sociability, culture, and historical artifice have been stripped away—was too insubstantial to bear any actual moral weight. The debates surrounding New World peoples are especially instructive on this point, given the paradoxical fact that Amerindians, South Pacific Islanders, and other newly discovered peoples were often presented in modern philosophical writings as empirical examples of purely natural humans, that is, as those who inhabit a state of nature. It might seem that, from the standpoint of a social contractarian and modern natural right perspective, one could not be more human than a natural or pure human, but it was precisely those who were so identified theoretically who were ultimately most easily dehumanized in practice.

The defence of non-Europeans against European imperial powers and the development of anti-imperialist arguments depended not only upon potentially egalitarian and humanitarian concepts (which, despite their exclusionary tendencies, at least countered the idea that non-Europeans were inherently inferior in some fundamental sense), but also, *secondly*, upon reconceptualizing the relationship between cultural diversity and humanity. In the view of a number of Enlightenment anti-imperialists, what most noticeably differentiates humans—their various and often incompatible or competing cultural systems of meanings and values—is integral to the human condition. Humans, in other words, were theorized as fundamentally cultural beings or *cultural agents*, as I have put it so as to emphasize the symbiotic relationship that these anti-imperialists discern between human reason, freedom, and imagination, and humans' social and cultural contexts. To view human beings in this way acknowledges their status as artful, reasoned, and free individuals who are partly shaped by their social and cultural contexts, yet who also through their actions and through changing perceptions alter such contexts themselves. Standard readings of Diderot and Kant, in particular, have generally ignored the ample textual evidence to support such a view and argue instead that they held humans to be respectively either materially determined automatons or, at bottom, 'noumenal' metaphysical subjects. As I have argued at length in the preceding chapters, such interpretive misconceptions fail to illuminate the specific manner in which Diderot and Kant theorize humanity and (what we would today describe as) cultural diversity and, accordingly, how they engage in anti-imperialist arguments. The changing understanding of New World peoples is represented well by the contrast that can be drawn between, on the one hand, noble savage theory and most social contract accounts of Amerindians (which portray them as living solely by the light of Nature, by either natural instincts or natural laws) and, on the other, the political theories of Diderot, Kant, and Herder, which view New World inhabitants as fellow cultural beings (rather than as pure or natural humans).

Third, closely related to the idea that humans are fundamentally cultural agents is the view that differences in social practices and cultural norms—even among the peoples who seemed strangest and most 'exotic' to European observers, such as Amerindians, Hottentots, and South Pacific Islanders—are often incommensurable and do not imply that the peoples themselves or the individual bearers of such distinct ways of life are inferior. By incommensurability, I mean the idea that, with regard to certain practices, institutions, or concepts, there are no universal standards that one could use to rank them as better or worse, superior or inferior. Under conditions of incommensurability, one can at best draw upon partial, incomplete, and plural standards, since there is no single norm, principle, or value with which they can be compared and judged. Some sense of moral incommensurability, while closely related to the second idea of humans as cultural agents, by no means follows necessarily from it. Some early modern thinkers, for instance, held that Amerindians were civil beings who led ordered and rationally comprehensible ways of life. Perhaps the most notable of these thinkers was Las Casas, whose personal moral indignation against Spanish imperial aggression gave rise to his spirited defence of Amerindians against imperial assaults, which hastened the demise of the belief that aboriginals were natural slaves. But Las Casas was not an opponent of imperialism as such, nor was he a thoroughgoing critic of the anthropological assumptions that grounded the predominant justifications of European empires. While he took Amerindians to be social and cultural beings, he nevertheless categorized them explicitly as inferior peoples because their specific cultural values and practices were thought to be inferior in comparison to those of Christian societies. Thus, Las Casas ranked the known peoples of the globe in his *Apologetica Historia* and explained that Europe's civilizing mission could raise inferior peoples, who were said to be on the lower end of this universal scale of progress, to the heights of Christian understanding.[29] Given the trenchant criticisms that Diderot, Kant, and Herder level against European institutions, beliefs, and practices, the triumphalism that lay behind such imperialist cross-cultural judgements became increasingly suspect. Under the influence primarily of Rousseau, and thus given their view of European social and political life as inegalitarian, corrupt, and often oppressive, Diderot, Kant, and Herder found it delusional to think that European institutions, mores, practices, or religious beliefs should serve as the benchmark against which other peoples ought to be judged. On the whole, the transformation in their thinking about human nature in relation to cultural pluralism led also to an appreciation of the plurality of cultural perspectives and forms of life that ultimately had significant consequences for their political theories. As Herder argues in his *Letters on the Advancement of Humanity*,

> There is no such thing as a specially favoured nation (*Favoritvolk*) on earth . . . there cannot, therefore, be any order of rank. . . . Least of all must we think of European culture as a universal standard of human values. To apply such a standard is not just misleading; it is meaningless. . . . The culture of *man* is not the culture of the *European*; it manifests itself according to place and time in *every* people. (18:247–49)

Ultimately, Diderot, Kant, and Herder undermine the imperial language of inferiority and superiority, and concomitantly the assumption that peoples are commensurable, which informed many defences of European empires.

There are two senses in which incommensurability plays a central role in the anti-imperialist political thought that I have identified, and it is important to see in what ways they are linked to the idea of humans as cultural agents. First, the idea of what Steven Lukes has called 'overall incommensurability' plays a significant role in the anti-imperialist political thought that I have explored. By 'overall incommensurability', I refer to the view that two groups cannot be compared according to a particular criterion because they are each so internally complex that it is impossible to make judgements of their relative worth as a whole. Thus, peoples (for example) are "rankable in too many different ways that cannot in turn be combined into a single way"; that is, "the various ways of ordering them . . . are non-congruent".[30] Simply stated, it is becomes easier to judge Amerindians, South Pacific Islanders, sub-Saharan Africans, and others as simply inferior when their societies are perceived as undifferentiated units. Once such peoples became theorized as artful and social individuals who live in societies with distinct practices, institutions, and value systems, even if such societies as a whole are viewed as less complex than European societies, it nevertheless becomes more difficult (though not of course impossible) to make sweeping judgements about their inferiority. The theory that humans are constitutively cultural agents and the doctrine of overall incommensurability are, then, conceptually related to one another, although it is obviously possible (consider Las Casas) to hold the former view without also endorsing the latter.

In addition to presenting a more nuanced, multifaceted understanding of humanity itself, and also specifically of New World peoples, Diderot, Kant, and Herder attack the view that there exists a universal standard that could be used to rank a wide variety of practices and beliefs (let alone entire peoples). They are all, to be sure, moral universalists in some sense, but for now it is important to stress in what sense they are also pluralists and how this pluralism is related to their commitment to a universal morality. This suggests a second and more complex form of incommensurability in their moral and political thought. Not only is it impossible to compare and rank peoples as whole entities, but a variety of specific institutions, practices, and beliefs are also not amenable to such judgements for there are no cross-cultural norms (or universal scales of value) with which (or along which) they could be compared and judged. As I have noted, understandings of the dominant patterns of land use, property relations, and the primary means of subsistence in a society played a crucial role in many modern debates about imperialism; sedentary agricultural societies in particular were viewed as radically distinct from societies that were nomadic and whose subsistence was based upon hunting, fishing, and herding. For many imperialist thinkers (for instance, international jurists such as Grotius and Vattel), an agriculturally based society constituted the prerequisite for a basic moral order; hence, pre-agricultural societies were thought to lack a moral and political status equal to that of European states on the stage of international politics. Moreover, from this perspective, given imperialists' frequent appropriations of Locke's account of property, not only do New World peoples thereby lack a sovereign status, but they also lack title to the lands that they were said to inhabit wastefully. According to Diderot, Kant, and Herder, however, these are precisely the kinds of cross-cultural judgements that one cannot make, for there are no cross-cultural standards with which one could make universal judgements about the superiority or inferiority of the diverse land-use practices that, in part, were seen to differentiate European from most non-European peoples.

Judgements, then, that nomadic lifestyles are not manifestly inferior to sedentary forms of life, and that many ways of life and understandings of value cannot be rank ordered, inform Enlightenment anti-imperialism. Yet, while a deep sense of moral incommensurability pervades Diderot, Kant, and Herder's political thinking, so too does a strong commitment to moral universalism. For all of them, the two are closely related, for the qualities that fundamentally characterize humanity and that deserve universal respect, in their view, are among the key sources of cultural differentiation, much of which lies beyond the purview of universal judgements. Diderot, Kant, and Herder distinguished between norms, practices, and institutions that, they argue, clearly violate human dignity and freedom, such as slavery, serfdom, imperialism, and the Indian caste system, and those that cannot and should not be judged according to such cross-cultural concepts, in part, because such judgements themselves violate humanity. To use the terminology that I have adopted in this book, the distinction here concerns when cultural agency ought to be respected morally and politically and when specific uses of cultural agency, as with the manifold actions and judgements of European imperialists, subvert the very grounds of cultural agency itself—the practical reason, freedom, imagination, skills, and self-cultivation (both individual and collective) that define humanity itself for Diderot, Kant, and Herder. Strikingly, as we have seen, these anti-imperialists do not simply limit the reach of universal principles in particular cases; rather, they theorize the relationship between the universal categories they posit (humanity, freedom, dignity, and the moral principles meant to safeguard them), on the one hand, and culturally varying norms, practices, and institutions, on the other, as complexly intertwined. Hence, for them, humanity is virtually synonymous with cultural difference, and thus the respect for the universal dignity of all humans necessarily implies a wide degree of respect for differing individual and collective ways of life.[31] The cogent manner with which they relate moral universalism and moral incommensurability in the course of their anti-imperialist political philosophies are hidden from view, however, by pervasive accounts of 'the Enlightenment' and what are often taken to be 'its' dogmatic veneration of moral universalism and concomitant denigration of cultural pluralism.

As I noted in the introduction, unlike the anti-slavery writings of the eighteenth century, Enlightenment-era anti-imperialist thought failed to generate a legacy that would be nurtured by prominent nineteenth-century thinkers. Thus, Enlightenment anti-imperialism remains a historical curiosity, for it emerges in European thought in the late eighteenth century among a variety of celebrated thinkers only to find itself as a marginalized philosophical viewpoint by the 1830s. In coming to terms with this intellectual shift, it is likely that, first, the range of languages of human diversity and, second, a change in the kind of intellectual sensibility that informed political thinking about 'European civilization' contributed to the decline of anti-imperialist thought.

Although arguments about changes in the broader intellectual context from the mid-eighteenth to the mid-nineteenth centuries are necessarily highly speculative, it is worth noting that the plurality of competing languages of diversity in the eighteenth century, in contrast to the narrower conceptualizations of (what is now often termed) cultural difference in the nineteenth century, may have had a role to play in this shift on questions of empire. The categories under which human diversity were theorized by the *philosophes* and *Aufklärer* of the eighteenth century included—among others—climate, national character, race, *moeurs*, *Kultur*, stadial accounts of social development, and sociological distinctions among agricultural, hunting, and pastoral lifestyles. This very diversity of languages about difference, and the variety of meanings ascribed to each one, may have enabled the development of unusual, and at times nuanced, accounts of cultural pluralism, since such concepts or explanations were often played off one another and combined in the most innovative accounts. In contrast, by the nineteenth century, the language of race, which was first developed in the influential natural histories of the eighteenth century by Buffon, Linnaeus, and Blumenbach, had overtaken other conceptual contenders and was much more frequently deployed in political writings to categorize non-European peoples. Similarly, the concept of the nation increasingly informed philosophical and anthropological understandings of (primarily European) peoples.[32]

To be sure, uncertainties and disagreements about the relative merits of different understandings of race and nation (and less often of other explanations of human diversity) and the standards with which one might be able, or not be able, to judge varying social practices, institutions, and whole peoples characterized nineteenth-century debates about cultural diversity. Nevertheless, the ideas of race and nation in earlier Enlightenment writings were still in a nascent state and had to contend with a number of alternative explanations and categories.[33] In eighteenth-century debates about human diversity, no single category, classificatory scheme, or set of explanations of cultural difference was hegemonic in the manner that racial typologies of non-European peoples dominated post-Enlightenment anthropological and political thought. Although at the cost of greater incoherence and instability, the diversity of approaches toward understanding cultural pluralism in the eighteenth century may have afforded a wider conceptual space for categorizing and explaining the diverse qualities and behavioural characteristics of peoples.

At the same time, it should be noted that the most influential nineteenth-century thinkers who defended European imperialism usually did not rely upon, and indeed often argued against, racist contentions about the intrinsic inferiority of foreign peoples. The idea of nationhood as a status that only some peoples, through a gradual process of progressive development, had achieved historically, one which indicated that such peoples could govern themselves and should help less fortunate peoples to do so, lay at the heart of John Stuart Mill's justification of British imperial rule over India.[34] As, Mill contends, "Despotism is a legitimate mode of government in dealing with barbarians, provided the end be their improvement."[35] Other prominent philosophers, such as Hegel and Marx, relied solely upon linear conceptions of social progress to tout either the civilizing possibilities of imperial rule or the ultimately productive development of feudal societies into capitalist economies, if only because communism itself could not be achieved without progressive changes both in the mode of production and in the ownership of the means of production. Like Mill, Hegel and Marx did not view non-European peoples as inherently backward; rather, with the help of imperial rule, such peoples would be lifted to a condition in which they could eventually govern themselves or, in the case of Marx, European imperialists would unwittingly prepare the ground for future revolutionary transitions to communism in the non-European world.[36] Other thinkers rested their imperialist arguments upon the national glory and political energy that would likely result from conquest abroad; thus, for Tocqueville, the social stresses and strains of democratizing and modernizing France could be partly alleviated by the grand venture of colonizing Algeria.[37]

This points to an important feature of Enlightenment anti-imperialism that cannot be fully captured by the three philosophical developments that I sketched earlier, since a key difference between the critics of empire in the eighteenth century and the imperialist political thinkers in the nineteenth century is one of intellectual sensibility or disposition, rather than entirely a difference in philosophical argumentation about human nature, cultural difference, and moral judgement. As we have seen, Diderot, Kant, and Herder were deeply critical of European states, for they viewed them as violent, absolutist, war-seeking, aggressive, and corrupt. While they valued the semblance of the rule of law that governments could at their best achieve, they also believed that actual European governments and societies were very far indeed from the ideal forms of governance that their political writings theorized; accordingly, they treated the very concept of 'civilization' with derision. The myriad social and political changes that the French Revolution ushered in eventually seemed to yield a political sensibility among many nineteenth-century European political thinkers that made them far more sanguine about the achievements of 'European civilization' than their eighteenth-century forebears. They were thus more amenable to the view that Europe had genuinely advanced beyond the non-European world and, hence, they were more open to the idea that it should forcibly lead non-European peoples toward a higher form of political rule, economic rationality, and social development. This was to be true even for those nineteenth-century thinkers who were, however differently, social critics who sought to engage in the reform of European societies and governments, such as John Stuart Mill, Tocqueville, Hegel, and Marx, each of whom in his own way considered the social, economic, and political changes from 1789 onward as truly significant advances toward more just societies. In contrast, Diderot (who died five years before the storming of the Bastille), and even Kant and Herder (who both held some hope that the French Revolution might inspire positive reforms in European societies and political systems) ultimately remained deeply disenchanted with the European states of their day.

This sense of distance from their own societies and governments fostered a sense of irony and scepticism about the grandiose claims that state (and imperial) authorities made about the political achievements of European civilization. In this respect, as I have noted, Diderot, Kant, and Herder were all profoundly influenced by their philosophical engagements with Rousseau. Intellectual temperaments characterized by a deep disenchantment with, irony toward, and scepticism about European political systems might not themselves foster a hatred of European empires, but they clearly undercut many of the pretensions that usually accompany civilizing imperialism. Their antipathy toward orthodox forms of religious authority further underscored their hatred of imperial paternalism and thus their discomfort with any form of missionary zealotry; it is telling, along these lines, that Kant derided justifications of European imperial incursions as "Jesuitism".[38] 'Europe', as Diderot, Kant, and Herder understood it in their anti-imperialist political philosophies, was very far indeed from the models of political justice that they theorized; indeed, for them, Europe was the primary source of social and political injustice around the world, rather than the standard-bearer of liberty or rights for the rest of humanity that should either inspire other peoples or be violently forced upon them.[39] In the end, this political sensibility animated many of their vehement arguments against the ideological bases of European imperial rule over non-European peoples.

IN CONTRAST to widespread accounts of 'the Enlightenment', the late eighteenth-century anti-imperialists studied in this book fold into their view of humanity the particularities of human life—the varied understandings and responses that draw upon memory, imagination, inherited practices, and customs. In their view, humans possess certain universal capacities that allow us to develop, sustain, and revise a wide variety of cultural practices. For Diderot, Kant, and Herder, these universal capacities consist most fundamentally of freedom and hence the ability to engage in imaganitive, aesthetic, instrumental, and moral reasoning. But their understandings of reason and freedom are not homogenous, for they view them as necessarily contextualized and open ended. Moreover, for them, cultural diversity cannot be reduced to reason and freedom even though these are the necessary prerequisites for the generation, maintenance, and transformation of plural practices and beliefs. The pluralism of human life exists precisely because humans' conscious and free (and at times unwitting and contingent) *interactions* with climate, technology, social and political conditions, and other factors engender a multiplicity of norms and institutions. There is a close relationship, then, between the philosophical anthropologies of Diderot, Kant, and Herder and their understandings of cultural pluralism and social life. Respecting human freedom came to mean, among other things, respecting the cultural pluralism that in part signifies our very humanity; it also meant that political criticism should be directed toward establishing the most fruitful conditions possible for the sustenance of this differentiated sense of humanity. Such conditions are often undermined and corrupted, in their view, by a variety of social, political, and religious practices, beliefs, and institutions. For these thinkers, European states were by far the worst offenders in this respect, for throughout the globe they routinely and oppressively denied individuals and whole peoples the freedoms necessary for the cultivation of their humanity, that is, for the workings of their cultural agency, and thus for a flourishing pluralism. Such views fuel these thinkers' antipathy toward the pathologies of state power generally as well as their attack more specifically upon the violent and homogenizing paternalism of imperial power.

I have considered the following questions: Which understandings of non-European peoples, cultural pluralism, liberty, and human nature engendered or impeded anti-imperialist sentiments? What are the key arguments that were made against European imperialism by thinkers such as Diderot, Kant, and Herder, and what does this tell us about (a) historiographical debates about 'the Enlightenment' and (b) the contested meanings of, and relationships among, humanity, cultural pluralism, and moral judgement? The responses I have offered throughout this book provide the beginnings of a more nuanced conception of Enlightenment-era political thought and a striking set of arguments about the moral and political consequences of different understandings of the relationship between humanity and cultural difference. By studying this strand of Enlightenment political thought through the lenses of imperialism, understandings of the non-European world, and theories of human nature and cultural diversity, one can discern philosophical commitments to a shared humanity that partly transcend, yet are partly defined by, cultural difference; a philosophical disposition that engages in cross-cultural judgements and yet folds into its ethical worldview an assumption of a deep moral incommensurability that constrains or disallows many cross-cultural judgements; and a critique of state-sponsored or state-sanctioned injustices that demands a respect for cultural difference, while also drawing upon an understanding of human freedom as a universal good. Among the more remarkable features of such writings—an aspect that should give pause to those who theorize an intractable conceptual divide between universalism and relativism in moral and political thought—is that an increasingly acute awareness of the *irreducible plurality* and *partial incommensurability* of social forms, moral values, and political institutions engendered a historically uncommon, inclusive moral *universalism*.[40] The conventional distinctions that many contemporary political theorists explicitly deploy or tacitly assume fail to capture the often counter-intuitive philosophical strategies and outlooks of the anti-imperialist current of Enlightenment political thought. Indeed, if a central reason to study the history of political thought is to gain the perspective of another set of assumptions and arguments that are shaped by different historical sensibilities and directed toward distinct political phenomena, and thus to defamiliarize our otherwise complacent political and ethical beliefs and priorities, then the study of Enlightenment anti-imperialism offers productive opportunities for such a task.

Notes

Chapter One
Introduction: Enlightenment Political Thought and the Age of Empire

1. In the concluding chapter, I address the question of whether one can mean-ingfully write of 'the Enlightenment' or whether there is a substantive meaning that we can attach to the term 'Enlightenment' that would make sense across multiple Enlightenments.

2. I use the terms 'empire' and 'imperialism' in a broad sense to indicate either the formal or the informal rule of one society over another society, especially (but not only) those cases when the metropole and the colonized territories are dis-tant, such as European imperial rule over non-European peoples. In some cases, empire involves extensive settlements and the introduction of many colonists from the metropole, while in others relatively few individuals from the metropole are present in the colonized territory. In some cases, a colonized society is ruled directly by another government; in others, imperial rule is relatively indirect, through (for instance) military officers, religious authorities, and / or directors of imperial trading companies. Diderot, Kant, and Herder were critics of both for-mal and more informal imperial rule over non-European peoples. On the range of practices, institutions, and forms of rule associated with 'empire', 'imperialism', and 'colonization', see Richard Koebner, *Empire* (Cambridge: Cambridge Uni-versity Press, 1961); M. I. Finley, "Colonies—An Attempt at a Typology", *Trans-actions of the Royal Historical Society*, 26 (1976): 167–88; J. S. Richardson, "Im-perium Romanum: Empire and the Language of Power", *Journal of Roman Studies*, 81 (1991): 1–9; Michael W. Doyle, *Empires* (Ithaca: Cornell University Press, 1986); and Anthony Pagden, *Peoples and Empires: A Short History of Euro-pean Migration, Exploration, and Conquest, from Greece to the Present* (New York: Modern Library, 2001). On the political languages and narratives that accom-panied, and helped to support, the rise of modern European empires, see David Armitage, *The Ideological Origins of the British Empire* (Cambridge: Cambridge University Press, 2000); and Anthony Pagden, *Lords of All the World: Ideologies of Empire in Spain, Britain and France c. 1500–c. 1800* (New Haven: Yale Univer-sity Press, 1995).

3. In the eighteenth century (and, indeed, today as well), the boundaries be-tween Europe and the non-European worlds were hotly contested, for 'Europe' could signify a relatively small set of Western European countries or, more expan-sively, all of what was traditionally conceived to be Christendom. See J.G.A. Pocock, "Some Europes in Their History" in *The Idea of Europe: From Antiquity to the European Union*, ed. Anthony Pagden (Cambridge and Washington, D.C.: Cambridge University Press and Woodrow Wilson Center Press, 2002), 55–71; and Larry Wolff, *Inventing Eastern Europe: The Map of Civilization on the Mind of the Enlightenment* (Stanford: Stanford University Press, 1994).

4. All scholars who work on the question of empire in modern European polit-

ical theory benefit from Anthony Pagden's valuable scholarship, but a book-length study of anti-imperialist political thought in the age of Enlightenment remains a lacuna in the scholarly literature, an especially curious one given its historical and philosophical distinctiveness.

5. David Brion Davis, *The Problem of Slavery in the Age of Revolution, 1770–1823* (Ithaca: Cornell University Press, 1975); and Robin Blackburn, *The Overthrow of Colonial Slavery, 1776–1848* (New York: Verso, 1988).

6. For instance, in some of Michel de Montaigne's essays, which I discuss in chapter 2.

7. See Francisco de Vitoria, "De Indis" in *Political Writings*, eds. Anthony Pagden and Jeremy Lawrance (Cambridge: Cambridge University Press, 1991), 233–292; Bartolomé de Las Casas, *In defense of the Indians: The defense of the Most Reverend Lord, Don Fray Bartolomé de las Casas, of the Order of Preachers, late Bishop of Chiapa, against the persecutors and slanderers of the peoples of the New World discovered across the seas*, ed. Stafford Poole (DeKalb: Northern Illinois University Press, 1974); Bartolomé de Las Casas, *The Devastation of the Indies: A Brief Account* (Baltimore: Johns Hopkins University Press, 1992).

8. See, for example, Jeremy Bentham, *Colonies, Commerce, and Constitutional Law: Rid Yourselves of Ultramaria and other writings on Spain and Spanish America*, ed. Philip Schofield (Oxford: Clarendon, 1995); Jean-Antoine-Nicolas de Caritat, marquis de Condorcet, *Condorcet: Selected Writings*, ed. Keith Michael Baker (Indianapolis: Bobbs-Merrill, 1976); Adam Smith, *An Inquiry into the Nature and Causes of the Wealth of Nations*, ed. R. H. Campbell and A. S. Skinner (Indianapolis: Liberty Fund, 1981), 2: 556–641.

9. Edmund Burke, *The Writings and Speeches of Edmund Burke*, vol. 5, *India: Madras and Bengal, 1774–1785*, and vol. 6, *India, the launching of the Hastings impeachment, 1786–1788*, ed. P. J. Marshall (Oxford: Clarendon, 1981 and 1991). See also Frederick G. Whelan, *Edmund Burke and India: Political Morality and Empire* (Pittsburgh: University of Pittsburgh Press, 1996); and David Bromwich, introduction to *On Empire, Liberty, and Reform: Speeches and Letters*, by Edmund Burke (New Haven: Yale University Press, 2000), 1–39.

10. See, for instance, Uday Singh Mehta, *Liberalism and Empire: A Study in Nineteenth-Century British Liberal Thought* (Chicago: University of Chicago Press, 1999).

11. See Nicholas K. Robinson, *Edmund Burke: A Life in Caricature* (New Haven: Yale University Press, 1996); and especially Conor Cruise O'Brien, *The Great Melody: A Thematic Biography and Commented Anthology of Edmund Burke* (Chicago: University of Chicago Press, 1992).

12. Benjamin Constant, "The spirit of conquest and usurpation and their relation to European civilization" in *Political Writings*, ed. and trans. Biancamaria Fontana (Cambridge: Cambridge University Press, 1988), 45–167.

13. On this shift within British and French political thought from the late eighteenth to the mid-nineteenth centuries, see Jennifer Pitts, *The Turn To Empire* (Princeton: Princeton University Press, forthcoming).

14. This feature of Enlightenment thought is beginning to be appreciated more fully, and not simply in the conventional manner of viewing Paris as the centre from which such thought radiated. See, for instance, Fania Oz-Salzberger,

Translating the Enlightenment (Oxford: Clarendon, 1995), on the impact of Scottish philosophy upon the German intellectual tradition; Jonathan I. Israel, *Radical Enlightenment: Philosophy and the Making of Modernity, 1650–1750* (Oxford: Oxford University Press, 2001), on the intellectual relationships among a diverse group of modern thinkers across generations and nationalities; and J.G.A. Pocock, *Barbarism and Religion*, vol. 1, *The Enlightenments of Edward Gibbon, 1737–1764* and vol. 2, *Narratives of Civil Government* (Cambridge: Cambridge University Press, 1999), on the cross-currents among Arminian, English, Scottish, and Parisian Enlightenments.

15. On the concept of 'culture' and its history, see Alfred Kroeber and Clyde Kluckhohn, "Culture: A Critical Review of Concepts and Definitions", *Papers of the Peabody Museum of American Archeology and Ethnology*, 47 (1952); Raymond Geuss, "Kultur, Bildung, Geist", in *Morality, Culture, and History: Essays on German Philosophy* (Cambridge: Cambridge University Press, 1999), 29–50; K. Anthony Appiah, "The Multiculturalist Misunderstanding", *The New York Review of Books*, 9 October 1997; Adam Kuper, *Culture: The Anthropologists' Account* (Cambridge: Harvard University Press, 1999); and James Swenson, "A small change in terminology or a Great Leap Forward? Culture and civilization in revolution." *MLN*, 112 (1997): 322–48.

16. Edmund Burke, "An Appeal from the New to the Old Whigs" [1791], *The Works of the Right Honourable Edmund Burke*, vol. 4 (London: J. C. Nimmo), 176.

Chapter Two
Toward a Subversion of Noble Savagery:
From Natural Humans to Cultural Humans

1. The term 'le bon sauvage' was not typically used by the thinkers under study here, although the term was used in French from the sixteenth century onward. Instead, they write of 'les sauvages', 'l'état sauvage', or 'la vie primitive', and so on. In English, the term 'noble savage' appears to have been coined by John Dryden in *The Conquest of Grenada* (1670): "I am as free as Nature first made man / Ere the base laws of servitude began / When wild in woods the noble savage ran". I use the term in this chapter, then, as a label for what can be retrospectively described as a tradition of thought about a variety of non-European (usually nomadic, or ostensibly nomadic) peoples, though such a 'tradition' was not always, of course, understood as such and was internally diverse. The kinds of portrayals I examine above, however, generated an intense series of debates in print and in conversation from the sixteenth century onward among a wide array of thinkers about whether the lives of 'wild men', 'savages', and 'primitives' were more just, more 'natural', and happier than the lives of cultivated Europeans. In this sense, writings that extol noble savagery were often seen to have a cohesion that, in effect, amounted to the view that there was an identifiable tradition of thinking along these lines that one could contest or support.

2. David Brion Davis, "At the Heart of Slavery", *The New York Review of Books*, 17 October 1996, 54.

3. See Edward Dudley and Maximillian E. Novak, eds., *The Wild Man Within:*

An Image in Western Thought from the Renaissance to Romanticism (Pittsburgh: University of Pittsburgh Press, 1972); and Arthur Lovejoy and George Boas, *Primitivism and Related Ideas in Antiquity* (Baltimore: Johns Hopkins University Press, 1997; originally 1935). For a survey of the range of positive and negative portrayals of Amerindians and South Pacific Islanders, see P. J. Marshall and Glyndwr Williams, *The Great Map of Mankind* (Cambridge: Harvard University Press, 1982), 187–226, 258–98; and V. G. Kiernan, "Noble and ignoble savages" in *Exoticism in the Enlightenment*, ed. G. S. Rousseau and Roy Porter (Manchester: Manchester University Press, 1990), 86–116. On the development of exotic representations of Amerindians, see Margaret T. Hodgen, *Early Anthropology in the Sixteenth and Seventeenth Centuries* (Philadelphia: University of Pennsylvania Press, 1964), 354ff; and Gilbert Chinard, *L'Amérique et le rêve exotique dans la littérature française au XVIIe et au XVIIIe siècle* (Paris: E. Droz, 1934). See also J. H. Elliot, "The discovery of America and the discovery of man", *Proceedings of the British Academy*, 58 (1972): 102–25; Melvin Richter, "Europe and *the Other* in Eighteenth-Century Thought", *Politisches Denken* (1997): 25–47.

4. On the religious roots of noble savage perspectives, see Michèle Duchet, *Anthropologie et Histoire au siècle des lumières* (Paris: François Maspero, 1971), 25–64; and Geoffrey Atkinson, *Les relations de voyages du XVIIe siècle et l'évolution des idées: Contribution à l'étude de la formation de l'esprit au XVIIIe siècle* (Paris: Libraire Ancienne Edouard Champion, 1924), 63–81.

5. Amerigo Vespucci, *Letters from a New World*, ed. Luciano Formisano, trans. David Jacobson (New York: Marsilio, 1992), 49–50.

6. Michel de Montaigne, *The Complete Essays of Montaigne*, ed. and trans. Donald Frame (Stanford: Stanford University Press, 1958), 153. Hereafter references to this work are given in parentheses in the text.

7. See the subtle reading along these lines by Edwin M. Duval, "Lessons of the New World: Design and Meaning in Montaigne's 'Des Cannibales' (I:31) and 'Des Coches' (III:6)", *Yale French Studies*, 64 (1983): 95–112.

8. See Arthur J. Slavin, "The American Principle from More to Locke" in *First Images of America: The Impact of the New World on the Old*, vol. 1, ed. Fredi Chiappelli: (Berkeley: University of California Press, 1976), 147–149; and William Shakespeare, *The Tempest* (Act 2, Scene 1):

Gonzalo:
. . . no kind of traffic
Would I admit: no name of magistrate:
Letters should not be known: riches, poverty,
And use of service—none: contract, succession,
Bourn, bound of land, tilth, vineyard—none:
No use of metal, corn, or wine, or oil:
No occupation, all men idle, all:
And women too, but innocent and pure:
No sovereignty. . . .

9. Given the gendered language in this passage, such natural titles presumably include those given to men in particular to inherit property equally only among

themselves. As we will see, the relationship between the sexes in New World societies was of great interest to Lahontan, Rousseau, and Diderot.

10. For a treatment of the theme of Stoicism in Montaigne's treatment of New World peoples, see David Quint, *Montaigne and the Quality of Mercy* (Princeton: Princeton University Press, 1998), 75–101.

11. To this might be added Montaigne's general comment upon New World peoples as such in "Of Coaches": "Most of the responses of these people and most of our dealings with them show that they were not at all behind us in natural brightness of mind and pertinence", although this could also be interpreted as a comment upon their native intelligence and innate capacity, rather than upon the impressiveness of the exercise of their faculties in social life (693).

12. John Locke, *An Essay concerning the true original, extent, and end of civil government*, in *Two Treatises of Government*, ed. Peter Laslett (Cambridge: Cambridge University Press, 1960), §49. See Herman Lebovics, "The Uses of America in Locke's *Second Treatise of Government*", *Journal of the History of Ideas*, 47 (1986): 567–81.

13. Baron de Lahontan, *Dialogues Curieux entre l'Auteur et un Sauvage de bons sens qui a voyagé et Mémoires de l'Amérique Septentrionale*, ed. Gilbert Chinard (Paris: A. Margraff, 1931), 95; see also 116. Cf. Montaigne (156). Hereafter references to Lahontan's *Dialogues* are given by page number in parentheses in the text; translations are mine.

14. For an analysis of the dialogic device used by Lahontan, see Roger Mercier, "Image de l'autre et image de soi-même dans le discours ethnologique au XVIIIe siècle", *Studies on Voltaire and the Eighteenth Century*, 154 (1976): 1417–35.

15. On Lahontan's use of 'natural religion' in the *Dialogues*, see Anthony Pagden, *European Encounters with the New World* (New Haven: Yale University Press, 1993), 123–26.

16. Norman Hampson, *The Enlightenment* (Harmondsworth: Penguin, 1968), 107. See Gottfried Wilhelm Leibniz, *Writings on China*, ed. and trans. Daniel J. Cook and Henry Rosemont, Jr. (Chicago: Open Court, 1994). See also Walter W. Davis, "China, the Confucian Ideal, and the European Age of Enlightenment" and Donald F. Lach, "Leibniz and China" and "The Sinophilism of Christian Wolff", all in *Discovering China: European Interpretations in the Enlightenment*, ed. Julia Ching and Willard G. Oxtoby (Rochester: University of Rochester Press, 1992).

17. Jean-Jacques Rousseau, *Oeuvres complètes*, 5 vols., Bibliothèque de la Pléiade, ed. Bernard Gagnebin and Marcel Raymond (Paris: Gallimard, 1959–95), 3:11. On the connections between the concept of despotism and understandings of the Far East, see Melvin Richter, "Despotism" in *Dictionary of the History of Ideas* (New York: Scribner, 1973); and Franco Venturi, "Oriental Despotism", *Journal of the History of Ideas*, 24 (1963): 133–142.

18. David Hume, *An Enquiry Concerning Human Understanding* [1748], in *Enquiries concerning human understanding and concerning the principles of morals*, ed. L.A. Selby-Bigge, revised by P. H. Nidditch (Oxford: Oxford University Press, 1975), 84.

19. Baron Lahontan, *New Voyages to North America* (London: H. Bonwicke, 1703), vol. I, 270 ("A Discourse of the Interest of the French, and of the English, in North America"), and 182 (Letter XXIII, 25 October 1692).

20. Hereafter references for Rousseau's writings are given in parentheses in the main text and are from the standard Pléiade edition: Rousseau, *Oeuvres complètes*, vol. 3 (1964). Unless otherwise noted, translations are from the following two editions: Jean-Jacques Rousseau, *The Discourses and other early political writings*, ed. and trans. Victor Gourevitch (Cambridge: Cambridge University Press, 1997); and Jean-Jacques Rousseau, *The Social Contract and other later political writings*, ed. and trans. Victor Gourevitch (Cambridge: Cambridge University Press, 1997).

21. Rousseau, *Oeuvres complètes* (1990), 5:394. Cf. Rousseau's comments about travel and education in his *Emile*, trans. Allan Bloom (New York: Basic Books, 1979), 450–71.

22. In "Of Cannibals", Montaigne argues exactly the opposite point concerning the professions that are most likely to yield a less subjective travel narrative (151–52). The better educated and more intellectually refined the traveller, he argues, the more likely the resulting travel accounts will be embellished with distorting analyses and judgements.

23. On the structure of Rousseau's theorization of the state of nature, see Victor Goldschmidt, *Anthropologie et Politique: Les principes du système de Rousseau* (Paris: Librairie Philosophique J. Vrin, 1974), 231ff.

24. Judith Shklar, *Men and Citizens: A Study of Rousseau's Social Theory* (Cambridge: Cambridge University Press, 1969), 12–32.

25. Francisco de Vitoria, "On the American Indians" (1539) in his *Political Writings*, ed. Anthony Pagden and Jeremy Lawrance (Cambridge: Cambridge University Press, 1991), 239–51.

26. For a discussion of some of the early modern origins of climate theory, see M. J. Tooley, "Bodin and the Medieval Theory of Climate", *Speculum*, 28 (1953): 64–83. For a comprehensive discussion of the history of geographical and climatological accounts of humanity, see Clarence J. Glacken, *Traces on the Rhodian Shore: Nature and Culture in Western Thought from Ancient Times to the End of the Eighteenth Century* (Berkeley: University of California Press, 1967), especially 551–622.

27. Montesquieu, *The Spirit of the Laws*, ed. and trans. Anne Cohler, Basia Miller, and Harold Stone (Cambridge: Cambridge University Press, 1989), 234 (Book 14, chapter 2).

28. For a representative and vivid account of one such phenomenon, see Roger Shattuck, *The Forbidden Experiment: The Story of the Wild Boy of Aveyron* (London: Secker and Warburg, 1980).

29. For a thorough examination of this aspect of Rousseau's thought in the context of historical and contemporary anthropological and genetic theories, see Robert Wokler, "Perfectible Apes in Decadent Cultures: Rousseau's Anthropology Revisited", *Daedalus*, 107, no. 3 (Summer 1978): 107–34.

30. On Rousseau's use of Prévost's collection of travel literature, see G. Pire, "Jean-Jacques Rousseau et les relations de voyages", *Revue d'histoire littéraire de la France*, 56, no. 3 (1956): 355–78.

31. Only one experiment, Rousseau attests, could unequivocally settle the orangutan issue, but it would only be taken up by the "crudest observers" and, in any case, would perhaps require more than one generation to verify the results. Rousseau thus suggests obliquely that the sure demonstration of his hypothesis would require a human and an orangutan to attempt sexual reproduction. However, before knowing with certainty that orangutans were human, the test could not be "tried in innocence" (211).

32. See Arthur O. Lovejoy, "The Supposed Primitivism of Rousseau's Discourse on Inequality", in *Essays in the History of Ideas* (Baltimore: Johns Hopkins Press, 1948), 14–37; and Tzvetan Todorov, *On Human Diversity: Nationalism, Racism, and Exoticism in French Thought*, trans. Catherine Porter (Cambridge: Harvard University Press, 1993), 277–82.

33. Jean-Jacques Rousseau, "La Découverte du Nouveau Monde", in *Œuvres complètes* (1961), 2:828.

34. See Jerome Schwartz, *Diderot and Montaigne: The Essais and the shaping of Diderot's humanism* (Genève: Libraire Droz, 1966).

35. François de Fénelon, *Telemachus, son of Ulysses*, ed. and trans. Patrick Riley ([1699] Cambridge University Press, 1994); see especially 108–14 (on the inhabitants of "Bétique"). Rousseau was also deeply influenced by this aspect of Fénelon's thought.

36. "Lettre de Voltaire à Jean-Jacques Rousseau" (30 August 1755) in Rousseau, *Oeuvres complètes*, 3:1379.

37. For an influential example of such a reading, see Tzvetan Todorov, *On Human Diversity*, 276–77.

38. Here I am in agreement with Wilda Anderson, *Diderot's Dream* (Baltimore: Johns Hopkins University Press, 1990), 127–67.

39. On this aspect of Rousseau's thought, see Jean Starobinski, *Jean-Jacques Rousseau: Transparency and Obstruction*, trans. Arthur Goldhammer (Chicago: University of Chicago Press, 1988), 22–32; Asher Horowitz, "'Laws and Customs Thrust Us Back into Infancy': Rousseau's Historical Anthropology", *The Review of Politics*, 52, No. 2 (Summer 1990): 215–41; Arthur M. Melzer, *The Natural Goodness of Man: On the System of Rousseau's Thought* (Chicago: The University of Chicago Press, 1990), 49–58. See also J. A. Passmore, "The Malleability of Man in Eighteenth-Century Thought" in *Aspects of the Eighteenth Century*, ed. Earl R. Wasserman (Baltimore: Johns Hopkins Press, 1965), 21–46.

40. Unless otherwise noted, quotations of Diderot's writings in this chapter are from Denis Diderot, *Political Writings*, ed. and trans. John Hope Mason and Robert Wokler (Cambridge: Cambridge University Press, 1992).

41. Jean-Jacques Rousseau, *The Collected Writings of Rousseau*, vol. 5, *The Confessions and Correspondence, Including the Letters to Malsherbes*, ed. Christopher Kelly, Roger D. Masters, and Peter G. Stillman, and trans. Christopher Kelly (Hanover: University Press of New England, 1995), 575 (Letter to Malsherbes, 12 January 1762). See also Maurice Cranston, *Jean-Jacques: The Early Life and Work of Jean-Jacques Rousseau, 1712–1754* (Chicago: University of Chicago Press, 1982), 226–29.

42. Rousseau, *Collected Writings*, 5:295.

43. Rousseau, ibid., 5:326.

44. As Rousseau writes in the *Confessions*, the passage "about the philosopher who reasons with himself while blocking his ears in order to harden himself to the moans of an unfortunate man is of his [Diderot's] making, and he provided me with others still stronger that I could not resolve to use." Rousseau, ibid. On both the friendship and the rift between Rousseau and Diderot, see Jean Fabre, "Deux Frères Ennemis: Diderot et Jean-Jacques", *Diderot Studies*, 3: 155–213; see also George R. Havens, "Diderot, Rousseau, and *Discours sur l'Inégalité*", *Diderot Studies*, 3: 219–62.

45. See Arthur M. Wilson's definitive intellectual biography, *Diderot* (New York: Oxford University Press, 1972), 841, n. 63.

46. This theme is made explicit immediately in the subtitle to *Madame de La Carlière*: "Sur l'inconséquence du jugement public de nos actions particulières" ["On the inconsistency of the public judgement of our private actions"].

47. Denis Diderot, *Oeuvres complètes de Diderot*, vol. 2, ed. Jules Assézat and Maurice Tourneux (Paris: Garnier Frères, 1875), 206, 203.

48. The *Supplément* first appeared in the privately circulated periodical that was edited by Diderot's friend Friedrich Grimm, *Correspondance Littéraire*, in 1773 and 1774. Diderot continued to make changes and additions to these early versions. The *Supplément* was first published posthumously in 1796. The two French editions that I have consulted are Denis Diderot, *Supplément au Voyage de Bougainville*, ed. Herbert Dieckmann (Gèneve: Droz, 1955); and Diderot, *Supplément au Voyage de Bougainville, publié d'après le manuscrit de Leningrad*, ed. Gilbert Chinard (Paris: E. Droz, 1935). The Dieckmann edition of the *Supplément* will be the basis for what is becoming the standard critical edition of Diderot's writings: *Oeuvres complètes*, ed. Herbert Dieckmann, Jean Fabre, and Jacques Proust (Paris: Hermann, 1975–). The volume of Diderot's political writings in this edition is still forthcoming. (As indicated in note 40, all citations of and quotations from the *Supplément* are from Diderot, *Political Writings*).

49. On the sophisticated literary configuration of Diderot's *Supplément* and the philosophical opportunities it affords him, see Dena Goodman, "The Structure of Political Argument in Diderot's *Supplément au Voyage de Bougainville*", *Diderot Studies*, 21 (1983): 123–37; and Goodman, *Criticism in Action: Enlightenment Experiments in Political Writing* (Ithaca: Cornell University Press, 1989), 169–229. See also Claudia Moscovici, "An Ethics of Cultural Exchange: Diderot's *Supplément au Voyage de Bougainville*", *CLIO*, 30 (2001): 289–307; and Ralph Leigh, "Diderot's Tahiti", *Studies in the Eighteenth Century*, 5 (1983): 113–28.

50. Diderot, *Oeuvres complètes*, ed. Dieckmann, Fabre, and Proust, 4:334. In this work, Diderot even cites New World "savages" as examples of such creatures, a view that he jettisons in later writings such as the *Supplément* and his contributions to the *Histoire des deux Indes*.

51. Bougainville, Louis Antoine de, *Voyage Autour du Monde: Par la frégate la Boudeuse et la flute l'Étoile* ([1771] Paris: Club des Libraires de France, 1958), 137. On European understandings of Tahiti and, more generally, of the South Pacific, see Neil Rennie, *Far-Fetched Facts: The Literature of Travel and the Idea of the South Seas* (Oxford: Clarendon, 1995); Roy Porter, "The Exotic as Erotic: Captain Cook at Tahiti" in *Exoticism in the Enlightenment*, ed. Roy Porter and G. S. Rousseau (Manchester: Manchester University Press, 1990), 117–44; and Alan

Frost, "The Pacific Ocean: The Eighteenth Century's 'New World'", *Studies on Voltaire and the Eighteenth Century*, 152 (1976): 779–822.

52. See M. L. Perkins, "Community Planning in Diderot's *Supplément au Voyage de Bougainville*", *Kentucky Romance Quarterly*, 21 (1974): 399–417.

53. See Frederick Whelan, "Population and Ideology in the Enlightenment", *History of Political Thought*, 12, no. 1 (1991): 35–72.

54. Demography also furnishes the standard that Rousseau prescribes in *On the Social Contract* as the one valid criterion of political welfare per se, regardless of the many historical and institutional differences among polities: "What is the aim of the political association? It is the preservation and prosperity of its members. And what is the surest sign that they are preserving themselves and prospering? It is their number and their population. . . . All other things being equal, the Government under which the Citizens, without resort to external means, without naturalizations, without colonies, populate and multiply is without fail the best: that under which a people dwindles and wastes away is the worst. Calculators, it is now up to you: count, measure, compare." (419–420, Book III, chapter 9: "Of the signs of a good government")

55. See Diderot's article "Encyclopédie" from the *Encyclopédie* (partly reprinted in Diderot, *Political Writings*, 21–27) for his understanding of this massive, multivolume project.

56. Twice in the *Supplément* Diderot raises the difficulty of formulating cross-culturally valid criteria of judgement for assessing the political health of societies. In each instance, he points to the conjunction of the common good and individual utility.

57. On self-interest and its relationship to virtue in eighteenth-century French philosophical writings, see Mark Hulliung, *The Autocritique of Enlightenment* (Cambridge: Harvard University Press, 1994), 9–37.

58. In addition to travel writings, actual historical visits by New World individuals to Europe in the eighteenth century provoked an intense interest in foreign peoples. For instance, as Diderot notes in the *Supplément*, a Tahitian named Autourou accompanied Bougainville on his journey back to France and spent a few weeks in Paris, attending operas and some of the salons before embarking on commercial trading ships back to Tahiti. See Bougainville's account of Autourou's visit in his *Voyage autour du monde*, 148–151.

59. Some of Diderot's arguments along these lines recall (and may have been influenced by) Lahontan's arguments about Huron women.

60. The Polly Baker story appeared in English journals in 1747, originating purportedly with Benjamin Franklin, and later was included by Abbé Raynal in the *Histoire des deux Indes*. For an extended treatment of this popular eighteenth-century story, see Max Hall, *Benjamin Franklin and Polly Baker: The History of a Literary Deception* (Chapel Hill: University of North Carolina Press, 1960).

61. Despite such arguments, Diderot's comments about women (for instance, in the essay "Sur les Femmes") are on the whole a curious mix of egalitarian and hierarchical views. For a discussion of Diderot's arguments in the context of the *philosophes'* writings about women, see Sylvana Tomaselli, "The Enlightenment Debate on Women", *History Workshop*, 20 (Autumn 1985): 101–24. See also A. Sfragaro, "La Représentation de la femme chez Diderot", *Studies on Voltaire and*

the Eighteenth Century, 193 (1980): 1893–99. Cf. Mary Trouille, "Sexual/Textual Politics in the Enlightenment: Diderot and D'Epinay Respond to Thomas's Essay on Women", *The Romanic Review*, 85, no. 2 (March 1994): 191–210.

62. In an early fragment, Rousseau writes: "Let us begin by considering women deprived of their freedom by the tyranny of men, and men the masters of everything . . . everything in their hands, they seized it by I know not what natural right which I could never quite understand, and which may well have no other foundation than main force." (*Oeuvres complètes*, Pléiade ed., 2:1254) By the time of the first and second *Discourses*, however, Rousseau had rejected such a view and endorsed instead a natural hierarchy between men and women.

63. See Melvin Richter, "The Comparative Study of Regimes and Societies in the Eighteenth Century", in *The Cambridge History of Eighteenth-Century Political Thought*, ed. Mark Goldie and Robert Wokler (Cambridge: Cambridge University Press, forthcoming).

64. The question of whether one can nonethnocentrically practise anthropology, and how one can assess varying interpretations of foreign peoples, is, of course, an ongoing debate, the genealogy of which can be traced to many of the early modern debates over New World peoples. A particularly telling and heated skirmish in cultural anthropology along these lines concerns competing accounts of why Captain Cook was killed by Hawaiians in 1779. See Gannath Obeyesekere, *The Apotheosis of Captain Cook: European Mythmaking in the Pacific* (Princeton: Princeton University Press, 1992); and Marshall Sahlins, *How "Natives" Think: About Captain Cook, for example* (Chicago: University of Chicago Press, 1995).

65. See Michèle Duchet, "Le 'Supplément au voyage de Bougainville' et la collaboration de Diderot à 'L'Histoire des deux Indes' ", *Cahiers de l'Association Internationale des Études Françaises*, 13 (1961): 173–87.

66. I borrow the term 'multidimensional social theory' from Steven Seidman, *Liberalism and the Origins of European Social Theory* (Berkeley: University of California Press, 1983), 33. Seidman argues that although many sociologists have viewed the development of multidimensional accounts of society (which theorize the symbiotic relationship between human agency and social structure in a methodologically sophisticated fashion) as a nineteenth-century revolt against the presuppositions of social contractarianism and other theories that were considered to presuppose methodological individualism, the roots of a multidimensional social theory can in fact be found in a variety of eighteenth-century Enlightenment writings.

67. As Clifford Geertz has noted, a significant overlap exists between protohumans' cultural history and humans' phylogenetic development. Since *Australopithecines* (pre-*homo sapiens*) began making tools, engaged in social practices such as organized hunting and lived in familial/social units (thereby leading a rudimentary cultural life), *homo sapiens* originated and developed physiologically within a cultural context. Accordingly, "culture, rather than being added on, so to speak, to a finished or virtually finished animal, was ingredient, and centrally ingredient, in the production of that animal itself." (47) In brief, from this perspective, the structure of our brains and our complex nervous system are partly cultural products. Thus, because "our central nervous system—and most partic-

ularly its crowning curse and glory, the neocortex—grew up in great part in inter-action with culture, it is incapable of directing our behaviour or organizing our experience without the guidance provided by systems of significant symbols." (49) See Clifford Geertz, "The Impact of the Concept of Culture on the Concept of Man" in *The Interpretation of Cultures* (New York: Basic Books, 1973).

68. Ibid., 49.

69. Ibid., 34.

70. Adam Ferguson, *An Essay on the History of Civil Society*, ed. Fania Oz-Salzberger ([1767] Cambridge: Cambridge University Press, 1995), 12, 14.

Chapter Three
Diderot and the Evils of Empire: The *Histoire des deux Indes*

1. The *Histoire* was first published in 1772 (with an imprint of 1770). It was published in extensively revised and enlarged forms in 1774 and 1780. There were numerous editions that followed with further alterations. All of Diderot's contributions can be found from the 1780 edition onward. Anthony Strugnell is now at work on a modern critical edition of the *Histoire*, which will be published by the Voltaire Foundation. Since this edition has not yet been published, there is no standard edition that is used to cite the *Histoire*; moreover, volume and page numbers differ from edition to edition. Thus, I have cited Raynal's *Histoire* by book and chapter in parentheses in the text (the *Histoire* is divided into 19 books, a division that is consistent across most editions). I have used the following edition: Guillaume-Thomas Raynal, *Histoire philosophique et politique des établisse-ments et du commerce des Européens dans les deux Indes*, 10 vols. (Genève: Jean-Leonard Pellet, 1780). A small selection of Diderot's contributions to the *Histoire* has been translated into English; see Diderot, *Political Writings*, ed. Mason and Wokler, 169–214. The translations of the *Histoire* in this essay are usually mine, since most are from passages not included in the Mason/Wokler selection; in some cases, I have drawn upon their edition, sometimes altering their transla-tion in light of the French text.

2. The philological work that has been done on the *Histoire* is complex and although we do not know the author of every passage, the cache of Diderot's manuscripts in the Fonds Vandeul (the collection of Diderot papers at the Bibli-othèque Nationale in Paris) that came to light in the 1950s has alerted scholars to his contributions. Thus, until fairly recently, although Diderot's participation in the *Histoire* had been rumoured since the 1770s, there was no evidence that could indicate what his specific contributions may have been. For a comprehen-sive analysis of these manuscripts that links them to sections of Raynal's *Histoire*, see Michèle Duchet, *Diderot et l'Histoire des deux Indes ou l'Écriture Fragmen-taire* (Paris: Libraire A.-G. Nizet, 1978). I have used this study as my guide to locate all of Diderot's contributions. On the issue of various contributors and their relationship to the anti-imperialism of the *Histoire*, see Yves Benot, "Di-derot, Pechmeja, Raynal et l'anticolonialisme", *Europe*, 41 (1963): 137–53.

3. Edmund Burke, letter to Richard Champion, 13 June 1777, in *The Corre-spondence of Edmund Burke*, vol. 3 (Cambridge: Cambridge University Press; Chicago: The University of Chicago Press, 1958–78), 353.

4. Robert Darnton, *The Forbidden Best-Sellers of Pre-revolutionary France* (New York: Norton, 1996), 22–82.

5. See J.G.A. Pocock, "Commerce, Settlement and History: A Reading of the *Histoire des deux Indes*", in *Articulating America: Fashioning a National Political Culture in Early America, Essays in Honor of J. R. Pole*, ed. Rebecca Starr (Lanham: Rowman & Littlefield, 2000), 15–44. See also Anthony Strugnell, "Postmodernism versus Enlightenment and the problem of the Other in Raynal's *Histoire des deux Indes*", *Studies on Voltaire and the Eighteenth Century*, 341 (1996): 169–82; and William R. Womack, "Eighteenth-century themes in the *Histoire philsophique et politique des deux Indes* of Guillaume Raynal", *Studies on Voltaire and the Eighteenth Century*, 96: 129–265. For insightful collections of essays on the *Histoire*, see Hans-Jürgen Lüsebrink and Manfred Tietz, eds., *Lectures de Raynal: L'Histoire des deux Indes en Europe et en Amérique au XVIIIe siècle, Studies on Voltaire and the Eighteenth Century*, vol. 286 (Oxford: Voltaire Foundation, 1991); Hans-Jürgen Lüsebrink and Anthony Strugnell, eds., *L'Histoire des deux Indes: Réécriture et polygraphie, Studies on Voltaire and the Eighteenth Century*, vol. 333 (Oxford: Voltaire Foundation, 1995). Forthcoming dissertations by Anoush Terjanian (Johns Hopkins University) and Sunil Agnani (Columbia University) will shed further light on this rich and influential, yet still understudied, text.

6. As Diderot writes, "The [commercial] exchanges should be free. If I want to seize by force what is refused me, or to use violence to have something which is not wanted forcibly accepted, then I could legitimately be either put in chains or driven away. If I get hold of the foreign commodity without offering the price for it, or I take it away by stealth, I am a thief who can be killed without remorse." (XIII, 1)

7. Diderot, "Droit Naturel", in *Political Writings*, 10.

8. Thus, a "universal morality" is not simply "inherent in the nature of man, [but] is also inherent in the nature of societies" (XIX, 14).

9. A fine study of this turn in Diderot's thought is Anthony Strugnell, *Diderot's politics: A study of the evolution of Diderot's political thought after the Encyclopédie* (The Hague: Nijhoff, 1973). See also the essays in Peter France and Anthony Strugnell, eds. *Diderot, les dernières années, 1770–84: Colloque du bicentenaire, 2–5 Septembre 1984 à Edimbourg* (Edinburgh: Edinburgh University Press, 1985).

10. Rousseau criticizes the universal dimension of Diderot's account of the general will in what has come to be known as the "Geneva Manuscript", an early draft of *Du Contrat Social*. See Rousseau, *The Social Contract and other later political writings*, 153–59. For an account of Diderot's influence (both positive and negative) upon Rousseau's theory of the general will, see Robert Wokler, "The influence of Diderot on the political theory of Rousseau: Two aspects of a friendship", *Studies on Voltaire and the Eighteenth Century*, 132 (1975): 55–111. See also Jacques Proust, "La contribution de Diderot à l'Encylopédie et les théories du droit naturel", *Annales Historiqes de la Revolution Française* (1963): 257–86. For a comprehensive history of the concept of the general will in modern French religious and political thought, see Patrick Riley, *The General Will Before Rousseau* (Princeton: Princeton University Press, 1986).

11. The *Réfutation suivie de l'ouvrage d'Hélvetius intitulé L'Homme* (see Diderot, *Oeuvres Philosophiques*, ed. P. Vernière [Paris: Garnier, 1956]) is a work that most clearly marks his split with materialist philosophy, which was further deepened by the increasing humanism in later works, including parts of the *Supplément* and especially his contributions to the *Histoire*. See D. C. Creighton, "Man and Mind in Diderot and Helvétius", *Publications of the Modern Language Association* (1956): 705-24. Diderot's heightened commitment to humanistic concepts and principles in his later thought may have aided the development not only of his anti-imperialist thought, but also of his increasingly tolerant and inclusive arguments about Jews. On the latter subject, see Leon Schwartz, *Diderot and the Jews* (Rutherford: Fairleigh Dickinson University Press, 1981).

12. Cf. Lester G. Crocker, "Diderot and the Idea of Progress", *Romanic Review* (1938): 151-59.

13. On the idea of customary moralities in Diderot, see Arthur M. Wilson, "The concept of '*moeurs*' in Diderot's social and political thought" in *The Age of Enlightenment: Studies presented to Theodore Bestermann*, ed. W. H. Barber (Edinburgh: Oliver & Boyd, 1967), 188-199.

14. The European discourse about the relationship among travel, commerce, and the rights of hospitality can be traced to the pre-Socratics as well as to the classical epics; as Anthony Pagden has argued, the right to hospitality is tacitly invoked in Virgil's *Aeneid*, and it reemerges crucially in the early modern theological debates about communication and the interaction of peoples abroad in light of the conquest of the New World. As I will show in chapter 5, Immanuel Kant subverted the traditionally imperialist tendencies of such arguments by using the idea of cosmopolitan right (a right to hospitality) to attack European imperialism. See Anthony Pagden, "Stoicism, Cosmopolitanism, and the Legacy of European Imperialism", *Constellations*, 7, no. 1 (March 2000), 3-22.

15. On this theme of travel and empire, see Pagden, *European Encounters with the New World*, 156-69.

16. Cf. Book XI, chapter 1: "We have seen immense countries invaded and laid waste; their innocent and peaceful inhabitants either massacred or loaded with chains; a dreadful solitude established upon the ruins of a numerous population; ferocious usurpers destroying one another, and heaping their dead bodies upon those of their victims."

17. On the distinction between active and passive injustice, and between misfortune and injustice, see Judith N. Shklar, *The Faces of Injustice* (New Haven: Yale University Press, 1990), chapter 2.

18. See Boyd Stanley Schlenther, "Religious Faith and Commercial Empire" and Patrick K. O'Brien, "Inseparable Connections: Trade, Economy, Fiscal State, and the Expansion of Empire, 1688-1815" in *The Oxford History of the British Empire*, vol. 2, *The Eighteenth Century*, ed. P. J. Marshall, respectively 128-50, 53-77 (Oxford: Oxford University Press, 1998).

19. The classic study of modern intellectual history along these lines remains Albert Hirschman, *The Passions and the Interests: Political Arguments for Capitalism before Its Triumph* (Princeton: Princeton University Press, 1977), recently republished in a twentieth anniversary edition with a foreword by Amartya Sen.

20. In German, such shades of meaning can be made explicit, as with *Verkehr*

and *Wechselwirkung*, which are both generally translated into English as *commerce*. Thus, as we will further see in chapter 5, Immanuel Kant moves between the two terms, sometimes using *Verkehr* (a term that he sometimes uses to denote contract, trade, or market-based interactions) and other times drawing upon the broader *Wechselwirkung* to indicate the communicative and interactive aspects of commerce. Politically, such nuances allowed Kant both to attack the injustices of imperialism as the horrid practices of "the commercial states of our part of the world", while also celebrating the future potential of the "spirit of commerce" in fostering peace among nations, a spirit also more narrowly described by Kant at one point as "the power of money" (Immanuel Kant, *Kants gesammelte Schriften, herausgegeben von der Preussischen Akademie der Wissenschaften zu Berlin* [Berlin: Walter de Gruyter, 1902–], 8:358; 8:368). Kant's use of the Latin *commercium* as well as its German offshoots is foreshadowed (and indeed may have been influenced) by Diderot's varied understanding of the concept of commerce in the *Histoire*.

21. Montesquieu, *The Spirit of the Laws* [1748], Book V, chapter 6, on the "spirit of commerce". Montesquieu was well aware of many of the injustices of imperial rule, although he was not a thoroughgoing opponent of European imperialism in the manner of Diderot. It should also be noted that, in *The Spirit of the Laws*, Montesquieu could display a nuanced sense of both the benefits and the potential costs, sometimes quite severe, in terms of disorder and inequality, of commerce. Thus, while he is still primarily remembered along these lines as a celebrant of commerce, he may well be more accurately placed with thinkers such as Diderot, aware of both the promise and the perils of modern commerce, though perhaps without quite the same level of ambivalence that we find in the *Histoire*.

22. In Book VII, chapter 24, Diderot paraphrases Cassiodorus, the sixth-century historian and monk, to make a related argument: "To acquire gold by sacrificing men is a crime. To go in search of it across the perils of the sea is a folly. To amass it by corruption and vices is base. The only profits that are just and honest are those that are acquired without injury to any person; and we never can possess, without remorse, what we have obtained at the expense of other men's happiness."

23. Cf. Immanuel Kant: "China and Japan (*Nipon*), which had given such guests a try, have therefore wisely [placed restrictions on them], the former allowing them access but not entry [*den Zugang, aber nicht den Eingang*], the latter even allowing access to only a single European people, the Dutch, but excluding them, like prisoners, from community with the natives" (Kant, *Kants gesammelte Schriften*, 8:359).

24. Cf. Book XIX, chap. 15: "The insatiable thirst for gold has given birth to the most infamous and atrocious of all trades, that of slaves. People speak of crimes against nature and they do not cite slavery as the most horrific. The majority of European nations are soiled by it, and a vile self-interest has stifled in human hearts all the feelings we owe to our fellow humans."

25. See C.L.R. James, *The Black Jacobins: Toussaint L'Ouverture and the San Domingo Revolution*, 2nd rev. ed. ([1938] New York: Vintage, 1963), 24–25, 171, 250. Diderot's famous passage was a revision of an earlier contribution to

the 1774 edition that had prophesied a "Black Spartacus". Diderot's contribution for the 1780 edition closely paraphrased an anti-imperialist passage in Sebastien Mercier's popular novel, *L'An 2440*, in which an eighteenth-century Frenchman wakes up to find himself in the year 2440. In a Paris square, he sees a statue of a black 'liberator'; the pedestal describes the figure as the man who liberated the New World from European oppression, at which the Frenchman cries in joy. See Yves Benot, *Diderot: De l'athéisme à l'anticolonialisme* (Paris: François Maspero, 1970), 212–15.

26. For instance, later in Book XI, chap. 24, Diderot writes in the voice of a slave who addresses slaveowners and the defenders of slavery: "Men or demons, whoever you are, do you dare to justify the attacks on my independence by the law of the strongest? What! The person who wants to make me a slave is not guilty, but is making use of his rights? What are these rights? Who has given them such a sacred character that they can silence my rights? By nature I have the right to defend myself; by nature you do not have the right to attack me. If you think that because you are stronger and more clever than me you have authority to oppress me, do not complain if my swift arm tears open your chest to find your heart. Do not complain when you feel, in your cut-up intestines, the taste of death, which I have stirred in with your food. I am stronger or more clever than you; it is your turn to be victim. Now expiate the crime of having been an oppressor."

27. Anatole Feugère, "La Doctrine Révolutionnaire de Raynal et de Diderot d'après l'*Histoire des Indes*", *Mercure de France* (1913), 498–517.

Chapter Four
Humanity and Culture in Kant's Politics

1. Citations from the *Critique of Pure Reason* refer to the standard 'A' and 'B' pagination, and the quotations are from Immanuel Kant, *Critique of Pure Reason*, trans. Werner S. Pluhar (Indianapolis: Hackett, 1996); I have also consulted Immanuel Kant, *Critique of Pure Reason*, ed. and trans. Allen W. Wood and Paul Guyer (Cambridge: Cambridge University Press, 1998). Citations of Kant's other writings in this and the following chapter are from the standard Prussian Academy edition (volume followed by page number): Immanuel Kant, *Kants gesammelte Schriften, herausgegeben von der Preussischen Akademie der Wissenschaften zu Berlin* (Berlin: Walter de Gruyter, 1902–). Quotations from the *Idea for a Universal History*, *Conjectures on the Beginning of Human History*, and Kant's reviews of Herder's *Ideas* are from Immanuel Kant, *Political Writings*, 2nd ed., ed. Hans Reiss, trans. H. B. Nisbet (Cambridge: Cambridge University Press, 1991). Quotations from *What is Enlightenment?*, the *Groundwork*, *The Critique of Practical Reason*, *Theory and Practice*, *Toward Perpetual Peace*, and *The Metaphysics of Morals* are from Immanuel Kant, *Practical Philosophy*, ed. and trans. Mary Gregor (Cambridge: Cambridge University Press, 1996). Quotations from *Religion Within the Boundaries of Mere Reason* and *The End of All Things* are from Immanuel Kant, *Religion and Rational Theology* (Cambridge: Cambridge University Press, 1997), ed. and trans. Allen W. Wood and George Di Giovanni. Quotations from the *Critique of Judgement* are from Immanuel Kant,

Critique of Judgment, trans. Werner S. Pluhar (Indianapolis: Hackett, 1987); I have also consulted Immanuel Kant, *Critique of the Power of Judgment*, ed. Paul Guyer, trans. Paul Guyer and Eric Matthews (Cambridge: Cambridge University Press, 2000). Quotations from the *Anthropology* are from Immanuel Kant, *Anthropology from a Pragmatic Point of View*, ed. and trans. Mary J. Gregor (The Hague: Martinus Nijhoff, 1974). Quotations from Kant's lectures on ethics are from Immanuel Kant, *Lectures on Ethics*, ed. Peter Heath and J. B. Schneewind, trans. Peter Heath (Cambridge: Cambridge University Press, 1997). At times, I have altered these English language quotations in light of my own translations in order to achieve greater clarity and terminological consistency.

2. I examine Kant's philosophy of history in the final section of this chapter.

3. The background issue in this controversy concerned not only the long-running debates over the status of scriptural truth, but the newly emerging dialogue about race. For Forster, the crucial underlying issue centred on whether humanity derived from a common source or from biologically distinct multiple sources. Forster backed the latter view and held accordingly that Europeans and Africans were members of different species. Kant, for his part, had long thought the multiple origin, multiple species theory absurd; thus, one advantage of critically appropriating Genesis as a narrative of origin rested upon its presentation of a first couple from which *all* humanity derives. For an account of the Kant-Forster debate, see Susan Meld Shell, *The Embodiment of Reason: Kant on Spirit, Generation, and Community* (Chicago: University of Chicago Press, 1996), 191–201; David Bindman, *Ape to Apollo: Aesthetics and the Idea of Race in the 18th Century* (Ithaca: Cornell University Press, 2002), 151–81; and Urs Bitterli, *Die "Wilden" und die "Zivilisierten": Grundzüge einer Geistes- und Kulturgeschichte der europäisch-überseeischen Begegnung* (Munich: Verlag C. H. Beck, 1976), 345–48. For a general survey of Forster's political thought and anthropology, see Frederick Beiser, *Enlightenment, Revolution, and Romanticism: The Genesis of Modern German Political Thought, 1790–1800* (Cambridge: Harvard University Press, 1992), 154–85; see also Russell A. Berman, *Enlightenment or Empire: Colonial Discourse in German Culture* (Lincoln: University of Nebraska Press, 1998), 21–64.

4. See John H. Zammito, *The Genesis of Kant's "Critique of Judgment"* (Chicago: University of Chicago Press, 1992), 207–13.

5. It is ironic, then, that Forster had viewed Kant's essay as a traditional affirmation of Scripture. Kant would later generate enormous controversy with his *Religion within the Boundaries of Mere Reason* (1793). The Prussian state eventually forced Kant to stop lecturing and writing about religion on the grounds that he appeared to doubt the revealed truth of the Scriptures. For a comparative analysis of Kant's and Herder's uses of Genesis, and accordingly of their theories of human nature, see Allen W. Wood, *Kant's Ethical Thought* (Cambridge: Cambridge University Press, 1999), 226–35.

6. I elaborate Kant's account of sociability, especially in relation to his aesthetics and to Rousseau's social theory, in the seventh section of this chapter.

7. In a footnote to the *Religion* (published four years earlier), the "faculty of desire" includes actual or potential desires for objects that are not consciously chosen or affirmed in any respect. Clearly, by the time of *The Metaphysics of Morals*, Kant had settled on a slightly different and narrower conception of this term.

8. Here I am in agreement with Frederick Neuhouser, *Fichte's Theory of Subjectivity* (Cambridge: Cambridge University Press, 1990), 146.

9. I later discuss the natural predispositions related to desire and freedom that Kant identifies in the *Religion*.

10. To be sure, Kant's delineation of the transformation of antecedent values in the *Conjectures* remains underspecified. His examples usually focus more on creation than on the reception of inherited values and practices because of the artificiality of the situation he discusses—a world in which values must be created de novo. Later, I examine moments in which Kant theorizes the inheritance and transformation of antecedent values. Kant was attuned to the power of inherited traditions and the social forms they took in everyday life, and his concept of 'enlightenment' is meant precisely to subject the traditions within which humans live to critical inquiry, rather than to accept them (and their possible injustices) passively. On the whole, while Herder's concept of *Bildung* offers a more detailed discussion of *cultural* transformation, Herder and Kant in fact develop rather similar insights along these lines.

11. In the *Conjectures*, humans' social nature appeared to be a necessary assumption for a normative understanding of human beings; in the *Religion*, it appears necessary for the purposes of discussing the constitutive aspects of human beings with regard to "the faculty of desire and the exercise of the power of choice." I return later to the concept of sociability in Kant's thought.

12. Henry E. Allison, *Kant's Theory of Freedom* (Cambridge: Cambridge University Press, 1990), 189. See also Lewis White Beck, "Kant's Two Conceptions of the Will in Their Political Context", in *Kant & Political Philosophy: The Contemporary Legacy* (New Haven: Yale University Press, 1993), 38–49.

13. See also *The Metaphysics of Morals*: "The faculty of desire whose inner determining ground, hence even what pleases it [*selbst das Belieben*], lies within the subject's reason is called the will [*Wille*]. . . . The will [*Wille*] itself, strictly speaking, has no determining ground; insofar as it can determine choice, it is instead practical reason itself." (6:213) See Yirmiyahu Yovel, "Kant's Practical Reason as Will: Interest, Recognition, Judgment, Choice". *Review of Metaphysics*, 52, no. 2 (1998): 267–94.

14. Rather, the latter view of humanity is meant to provide a regulative ideal for our moral judgements and can thus be used to counteract the injustices and oppressions that can arise from the former view of humanity, from the use of our cultural agency.

15. For Kant, the concept of *Kultur* is by no means "completely asocial", as some commentators have suggested. See, for instance, Raymond Geuss, "Kultur, Bildung, Geist", in *Morality, Culture, and History: Essays on German Philosophy* (Cambridge: Cambridge University Press, 1999), 33.

16. I refer to this kind of society here as 'modern', but, as I show later, the complex (and oppressive) cultural life that Kant discusses appears to refer to any settled, agriculturally based society, including presumably premodern settled societies (but not, for instance, hunting societies or nomadic/pastoral societies, which are Kant's two other broad categories of peoples).

17. I discuss later the effects of this dual use of the term 'culture' on Kant's understanding of non-European hunting and pastoral peoples.

18. For the concept of skill, see also the *Anthropology*, 7:323.

19. Translation by Allen Wood in Kant, *Practical Philosophy*, xvii.

20. See Allen W. Wood, general introduction to Kant, *Practical Philosophy*; Richard L. Velkley, *Freedom and the End of Reason: On the Moral Foundation of Kant's Critical Philosophy* (Chicago: University of Chicago Press, 1989), 61–88; and Beiser, *Enlightenment, Revolution, and Romanticism*, 32–36. See also Shell, *The Embodiment of Reason*, 81–87; and J. B. Schneewind, *The Invention of Autonomy: A History of Modern Moral Philosophy* (Cambridge: Cambridge University Press, 1998), 487–92. The classic analysis of Rousseau's impact on Kant is Ernst Cassirer, "Kant and Rousseau", in *Rousseau, Kant, Goethe: Two Essays*, trans. James Gutmann, Paul Oskar Kristeller, and John Herman Randall, Jr. (Princeton: Princeton University Press, 1945), 1–60.

21. In an incisive essay, Christine Korsgaard notes that Kant sometimes uses 'humanity' to refer to our personality. But in those cases, she argues, 'humanity' simply refers to our *perfected* ability to set purposes. This implies that the usage of humanity as personality is *simply* a perfected variant of the concept of humanity as cultural agency. My discussion above will show in what sense this is true for Kant, but this nevertheless elides what I contend are the two clearly distinguishable concepts of humanity in Kant's thought. As I argue above, the sense of a dignified humanity in Kant is a *distinct* conception of humanity that draws upon a *different* account of practical reason and freedom than that of cultural agency, and thus is not *simply* a version, perfected or otherwise, of our cultural agency. See Christine M. Korsgaard, "Kant's Formula of Humanity", in *Creating the Kingdom of Ends* (Cambridge: Cambridge University Press, 1996), 114. See also Korsgaard, *The Sources of Normativity* (Cambridge: Cambridge University Press, 1996), 122. Cf. Thomas E. Hill, Jr., *Dignity and Practical Reason* (Ithaca: Cornell University Press, 1992), 38–57; and Mary Gregor, *Laws of Freedom* (New York: Barnes & Noble, 1963), 168–69.

22. The further question, of course, is whether the very idea of human dignity, or the fundamental moral principle ('the categorical imperative') that we should respect the humanity in our persons, can be philosophically justified (that is, rationally proven, or given a solid foundation). I have not dealt with this question in this chapter, given that I have focused instead on elucidating Kant's understanding of these claims, reconstructing the social and political concerns that help give rise to them, and explaining how they inform his attitudes toward culture, imperialism, and his practical philosophy in general. Although I cannot argue the point here, my contention along these lines is that the question is not amenable to rational justification in any way that would avoid either a dogmatic assertion or a circular argument (the results, in my view, of Kant's two attempts to offer such justifications in the *Critique of Practical Reason* and *Groundwork* part III respectively). Much of Kant's approach, however, fits within the critical strictures within which he attempts to philosophize—his approach does not allow him to (and thus he does not) support the idea of human dignity with an authoritative appeal to God (or of some particular religious doctrine or revealed truth), to the fundamental organization of the natural world (or its intrinsic ends or purposes), to a rationally divinable meaning or end of history, or to theoretical reason (to a clear and distinct intuition of a moral framework or natural laws themselves). All that remains, for Kant, is (1) our varied experience on the one hand, which he saw as

the realm of our distinctive cultural agency, but also as the largely exploitative and oppressive social reality that gives rise (in his view) to the need for a concept of dignity in the first place, and (2) practical reason on the other. Kant's much discussed and criticized 'fact of reason' argument in the second *Critique* ultimately consists of a leap of rational or moral faith, one that may well be dogmatic, although it should be noted that it is a leap taken for what Kant understood to be humane and egalitarian purposes. In this sense, Kant's justification strategy for the ethical touchstone of his practical philosophy has much in common with the relevant arguments by Diderot about the general will of humanity and by Herder about the moral understanding and ideal of *Humanität*.

23. In the *Anthropology*, Kant notes that "the character of the [human] species" consists, first of all, in a "technical predisposition" or "predisposition for skill" that make humans "fit for manipulating things not in one particular way but in any way whatsoever, and so for using reason". Kant contends accordingly that the "characterization of man as a rational animal is already present in the form and organization of the human hand". Related to this, however, is the "pragmatic predisposition" which consists in "using other men skilfully for his purposes". (7:322, 323) Thus, our cultural agency is often bound up, in Kant's view, with our use as means for others' ends.

24. See 6:462.

25. I use 'metaphysical' here in the generic sense in which it is often deployed critically, whereby it refers to an affirmation of essences (the essential properties of things) or to grand cosmological realities.

26. See B xvi.

27. Kant writes that "although to the beings of sense there correspond beings of the understanding and there may indeed be beings of the understanding to which our sensible power of intuition has no reference whatsoever, yet our concepts of understanding, as mere forms of thought for our sensible intuition, do not in the least extend to them." (A253)

28. Perhaps one of Kant's more successful metaphors is his description of critical philosophy surveying a territory with grand ambitions, only to discover that it is a small island (and one that we cannot even know objectively, for Kant even denies objective knowledge of space and time). This is an "island . . . surrounded by a vast and stormy ocean, where illusion properly resides and many fog banks and much fast-melting ice feign new-found lands. This sea incessantly deludes the seafarer with empty hopes as he roves [*schwärmen*, also 'to rave', 'be fanatic'; religious and philosophical zealots are often castigated in Kant's writings as *Schwärmer*] through his discoveries, and thus entangles him in adventures that he can never relinquish, nor ever bring to an end." (A 235 / B 295) On the unknowability of noumena, see Rae Langton, *Kantian Humility: Our Ignorance of Things in Themselves* (Oxford: Oxford University Press, 1998), 15–47.

29. Even in the *Critique of Practical Reason*, where Kant makes his strongest truth claim about the moral law, the presumed unconditioned (and dignifying) aspect of ourselves is still not *understood*; the former vacuum of the unconditioned is filled only with a concept of our autonomy that is merely *practically* valid, but not theoretically knowable.

30. Frederick Beiser rightly notes that the question of "why . . . metaphysics

seem[ed] a necessity after Kant had declared it an impossibility in 1780" is "the central one for understanding the rise of post-Kantian idealism at the beginning of the nineteenth century." (Beiser, *The Fate of Reason: German Philosophy from Kant to Fichte* [Cambridge: Harvard University Press, 1987], 326.) On the appropriation of Kant's critical philosophy by thinkers who jettisoned the modesty of Kant's theories in favour of grander philosophical systems (which were often touted to be 'Kantian' systems of thought) and the impact that this had on later thinkers, such as Hegel, see Karl Ameriks, *Kant and the Fate of Autonomy: Problems in the Appropriation of the Critical Philosophy* (Cambridge: Cambridge University Press, 2000).

31. The Latin *cultura* refers to tending or cultivation, very often to the tending or cultivation of crops (agri-culture). Revealingly, the *OED* (2nd ed.) shows that the related Latin *culter* is the source of the English word coulter (or colter): the blade of a plough whose vertical cut in the soil "is then sliced horizontally by the share."

32. I discuss at length Kant's sociological distinction among hunting, pastoral, and agrarian peoples in the following chapter.

33. As Kant writes in the "Critique of Aesthetic Judgement", "That the ability to communicate one's mental state, even if this is only the state of one's cognitive powers, carries a pleasure with it, could easily be established (empirically and psychologically) from man's natural propensity to sociability. But that would not suffice for our aim here. When we make a judgement of taste, the pleasure we feel is something we require from everyone else as necessary" (5:218).

34. Daniel Gordon, *Citizens Without Sovereignty: Equality and Sociability in French Thought, 1670–1789* (Princeton: Princeton University Press, 1994). My following comments are indebted to this work.

35. While *société* was often used to denote small, informal associations in the seventeenth century, in the eighteenth century it often referred to a kind of community with some permanence, to actual spaces within which social interaction could regularly take place. Moreover, words like *social*, *sociabilité*, and *sociable* were little used in seventeenth-century French writings. Gordon's examination of the ARTFL database (the Project for American Research on the Treasury of the French Language, which maintains a large database on French literature and philosophy) shows that uses of *social* jump from 8 (in the seventeenth century) to 838 in the eighteenth century; for *sociabilité*, 0 to 66; for *sociable*, 16 to 222. While some seventeenth-century French political theorists of absolutism, such as Bossuet, argued that humans were naturally sociable, only with later thinkers like Pufendorf and, especially, *philosophes* like Diderot, does one find a defence of a relatively self-sustaining social sphere. See Gordon, *Citizens Without Sovereignty*, 53 and, more generally, 3–8, 43–85.

36. Kant, *Political Writings*, 220. Cf. 5:378. As Bhikhu Parekh well notes, "in the wrong hands" such comments by themselves could have dangerous, even "murderous", implications. These passages, however, do not substantiate the view, as I have shown and will continue to show in this and the following chapter, that for Kant "nature represented variety, reason uniformity, and *qua* rational beings, the good life was the same for all." (Parekh, *Rethinking Multiculturalism: Cultural Diversity and Political Theory* [Cambridge: Harvard University Press, 2000], 347, n. 9).

37. Kant was also concerned that Herder relied too uncritically upon ethnographic writings, which often offer directly contradictory characterizations of foreign peoples, in the course of making historical and political arguments. As Kant contends, "as it is, one may prove, if one wishes, from numerous descriptions of various countries . . . that Americans and Negroes are races that have sunk below the level of other members of the species in terms of intellectual abilities—or alternatively, on the evidence of no less plausible accounts, that they should be regarded as equal in natural ability to all the other inhabitants of the world. Thus, the philosopher is at liberty to choose whether he wishes to assume natural difference or to judge everything by the principle *tout comme chez nous*, with the result that all the systems he constructs on such unstable foundations must take on the appearance of ramshackle hypotheses." Kant, *Political Writings*, 217.

38. Similarly, in the *Conjectures*, Kant discusses *Emile* and the *Social Contract* not to endorse any of the arguments therein, but to argue that Rousseau teaches us to be aware of the long and difficult path that lies ahead in reforming our social and political practices and institutions. Kant argues that the two *Discourses*, on the one hand, and *Emile* and the *Social Contract*, on the other, are not "contradictory", for the latter two works attempt to solve the "difficult problem" posed by the first two writings (see 8:115–17).

39. See also 6:306.

40. See also *Critique of Judgement*, 5:433.

41. This is Kant's list of the realms of taste in the *Anthropology*.

42. In one of the most intriguing moments of the "Critique of Aesthetic Judgement", which is rife with moral language, Kant argues at length that judgements concerning beauty are analogous to moral judgements and that aesthetic judgements thereby prepare the ground for morality. "[T]he beautiful", Kant contends, "is the symbol of the morally good". For instance, "[w]e call buildings or trees majestic and magnificent, or landscapes cheerful and gay; even colors are called innocent, humble, or tender, because they arouse sensations in us that are somehow analogous to the consciousness we have in a mental state produced by moral judgements." See Kant's arguments at 5:353–54. On the connections between moral and aesthetic judgments, see Paul Guyer, *Kant and the Claims of Taste*, 2nd ed. (Cambridge: Cambridge University Press, 1997), 312–50; and Samuel Fleischacker, *A Third Concept of Liberty: Judgment and Freedom in Kant and Adam Smith* (Princeton: Princeton University Press, 1999), 23–87.

43. I discuss Kant's concept of cosmopolitan right, which offers the political version of such claims, in the following chapter.

44. This is discussed in a section of the *Doctrine of Virtue* (§§ 34–35) entitled "Sympathetic feeling is generally a duty."

45. For instance, see a number of the essays in Martha Nussbaum, *For Love of Country: Debating the Limits of Patriotism*, ed. Joshua Cohen (Boston: Beacon Press, 1996).

46. "Notes on the lectures of Mr. Kant on the metaphysics of morals" taken by Johann Friedrich Vigilantius, beginning on 14 October 1793.

47. Edmund Burke, *Reflections on the Revolution in France*, ed. J.G.A. Pocock (Indianapolis: Hackett, 1987), 41.

48. See also 6:473. Although this aspect of Kant's ethical thought is not often

appreciated, here we see Kant practising moral judgement in the manner that he himself recommends. Far from formalistically abstracting away from the particularities of the situation, Kant socially and politically contextualizes the practice of beneficence in his day to assess its moral worthiness.

49. See 6:241.

50. This is the Hobbesian side of Kant's theory of justice, as Jeremy Waldron and Richard Tuck have noted (Waldron, "Kant's Positivism" in *The Dignity of Legislation* [Cambridge: Cambridge University Press, 1999], 36–62; and Tuck, *The Rights of War and Peace: Political thought and the international order from Grotius to Kant* [Oxford: Oxford University Press, 1999], 207–14).

51. Cf. Robert Pippin's discussion of Kant's theory of justice, which highlights the political consequences for Kant of treating humanity as an end-in-itself (Pippin, *Idealism as Modernism: Hegelian Variations* [Cambridge: Cambridge University Press, 1997]), 56–91). See also Allen D. Rosen, *Kant's Theory of Justice* (Ithaca: Cornell University Press, 1993), 62–65.

52. Kant asserts repeatedly that the concept of *moral* virtue concerns the ideal of pure ethical practice, acting with the proper (inner) incentives (not for mere personal gain), while the concept of *political* right focuses only on the external conditions of state coercion in order to ensure, for instance, that a law is followed or that a contract is kept. See, for instance, 6:232.

53. See also "What is Enlightenment?" 8:35.

54. John Christian Laursen has incisively probed this "subversive" aspect of Kant's politics, one that he argues is based upon both an incorporation of scepticism and a communicative, open-ended response to it. See Laursen, "Scepticism and Intellectual Freedom: The Philosophical Foundations of Kant's Politics of Publicity", *History of Political Thought*, 10, no. 3 (Autumn 1989): 439–55; and Laursen, "The Subversive Kant: The Vocabulary of 'Public' and 'Publicity'" in *What is Enlightenment? Eighteenth-Century Answers and Twentieth-Century Questions*, ed. James Schmidt (Berkeley: University of California Press, 1996), 253–69.

55. See 19:595–96. For an analysis of Kant's early political thought as revealed in his reflections and in his notes on natural jurisprudence, see Frederick Beiser, *Enlightenment, Revolution, and Romanticism*, 27–36.

56. See 6:341–42. Kant argues: "A powerful ruler in our time [King Louis XVI] therefore made a very serious error in judgement when, to extricate himself from the embarrassment of large state debts, he left it to the people to take this burden on itself and distribute it as it saw fit; for then the legislative authority naturally came into the people's hands, not only with regard to the taxation of subjects but also with regard to the government, namely to prevent it from incurring new debts by extravagance or war. The consequence was that the monarch's sovereignty [*Herrschergewalt*] wholly disappeared (it was not merely suspended) and passed to the people, to whose legislative will the belongings of every subject became subjected."

57. For a collection of speeches given at or presented to the Convention during the trial of King Louis XVI, see Michael Walzer, ed., *Regicide and Revolution*, trans. Marian Rothstein (New York: Columbia University Press, 1992).

58. See Lewis White Beck, "Kant and the Right of Revolution", *Journal of the History of Ideas*, 32 (1971): 411–22.

59. See Allen Wood's introductory essay in Kant, *Religion and Rational Theology*, xvii. See also James Schmidt, "What is Enlightenment? A Question, Its Context, and Some Consequences", in *What is Enlightenment? Eighteenth-Century Answers and Twentieth-Century Questions*, ed. James Schmidt (Berkeley: University of California Press, 1996), especially 6–11.

60. In the preface to *The Conflict of the Faculties*, published in 1798 (after the death of Friedrich Wilhelm II and the dismissal of Wöllner in 1797), Kant printed both this letter and his response to the king. Kant justifies his return to publishing about religion in light of the fact that he made his promise specifically as his king's loyal subject; given that that particular king is now dead, Kant states that he is no longer under any obligation to restrict his activities. See 7:5–11.

61. Beiser, *Enlightenment, Revolution, and Romanticism*, 54.

62. See Moses Mendelssohn, "On the Question: What is Enlightenment?" in *What is Enlightenment? Eighteenth-Century Answers and Twentieth-Century Questions*, ed. James Schmidt, 53–57.

63. See George Cavallar, "Kant's Judgment on Frederick's Enlightened Absolutism", *History of Political Thought*, 14, no. 1 (Spring 1993): 103–32.

64. George Armstrong Kelly, *Idealism, Politics, and History: Sources of Hegelian Thought* (Cambridge: Cambridge University Press, 1969), 139.

65. On the nature of teleological judgements in Kant, see Rudolf A. Makkreel, *Imagination and Interpretation in Kant: The Hermeneutical Import of the Critique of Judgment* (Chicago: University of Chicago Press, 1990), chapters 6 and 7.

66. Joshua Foa Dienstag, *Dancing in Chains: Narrative and Memory in Political Theory* (Stanford: Stanford University Press, 1997), 3.

67. Cf. Kant's observations in the *Religion* about "radical evil" where he notes that violence among the indigenous peoples of the New World and violence of European states seem to suggest the tragic possibility that there is neither a naturally good "so-called" state of nature nor a just and peaceful civilized condition (6:33–34).

68. As Kant writes in *Theory and Practice*, "however uncertain I may always be and remain as to whether something better is to be hoped for the human race, this cannot infringe upon the maxim, and hence upon its presupposition, necessary for practical purposes, that it is practicable." (8:309)

69. In contrast, for a recent example of a reading of Kant's philosophy of history and, accordingly, his politics as Eurocentric, see James Tully, "The Kantian Idea of Europe: Critical and Cosmopolitan Perspectives", in *The Idea of Europe: From Antiquity to the European Union* (Cambridge and Washington, D.C.: Cambridge University Press and Woodrow Wilson Center Press, 2002), 331–58; cf. Anthony Pagden's introductory remarks in this volume, 15–17.

70. See Yirmiyahu Yovel, *Kant and the Philosophy of History* (Princeton: Princeton University Press, 1980), 140–46.

71. It is precisely this view that leads Kant to make deterministic claims such as the following from *Toward Perpetual Peace*: "When I say of nature, it *wills* that this or that happen, this does not mean, it lays upon us a *duty* to do it (for only practical reason, without coercion, can do that) but rather that nature itself does it, whether we will it or not (*fata volentum ducunt, nolentem trahunt* [The Fates

lead the willing, drive the unwilling (Seneca)])." (8:365) The fact that we can *consider* the flow of history as moving toward greater freedom and peace does not create a duty for us to seek this; rather, these goals should be sought because they are morally obligatory (they make it more likely that humans will be treated as ends in themselves, not as mere means). At the same time, working on the *assumption* that "nature" is on our side, whatever our particular choices and actions, gives us the *hope* necessary to work toward such a future. This is the moral psychological claim that underpins and animates Kant's philosophy of history.

Chapter Five
Kant's Anti-imperialism: Cultural Agency and Cosmopolitan Right

1. See *Kants gesammelte Schriften*, 6:387. Kant believed, then, that the powers of understanding are the highest of the human faculties—thus, not the simply physical, nor the simply rational, but the intermediate set of capacities that involve judgement, imagination, and aesthetics, all of which are necessarily informed by experience (i.e., humanity as cultural agency). It is striking that Kant is unwilling to privilege philosophical and scientific investigation (activities made possible largely by the "powers of spirit") as an objectively superior pursuit or to rank order various ways of life. Yet, this is precisely in keeping with what Kant himself implied was the chastening of his former elitism after having read Rousseau in the mid-1760s. Kant indicates, then, the centrality of one particular set of capacities as most distinctively human and, thus, proclaims that these powers are the highest of our faculties. These powers of understanding, however, simply generate a plurality of largely incommensurable ideas, practices, and lives. In other words, proclaiming the powers of the mind to be "highest" does not make one particular way of life superior to any other. As we will see, this is central to Kant's discussion of the diversity of peoples and imperialism.

2. In fact, Kant explicitly combines his understandings of Stoicism and Epicureanism to argue that one's "valiant" commitment to virtue "ought to aim at a frame of mind" that brings "an agreeable enjoyment to life" and that conduces to a generally "cheerful spirit". In contrast, he contends that "monkish ascetics, which from superstitious fear or hypocritical loathing of oneself goes to work with self-torture and mortification of the flesh, is not directed to virtue but rather to fantastically purging oneself of sin by imposing punishments on oneself. Instead of morally *repenting* sins (with a view to improving), it wants to do *penance* by punishments chosen and inflicted by oneself." Such forms of penance, Kant suggests, are simply oppressive acts of self-hatred that drain a moral life of all cheerfulness. In short, then, the body is not a thing to be loathed and punished. There are physical impulses, if not the body itself, which in some situations might lead individuals to violent or cruel acts—with that in mind, Kant argues, one should practice not a 'monkish asceticism', but an "ethical gymnastics" which "consists only in combatting natural impulses sufficiently to be able to master them when a situation comes up in which they threaten morality; hence it makes one valiant and cheerful in the consciousness of one's restored freedom." (6:485)

3. Cf. Georg Wilhelm Friedrich Hegel, *Philosophy of Right*, trans. T. M. Knox (Oxford: Clarendon, 1967), §192.

4. Kant writes that "this is how it is with all actions the motive of which is not the unconditional law of reason (duty) but an end that we have by choice [*willkürlich*] made their basis; for this belongs to the sum of all ends the attainment of which is called happiness, and one action can contribute more, another less to my happiness, and so be better or worse than the other." (8:282)

5. As Kant argues, "I must first be sure that I am not acting against my duty; only afterwards am I permitted to look around for happiness, to the extent that I can unite the state of being happy with that morally (not naturally) good state of mine." (8:283)

6. Kant's use of this juristic term—*res merae facultatis*—refers to the faculty of human choice and negative freedom that he discusses earlier in the *The Metaphysics of Morals*. As I later show, it also provides an illuminating link to his anthropological understanding of, and political judgements about, the diversity of human *groups*. *Res merae facultatis* concerns the cognitive faculty and freedom that constitute humans' distinctiveness, their cultural agency. As I noted earlier, Kant elaborates the relevant "faculty" accordingly: it is the "faculty to do or to refrain from doing as one pleases [*nach Belieben*]." This constitutes what Kant calls "human choice", "a choice that can indeed be affected but not determined by impulses". As he adds shortly thereafter, "*Freedom* of choice is this independence from being *determined* by sensible impulses; this is the negative concept of freedom." (6:213) The domain of this cultural agency is the space, what I have called the cultural space, within which we judge and act diversely—for instance, in our determinations of how and for what purposes we wish to develop ourselves. The standard use of the term *res merae facultatis* is described by Emmerich de Vattel (in his *Law of Nations*, which Kant had read), who writes the following of the "rights" of *merae facultatis*: "there are rights that consist in a simple *power* to do a thing; the Latin term is *iura merae facultatis*, rights unqualified as to their exercise. They are of such a nature that the possessor of them may use or not use them as he thinks fit, being absolutely free from any constraint in that respect, so that acts done in the exercise of these rights are acts of mere free will, which one may or may not do at one's pleasure." (*The Law of Nations or the Principles of Natural Law Applied to the Conduct and to the Affairs of Nations and of Sovereigns*, trans. Charles G. Fenwick [Buffalo: William S. Hein, 1995; originally published in 1758], chapter 8, 41–42.)

7. I emphasize the moral wrongs because Kant often gives special mention to the negative check provided by a categorical imperative as a regulative ideal. At the same time, of course, Kant by no means shies away from providing the positive concepts in light of which such negative judgements are based: most notably, human dignity and freedom. On Kant's use of negative limits to set boundaries for action and cognition in his ethics and epistemology, see Onora O'Neill, "Reason and Politics in the Kantian Enterprise", in *Constructions of Reason: Explorations of Kant's Practical Philosophy* (Cambridge: Cambridge University Press, 1989), especially 22–24.

8. Contrary to common interpretations, Kant believes that partial judgements and actions are *morally* permissible. With regard to helping others, for instance, Kant argues that one can legitimately privilege a friend or a family member in need over a needy distant stranger. Thus, even one who is engaged in a morally

inspired action or practice can privilege, for instance, filial duty over a duty to humanity in general. For the purposes of isolating instances of doing duty for duty's sake, Kant tends to use examples in which individuals act against their self-interest or against the advantage of their kin or friends, but his point in doing so is not to show that helping 'one's own' is immoral, but that it is much easier to determine that one has acted in a morally meritorious way if some sacrifice of one's own interests is involved. Moreover, as I showed in the last chapter, from the perspective of moral psychology, Kant believes that the idea of loving human-ity as a whole, i.e., a cosmopolitan ethos, generates only a very weak moral feel-ing. It is much more likely, he argues, for people to think and to act morally in local settings and with somewhat parochial interests and issues in mind. What is crucial, Kant argues, is that one should participate in such local spheres of life from a larger, humanitarian perspective; *this*, he contends, is not only possible and realistic (from the standpoint of an accurate moral psychology), but also necessary for any progressive ethical, social, and political development to occur.

9. Montesquieu, *The Spirit of the Laws*, 290 (Book 18, chapter 11).

10. See Rousseau, *Oeuvres complètes*, Pléiade ed. (1964), 3:560.

11. See Istvan Hont, "The language of sociability and commerce: Samuel Pu-fendorf and the theoretical foundations of the 'Four-Stages Theory'", in *The Lan-guages of Political Theory in Early-Modern Europe*, ed. Anthony Pagden (Cam-bridge: Cambridge University Press, 1987), 253–76; Christopher J. Berry, *Social Theory of the Scottish Enlightenment* (Edinburgh: University of Edinburgh Press, 1997).

12. See Richard H. Popkin, "The Philosophical Basis of Eighteenth-Century Racism" in *Racism in the Eighteenth Century*, ed. Harold E. Pagliaro (Cleveland: Case Western Reserve University Press, 1973), 245–62; Nicholas Hudson, "From 'Nation' to 'Race': The Origin of Racial Classification in Eighteenth-Cen-tury Thought", *Eighteenth-Century Studies*, 29, no. 3 (1996): 247–64; Robert Bernasconi, "Who Invented the Concept of Race? Kant's Role in the Enlighten-ment Construction of Race", in *Race*, ed. Robert Bernasconi (Oxford: Blackwell, 2001); Pierre Pluchon, *Nègres et juifs au XVIIIe siècle: Le racisme au siècle des lumiéres* (Paris: Tallandier, 1984). More generally, see also the essays in Peter Hulme and L. J. Jordanova, eds., *The Enlightenment and Its Shadows* (New York: Routledge, 1990). For an extensive historical and philosophical argument that the category of race is not only historically contingent, but both conceptually confused and scientifically implausible as an account of human diversity, see K. Anthony Appiah, "Race, Culture, Identity: Misunderstood Connections", *The Tanner Lectures on Human Values*, vol. 17, ed. Grethe B. Peterson (Salt Lake City: University of Utah Press, 1996), 51–136. On the need for political theorists to develop a critical theory of race in light of the importance of race in the histori-cal development of modern philosophy, see Thomas McCarthy, "Political Philos-ophy and the Problem of Race", in *Die Öffentlichkeit der Vernunft und die Ver-nunft der Öffentlichkeit*, ed. K. Günther and L. Wingert (Frankfurt: Suhrkamp Verlag, 2001).

13. Emmanuel Chukwudi Eze, ed., *Race and the Enlightenment: A Reader* (Oxford: Blackwell, 1997), 47.

14. David Hume, *Essays: Moral, Political, and Literary*, rev. ed., ed. Eugene F.

Miller (Indianapolis: Liberty Fund, 1987), 629–30. Hume was criticized for this remark by contemporaries, such as James Beattie, in *An Essay on the Nature and Immutability of Truth, in Opposition to Sophistry and Skepticism* (1770), who argued that past pronouncements of this kind by Aristotle to legitimate both slavery and imperialism, have been proven wrong. Beattie writes that "many nations" that Aristotle consigned to servitude "have shown themselves equal in genius to the most exalted of humankind." He contends that evidence gathered from travel reports demonstrates that a number of nonwhites are, indeed, "eminent" in "action and speculation", including Africans and [indigenous] Americans, let alone those of "[t]he empires of Peru and Mexico". He also argues that Europeans' achievements are the result not of any intrinsic superiority, but of "accidental discoveries" as well as the inventions of a "few individuals", for which all Europeans cannot take credit (see Eze, ed., *Race and the Enlightenment*, 34–36). Hume revised the footnote in question in 1776, perhaps because of this attack, but only to change "the Negroes, and indeed all other species of [nonwhite] men" to simply "the negroes", an alteration that made his claim less sweeping, but would not have satisfied Beattie, a self-described "friend of humanity". For the revised footnote that was first published posthumously in 1777, see Hume, *Essays*, 208.

15. Eze, ed., *Race and the Enlightenment*, 55.

16. Ibid., 49.

17. Ibid., 62–63.

18. "In the hot countries the human being matures in all aspects earlier, but does not, however, reach the perfection of those in the temperate zones. Humanity is at its greatest perfection in the race of whites. The yellow Indians do have a meagre talent. The Negroes are far below them and at the lowest point are a part of the American peoples. . . . The inhabitant of the temperate parts of the world, above all the central part, has a more beautiful body, works harder, is more jocular, more controlled in his passions, more intelligent than any other race of people in the world. That is why at all points in time these people have educated the others and controlled them with weapons. The Romans, Greeks, the ancient Nordic peoples, Genghis Khan, the Turks, Tamurlaine, the Europeans after Columbus's discoveries, they have all amazed the southern lands with their arts and weapons." (Ibid., 63–64)

19. On occasion, in the *Anthropology* (1798), Kant makes generic references to races in order to refer to the variety of human groups in the world, but without any hierarchical ordering of peoples of the kind that can be found in earlier publications.

20. Shell, *The Embodiment of Reason*, 387. Shell speculates that "[w]hat removes race from the forefront of Kant's anthropological interest may be, in part, a new understanding of human history emphasizing the cultural advances introduced by European peoples." (387) More precisely, in §83 of the *Critique of Judgement*, Kant details the cultural progress of *civilized* societies, not simply European ones, which not only fosters advances in the arts, sciences, and other refined pursuits, but also, in Kant's view, yields harsh inequalities, oppressive injustices, and the variety of evils that he associates with 'civilization'. In any case, my contention is that the more general trend in Kant's later writings that miti-

gates the role of the concept of race is his idea of "culture in general" (not simply a narrower use of culture as the practices and institutions of agricultural peoples, about which he clearly held mixed feelings) and concomitantly the concept of distinctively human freedom, which, I argue later, Kant applies consistently to *all* human peoples, including hunting and pastoralist peoples, in his anti-imperialist political philosophy.

21. This shift in Kant's published writings about human diversity and, incredibly, even his staunch anti-imperialism is not mentioned in many treatments of Kant on race and non-European peoples. See, for instance, Emmanuel Chukwudi Eze, "The Color of Reason: The Idea of 'Race' in Kant's Anthropology", in *Anthropology and the German Enlightenment: Perspectives on Humanity*, ed. Katherine M. Faull (Lewisburg: Bucknell University Press, 1995), 200–241. The most comprehensive and balanced treatment of Kant's writings on race, which considers them alongside the full range of his anthropological, moral, and political writings, is Robert B. Louden, *Kant's Impure Ethics: From Rational Beings to Human Beings* (Oxford: Oxford University Press, 2000).

22. That these two strands of theorizing human diversity seem to coexist in Kant's later thought, if not in his late published writings, is one of the fascinating pardoxes of an intellectual age rich with philosophical tensions. It should not come as a surpirse, however, for the long eighteenth century is the source both of radical anti-slavery and anti-imperialist thinking and of the early development of 'modern' biological sciences, which, of course, included the conceptualization of human races.

23. Kant contends that a study of the similarities among languages can provide clues to the migration patterns of various peoples. He writes, for instance, that "we see peoples whose unity of language enables us to recognize the unity of their descent, such as the Samoyeds on the Arctic Ocean on the one hand and on the other a people of similar language two hundred miles distant in the Altaian Mountains, between whom another, namely a Mongolian people given to horsemanship and hence to war [Kant believed that the horse was the first instrument of war], has thrust itself and so driven the former part of the tribe far away from the latter, into the most inhospitable Arctic regions, where they would certainly not have spread of their own inclination. . . ." He also notes that such links exist between the Lapps of Finland and Hungarians (8:364–65).

24. Kant argues that while serious conflicts still occur even after such separations, the continuing tensions are partly productive, for the threat of outsiders checks the possibility of utterly despotic conditions within both nonsettled and settled societies. Kant's sociological claim is based on his contention that defending one's society against another requires a certain amount of resources and that such wealth cannot be produced without at least a modicum of freedom, presumably of the kind and degree that would permit at least the most basic social interactions and economic activity (8:120).

25. See Barbara Arneil, *John Locke and America: The defence of English colonialism* (Oxford: Clarendon, 1996); James Tully, *An Approach to Political Philosophy: Locke in Contexts* (Cambridge: Cambridge University Press, 1993), 260ff; James Tully, "Aboriginal property and western theory: recovering a middle

ground", *Social Philosophy and Policy*, 11 (1994): 153–80; Pagden, *Lords of All the World*, 76–79.

26. A few pages later, Kant reiterates this argument: "The first working, enclosing, or, in general, transforming of a piece of land can furnish no title of acquisition to it. . . . [W]hoever expends his labor on land that was not already his has lost his pains and toil to who was first." (6:268–69)

27. According to Kant, this is also the ethical idea by which laws of the sea should be understood. Since groups or individuals are incapable of controlling the ocean as a whole, it should remain free for all to use. In contrast, to the extent that coastal waters are capable of being defended, they can be considered part of a people's territory—"for example, as far as a cannon shot can reach no one may fish, haul up amber from the ocean floor, and so forth, along the coast of a territory that already belongs to a certain state." (6:265)

28. Most discussions of Kant's politics treat his account of cosmopolitanism as simply another way of describing his theory of interstate, or international, relations. Such readings accord with some of Kant's generic uses of the term. Ultimately, however, from the mid-1790s onward in works such as *Toward Perpetual Peace* and *The Metaphysics of Morals*, Kant asserts that international right and cosmopolitan right are qualitatively distinct domains of justice. For examples of the more standard reading that tends to conflate Kant's concepts of international and cosmopolitan right, see the essays in an otherwise fine collection, James Bohman and Matthias Lutz-Bachmann, eds., *Perpetual Peace: Essays on Kant's Cosmopolitan Ideal* (Cambridge: MIT Press, 1997).

29. Cf. *Critique of Pure Reason*, B 372–B 374.

30. With regard to past relationships between Europe and Asia, Kant writes that "what the Romans called the Land *of the Sers* was China . . . [and] that silk was brought from there to Europe via *Greater Tibet* (presumably through *Lesser Tibet* and Bukhara, crossing Persia and so forth). This led to numerous reflections on the antiquity of this astonishing state [China] as compared with that of Hindustan, and on its connection with *Tibet* and through this with Japan". Kant goes on to complain that "the ancient community between Europe and Tibet . . . has never been rightly acknowledged" and thus attempts to "make plausible the early commerce of Europe with China across Tibet ([which occurred] perhaps even earlier than with Hindustan)." (8:359–60) See also Jeremy Waldron, "What is Cosmopolitan?" *Journal of Political Philosophy*, 8 (2000): 227–43.

31. Earlier in *The Metaphysics of Morals*, after having defended the "right to emigrate", Kant argues that the state "has the right to encourage immigration and settling by foreigners (colonists), even though his native subjects might look askance at this, provided that their private ownership of land is not curtailed by it." (6:338) This is the nonpejorative sense in which Kant sometimes uses the term "colonist", as a foreigner who settles on a nation's territory by permission of the governing authorities, as opposed to colonists who simply "conquer" other peoples and their territories, which he condemns outright as a result of this theory of cosmopolitan right. Kant also argues that it is unjust for a "defeated state or its subjects" to "lose their civil freedom through the conquest of their country, so that the state would be degraded to a colony and its subjects to bondage"

(6:348). A "colony" that is not manifestly unjust is one that is, in effect, a "province", and so the people has "its own constitution, its own legislation, and its own land, on which those who belong to another state are only foreigners". The "mother state" in such situations possesses executive authority, but the "daughter state . . . still governs itself". Such a hybrid state (*"civitas hybrida"*), for Kant, generally is made up of territories that are close together, and so Kant notes that this is the relationship that "Athens had with respect to various islands and that Great Britain now has with regard to Ireland." (6:348) In the latter case, however, Kant argues in a later passage that Great Britain is engaged in fundamentally violating the most basic rights of the Irish, for it is unjust when "a citizen . . . is excluded from the service of the state and the advantages this brings him because his religion is different from that of the court (as Great Britain has done to the Irish nation)." (6:368)

32. Pagden, *European Encounters with the New World*, 157. While pilgrims were usually respected, Pagden contends that they subjected themselves to the hardship of a long journey "only in order that they may return home purified. Their objective is the return itself, not the journey." (157)

33. Kant's defence of cross-cultural communication and transnational ties, which he uses ultimately as part of an effort to attack European imperialism, was traditionally used as a strategy to *defend* European imperial rule. Kant, therefore, in the course of appropriating the discourse of a right to commerce and communication, which Vitoria had discussed in his celebrated *relectio* on the Amerindians, transformed its traditional political implications. On the pre-Enlightenment uses of commerce and communication in the context of cosmopolitanism and empire, see Pagden, "Stoicism, Cosmopolitanism, and the Legacy of European Imperialism", 3–22. See also the discussion of "natural partnership and communication" in Vitoria, "On the American Indians" (1539) in his, *Political Writings*, 278–84; see also Fichte's version of cosmopolitan right, which was inspired by Kant: J. G. Fichte, *Foundations of Natural Right: According to the Principles of Wissenschaftslehre*, ed. Frederick Neuhouser, trans. Michael Baur (Cambridge: Cambridge University Press, 2000, originally published 1796–97), 332–34.

34. As I explained in the last chapter, such arguments about political progress constitute a *narrative* that Kant creates to convince his readers that such goals are not "chimerical" and that we should therefore work toward realizing them as best we can. They are not meant to be arguments that the world will necessarily work out for the best, and that we can relax and let "nature" do its work, a proposition that Kant rejects, due to both his deep pessimism and his strong belief in the importance of human agency.

35. Cf. Diderot, *Political Writings*, 175: "The Chinese may be bad politicians when they shut us out of their empire, but they are not unjust. Their country has sufficient population, and we [Europeans] are too dangerous as guests." Such similarities in the substance of arguments about empire, the ordering of arguments, and the use of particular examples indicate that Kant's discussion of cosmopolitan right was likely influenced by Diderot's anti-imperialist contributions to Abbé Raynal's widely read *Histoire des deux Indes* (which we know Kant's student, Herder, had read).

36. On some of the Chinese restrictions upon European, and in particular upon Portuguese, voyagers, see Urs Bitterli, *Cultures in Conflict: Encounters between European and Non-European Cultures, 1492–1800*, trans. Ritchie Robertson (Cambridge: Polity Press, 1989), 133–54. For a discussion of the many Japanese restrictions upon Dutch and other European merchants, see Marius B. Jansen, ed., *The Cambridge History of Japan*, vol. 5 (Cambridge: Cambridge University Press, 1989), 87–111.

37. Cf. Diderot, *Political Writings*, 175–76: "Both reason and equity permit the establishment of colonies, but they also mark out the principles from which one must not stray when founding them. . . . Either the country is deserted, or it is partly deserted and partly inhabited, or it is fully inhabited. If it is fully inhabited I can lay legitimate claim only to the hospitality and assistance which one man owes another. . . . If the country is partly deserted and partly occupied, then the deserted part is mine. . . . The forests, rivers and sea-shore are common to us both, unless their exclusive use was necessary to his livelihood. The only other thing he can demand from me is that I should be a peaceful neighbour and that my settlement should in no way threaten him. . . . An uninhabited and deserted country is the only one which can be appropriated. The first well-attested discovery was a capture of legitimate possession."

38. Fritz Medicus, "Kant's Philosophy of History", *Kant-Studien*, 54 (1900): 61–67; quoted in Wood, *Kant's Ethical Thought*, 341, n. 8; for a discussion of post-Enlightenment criticisms of Kant's anti-imperialism, see Georg Cavallar, *Pax Kantiana: Systematisch-historische Untersuchung des Entwurfs 'Zum ewigen Frieden' (1795) von Immanuel Kant* (Vienna: Böhlau Verlag, 1992), 235–44.

39. So prevalent was this view that even outside the framework of social contract thinkers like John Locke (who held famously that "in the beginning all the world was America"), a frequent assumption was that travelling in space to America was equivalent, in some sense, to travelling back in time to view not only Europe's, but humanity's, origins. Adam Ferguson, who criticized the view that New World inhabitants were asocial and purely natural, argued at the same time that a venerable tradition of European thinking about foreign peoples demonstrated that such a technique could provide accurate information of civilized Europe's own past. In *An Essay on the History of Civil Society* (1767), he writes, "Thucydides, notwithstanding the prejudice of his country against the name of *Barbarian*, understood that is was in the customs of barbarous nations [that] he was to study the more ancient manners of Greece." Speaking primarily of Amerindians, Ferguson continues, "It is in their present condition, that we are to behold, as in a mirrour, the features of our own progenitors; and from thence we are to draw our conclusions with respect to the influence of situations, in which, we have reason to believe, our fathers were placed. . . . If, in advanced years, we would form a just notion of our progress from the cradle, we must have recourse to the nursery, and from the example of those who are still in the period of life we mean to describe, take our representation of past manners, that cannot, in any other way, be recalled." (Ferguson, *An Essay on the History of Civil Society*, 80).

40. For a thorough treatment of the relationship between modern conceptions of international relations and theories of 'natural man' in social contract accounts, see Tuck, *The Rights of War and Peace*.

41. Kant argues the following: "According to some accounts, timid Portuguese believed the most beautiful interior parts of Africa to be peopled with [African] cannibals who even fattened humans up for slaughter. However, we should not attach credibility to such fables so easily because experience has taught us that these peoples only slaughter their prisoners of war whom they capture while still alive, and then with great ceremony. . . . Whenever [Europeans] did not know much about the country, someone would say that it was inhabited by cannibals, despite the fact that there are very few of these kinds of people or, even more correctly, none at all." Kant, *Lectures on Physical Geography*, in Eze, ed., *Race and the Enlightenment*, 59.

42. Moreover, as I will explain below, Kant did not seem to believe that hunters and pastoralists are in a position to submit to a civil authority on the model of the *Rechtstaat*; thus, they are not under a categorical duty to leave their condition voluntarily and join civil societies.

43. Cf. 7:320.

44. David Hume, "Of the Original Contract", in *Essays: Moral, Political, and Literary*, 471.

45. See 6:318.

46. In his handwritten notes, Kant writes that the social contract is "not a principle explaining the origin of civil society"; rather, it suggests "how it [a civil society] ought to be." See John Ladd's introduction to Kant's *The Metaphysical Elements of Justice* (Indianapolis: Library of Liberal Arts, 1965), xxx. For my discussion of the hypothetical nature of Kant's social contractarianism, I am particularly indebted to Patrick Riley, *Will and Political Legitimacy: A Critical Exposition of Social Contract Theory in Hobbes, Locke, Rousseau, Kant, and Hegel* (Cambridge: Harvard University Press, 1982), 125–27. For a fuller treatment, see Patrick Riley, *Kant's Political Philosophy* (Totowa, N.J.: Rowman & Littlefield, 1983).

47. Shortly thereafter, Kant explains his use of the terms "leisure" and "labour": "*Pastoral life* is not only leisurely, but also the most reliable means of support, for there is no lack of fodder for animals in a largely uninhabited country. *Agriculture* or the planting of crops, on the other hand, is extremely laborious, subject to the vagaries of climate, and consequently insecure; it also requires permanent settlements, ownership of land, and sufficient strength to defend the latter." (8:118)

48. Kant further expounds on this theme, that the life of agriculture fosters the creation of village communities that then necessitates the establishment of the state, in another key passage in the *Conjectures*: "Where people depend for their livelihood on the cultivation of the soil (and on the planting of trees in particular), they require permanent accommodation; and the defence of such property against all encroachment requires a large number of people who are prepared to assist one another. Hence those who adopted this way of life could no longer live in scattered family units, but had to stick together and set up village communities. . . . [This ultimately] meant that certain steps were taken to establish a civil constitution and the public administration of justice." (8:119)

49. As I have said, the state of nature *is* analogous, in Kant's view, to a non-hypothetical, empirical reality—namely, the international relations of states—but this is not here the issue in question.

Chapter Six
Pluralism, Humanity, and Empire in Herder's Political Thought

1. See Isaiah Berlin, "Herder and the Enlightenment", in *The Proper Study of Mankind*, ed. Henry Hardy and Roger Hausheer (New York: Farrar, Straus and Giroux, 1998), 359–435; Dorinda Outram, *The Enlightenment* (Cambridge: Cambridge University Press, 1995), 77–79; and Parekh, *Rethinking Multiculturalism*, 67–76.

2. On the sources that influenced Herder, which include Raynal's *Histoire*, see Max Rouché, *La philosophie de l'histoire de Herder* (Paris: Publications de la Faculté des Lettres de l'Université de Strasbourg, 1940), 135–84.

3. For an interpretation of Herder's historiography in light of previous theories of history, see Donald R. Kelley, *Faces of History: Historical Inquiry from Herodotus to Herder* (New Haven: Yale University Press, 2000), chapter 9. See also Alexander Gillies, "Herder's Approach to the Philosophy of History", *Modern Language Review*, 35 (1940); and Arthur O. Lovejoy, "Herder and the Enlightenment Philosophy of History", in *Essays in the History of Ideas*, ed. Arthur O. Lovejoy (Baltimore: Johns Hopkins Press, 1948), 166–82.

4. The most conspicuous missing theme is the crucial concept of humanity (*Humanität*), which Herder formulates and develops later in the *Ideas*, as I detail later.

5. Since translations of Herder do not normally include the pagination from German editions of Herder's writings, I have cited available English versions whenever possible, although, for greater fidelity to Herder's German and for conceptual consistency, I have at times altered these translations. My citations from *Yet Another Philosophy of History* are from Johann Gottfried Herder, *J. G. Herder on social and political culture*, ed. and trans. F. M. Barnard (Cambridge: Cambridge University Press, 1969); cited in the text as *SC*. For some of Herder's *Briefe zu Beförderung der Humanität* [*Letters on the Advancement of Humanity*], I have quoted Herder, *On World History: An Anthology*, ed. Hans Adler and Ernest A. Menze, trans. Ernest A. Menze with Michael Palma (London: M. E. Sharpe, 1997); cited in the text as *WH*. For the *Ideas*, I have cited (simply by page number in the text itself) what remains the only comprehensive English translation: Herder, *Outlines of a Philosophy of the History of Man*, trans. T. Churchill (London: J. Johnson, 1800). The standard German edition, which I have consulted for all of Herder's texts that I treat in this chapter, is Herder, *Sämtliche Werke*, 33 vols., ed. Bernard Ludwig Suphan (Berlin: Weidmannsche Buchhandlung, 1877–1913); the volumes that I address are 5 (*Yet Another Philosophy of History*), 13 (*Ideas*, Books I to X), 14 (*Ideas*, Books XI to XX), and 18 (*Letters on the Advancement of Humanity*). Citations of *Briefe* not available in English are from the Suphan edition and are indicated by volume number and page number, in which case the translations are mine.

6. In this respect, Herder's searing dismissal of philosophical generalities bears striking resemblance to Edmund Burke's sometimes traditionalist, though largely reformist, aspersions against political revolutionaries and the currents of philosophy that tend to eschew circumstance in favour of innovation. And, like those of

Burke, Herder's critical arguments are often misjudged as reactionary, whereas both thinkers base their arguments on the view that the social and political reforms that are called upon by self-professed enlightened thinkers and political actors are impeded by their arguments and strategies.

7. See Karl Menges, "Herder and the 'Querelle des Anciens et des Modernes'" in *Eighteenth-Century German Authors and Their Aesthetic Theories*, edited by R. Critchfield and W. Koepke (Columbia, S.C.: Camden House, 1988), 147–83.

8. It is important, then, not to take such deterministic and providential language too literally. See G. A. Wells, "Herder's Determinism", *Journal of the History of Ideas*, 19 (1958): 105–13; Wells, *Herder and After: A Study in the Development of Sociology* (The Hague: Mouton, 1959), 262–69; F. M. Barnard, "Herder's Treatment of Causation and Continuity in History", *Journal of the History of Ideas*, 24 (1963): 197–212.

9. For an example of the latter understanding of Herder's political thought, see Damon Linker, "The Reluctant Pluralism of J. G. Herder", *The Review of Politics*, 62 (2000): 267–93.

10. In addition to the concept of a *Volk*, Herder also writes of diverse national characters (*Nationalcharaktere*) and varying kinds of national happiness (*Nationalglückseligkeit*). As Raymond Geuss and others have noted, Herder (like Kant) does not use the term culture (*Kultur*) in the plural. Culture is part and parcel of humanity itself for Herder (again like Kant); humans are not, in this view, members of different cultures.

11. The fifth part was to have described the history of Europe from the Renaissance to Herder's own time. See Robert T. Clark, *Herder: His Life and Thought* (Berkeley: University of California Press, 1955), 308; F. M. Barnard, *Herder's Social and Political Thought: From Enlightenment to Nationalism* (Oxford: Clarendon, 1965), xix; and Rudolf Haym, *Herder*, vol. 2 (Berlin: Aufbau-Verlag, 1954), 236–48.

12. For a comparative analysis of Herder's and Rousseau's political theories, see F. M. Barnard, *Self-Direction and Political Legitimacy: Rousseau and Herder* (Oxford: Clarendon, 1988), especially 285–321.

13. On this aspect of Herder's thought, see Charles Taylor, "The Importance of Herder", in *Philosophical Arguments* (Cambridge: Harvard University Press, 2000), 79–99; Taylor, *Sources of the Self: The Making of the Modern Identity* (Cambridge: Harvard University Press, 1989), 368–376; Hans Aarsleff, "The Tradition of Condillac: The Problem of the Origin of Language in the Eighteenth Century and the Debate in the Berlin Academy before Herder", in *Studies in the History of Linguistics: Traditions and Paradigms*, ed. D. Hymes (Bloomington: Indiana University Press, 1974), 93–156; and Marc Crépon, *Les géographies de l'esprit: Enquête sur la caractérisation des peuples de Leibniz à Hegel* (Paris: Payot et Rivages, 1996), 131–46.

14. For an example of the concern that Herder's commitment to cultural difference and moral incommensurability might undermine the moral basis of his call for mutual respect, see Pagden, *European Encounters with the New World*, 179–81. Pagden argues that "Herder pushed the notion of incommensurability to the point where the very concept of a single human genus became, if not impossible to achieve, at least culturally meaningless." (180)

15. As Herder writes, "I wish I could extend the signification of the word *humanity*, so as to comprise in it everything I have said thus far on the noble conformity of man to reason and liberty, to finer senses and appetites, to the most delicate yet strong health, to the population and rule of the Earth; for man has not a more dignified word for his destination than what expresses himself, in whom the image of the creator lives imprinted as visibly as it can be here." (98)

16. Friedrich Meinecke, *Historism: The Rise of a New Historical Outlook*, trans. J. E. Anderson, foreword by Sir Isaiah Berlin (London: Routledge & Kegan Paul, 1972), 297. The original German edition, *Die Entstehung des Historismus*, was published in 1959.

17. Herder does not uncritically endorse the value of religion, for he suggests that religions eventually become dogmatic and removed from the spiritual yearnings that first engendered them. Religions are particularly vulnerable to this, Herder argues, because the signs and symbols on which they rely are not grounded in anything perceptible; thus, unlike other institutions, they cannot easily renew themselves because it is difficult, if not impossible, to bring religious signs, symbols, and other "arbitrary characters" into comparison with their referents. Moreover, the religious authorities that are instituted to oversee religious institutions and practices thereby become corrupt as the "signification of symbols" becomes opaque to them and to their adherents (see 252). Nevertheless, Herder argues, "religion alone introduced the first rudiments of civilization and science among all people". In addition, when religion is considered at its best, as a powerful symbol of the universal yearning for profound meaning, self-examination, and spiritual contemplation, it represents "the highest humanity of humankind", that is, the highest ideals that characterize human life as such (103).

18. See Samson B. Knoll, "Herder's concept of *Humanität*" in *Johann Gottfried Herder: Innovator through the ages*, ed. Wulf Koepke (Bonn: Bouvier Verlag Herbert Grundmann, 1982), 9–18.

19. See also pp. 167–168 for a discussion of the nomadic lifestyles of the Kalmuks and Mongols.

20. For a recent example of this argument, see Jared Diamond, *Guns, Germs, and Steel: The Fates of Human Societies* (New York: Norton, 1998), 157–75.

21. On the anti-statist elements of Herder's political thought, see F. M. Barnard, *Herder's Social and Political Thought*, 62–71.

22. Such arguments were popular among eighteenth-century critics of European chauvinism. For example, see the similar attack on David Hume's derogatory remarks about "Negroes" by the eighteenth-century thinker James Beattie (*An Essay on the Nature and Immutability of Truth, in Opposition to Sophistry and Skepticism* [1770]) in *Race and the Enlightenment*, 34–37.

23. Herder's thought, of course, was often not interpreted this way by succeeding generations of scholars and political actors. See G. A. Wells, *Herder And After*, 189–205; and Robert Reinhold Ergang, *Herder and the Foundations of German Nationalism* (New York: Columbia University Press, 1931).

24. See Edgar B. Schick, *Metaphorical organicism in Herder's early works: A study of the relation of Herder's literary idiom to his world-view* (The Hague: Mouton, 1971).

25. Anthony J. La Vopa, "Herder's *Publikum*: Language, Print, and Sociability

in Eighteenth-Century Germany," *Eighteenth-Century Studies*, 29, no. 1 (1996): 5–24.

26. On Hamann's thought, see Isaiah Berlin, *The Magus of the North: J. G. Hamann and the Origins of Modern Nationalism* (New York: Farrar, Straus & Giroux, 1993).

27. Beiser, *Enlightenment, Revolution, and Romanticism*, 189–97. Cf. Emil Adler, *Herder und die Deutsche Aufklärung* (Frankfurt: Europa Verlag, 1968), 53–68.

28. A recent study that comprehensively examines the earlier philosophical relationship between Kant and Herder is John H. Zammito, *Kant, Herder, and the Birth of Anthropology* (Chicago: University of Chicago Press, 2002).

Chapter Seven
Conclusion: The Philosophical Sources and Legacies of Enlightenment Anti-imperialism

1. Robert Wokler, "Projecting the Enlightenment", in *After MacIntyre*, ed. John Horton and Susan Mendus (Notre Dame: University of Notre Dame, 1994), 126.

2. Alasdair MacIntyre, *Whose Justice? Which Rationality?* (Notre Dame: University of Notre Dame Press, 1988), 6. Cf. MacIntyre, *After Virtue: A Study in Moral Theory*, 2nd ed. (Notre Dame: University of Notre Dame Press, 1984; 1981), 33–34: "In many pre-modern, traditional societies it is through his or her membership in a variety of social groups that the individual identifies himself or herself and is identified by others. I am brother, cousin and grandson, member of this household, that village, this tribe. *These are not characteristics that belong to human beings accidentally, to be stripped away in order to discover 'the real me'.* They are part of my substance, defining partially at least and sometimes wholly my obligations and my duties. Individuals inherit a particular space within an interlocking set of social relationships; lacking that space, they are nobody, or at best a stranger or an outcast." (emphasis added)

3. On this point, cf. Stephen Toulmin's arguments in *Cosmopolis*. As part of what Toulmin takes to be the radical transformation in philosophical and scientific discourse that occurred in the seventeenth century, thinkers began to favour as forms of practical knowledge, we are told, the written, the universal, the general, and the timeless, as opposed to the oral, the particular, the local, and the timely. About the study of foreign peoples, he asserts that "[w]hen modern philosophers dismissed ethnography and history as irrelevant to truly 'philosophical' inquiry, they excluded from their enterprise a whole realm of questions that had previously been recognized as legitimate topics of inquiry. From then on, *abstract axioms were in, concrete diversity was out.*" With reference to the eighteenth century, Toulmin notes that "[t]he Enlightenment philosophers" accepted this intellectual shift "in its entirety", though they also criticized some of the restrictive tendencies of the modern nation-state and inspired revolutionaries and others to attack some of the "inequalities built into the 'modern' scaffolding" (Toulmin, *Cosmopolis: The Hidden Agenda of Modernity* [Chicago: University of Chicago Press, 1990], 33, 142, 168, respectively).

4. On the larger (and dubious) connections that some scholars have made between eighteenth-century political thought and 'modernity' or modern life in general, see James Schmidt, "What Enlightenment Project?" *Political Theory*, 28, no. 6 (December 2000): 734–57.

5. John Gray, "After the New Liberalism", *Social Research*, 61, no. 3 (Fall 1994): 726; reprinted in John Gray, *Enlightenment's Wake : Politics and Culture at the Close of the Modern Age* (New York : Routledge, 1995).

6. John Gray, "After the New Liberalism", 726.

7. See his discussion of the primary characteristics of 'the Enlightenment' in John Gray, *Isaiah Berlin* (Princeton: Princeton University Press, 1996), 138–40.

8. Pocock, *Barbarism and Religion*, 1:5.

9. It is an open question whether this has in fact been resisted even in some of the most sophisticated accounts of eighteenth-century philosophy and political thought. Does Ernst Cassirer's classic description of the *Geist* of Enlightenment, for example, constitute an attempt to articulate the vague and indeterminate self-understanding of a carefully delineated group of thinkers, however controversial and contestable this might be, or does it dogmatically reify a concrete, more substantial set of arguments that is then projected on to an entire intellectual age? The former question will admit of multiple plausible answers, of which Cassirer's can only be one, but my point here is that the latter is a qualitatively distinct intellectual agenda, one that carries far greater (and potentially counter-productive) risks in its treatment of a diverse philosophical era. See Ernst Cassirer, *The Philosophy of the Enlightenment*, trans. Fritz C. A. Koelln and James P. Pettegrove (Princeton: Princeton University Press, 1951; originally, *Die Philosophie der Aufklärung* [Tübingen, 1932]), 3–36.

10. Cf. Peter Gay, *The Enlightenment: The Rise of Modern Paganism* (New York: Norton, 1977; 1966), 3–19; David Carrithers, "The Enlightenment Science of Society", in *Inventing Human Science: Eighteenth-Century Domains* (Berkeley: The University of California Press, 1995), 232–70; and Israel, *Radical Enlightenment*, preface.

11. For example, see the vigorous arguments by Bhikhu Parekh, "Moral philosophy and its anti-pluralist bias", in *Philosophy and Pluralism*, ed. David Archard (Cambridge: Cambridge University Press, 1996), Royal Institute of Philosophy Supplement 40, 117–34.

12. Judith N. Shklar, "Politics and the Intellect", in *Political Thought and Political Thinkers*, ed. Stanley Hoffmann (Chicago: University of Chicago Press, 1998), 94.

13. The diversity of Enlightenments that recent scholars have attempted to classify include (among many others) a variety of national Enlightenments, the 'high' Enlightenments of the *philosophes* and *Aufklärer*, and the 'low' Enlightenments of pamphleteers and pornographers, as well as moderate and radical Enlightenments, early and late Enlightenments, Arminian religious Enlightenments, and radically materialist Spinozist Enlightenments. See Roy Porter and Mikulás Teich, eds., *The Enlightenment in National Context* (Cambridge: Cambridge University Press, 1981); Robert Darnton, *The Literary Underground of the Old Regime* (Cambridge: Harvard University Press, 1982); Margaret C. Jacob, *The Radical Enlightenment: Pantheists, Freemasons and Republicans* (London: Allen

& Unwin, 1981); Pocock, *Barbarism and Religion*, vol. 1; and Israel, *Radical Enlightenment*.

14. Cf. Graeme Garrard, "Rousseau, Maistre, and the Counter-Enlightenment", *History of Political Thought*, 15, no. 1 (1994): 97–120.

15. Michel Foucault, "What is Enlightenment?" in *The Foucault Reader*, ed. Paul Rabinow, trans. Catherine Porter (New York: Pantheon, 1984), 45.

16. On the general issues raised by such a question, see Martin Hollis, "Is Universalism Ethnocentric?" in *Multicultural Questions*, ed. Christian Joppke and Steven Lukes (Oxford: Oxford University Press, 1999), 27–43; and Seyla Benhabib, " 'Nous' et 'les Autres': The Politics of Complex Cultural Dialogue in a Global Civilization" in *Multicultural Questions*, 44–62.

17. Thus, my arguments in this section are confined to the strand of anti-imperialist political theory that I have elaborated in the previous chapters. Some of what I will argue will not apply entirely to other currents of eighteenth-century anti-imperialist thought, those for instance that argued against European imperialism partly upon commercial, economic grounds (e.g., Adam Smith) or anti-imperialist philosophies that were premised explicitly upon a nonimperial civilizing process (e.g., Condorcet). On Adam Smith, see Donald Winch, *Classical Political Economy and Colonies* (Cambridge: Harvard University Press, 1965), chapter 2; on Condorcet, see Jean Starobinski, "The Word *Civilization*" in *Blessings in Disguise; or, The Morality of Evil*, trans. Arthur Goldhammer (Cambridge: Harvard University Press, 1993), 1–35.

18. *Histoire des deux Indes*, Book IX, chapter 20.

19. *Histoire des deux Indes*, Book XI, chapter 24.

20. As Paul Hazard notes, in many respects, the rise of travel literature led European thinkers "from a world of intellectual stability into one of movement and flux." (Hazard, *The European Mind: 1680–1715*, trans. J. Lewis May [Cleveland: Meridian, 1963], 28.) See also Henry Vyverberg, *Human Nature, Cultural Diversity, and the French Enlightenment* (Oxford: Oxford University Press, 1989), 88–97.

21. David Hume, *An Enquiry Concerning the Principles of Morals*, in *Enquiries Concerning Human Understanding and Concerning the Principles of Morals*, ed. L. A. Selby-Bigge, rev. P. H. Nidditch (Oxford: Clarendon, 1975), 174.

22. Georges Gusdorf, *L'avènement des sciences humaines au siècle des lumières* (Paris: Payot, 1973). See also the essays in Christopher Fox, Roy Porter and Robert Wokler, eds., *Inventing Human Science: Eighteenth-Century Domains* (Berkeley: University of California Press, 1995); and Sergio Moravia, "The Enlightenment and the Sciences of Man", *History of Science*, 18 (1980): 247–68.

23. John Locke, *An Essay concerning Human Understanding*, ed. Peter H. Nidditch (Oxford: Clarendon Press, 1975), 454. Further pagination from this edition is noted in parentheses in the main text.

24. See Lewis Hanke, *Aristotle and the American Indians* (Chicago: Henry Regnery, 1959), 12–27; Hanke, *All Mankind is One: A Study of the Disputation Between Bartolomé de Las Casas and Juan Ginés de Sepúlveda in 1550 on the Intellectual and Religious Capacity of the American Indians* (DeKalb: Northern Illinois University Press, 1974), 3–56; and Anthony Pagden, *The Fall of Natural*

Man: The American Indian and the Origins of Comparative Ethnology, 2nd ed. (Cambridge: Cambridge University Press, 1986), 38–47.

25. See, for example, the discussion of the "universal aspiration" and its relationship to early modern debates about New World peoples in James Q. Wilson, *The Moral Sense* (New York: Free Press, 1993), 207–09.

26. Cf. Hannah Arendt on stateless persons: "man had hardly appeared as a completely emancipated, completely isolated being who carried his dignity within himself without reference to some larger encompassing order, when he disappeared again. . . . From the beginning the paradox involved in the declaration of inalienable human rights was that it reckoned with an 'abstract' human being who seemed to exist nowhere, for even savages lived in some kind of social order." (Hannah Arendt, *The Origins of Totalitarianism*, new ed. with added prefaces [New York: Harcourt Brace, 1979], 291.) Of course, theorizing "savages" as participants in a genuinely social order was itself an achievement in the context of the prevalent understandings of Amerindians and other New World peoples. As I have argued, to view them in this way, humans as such needed to be conceptualized as constitutively cultural agents. This thicker and particularized understanding of the human subject made humanity less abstract and more likely to be effective as a universal moral concept.

27. On this 'agriculturalist argument', see Tuck, *The Rights of War and Peace*; and Richard Tuck, "Natural Rights and Empire", paper presented at the American Political Science Association conference, San Francisco, 1996. See also Pagden, *Lords of all the World*, 76–79; and Anthony Pagden, "Dispossessing the Barbarian: The Language of Spanish Thomism and the Debate over the Property Rights of the American Indians", in *The Languages of Political Theory in Early-Modern Europe*, ed. Anthony Pagden (Cambridge: Cambridge University Press, 1986), 79–98.

28. Of course, the belief that Amerindians were simply savage creatures (i.e., 'wild men' who lacked self-control and thus could not govern themselves) continued to hold sway in the popular and intellectual imagination. On this, see Dudley and Novak, eds., *The Wild Man Within*. The idea of an inherent—i.e., a biological or genetic—inferiority was to take centre stage in writings and speeches about imperial politics in the nineteenth century when the language of race fully entered European political discourse.

29. Pagden, *The Fall of Natural Man*, 137–44.

30. Steven Lukes, *Moral Conflict and Politics* (Oxford: Clarendon Press, 1991), 34, and in general, chapter 3, "Incommensurability in Science and Ethics", 33–49. See also Steven Lukes, "Berlin's dilemma: The distinction between relativism and pluralism", *Times Literary Supplement*, 27 March 1998, pp. 8–10. Cf. Joseph Raz, "Incommensurability and Agency", in *Incommensurability, Incomparability, and Practical Reason* ed. Ruth Chang (Cambridge: Harvard University Press, 1997), 110–28; and Bernard Williams, *Ethics and the Limits of Philosophy* (Cambridge: Harvard University Press, 1985), 156–60.

31. Cf. Dena Goodman, "Difference: An Enlightenment Concept", in *What's Left of Enlightenment?* ed. Keith Michael Baker and Peter Hanns Reill (Stanford: Stanford University Press, 2001), 129–47. See also Gay, *The Enlightenment*, 2: 319–43.

32. For accounts of the early development of the concepts of 'race' and 'nation', see George W. Stocking, Jr., *Race, Culture, and Evolution: Essays in the History of Anthropology* (New York: Free Press, 1968); Hugh Seton-Weston, "Race and Nation", in *Nations and States* (Boulder: Westview, 1977), 355–81; and Hudson, "From 'Nation' to 'Race'", 247–64.

33. Cf. Istvan Hont, "The Permanent Crisis of a Divided Mankind: 'Contemporary Crisis of the Nation-State' in Historical Perspective", in *Contemporary Crisis of the Nation-State?* ed. John Dunn (Oxford: Blackwell, 1995), 166–231.

34. Pratap B. Mehta, "Liberalism, Nation, and Empire: The Case of J. S. Mill", paper presented at the American Political Science Association conference, San Francisco, 1996.

35. John Stuart Mill, *On Liberty and other writings*, ed. Stefan Collini (Cambridge: Cambridge University Press, 1989), 13.

36. Hegel, *Philosophy of Right*, 212–23; Karl Marx, *Karl Marx on Colonialism and Modernization*, ed. Shlomo Avineri (New York: Doubleday, 1968).

37. See Alexis de Tocqueville, *Writings on Empire and Slavery*, ed. and trans. Jennifer Pitts (Baltimore: Johns Hopkins University Press, 2001); Jennifer Pitts, "Introduction", ibid.; and Melvin Richter, "Tocqueville on Algeria", *Review of Politics*, 25 (1963).

38. Earlier Enlightenment denunciations of imperial injustices explicitly linked European missionary work with brutal military conquests and the loss of political independence for non-European peoples. Consider, for instance, Bayle's defence of the Japanese explusion of Christian missionaries as a rational response to the first stage of what, in his view, would inevitably become a full-fledged imperial assault. See Bayle's entry for "Japan" in his *Dictionnaire historique et critique* (1697); Pierre Bayle, *Political Writings*, ed. and trans. Sally L. Jenkinson (Cambridge: Cambridge University Press, 2000), 128–35.

39. It is important to note that the lack of German colonies in the non-European world, the success of the American colonists' revolt against the British, and the decline of French colonial holdings in the late eighteenth century (as a result largely of the Seven Years' War) did *not* lead Diderot, Kant, and Herder to believe that European empires were in decline and, thus, that they represented an antiquated form of political rule. In fact, each of them considered European imperialism to be an increasingly important factor in international relations, regardless of the changing fortunes of particular imperial states and the fact that not all European societies had yet taken part in imperial rule abroad. It was precisely because of their concerns about the growing strength of imperial politics that they saw Europe as the chief instigator of injustices throughout the world.

40. In contrast, the development of less pejorative views of non-European peoples and of a more inclusive moral outlook is often portrayed simply as a move toward relativism and away from any form of universalism. See, for instance, Alan Frost, "The perception of culture's relativity in the second half of the eighteenth century", *Studies in the Eighteenth Century*, 5 (1983): 131.

Works Cited

Aarsleff, Hans. "The Tradition of Condillac: The Problem of the Origin of Language in the Eighteenth Century and the Debate in the Berlin Academy before Herder." In *Studies in the History of Linguistics: Traditions and Paradigms*, edited by D. Hymes, 93–156. Bloomington: Indiana University Press, 1974.

Adler, Emil. *Herder und die Deutsche Aufklärung*. Frankfurt: Europa Verlag, 1968.

Allison, Henry E. *Kant's Theory of Freedom*. Cambridge: Cambridge University Press, 1990.

Ameriks, Karl. *Kant and the Fate of Autonomy: Problems in the Appropriation of the Critical Philosophy*. Cambridge: Cambridge University Press, 2000.

Anderson, Wilda. *Diderot's Dream*. Baltimore: Johns Hopkins University Press, 1990.

Appiah, K. Anthony. "Race, Culture, Identity: Misunderstood Connections", in *The Tanner Lectures on Human Values*. Vol. 17, edited by Grethe B. Peterson, 51–136. Salt Lake City: University of Utah Press, 1996.

———. "The Multiculturalist Misunderstanding", *The New York Review of Books*, 9 October 1997.

Arendt, Hannah. *The Origins of Totalitarianism*. New ed. with added prefaces. New York: Harcourt Brace, 1979.

Armitage, David. *The Ideological Origins of the British Empire*. Cambridge: Cambridge University Press, 2000.

Arneil, Barbara. *John Locke and America: The defence of English colonialism*. Oxford: Clarendon, 1996.

Atkinson, Geoffrey. *Les relations de voyages du XVIIe siècle et l'évolution des idées: Contribution à l'étude de la formation de l'esprit au XVIIIe siècle*. Paris: Libraire Ancienne Edouard Champion, 1924.

Augustine, Saint, Bishop of Hippo. *The city of God against the pagans*. Edited and translated by R. W. Dyson. Cambridge: Cambridge University Press, 1998.

Barnard, F. M. "Herder's Treatment of Causation and Continuity in History". *Journal of the History of Ideas*, 24 (1963): 197–212.

———. *Herder's Social and Political Thought: From Enlightenment to Nationalism*. Oxford: Clarendon, 1965.

———. *Self-Direction and Political Legitimacy: Rousseau and Herder*. Oxford: Clarendon, 1988.

Bayle, Pierre. *Political Writings*. Edited and translated by Sally L. Jenkinson. Cambridge: Cambridge University Press, 2000.

Beattie, James. *An Essay on the Nature and Immutability of Truth, in Opposition to Sophistry and Skepticism* (1770). Excerpted in *Race and the Enlightenment: A Reader*, edited by Emmanuel Chukwudi Eze, 34–37. Oxford: Blackwell, 1997.

Beck, Lewis White. "Kant and the Right of Revolution". *Journal of the History of Ideas*, 32 (1971): 411–22.

————. "Kant's Two Conceptions of the Will in Their Political Context." In *Kant & Political Philosophy: The Contemporary Legacy*, 38–49. New Haven: Yale University Press, 1993.

Beiser, Frederick. *The Fate of Reason: German Philosophy from Kant to Fichte*. Cambridge: Harvard University Press, 1987.

————. *Enlightenment, Revolution, and Romanticism: The Genesis of Modern German Political Thought, 1790–1800*. Cambridge: Harvard University Press, 1992.

Benhabib, Seyla. "'Nous' et 'les Autres': The Politics of Complex Cultural Dialogue in a Global Civilization." In *Multicultural Questions*, edited by Christian Joppke and Steven Lukes, 44–62. Oxford: Oxford University Press, 1999.

Benot, Yves. "Diderot, Pechmeja, Raynal et l'anticolonialisme". *Europe*, 41 (1963): 137–53.

————. *Diderot: De l'athéisme à l'anticolonialisme*. Paris: François Maspero, 1970.

Bentham, Jeremy. *Colonies, Commerce, and Constitutional Law: Rid Yourselves of Ultramaria and other writings on Spain and Spanish America*. Edited by Philip Schofield. Oxford: Clarendon, 1995.

Berlin, Isaiah. *The Magus of the North: J. G. Hamann and the Origins of Modern Nationalism*. New York: Farrar, Straus and Giroux, 1993.

————. "Herder and the Enlightenment". In *The Proper Study of Mankind*, edited by Henry Hardy and Roger Hausheer, 359–435. New York: Farrar, Straus and Giroux, 1998.

Berman, Russell A. *Enlightenment or Empire: Colonial Discourse in German Culture*. Lincoln: University of Nebraska Press, 1998.

Bernasconi, Robert. "Who Invented the Concept of Race? Kant's Role in the Enlightenment Construction of Race". In *Race*, edited by Robert Bernasconi. Oxford: Blackwell, 2001.

Berry, Christopher J. *Social Theory of the Scottish Enlightenment*. Edinburgh: University of Edinburgh Press, 1997.

Bindman, David. *Ape to Apollo: Aesthetics and the Idea of Race in the 18th Century*. Ithaca: Cornell University Press, 2002.

Bitterli, Urs. *Die "Wilden" und die "Zivilisierten": Grundzüge einer Geistes- und Kulturgeschichte der europäisch-überseeischen Begegnung*. Munich: Verlag C. H. Beck, 1976.

————. *Cultures in Conflict: Encounters between European and Non-European Cultures. 1492–1800*. Translated by Ritchie Robertson. Cambridge: Polity Press, 1989.

Blackburn, Robin. *The Overthrow of Colonial Slavery, 1776–1848*. New York: Verso, 1988.

Bohman, James, and Matthias Lutz-Bachmann, eds. *Perpetual Peace: Essays on Kant's Cosmopolitan Ideal*. Cambridge: MIT Press, 1997.

Bougainville, Louis Antoine de. *Voyage Autour du Monde: Par la frégate la Boudeuse et la flute l'Étoile*. [1771]. Paris: Club des Libraires de France, 1958.

Bromwich, David. Introduction to *On Empire, Liberty, and Reform: Speeches and Letters*, by Edmund Burke. New Haven: Yale University Press, 2000.

Burke, Edmund. "An Appeal from the New to the Old Whigs" [1791]. In *The Works of the Right Honourable Edmund Burke*, vol. 4. London: J. C. Nimmo, 1887.

———. *The Correspondence of Edmund Burke*. Vol. 3. Cambridge: Cambridge University Press; Chicago: University of Chicago Press, 1958–78.

———. *The Writings and Speeches of Edmund Burke*. Vol. 5, *India: Madras and Bengal, 1774–1785*, edited by P. J. Marshall. Oxford: Clarendon, 1981.

———. *Reflections on the Revolution in France*. Edited by J.G.A. Pocock. Indianapolis: Hackett, 1987.

———. *The Writings and Speeches of Edmund Burke*. Vol. 6, *India, the launching of the Hastings impeachment, 1786–1788*, edited by P. J. Marshall. Oxford: Clarendon, 1991.

Carrithers, David. "The Enlightenment Science of Society." In *Inventing Human Science: Eighteenth-Century Domains*, 232–70. Berkeley: The University of California Press, 1995.

Cassirer, Ernst. "Kant and Rousseau" In *Rousseau, Kant, Goethe: Two Essays*, translated by James Gutmann, Paul Oskar Kristeller, and John Herman Randall, Jr., 1–60. Princeton: Princeton University Press, 1945.

———. *The Philosophy of the Enlightenment*. Translated by Fritz C.A. Koelln and James P. Pettegrove. Princeton: Princeton University Press, 1951.

Cavallar, Georg. *Pax Kantiana: Systematisch-historische Untersuchung des Entwurfs 'Zum ewigen Frieden' (1795) von Immanuel Kant*. Vienna: Böhlau Verlag, 1992.

Cavallar, George. "Kant's Judgment on Frederick's Enlightened Absolutism". *History of Political Thought*, 14, no. 1 (Spring 1993): 103–32.

Chinard, Gilbert. *L'Amérique et le rêve exotique dans la littérature française au XVIIe et au XVIIIe siècle*. Paris: E. Droz, 1934.

Clark, Robert T. *Herder: His Life and Thought*. Berkeley: University of California Press, 1955.

Condorcet, Jean-Antoine-Nicolas de Caritat, marquis de. *Condorcet: Selected Writings*. Edited by Keith Michael Baker. Indianapolis: Bobbs-Merrill, 1976.

Constant, Benjamin. "The spirit of conquest and usurpation and their relation to European civilization". In *Political Writings*, edited and translated by Biancamaria Fontana, 45–167. Cambridge: Cambridge University Press, 1988.

Cranston, Maurice. *Jean-Jacques: The Early Life and Work of Jean-Jacques Rousseau, 1712–1754*. Chicago: University of Chicago Press, 1982.

Creighton, D. C. "Man and Mind in Diderot and Helvétius". *Publications of the Modern Language Association* (1956): 705–24.

Crépon, Marc. *Les géographies de l'esprit: Enquête sur la caractérisation des peuples de Leibniz à Hegel*. Paris: Payot et Rivages, 1996.

Crocker, Lester G. "Diderot and the Idea of Progress". *Romanic Review* (1938): 151–59.

Darnton, Robert. *The Literary Underground of the Old Regime*. Cambridge: Harvard University Press, 1982.

———. *The Forbidden Best-sellers of Pre-revolutionary France*. New York: Norton, 1996.

Davis, David Brion. *The Problem of Slavery in the Age of Revolution, 1770–1823*. Ithaca: Cornell University Press, 1975.

———. "At the Heart of Slavery". *The New York Review of Books*, 17 October 1996.

Davis, Walter W. "China, the Confucian Ideal, and the European Age of Enlightenment" in *Discovering China: European Interpretations in the Enlightenment*, edited by Julia Ching and Willard G. Oxtoby. Rochester: University of Rochester Press, 1992.

Diamond, Jared. *Guns, Germs, and Steel: The Fates of Human Societies*. New York: Norton, 1998.

Diderot, Denis. *Oeuvres complètes de Diderot*. Vol. 2, edited by Jules Asségat and Maurice Tourneux. Paris: Garnier Frères, 1875.

———. *Supplément au Voyage de Bougainville, publié d'après le manuscrit de Leningrad*. Edited by Gilbert Chinard. Paris: E. Droz, 1935.

———. *Supplément au Voyage de Bougainville*. Edited by Herbert Dieckmann. Gèneve: Droz, 1955.

———. *Réfutation suivie de l'ouvrage d'Hélvetius intitulé L'Homme*. In *Oeuvres Philosophiques*, edited by P. Vernière. Paris: Garnier, 1956.

———. *Oeuvres complètes*. Vol. 4 edited by Herbert Dieckmann, Jean Fabre, and Jacques Proust. Paris: Hermann, 1975.

———. *Political Writings*. Edited and translated by John Hope Mason and Robert Wokler. Cambridge: Cambridge University Press, 1992.

Dienstag, Joshua Foa. *Dancing in Chains: Narrative and Memory in Political Theory*. Stanford: Stanford University Press, 1997.

Doyle, Michael W. *Empires*. Ithaca: Cornell University Press, 1986.

Duchet, Michèle. "Le 'Supplément au voyage de Bougainville' et la collaboration de Diderot à 'L'Histoire des deux Indes'". *Cahiers de l'Association Internationale des Études Françaises*, 13 (1961): 173–87.

———. *Anthropologie et Histoire au siècle des lumières*. Paris: François Maspero, 1971.

———. *Diderot et l'Histoire des deux Indes ou l'Écriture Fragmentaire*. Paris: Libraire A.-G. Nizet, 1978.

Dudley, Edward, and Maximillian E. Novak, eds. *The Wild Man Within: An Image in Western Thought from the Renaissance to Romanticism*. Pittsburgh: University of Pittsburgh Press, 1973.

Duval, Edwin M. "Lessons of the New World: Design and Meaning in Montaigne's "Des Cannibales" (I:31) and "Des Coches" (III: 6)." *Yale French Studies*, no. 64 (1983): 95–112.

Elliot, J. H. "The discovery of America and the discovery of man". *Proceedings of the British Academy*, 58 (1972): 102–25.

Ergang, Robert Reinhold. *Herder and the Foundations of German Nationalism*. New York: Columbia University Press, 1931.

Eze, Emmanuel Chukwudi. "The Color of Reason: The Idea of 'Race' in Kant's Anthropology". In *Anthropology and the German Enlightenment: Perspectives on Humanity*, edited by Katherine M. Faull, 200–241. Lewisburg: Bucknell University Press, 1995.

———, ed. *Race and the Enlightenment: A Reader*. Oxford: Blackwell, 1997.

Fabre, Jean. "Deux Frères Ennemis: Diderot et Jean-Jacques". *Diderot Studies*, 3: 155–213.

Fénelon, François de Salignac de La Mothe. *Telemachus, son of Ulysses*. Edited and translated by Patrick Riley. [1699]. Cambridge: Cambridge University Press, 1994.

Ferguson, Adam. *An Essay on the History of Civil Society*. Edited by Fania Oz-Salzberger. [1767]. Cambridge: Cambridge University Press, 1995.

Feugère, Anatole. "La Doctrine Révolutionnaire de Raynal et de Diderot d'après l'*Histoire des Indes*". *Mercure de France* (1913): 498–517.

Fichte, J. G. *Foundations of Natural Right: According to the Principles of the Wissenschaftslehre*. Edited by Frederick Neuhouser, translated by Michael Baur. [1796–97]. Cambridge: Cambridge University Press, 2000.

Finley, M. I. "Colonies—An Attempt at a Typology". *Transactions of the Royal Historical Society*, 26 (1976): 167–88.

Fleischacker, Samuel. *A Third Concept of Liberty: Judgment and Freedom in Kant and Adam Smith*. Princeton: Princeton University Press, 1999.

Foucault, Michel. "What is Enlightenment?" In *The Foucault Reader*, edited by Paul Rabinow, translated by Catherine Porter. New York: Pantheon, 1984.

Fox, Christopher, Roy Porter, and Robert Wokler, eds. *Inventing Human Science: Eighteenth-Century Domains*. Berkeley: University of California Press, 1995.

France, Peter, and Anthony Strugnell, eds. *Diderot, les dernières années, 1770–84: Colloque du bicentenaire, 2–5 Septembre 1984 à Edimbourg*. Edinburgh: Edinburgh University Press, 1985.

Frost, Alan. "The Pacific Ocean: The Eighteenth Century's 'New World'". *Studies on Voltaire and the Eighteenth Century*, 152 (1976): 779–822.

———. "The perception of culture's relativity in the second half of the eighteenth century". *Studies in the Eighteenth Century*, 5 (1983).

Garrard, Graeme. "Rousseau, Maistre, and the Counter-Enlightenment". *History of Political Thought*, 15, no. 1 (1994): 97–120.

Gay, Peter. *The Enlightenment: An Interpretation*. Vol. 1, *The Rise of Modern Paganism*, and vol. 2: *The Science of Freedom*. New York: Norton, 1977; originally 1966 and 1969.

Geertz, Clifford. "The Impact of the Concept of Culture on the Concept of Man". In *The Interpretation of Cultures*. New York: Basic Books, 1973.

Geuss, Raymond. "Kultur, Bildung, Geist". In *Morality, Culture, and History: Essays on German Philosophy*, 29–50. Cambridge: Cambridge University Press, 1999.

Gillies, Alexander. "Herder's Approach to the Philosophy of History". *Modern Language Review*, 35 (1940).

Glacken, Clarence J. *Traces on the Rhodian Shore: Nature and Culture in Western Thought from Ancient Times to the End of the Eighteenth Century*. Berkeley: University of California Press, 1967.

Goldschmidt, Victor. *Anthropologie et Politique: Les principes du système de Rousseau*. Paris: Librairie Philosophique J. Vrin, 1974.

Goodman, Dena. "The Structure of Political Argument in Diderot's *Supplément au Voyage de Bougainville*". *Diderot Studies*, 21 (1983): 123–37.

———. *Criticism in Action: Enlightenment Experiments in Political Writing*. Ithaca: Cornell University Press, 1989.

———. "Difference: An Enlightenment Concept". In *What's Left of Enlightenment? A Postmodern Question*, edited by Keith Michael Baker and Peter Hanns Reill, 129–47. Stanford: Stanford University Press, 2001.

Gordon, Daniel. *Citizens Without Sovereignty: Equality and Sociability in French Thought, 1670–1789*. Princeton: Princeton University Press, 1994.

Gray, John. "After the New Liberalism". *Social Research*, 61, no. 3 (Fall 1994): Reprinted in John Gray, *Enlightenment's Wake: Politics and Culture at the Close of the Modern Age*. New York: Routledge, 1995.

———. *Isaiah Berlin*. Princeton: Princeton University Press, 1996.

Gregor, Mary. *Laws of Freedom*. New York: Barnes and Noble, 1963.

Gusdorf, Georges. *L'avènement des sciences humaines au siècle des lumières*. Paris: Payot, 1973.

Guyer, Paul. *Kant and the Claims of Taste*. 2nd ed. Cambridge: Cambridge University Press, 1997.

Hall, Max. *Benjamin Franklin and Polly Baker: The History of a Literary Deception*. Chapel Hill: University of North Carolina Press, 1960.

Hampson, Norman. *The Enlightenment*. Harmondsworth: Penguin, 1968.

Hanke, Lewis. *Aristotle and the American Indians*. Chicago: Henry Regnery, 1959.

———. *All Mankind is One: A Study of the Disputation Between Bartolomé de Las Casas and Juan Ginés de Sepúlveda in 1550 on the Intellectual and Religious Capacity of the American Indians*. DeKalb: Northern Illinois University Press, 1974.

Havens, George R. "Diderot, Rousseau, and *Discours sur l'Inégalité*". *Diderot Studies*, 3: 219–62.

Haym, Rudolf. *Herder*. Vol. 2. Berlin: Aufbau-Verlag, 1954.

Hazard, Paul. *The European Mind: 1680–1715*. Translated by J. Lewis May. Cleveland: Meridian, 1963.

Hegel, Georg Wilhelm Friedrich. *Philosophy of Right*. Translated by T. M. Knox. Oxford: Clarendon, 1967.

Herder, Johann Gottfried. *Outlines of a Philosophy of the History of Man*. Translated by T. Churchill. London: J. Johnson, 1800.

———. *Sämtliche Werke*. 33 vols. Edited by Bernard Ludwig Suphan. Berlin: Weidmannsche Buchhandlung, 1877–1913.

———. *J. G. Herder on social and political culture*. Edited and translated by F. M. Barnard. Cambridge: Cambridge University Press, 1969.

———. *On World History: An Anthology*. Edited by Hans Adler and Ernest A. Menze, translated by Ernest A. Menze with Michael Palma. London: M. E. Sharpe, 1997.

Hill, Thomas E., Jr. *Dignity and Practical Reason*. Ithaca: Cornell University Press, 1992.

Hirschman, Albert. *The Passions and the Interests: Political Arguments for Capitalism before Its Triumph*. Princeton: Princeton University Press, 1977.

Hodgen, Margaret T. *Early Anthropology in the Sixteenth and Seventeenth Centuries*. Philadelphia: University of Pennsylvania Press, 1964.

Hollis, Martin. "Is Universalism Ethnocentric?" In *Multicultural Questions*, edited by Christian Joppke and Steven Lukes, 27–43. Oxford: Oxford University Press, 1999.

Hont, Istvan. "The language of sociability and commerce: Samuel Pufendorf and the theoretical foundations of the 'Four-Stages Theory'". In *The Languages of Political Theory in Early-Modern Europe*, edited by Anthony Pagden, 253–76. Cambridge: Cambridge University Press, 1987.

———. "The Permanent Crisis of a Divided Mankind: 'Contemporary Crisis of the Nation-State' in Historical Perspective". In *Contemporary Crisis of the Nation-State?* edited by John Dunn, 166–231. Oxford: Blackwell, 1995.

Horowitz, Asher. "'Laws and Customs Thrust Us Back into Infancy': Rousseau's Historical Anthropology". *The Review of Politics*, 52, no. 2 (Summer 1990): 215–41.

Hudson, Nicholas. "From 'Nation' to 'Race': The Origin of Racial Classification in Eighteenth-Century Thought". *Eighteenth-Century Studies*, 29, no. 3 (1996): 247–64.

Hulliung, Mark. *The Autocritique of Enlightenment*. Cambridge: Harvard University Press, 1994.

Hulme, Peter, and L. J. Jordanova, eds. *The Enlightenment and Its Shadows*. New York: Routledge, 1990.

Hume, David. *Enquiries Concerning Human Understanding and Concerning the Principles of Morals*. Edited by L. A. Selby-Bigge, revised by P. H. Nidditch. Oxford: Clarendon, 1975.

———. *Essays: Moral, Political, and Literary*. Rev. ed. Edited by Eugene F. Miller. Indianapolis: Liberty Fund, 1987.

Israel, Jonathan I. *Radical Enlightenment: Philosophy and the Making of Modernity, 1650–1750*. Oxford: Oxford University Press, 2001.

Jacob, Margaret C. *The Radical Enlightenment: Pantheists, Freemasons and Republicans*. London: Allen and Unwin, 1981.

James, C.L.R. *The Black Jacobins: Toussaint L'Ouverture and the San Domingo Revolution*. 2nd rev. ed. New York: Vintage 1963; originally 1938.

Jansen, Marius B., ed. *The Cambridge History of Japan*. Vol. 5. Cambridge: Cambridge University Press, 1989.

Kant, Immanuel. *Kants gesammelte Schriften, herausgegeben von der Preussischen Akademie der Wissenschaften zu Berlin*. Berlin: Walter de Gruyter, 1902–.

———. *Anthropology from a Pragmatic Point of View*. Edited and translated by Mary J. Gregor. The Hague: Martinus Nijhoff, 1974.

———. *Critique of Judgment*. Translated by Werner S. Pluhar. Indianapolis: Hackett Publishing Company, 1987.

———. *Political Writings*. 2nd ed. Edited by Hans Reiss, translated by H. B. Nisbet. Cambridge: Cambridge University Press, 1991.

———. *Critique of Pure Reason*. Translated by Werner S. Pluhar. Indianapolis: Hackett, 1996.

———. *Practical Philosophy*. Edited and translated by Mary Gregor. Cambridge: Cambridge University Press, 1996.

———. *Lectures on Ethics*. Edited by Peter Heath and J. B. Schneewind, translated by Peter Heath. Cambridge: Cambridge University Press, 1997.

———. *Religion and Rational Theology*. Edited and translated by Allen W. Wood and George Di Giovanni. Cambridge: Cambridge University Press, 1997.

———. *Critique of Pure Reason*. Edited and translated by Allen W. Wood and Paul Guyer. Cambridge: Cambridge University Press, 1998.

———. *Critique of the Power of Judgment*. Edited by Paul Guyer, and translated by Paul Guyer and Eric Matthews. Cambridge: Cambridge University Press, 2000.

Kelley, Donald R. *Faces of History: Historical Inquiry from Herodotus to Herder.* New Haven: Yale University Press, 2000.

Kelly, George Armstrong. *Idealism, Politics, and History: Sources of Hegelian Thought.* Cambridge: Cambridge University Press, 1969.

Kiernan, V. G. "Noble and ignoble savages". In *Exoticism in the Enlightenment,* edited by G. S. Rousseau and Roy Porter, 86–116. Manchester: Manchester University Press, 1990.

Kluckhohn, Clyde, and Alfred Kroeber, "Culture: A Critical Review of Concepts and Definitions". In *Papers of the Peabody Museum of American Archeology and Ethnology,* vol. 47 (1952).

Knoll, Samson B. "Herder's concept of *Humanität*". In *Johann Gottfried Herder: Innovator through the ages,* edited by Wulf Koepke, 9–18. Bonn: Bouvier Verlag Herbert Grundmann, 1982.

Koebner, Richard. *Empire.* Cambridge: Cambridge University Press, 1961.

Korsgaard, Christine M. "Kant's Formula of Humanity". In *Creating the Kingdom of Ends.* Cambridge: Cambridge University Press, 1996.

———. *The Sources of Normativity.* Cambridge: Cambridge University Press, 1996.

Kuper, Adam. *Culture: The Anthropologists' Account.* Cambridge: Harvard University Press, 1999.

Lach, Donald F. "Leibniz and China" and "The Sinophilism of Christian Wolff". In *Discovering China: European Interpretations in the Enlightenment,* edited by Julia Ching and Willard G. Oxtoby. Rochester: University of Rochester Press, 1992.

Ladd, John. Introduction to *The Metaphysical Elements of Justice,* by Immanuel Kant. Edited by John Ladd. Indianapolis: Library of Liberal Arts, 1965.

Lahontan, Louis Armand de Lom d'Arce, baron de. *New Voyages to North America.* Vol. 1. London: H. Bonwicke, 1703.

———. *Dialogues Curieux entre l'Auteur et un Sauvage de bons sens qui a voyagé et Mémoires de l'Amérique Septentrionale.* Edited by Gilbert Chinard. Paris: A. Margraff, 1931.

Langton, Rae. *Kantian Humility: Our Ignorance of Things in Themselves.* Oxford: Oxford University Press, 1998.

Las Casas, Bartolomé de. *In defense of the Indians: The defense of the Most Reverend Lord, Don Fray Bartolomé de las Casas, of the Order of Preachers, late Bishop of Chiapa, against the persecutors and slanderers of the peoples of the New World discovered across the seas.* Edited by Stafford Poole. DeKalb: Northern Illinois University Press, 1974.

———. *The Devastation of the Indies: A Brief Account.* Baltimore: Johns Hopkins University Press, 1992.

Laursen, John Christian. "Scepticism and Intellectual Freedom: The Philosophical Foundations of Kant's Politics of Publicity". *History of Political Thought,* 10, no. 3 (Autumn 1989): 439–55.

———. "The Subversive Kant: The Vocabulary of 'Public' and 'Publicity'". In *What is Enlightenment? Eighteenth-Century Answers and Twentieth-Century Questions,* edited by James Schmidt, 253–69. Berkeley: University of California Press, 1996.

La Vopa, Anthony J. "Herder's *Publikum*: Language, Print, and Sociability in Eighteenth-Century Germany". *Eighteenth-Century Studies*, 29 (1996): 5–24.

Lebovics, Herman. "The Uses of America in Locke's *Second Treatise of Government*". *Journal of the History of Ideas*, 47 (1986): 567–81.

Leibniz, Gottfried Wilhelm. *Writings on China*. Edited and translated by Daniel J. Cook and Henry Rosemont, Jr. Chicago: Open Court, 1994.

Leigh, Ralph. "Diderot's Tahiti". *Studies in the Eighteenth Century*, 5 (1983): 113–28.

Linker, Damon. "The Reluctant Pluralism of J. G. Herder". *The Review of Politics*, 62 (2000): 267–93.

Locke, John. *An Essay concerning the true original, extent, and end of civil government*. In *Two Treatises of Government*, edited by Peter Laslett. Cambridge: Cambridge University Press, 1960.

———. *An Essay concerning Human Understanding*. Edited by Peter H. Nidditch. Oxford: Clarendon, 1975.

Louden, Robert B. *Kant's Impure Ethics: From Rational Beings to Human Beings*. Oxford: Oxford University Press, 2000.

Lovejoy, Arthur, and George Boas. *Primitivism and Related Ideas in Antiquity*. Baltimore: Johns Hopkins University Press, 1997; originally 1935.

Lovejoy, Arthur O. "Herder and the Enlightenment Philosophy of History". In *Essays in the History of Ideas*, edited by Arthur O. Lovejoy, 166–82. Baltimore: Johns Hopkins University Press, 1948.

———. "The Supposed Primitivism of Rousseau's Discourse on Inequality". In *Essays in the History of Ideas*, 14–37. Baltimore: Johns Hopkins Press, 1948.

Lukes, Steven. *Moral Conflict and Politics*. Oxford: Clarendon, 1991.

———. "Berlin's dilemma: The distinction between relativism and pluralism". *Times Literary Supplement*, 27 March 1998, pp. 8–10.

Lüsebrink, Hans-Jürgen, and Manfred Tietz, eds. *Lectures de Raynal: L'Histoire des deux Indes en Europe et en Amérique au XVIIIe siècle*. Studies on Voltaire and the Eighteenth Century, vol. 286. Oxford: Voltaire Foundation, 1991.

Lüsebrink, Hans-Jürgen, and Anthony Strugnell, eds. *L'Histoire des deux Indes: Réécriture et polygraphie*. Studies on Voltaire and the Eighteenth Century, vol. 333. Oxford: Voltaire Foundation, 1995.

MacIntyre, Alasdair. *After Virtue: A Study in Moral Theory*. 2nd ed. Notre Dame: University of Notre Dame Press, 1984.

———. *Whose Justice? Which Rationality?* Notre Dame: University of Notre Dame Press, 1988.

Makkreel, Rudolf A. *Imagination and Interpretation in Kant: The Hermeneutical Import of the Critique of Judgment*. Chicago: University of Chicago Press, 1990.

Marshall, P. J., and Glyndwr Williams. *The Great Map of Mankind*. Cambridge: Harvard University Press, 1982.

Marx, Karl. *Karl Marx on Colonialism and Modernization*. Edited by Shlomo Avineri. New York: Doubleday, 1968.

McCarthy, Thomas. "Political Philosophy and the Problem of Race". In *Die Öffentlichkeit der Vernunft und die Vernunft der Öffentlichkeit*, edited by K. Günther and L. Wingert. Frankfurt: Suhrkamp Verlag, 2001.

Medicus, Fritz. "Kant's Philosophy of History". *Kant-Studien*, 54 (1900): 61–67.

Mehta, Pratap B. "Liberalism, Nation, and Empire: The Case of J. S. Mill". Paper presented at the American Political Science Association conference, San Francisco, 1996.

Mehta, Uday Singh. *Liberalism and Empire: A Study in Nineteenth-Century British Liberal Thought*. Chicago: University of Chicago Press, 1999.

Meinecke, Friedrich. *Historism: The Rise of a New Historical Outlook*. Translated by J. E. Anderson, foreword by Sir Isaiah Berlin. London: Routledge and Kegan Paul, 1972; 1959.

Melzer, Arthur M. *The Natural Goodness of Man: On the System of Rousseau's Thought*. Chicago: University of Chicago Press, 1990.

Mendelssohn, Moses. "On the Question: What is Enlightenment?" In *What is Enlightenment? Eighteenth-Century Answers and Twentieth-Century Questions*, edited by James Schmidt, 53–57. Berkeley: University of California Press, 1996.

Menges, Karl. "Herder and the 'Querelle des Anciens et des Modernes'". In *Eighteenth-Century German Authors and Their Aesthetic Theories*, edited by R. Critchfield and W. Koepke, 147–83. Columbia, S.C.: Camden House, 1988.

Mercier, Roger. "Image de l'autre et image de soi-même dans le discours ethnologique au XVIIIe siècle". *Studies on Voltaire and the Eighteenth Century*, 154 (1976): 1417–35.

Mill, John Stuart. *On Liberty and other writings*. Edited by Stefan Collini. Cambridge: Cambridge University Press, 1989.

Montaigne, Michel de. *The Complete Essays of Montaigne*. Edited and translated by Donald Frame. Stanford: Stanford University Press, 1958.

Montesquieu, Charles de Secondat, baron de. *The Spirit of the Laws*. Edited and translated by Anne Cohler, Basia Miller, and Harold Stone. Cambridge: Cambridge University Press, 1989.

Moravia, Sergio. "The Enlightenment and the Sciences of Man". *History of Science*, 18 (1980): 247–68.

Moscovici, Claudia. "An Ethics of Cultural Exchange: Diderot's *Supplément au Voyage de Bougainville*". *CLIO*, 30 (2001): 289–307.

Neuhouser, Frederick. *Fichte's Theory of Subjectivity*. Cambridge: Cambridge University Press, 1990.

Nussbaum, Martha. *For Love of Country: Debating the Limits of Patriotism*. Edited by Joshua Cohen. Boston: Beacon Press, 1996.

O'Brien, Conor Cruise. *The Great Melody: A Thematic Biography and Commented Anthology of Edmund Burke*. Chicago: University of Chicago Press, 1992.

O'Brien, Patrick K. "Inseparable Connections: Trade, Economy, Fiscal State, and the Expansion of Empire, 1688–1815". In *The Oxford History of the British Empire*, vol. 2, *The Eighteenth Century*, edited by P. J. Marshall, 53–77. Oxford: Oxford University Press, 1998.

O'Neill, Onora. "Reason and Politics in the Kantian Enterprise". In *Constructions of Reason: Explorations of Kant's Practical Philosophy*. Cambridge: Cambridge University Press, 1989.

Obeyesekere, Gannath. *The Apotheosis of Captain Cook: European Mythmaking in the Pacific*. Princeton: Princeton University Press, 1992.

Outram, Dorinda. *The Enlightenment*. Cambridge: Cambridge University Press, 1995.

Oz-Salzberger, Fania. *Translating the Enlightenment*. Oxford: Clarendon, 1995.

Pagden, Anthony. *The Fall of Natural Man: The American Indian and the Origins of Comparative Ethnology*. 2nd ed. Cambridge: Cambridge University Press, 1986).

———. "Dispossessing the Barbarian: The Language of Spanish Thomism and the Debate over the Property Rights of the American Indians". In *The Languages of Political Theory in Early-Modern Europe*, edited by Anthony Pagden, 79–98. Cambridge: Cambridge University Press, 1986.

———. *European Encounters with the New World*. New Haven: Yale University Press, 1993.

———. *Lords of All the World: Ideologies of Empire in Spain, Britain and France c.1500–c.1800*. New Haven: Yale University Press, 1995.

———. "Stoicism, Cosmopolitanism, and the Legacy of European Imperialism". *Constellations*, 7, no. 1 (March 2000): 3–22.

———. *Peoples and Empires: A Short History of European Migration, Exploration, and Conquest, from Greece to the Present*. New York: Modern Library, 2001.

Parekh, Bhikhu. "Moral philosophy and its anti-pluralist bias". In *Philosophy and Pluralism*, edited by David Archard, 117–134. Cambridge: Cambridge University Press, 1996.

———. *Rethinking Multiculturalism: Cultural Diversity and Political Theory*. Cambridge: Harvard University Press, 2000.

Passmore, J. A. "The Malleability of Man in Eighteenth-Century Thought". In *Aspects of the Eighteenth Century*, edited by Earl R. Wasserman, 21–46. Baltimore: Johns Hopkins Press, 1965.

Perkins, M. L. "Community Planning in Diderot's *Supplément au Voyage de Bougainville*". *Kentucky Romance Quarterly*, 21 (1974): 399–417.

Pippin, Robert P. *Idealism as Modernism: Hegelian Variations*. Cambridge: Cambridge University Press, 1997.

Pire, G. "Jean-Jacques Rousseau et les relations de voyages". *Revue d'histoire littéraire de la France*, 56, no. 3 (1956): 355–78.

Pitts, Jennifer. Introduction to *Writings on Empire and Slavery* by Alexis de Tocqueville. Edited and translated by Jennifer Pitts. Baltimore: Johns Hopkins University Press, 2001.

———. *The Turn to Empire*. Princeton: Princeton University Press, forthcoming.

Pluchon, Pierre. *Nègres et juifs au XVIIIe siècle: Le racisme au siècle des lumiéres*. Paris: Tallandier, 1984.

Pocock, J.G.A. *Barbarism and Religion*. Vol. 1, *The Enlightenments of Edward Gibbon, 1737–1764*. Vol. 2, *Narratives of Civil Government*. Cambridge: Cambridge University Press, 1999.

———. "Commerce, Settlement and History: A Reading of the *Histoire des deux Indes*". In *Articulating America: Fashioning a National Political Culture in Early America, Essays in Honor of J. R. Pole*, edited by Rebecca Starr, 15–44. Lanham: Rowman and Littlefield, 2000.

————. "Some Europes in Their History". In *The Idea of Europe: From Antiquity to the European Union*, edited by Anthony Pagden, 55–71. Cambridge and Washington, D.C.: Cambridge University Press and Woodrow Wilson Center Press, 2002.

Popkin, Richard H. "The Philosophical Basis of Eighteenth-Century Racism". In *Racism in the Eighteenth Century*, edited by Harold E. Pagliaro, 245–62. Cleveland: Case Western Reserve University Press, 1973.

Porter, Roy. "The Exotic as Erotic: Captain Cook at Tahiti". In *Exoticism in the Enlightenment*, edited by Roy Porter and G. S. Rousseau, 117–44. Manchester: Manchester University Press, 1990.

Porter, Roy, and Mikulás Teich, eds. *The Enlightenment in National Context*. Cambridge: Cambridge University Press, 1981.

Proust, Jacques. "La contribution de Diderot à l'Encylopédie et les théories du droit naturel". *Annales Historiqes de la Revolution Française* (1963): 257–86.

Quint, David. *Montaigne and the Quality of Mercy*. Princeton: Princeton University Press, 1998.

Raynal, Guillaume-Thomas. *Histoire philosophique et politique des établissements et du commerce des Européens dans les deux Indes*. 10 vols. Genève: Jean-Leonard Pellet, 1780.

Raz, Joseph. "Incommensurability and Agency". In *Incommensurability, Incomparability, and Practical Reason*, edited by Ruth Chang, 110–28. Cambridge: Harvard University Press, 1997.

Rennie, Neil. *Far-Fetched Facts: The Literature of Travel and the Idea of the South Seas*. Oxford: Clarendon, 1995.

Richardson, J. S. "Imperium Romanum: Empire and the Language of Power", *Journal of Roman Studies*, 81 (1991): 1–9.

Richter, Melvin. "Tocqueville on Algeria". *Review of Politics*, 25 (1963).

————. "Despotism" in *Dictionary of the History of Ideas*. New York: Scribner, 1973.

————. "Europe and *the Other* in Eighteenth-Century Thought." *Politisches Denken* (1997): 25–47.

————. "The Comparative Study of Regimes and Societies in the Eighteenth Century". In *The Cambridge History of Eighteenth-Century Political Thought*, edited by Mark Goldie and Robert Wokler. Cambridge: Cambridge University Press, forthcoming.

Riley, Patrick. *Will and Political Legitimacy: A Critical Exposition of Social Contract Theory in Hobbes, Locke, Rousseau, Kant, and Hegel*. Cambridge: Harvard University Press, 1982.

————. *Kant's Political Philosophy*. Totowa, N.J.: Rowman and Littlefield, 1983.

————. *The General Will Before Rousseau*. Princeton: Princeton University Press, 1986.

Robinson, Nicholas K. *Edmund Burke: A Life in Caricature*. New Haven: Yale University Press, 1996.

Rosen, Allen D. *Kant's Theory of Justice*. Ithaca: Cornell University Press, 1993.

Rouché, Max. *La philosophie de l'histoire de Herder*. Paris: Publications de la Faculté des Lettres de l'Université de Strasbourg, 1940.

Rousseau, Jean-Jacques. *Oeuvres complètes*. Bibliothèque de la Pléiade. Edited by Bernard Gagnebin and Marcel Raymond. 5 vols. Paris: Gallimard, 1959–95.

——. *Emile*. Translated by Allan Bloom. New York: Basic Books, 1979.

——. *The Collected Writings of Rousseau*. Vol. 5, *The Confessions and Correspondence, Including the Letters to Malesherbes*, edited by Christopher Kelly, Roger D. Masters, and Peter G. Stillman, translated by Christopher Kelly. Hanover: University Press of New England, 1995.

——. *The Discourses and other early political writings*. Edited and translated by Victor Gourevitch. Cambridge: Cambridge University Press, 1997.

——. *The Social Contract and other later political writings*. Edited and translated by Victor Gourevitch. Cambridge: Cambridge University Press, 1997.

Sahlins, Marshall. *How "Natives" Think: About Captain Cook, for example*. Chicago: University of Chicago Press, 1995.

Schick, Edgar B. *Metaphorical organicism in Herder's early works: A study of the relation of Herder's literary idiom to his world-view*. The Hague: Mouton, 1971.

Schlenther, Boyd Stanley. "Religious Faith and Commercial Empire". In *The Oxford History of the British Empire*, vol. 2, *The Eighteenth Century*, edited by P. J. Marshall, 128–50. Oxford: Oxford University Press, 1998.

Schmidt, James. "What is Enlightenment? A Question, Its Context, and Some Consequences." In *What is Enlightenment? Eighteenth-Century Answers and Twentieth-Century Questions*, edited by James Schmidt. Berkeley: University of California Press, 1996.

——. "What Enlightenment Project?" *Political Theory*, 28, no. 6 (2000): 734–57.

Schneewind, J. B. *The Invention of Autonomy: A History of Modern Moral Philosophy*. Cambridge: Cambridge University Press, 1998.

Schwartz, Jerome. *Diderot and Montaigne: The Essais and the shaping of Diderot's humanism*. Genève: Libraire Droz, 1966.

Schwartz, Leon. *Diderot and the Jews*. Rutherford: Fairleigh Dickinson University Press, 1981.

Seidman, Steven. *Liberalism and the Origins of European Social Theory*. Berkeley: University of California Press, 1983.

Seton-Weston, Hugh. "Race and Nation". In *Nations and States*, 355–81. Boulder: Westview, 1977.

Sfragaro, A. "La Représentation de la femme chez Diderot". *Studies on Voltaire and the Eighteenth Century*, 193 (1980): 1893–99.

Shattuck, Roger. *The Forbidden Experiment: the story of the Wild Boy of Aveyron*. London: Secker and Warburg, 1980.

Shell, Susan Meld. *The Embodiment of Reason: Kant on Spirit, Generation, and Community*. Chicago: University of Chicago Press, 1996.

Shklar, Judith N. *Men and Citizens: A Study of Rousseau's Social Theory*. Cambridge: Cambridge University Press, 1969.

——. *The Faces of Injustice*. New Haven: Yale University Press, 1990.

——. "Politics and the Intellect". In *Political Thought and Political Thinkers*, edited by Stanley Hoffmann. Chicago: University of Chicago Press, 1998.

Slavin, Arthur J. "The American Principle from More to Locke". In *First Images of America: The Impact of the New World on the Old*, vol. 1, edited by Fredi Chiappelli. Berkeley: University of California Press, 1976.

Smith, Adam. *An Inquiry into the Nature and Causes of the Wealth of Nations*.

Vol. 2, edited by R. H. Campbell and A. S. Skinner. Indianapolis: Liberty Fund, 1981.

Starobinski, Jean. *Jean-Jacques Rousseau: Transparency and Obstruction*. Translated by Arthur Goldhammer. Chicago: University of Chicago Press, 1988.

———. "The Word *Civilization*". In *Blessings in Disguise; or, The Morality of Evil*, translated by Arthur Goldhammer, 1–35. Cambridge: Harvard University Press, 1993.

Stocking, George W., Jr. *Race, Culture, and Evolution: Essays in the History of Anthropology*. New York: Free Press, 1968.

Strugnell, Anthony. *Diderot's politics: A study of the evolution of Diderot's political thought after the Encyclopédie*. The Hague: Nijhoff, 1973.

———. "Postmodernism versus Enlightenment and the problem of the Other in Raynal's *Histoire des deux Indes*". *Studies on Voltaire and the Eighteenth Century*, 341 (1996): 169–82.

Swenson, James. "A small change in terminology or a Great Leap Forward? Culture and civilization in revolution". *MLN*, 112 (1997): 322–48.

Taylor, Charles. *Sources of the Self: The Making of the Modern Identity*. Cambridge: Harvard University Press, 1989.

———. "The Importance of Herder". In *Philosophical Arguments*, 79–99. Cambridge: Harvard University Press, 2000.

Tocqueville, Alexis de. *Writings on Empire and Slavery*. Edited and translated by Jennifer Pitts. Baltimore: Johns Hopkins University Press, 2001.

Todorov, Tzvetan. *On Human Diversity: Nationalism, Racism, and Exoticism in French Thought*. Translated by Catherine Porter. Cambridge: Harvard University Press, 1993.

Tomaselli, Sylvana. "The Enlightenment Debate on Women". *History Workshop*, 20 (1985): 101–24.

Tooley, M. J. "Bodin and the Medieval Theory of Climate". *Speculum*, 28 (1953): 64–83.

Toulmin, Stephen. *Cosmopolis: The Hidden Agenda of Modernity*. Chicago: University of Chicago Press, 1990.

Trouille, Mary. "Sexual/Textual Politics in the Enlightenment: Diderot and D'Epinay Respond to Thomas's Essay on Women". *The Romanic Review*, 85, no. 2 (1994): 191–210.

Tuck, Richard. "Natural Rights and Empire". Paper presented at the American Political Science Association conference, San Francisco, 1996.

———. *The Rights of War and Peace: Political thought and the international order from Grotius to Kant*. Oxford: Oxford University Press, 1999.

Tully, James. *An Approach to Political Philosophy: Locke in Contexts*. Cambridge: Cambridge University Press, 1993.

———. "Aboriginal property and western theory: Recovering a middle ground". *Social Philosophy and Policy*, 11 (1994): 153–80.

———. "The Kantian Idea of Europe: Critical and Cosmopolitan Perspectives". In *The Idea of Europe: From Antiquity to the European Union*, 331–58. Cambridge and Washington, D.C.: Cambridge University Press and Woodrow Wilson Center Press, 2002.

Vattel, Emmerich de. *The Law of Nations or The Principles of Natural Law Ap-*

plied to the Conduct and to the Affairs of Nations and of Sovereigns. Translated by Charles G. Fenwick. [1758]. Buffalo: William S. Hein, 1995.

Velkley, Richard L. *Freedom and the End of Reason: On the Moral Foundation of Kant's Critical Philosophy.* Chicago: University of Chicago Press, 1989.

Venturi, Franco. "Oriental Despotism". *Journal of the History of Ideas*, 24 (1963): 133–42.

Vespucci, Amerigo. *Letters from a New World.* Edited by Luciano Formisano, translated by David Jacobson. New York: Marsilio, 1992.

Vitoria, Francisco de. "On the American Indians" (1539). In *Political Writings*, by Francisco de Vitoria. Edited by Anthony Pagden and Jeremy Lawrance, 233–92. Cambridge: Cambridge University Press, 1991.

Voltaire, François Marie Arouet de. "Lettre de Voltaire à Jean-Jacques Rousseau" (30 August 1755). In *Oeuvres complètes*, by Jean-Jacques Rousseau. Vol. 3. Bibliothèque de la Pléiade. Paris: Gallimard, 1964.

Vyverberg, Henry. *Human Nature, Cultural Diversity, and the French Enlightenment.* Oxford: Oxford University Press, 1989.

Waldron, Jeremy. "Kant's Positivism". In *The Dignity of Legislation*, 36–62. Cambridge: Cambridge University Press, 1999.

———. "What is Cosmopolitan?" *Journal of Political Philosophy*, 8 (2000): 227–43.

Walzer, Michael, ed. *Regicide and Revolution.* Translated by Marian Rothstein. New York: Columbia University Press, 1992.

Wells, G. A. "Herder's Determinism". *Journal of the History of Ideas*, 19 (1958): 105–13.

———. *Herder And After: A Study in the Development of Sociology.* The Hague: Mouton, 1959.

Whelan, Frederick. "Population and Ideology in the Enlightenment". *History of Political Thought.* 12, no. 1 (1991): 35–72.

———. *Edmund Burke and India: Political Morality and Empire.* Pittsburgh: University of Pittsburgh Press, 1996.

Williams, Bernard. *Ethics and the Limits of Philosophy.* Cambridge: Harvard University Press, 1985.

Wilson, Arthur M. "The concept of '*moeurs*' in Diderot's social and political thought". In *The Age of Enlightenment: Studies presented to Theodore Bestermann*, edited by W. H. Barber, 188–99. Edinburgh: Oliver and Boyd, 1967.

———. *Diderot.* New York: Oxford University Press, 1972.

Wilson, James Q. *The Moral Sense.* New York: Free Press, 1993.

Winch, Donald. *Classical Political Economy and Colonies.* Cambridge: Harvard University Press, 1965.

Wokler, Robert. "The influence of Diderot on the political theory of Rousseau: Two aspects of a friendship". *Studies on Voltaire and the Eighteenth Century*, 132 (1975): 55–111.

———. "Perfectible Apes in Decadent Cultures: Rousseau's Anthropology Revisited". *Daedalus*, 107 (1978): 107–34.

———. "Projecting the Enlightenment". In *After MacIntyre*, edited by John Horton and Susan Mendus. Notre Dame: University of Notre Dame, 1994.

Wolff, Larry. *Inventing Eastern Europe: The Map of Civilization on the Mind of the Enlightenment.* Stanford: Stanford University Press, 1994.

Womack, William R. "Eighteenth-century themes in the *Histoire philsophique et politique des deux Indes* of Guillaume Raynal". *Studies on Voltaire and the Eighteenth Century*, 96: 129–265.

Wood, Allen W. General introduction to *Practical Philosophy* by Immanuel Kant. Edited and translated by Mary Gregor. Cambridge: Cambridge University Press, 1996.

———. Introduction to *Religion and Rational Theology*, by Immanuel Kant. Edited and translated by Allen W. Wood and George Di Giovanni. Cambridge: Cambridge University Press, 1997.

———. *Kant's Ethical Thought*. Cambridge: Cambridge University Press, 1999.

Yovel, Yirmiyahu. *Kant and the Philosophy of History*. Princeton: Princeton University Press, 1980.

———. "Kant's Practical Reason as Will: Interest, Recognition, Judgment, Choice". *Review of Metaphysics*, 52, no. 2 (1998): 267–94.

Zammito, John H. *The Genesis of Kant's* "Critique of Judgment". Chicago: The University of Chicago Press, 1992.

———. *Kant, Herder, and the Birth of Anthropology*. Chicago: University of Chicago Press, 2002.

Index